Law, Crime and English Society, 1660–1830

This book examines how the law was made, defined, administered and used in eighteenth-century England. An international team of leading historians explore the ways in which legal concerns and procedures came to permeate society, and reflect on eighteenth-century concepts of corruption, oppression and institutional efficiency. These themes are pursued throughout in a broad range of contributions, which include studies of magistrates and courts, the forcible enlistment of soldiers and sailors, the eighteenth-century 'bloody code', the making of law basic to nineteenth-century social reform, the populace's extension of law's arena to newspapers, theologians' use of assumptions basic to English law, Lord Chief Justice Mansfield's concept of the liberty intrinsic to England and Blackstone's concept of the framework of English law. The result is an invaluable account of the legal bases of eighteenth-century society which is essential reading for historians at all levels.

NORMA LANDAU is the author of *The justices of the peace, 1679–1760*, published in 1984.

Law, Crime and English Society, 1660–1830

edited by

Norma Landau

University of California at Davis

PUBLISHED BY THE PRESS SYNDICATE OF THE UNIVERSITY OF CAMBRIDGE
The Pitt Building, Trumpington Street, Cambridge, United Kingdom

CAMBRIDGE UNIVERSITY PRESS
The Edinburgh Building, Cambridge CB2 2RU, UK
40 West 20th Street, New York, NY 10011–4211, USA
477 Williamstown Road, Port Melbourne, VIC 3207, Australia
Ruiz de Alarcón 13, 28014 Madrid, Spain
Dock House, The Waterfront, Cape Town 8001, South Africa

http://www.cambridge.org

First published 2002

Printed in the United Kingdom at the University Press, Cambridge

Typeface Plantin 10/12 pt   *System* LATEX 2$_\varepsilon$ [TB]

A catalogue record for this book is available from the British Library

ISBN 0 521 64261 2 hardback

In honour of John M. Beattie

Mentor, scholar, friend

Contents

Part 3 Society

    1772–1830   165
    RUTH PALEY

9   Religion and the law: evidence, proof and 'matter of fact',
    1660–1700   185
    BARBARA SHAPIRO

10 The press and public apologies in eighteenth-century
    London   208
    DONNA T. ANDREW

11 Origins of the factory acts: the Health and Morals of
    Apprentices Act, 1802   230
    JOANNA INNES

    John M. Beattie's publications   256
    Index   258

Figures

Contributors

DONNA T. ANDREW is a professor of modern British history at the University of Guelph in Canada. She is the author of *Philanthropy and police: London charity in the eighteenth century* (Princeton, 1989), the compiler of *London debating societies 1776–1799* (London Record Society, 1994) and, with Randall McGowen, joint author of *The Perreaus and Mrs Rudd: forgery and betrayal in eighteenth-century London* (Berkeley, 2001). She is currently completing a book entitled *The attack on aristocratic vice: cultural skirmishes in eighteenth-century England,* and beginning a new project on eighteenth-century London newspaper advertisement.

DOUGLAS HAY holds a joint appointment in the History Department and Osgoode Hall Law School, York University, Toronto. He is a contributor to and an editor of *Albion's fatal tree* (London and New York, 1975), *Policing and prosecution in Britain 1750–1850* (Oxford, 1989) and *Labour, law and crime: an historical perspective* (London and New York, 1987); and is joint author with Nicholas Rogers of *Eighteenth-century English society: shuttles and swords* (Oxford and New York, 1997). He has also written numerous articles and chapters which have appeared in journals and other collections. He is currently working on a study of the court of King's Bench, and a collaborative project on master and servant law in the British Empire.

JOANNA INNES is a fellow of Somerville College, Oxford, where she has taught since 1982. She has published extensively on social problems and policy in the long eighteenth century, and is currently at work on two volumes of her collected essays.

PETER KING is Professor of Social History at University College Northampton. He has published more than a dozen articles on the history of crime, law and society, is joint editor of *Chronicling poverty: the voices and strategies of the labouring poor 1640–1820* (London, 1997) and author of *Crime, justice and discretion in England 1740–1820* (Oxford, 2000).

NORMA LANDAU is a professor of history at the University of California at Davis. She is the author of *The justices of the peace, 1679–1760* (Berkeley, 1984) and of articles on the political, social, and legal history of eighteenth-century England. She is now working on two studies: on the regulation of migration within early modern England; and on the justices of the peace and their courts in eighteenth-century metropolitan London.

DAVID LIEBERMAN is the Jefferson E. Peyser Professor of Law and the Chair and Associate Dean of the Jurisprudence and Social Policy Program at the University of California, Berkeley. He is the author of *The province of legislation determined: legal theory in eighteenth-century Britain* (Cambridge, 1989) and other studies in the history of legal ideas. He is currently preparing for publication a critical edition of Jean Louis De Lolme's *The constitution of England*.

RANDALL MCGOWEN, professor of history at the University of Oregon, has co-authored with Donna Andrew *The Perreaus and Mrs Rudd: forgery and betrayal in eighteenth-century London* (Berkeley, 2001). He is also the author of numerous articles on punishment and the criminal law, and is currently at work on a book on the debate over forgery and capital punishment in early nineteenth-century England.

RUTH PALEY works at the History of Parliament Trust where she is responsible for *The history of the House of Lords, 1660–1832*. She is the editor of *Justice in eighteenth-century Hackney: the justicing notebook of Henry Norris and the Hackney petty sessions book* (London Record Society, 1991), and has published articles on policing in eighteenth- and nineteenth-century London. She is currently preparing, in collaboration with Elaine A. Reynolds, to write about the history of policing London from 1700 to 1839, and is editing a volume of criminal cases that were tried in London from 1700 to 1875.

NICHOLAS ROGERS is a professor of history at York University, Toronto. He is the author of *Whigs and cities: popular politics in the age of Walpole and Pitt* (Oxford and New York, 1989); *Crowds, culture and politics in Georgian Britain* (Oxford and New York, 1998); and, with Douglas Hay, of *Eighteenth-century English society: shuttles and swords* (Oxford and New York, 1997). He is currently completing a book on naval impressment and its opponents in Georgian Britain and the Atlantic seaboard.

BARBARA SHAPIRO, professor in the Graduate School at the University of California, Berkeley, is the author of *John Wilkins 1614–72: an intellectual biography* (Berkeley, 1968), *Probability and certainty in seventeenth-century England: a study of the relationships between natural science, religion, history, law, and literature* (Princeton, 1983), *'Beyond reasonable doubt' and 'probable cause': historical perspectives on the Anglo-American law of evidence* (Berkeley, 1991) and *A culture of fact: England 1550–1720* (Ithaca, 2000). She is currently working on English political thought in the sixteenth and seventeenth centuries.

1   Introduction

Norma Landau

This volume is a tribute to John Beattie, whose work is fundamental to the burgeoning study of crime and the courts in early modern England, and whose enthusiastic interest in the work of his fellow historians is one of the attractions of eighteenth-century English history. On his retirement, John's current students and colleagues at the University of Toronto published a *Festschrift* in his honour.[1] This is therefore the second volume dedicated to John. Of the contributors to this volume, some were John's students as undergraduates, others his graduate students, and all enjoy his friendship. John is an extraordinary scholar: not only acute, persistent, and insightful in his own work, but generous in giving his time, advice, and aid to others. John's work has made our work better; his presence has enhanced our enjoyment of our work. This volume is one way in which we say 'thank you'.

The chapters in this volume develop themes raised by John Beattie's second and third books, *Crime and the courts in England, 1660–1800* and *Policing and punishment in London, 1660–1750*.[2] The foundation of both books is analysis of the charges of felonious conduct brought before Quarter Sessions, Assizes, and the Old Bailey (London and Middlesex's Assizes), and the way in which these courts dealt with these allegations. The evidential core of the books are the allegations themselves – charges presented according to the dictates of legal formulae, written on dirty strips in a now obsolete hand, and annotated with the scribbled Latin shorthand of the court's clerks as they recorded the court's verdict and sentence on each allegation.[3]

Mastery and analysis of such records is in itself a formidable achievement – an achievement prognosticated by Beattie's first book, *The English*

---

[1] G. Smith, A. May and S. Devereaux, *Criminal justice in the old world and the new* (Toronto, 1998).

[2] J. M. Beattie, *Crime and the courts in England, 1660–1800* (Princeton, 1986), and *Policing and punishment in London, 1660–1750: urban crime and the limits of terror* (Oxford, 2001).

[3] For problems intrinsic to analysis of indictments, see J. M. Beattie, 'Towards a study of crime in eighteenth-century England: a note on indictments', in P. Fritz and D. Williams, eds., *The triumph of culture* (Toronto, 1972).

court in the reign of George I.[4] This book, on George I's household, like Beattie's two later books on the criminal courts, is founded on arcane documents, in this case household accounts, which Beattie uses to delineate the way in which the king's household functioned. As in his later work, Beattie here uses analysis of administration as a means of posing questions resonating beyond administrative structure. This book examines the distribution and nature of the court's patronage, an issue central to the debate about the early Hanoverian constitution. So, too, in ways foreshadowing Beattie's analysis of the administration of the criminal law, his analysis of the administration of the household disclosed something quite unexpected: George I's efforts to make his court the centre of political life when he could not rely on his son to fulfil the monarch's role as social centre of England's politics.[5] Beattie thereby revealed that a cliché which had shaped depiction of early Hanoverian politics – that George I was interested neither in England nor its throne – was simply wrong. As Beattie demonstrated, George I took an active part in England's political life; and this reassessment of the first Hanoverian monarch's political role, coupled with Beattie's analysis of the functioning and importance of the royal court, is a major contribution to current depictions of English politics.

Beattie's second and third books examine another variety of royal court – the criminal courts. Like his book on the royal household, these too delineate the way in which a court works, the ways in which it changed, and the ways in which both functions and their change reveal the structures and stresses of the society it governed. Beattie's work has brought a new perspective to the study of the eighteenth-century criminal law, a subject whose study had been defined by Sir Leon Radzinowicz's *A history of English criminal law*.[6] This distinguished work was the first to give an extended historical analysis of the criminal law that went beyond the statute law, and it did so by looking at opinion about the law and its administration. As one would therefore expect, Radzinowicz's *History* is a masterful orchestration of voices criticizing the criminal law, declaring it corrupt, ineffective, illogical, asystematic, arbitrary, antithetic to the ends of justice, and therefore in need of drastic reform.

Such an emphasis was highly compatible with what Butterfield termed the 'Whig interpretation' of English history,[7] an interpretation that shaped

---

[4] (Cambridge, 1967).

[5] See also J. M. Beattie, 'The court of George I in English politics', *English Historical Review*, vol. 81 (1966).

[6] Sir L. Radzinowicz, *A history of English criminal law and its administration from 1750*, vols. I–IV (London, 1948–68), vol. V with R. Hood (London, 1986).

[7] Sir H. Butterfield, *The Whig interpretation of history* (London, 1931).

the historiography of eighteenth-century England until the middle of the twentieth century. The Whig interpretation's thrust was analysis of the evolution of English progress, and as Radzinowicz's first sentence proclaimed, he was heir to this tradition: 'Lord Macaulay's generalisation that the history of England is the history of progress is as true of the criminal law as of the other social institutions of which it is a part.'[8] Radzinowicz began his delineation of the progress of the criminal law in the mid-eighteenth century, a choice which when combined with his Whiggish proclivity branded the eighteenth-century criminal law as interesting chiefly for the scope it provided for reform. Here again Radzinowicz's analysis accorded with that of the Whig interpretation, in which the eighteenth century featured as a hiatus in the story of English progress, an era possessing the political structures which, as the nineteenth century showed, could be the engine of progress, but which were employed in a manner corrupting both the structures and those who ran them. Since, in the Whigs' view, the English had the structures requisite for good government but did not use those structures as they would be used in the nineteenth century, then it could be assumed that much of what a later era considered good government simply did not appear in eighteenth-century England.

While the interpretive tradition founded by Sir Lewis Namier challenged the Whig depiction of eighteenth-century political institutions, it too provided an historiographical environment congenial to Radzinowicz's presentation. Namier devoted his histories to demonstrations that the eighteenth-century constitution and its political structures differed fundamentally from those characterizing the politics and constitution of the next two centuries.[9] As a result, he focused on those activities and episodes which Whig historians had cited as prime examples of the age's corruption, evaluating them in a light quite different from that brought by the Whigs, but not directing attention to eighteenth-century governmental activities neglected in Whig historiography's depiction of the need for reform. While Namierite historiography therefore presents eighteenth-century England as governed through structures fundamentally different from those of the Victorian era and adequate for its needs, it does so by assigning different values to the Whig depiction of a government that did little rather than by presenting evidence of hitherto neglected governmental activity. Since Radzinowicz presents the eighteenth-century criminal law as a striking example of the ineffective and minimal

---

[8] Radzinowicz, *History of English criminal law*, vol. I, p. ix.
[9] Sir L. B. Namier, *England in the age of the American revolution* (2nd edn, London, 1963); Sir L. B. Namier, *The structure of politics at the accession of George III* (rev. edn, London, 1957).

government of eighteenth-century England, a new view of that law would also provide a new perspective on eighteenth-century England.

Beattie's work provides just such a new view. Rather than measuring the eighteenth-century criminal law against modern expectations of law, Beattie instead presents the criminal law as contemporaries thought it worked. As a result, features of the law which to modern eyes, as to reformers, seem inefficacious, illogical and arbitrary appear in Beattie's analysis as integral to its system. According to Beattie, the major goal of eighteenth-century criminal law was deterrence. And so Parliament enacted what later ages would christen 'the bloody code' – over 200 laws decreeing that the penalty for acts detailed in these laws was death. However, as Beattie states, effective deterrence demands not hundreds of hangings, but instead a relatively few terrifying examples of the awe-inspiring power of the law. Therefore, judges and jurors had to select those to be sent to the gallows from among those indicted for capital crimes. In so doing, they made decisions which later ages would deride as arbitrary and illogical: judges secured the monarch's pardon for a large proportion of the capitally convicted; juries routinely convicted defendants of a lesser offence, and so a less severely punished offence, than that for which a defendant was indicted, and they did so even when it was manifestly clear that the defendant had indeed committed the offence for which he had originally been indicted. Beattie's interpretation therefore transforms the judge and jury's seemingly illogical and arbitrary decisions into rational choices made within a system demanding that they make such choices.[10] Indeed, as he shows, features of the eighteenth-century criminal trial which to modern eyes appear absurdly unfair functioned so as to aid judge and jury in making these decisions. So, for example, the rule that defendants defend themselves, that they use lawyers to address points of law only, meant that judge and jury could assess the character of defendants and the way they responded to the charges against them. When, in the early nineteenth century, Parliament replaced the bloody code with a penal regime emphasizing not deterrence but instead the reformation of criminals through imprisonment, judge and jury no longer selected from among all convicts those suitable for exemplary death, and the eighteenth-century trial lost its rationale. In its turn, that trial was by 1836 replaced with a new structure, a structure featuring the combat of lawyers.[11] As is evident,

[10] For an analysis showing that, when recommending pardons for those convicted of capital crimes, judges used criteria similar to those used today, see P. King, 'Decision makers and decision-making in the English criminal law, 1750–1800', *Historical Journal*, vol. 27 (1984).

[11] For eighteenth-century trials, see: J. M. Beattie, 'Crime and the courts in Surrey', in J. S. Cockburn, ed., *Crime in England, 1550–1800* (London, 1977); Beattie, *Crime and*

Beattie's analysis integrates punishment – and so the bloody code and its change – with both the court's decisions and its structures for making decisions.[12]

In examining punishments for criminal offences, Beattie necessarily engages with statute law and Parliament, and so with the artifacts and institution traditionally presented as the defining structures of English history. Since Beattie presents a new interpretation of the punishment of offenders in later Stuart and Hanoverian England, his interpretation challenges both Whig and Namierite characterizations of eighteenth-century government. According to the standard interpretations, the bloody code was acquired in a fit of absence of mind, enacted by a parliament uninterested in debating any of the numerous extensions of the death penalty it so placidly approved.[13] In contrast, Beattie's analysis of the sentences inflicted upon those convicted at Quarter Sessions and Assizes shows that there was continual experimentation with punishment in later Stuart England, as judges and juries searched for a punishment less dire than hanging which would nonetheless deter crime. Eventually, England's governors found such a punishment in transportation. In Beattie's analysis, the Transportation Act of 1718 therefore emerges as the logical culmination of several decades of thought about punishment and its consequences, thought hitherto unrecognized because its record was the courts' action rather than the pamphlets and publications of parliamentary debates which reveal later eras' concerns about public policy. So, too, Beattie's presentation provides a context both for the courts' actions and for the enactment of major parts of the bloody code. As he shows, both the Transportation Act and early eighteenth-century legislation extending capital punishment to theft by servants, to shoplifting and theft from stables and warehouses, and to all varieties of house-breaking can be traced to pressure brought by the City of London on Parliament to deal more effectively with metropolitan crime. Indeed, Beattie identifies the Recorder of London as the member of Parliament who devised

---

the courts, chaps. 7 and 8; J. M. Beattie, 'Scales of justice: defense counsel and the English criminal trial in the eighteenth and nineteenth centuries', Law and History Review, vol. 9 (1991); Beattie, Policing and punishment, chap. 6; J. H. Langbein, 'The criminal trial before the lawyers', University of Chicago Law Review, vol. 45 (1978); J. H. Langbein, 'Shaping the eighteenth-century criminal trial: a view from the Ryder sources', University of Chicago Law Review, vol. 50 (1983); J. H. Langbein, 'The prosecutorial origins of defence counsel in the eighteenth century: the appearance of solicitors', Cambridge Law Journal, vol. 58 (2000).

[12] J. Innes and J. Styles, 'The crime wave: recent writing on crime and criminal justice in eighteenth-century England', in A. Wilson, ed., Rethinking social history: English society 1570–1920 and its interpretation (Manchester, 1993), pp. 233–9.

[13] Radzinowicz, History of English criminal law, vol. I, p. 35; W. H. Lecky, England in the eighteenth century, new edn, vol. VII (New York, 1903), p. 320.

and ensured both passage and implementation of the Transportation Act.[14]

Such discovery of the thought, motivation and agency animating eighteenth-century legislation constitutes a new view both of early eighteenth-century England and of the course of eighteenth-century English history. Traditionally, the early eighteenth century was 'pudding time', the era in which the complacent victors of seventeenth-century battles enjoyed their supremacy while forgetting their principles, an era characterized by 'the sullen torpor of the Jacobite sympathisers, and the cynical acquiescence in evil of the Walpolean Whigs', and so an era whose elite's behaviour was contrasted to the 'heightened sense' of social responsibility exhibited in the later eighteenth century, when the banner of reform was raised aloft and the way prepared for the triumphs of the nineteenth century.[15] In contrast, Beattie has presented an early eighteenth century interested and active in the concerns supposedly characteristic only of later eras, concerns heretofore hidden because of the ways in which this society's courts, its uses of its courts and of Parliament, and its concepts of the use of courts and the law differed from those of later eras. The chapters in this volume build on Beattie's insights.

Law-making and the state

Two chapters build upon Beattie's contribution to current investigation of the making of law in eighteenth-century England, and a third reflects upon the law as both bulwark and barrier to the power of the state. Given both Whig and Namierite depictions of eighteenth-century politics and the constitution, it is not surprising that, until relatively recently, historians have devoted little attention to laws enacted in the eighteenth century. After all, even contemporaries found Parliament uninteresting. According to Henry Fox, 'A bird might build her nest in the Speaker's chair, or in his peruke. There won't be a debate that can disturb her.'[16] Nor have historians found the legislation which Parliament did pass either impressive or effective. The Webbs, who wrote the definitive depiction of eighteenth-century local government, thought the laws passed by eighteenth-century

[14] J. M. Beattie, 'The cabinet and the management of death at Tyburn after the revolution of 1688', in L. Schwoerer, ed., *The revolution of 1688–89: changing perspectives* (Cambridge, 1992); J. M. Beattie, 'London crime and the making of the "bloody code", 1689–1718', in L. Davison *et al.*, eds., *Stilling the grumbling hive: the response to social and economic problems in England, 1689–1750* (Stroud and New York, 1992); Beattie, *Policing and punishment*, chaps. 7, 8, 9.

[15] S. and B. Webb, *English local government from the revolution to the municipal corporations act*, vol. I, *The parish and the county* (London, 1908), p. 364.

[16] R. Pares, *King George III and the politicians* (London, 1953), p. 4.

Parliaments 'had next to no effect on the way in which the country was governed in practice'.[17] Beattie's work, revealing the thought and experimentation buttressing eighteenth-century penal legislation, and the quite evident effect that legislation had on courts' trials, verdicts and sentences, has therefore made a major contribution to new interpretations of lawmaking in eighteenth-century England.

These new interpretations build on Sheila Lambert's and Peter Thomas' analyses of the way in which eighteenth-century Parliaments organized themselves so as to pass legislation, analyses arguing that such organization was very effective. The proof, as Julian Hoppit, John Styles and Joanna Innes have shown, is the legislation itself: there was a lot of it, and that in itself was new. In the 203 years from 1485 to 1688, excluding 1642 to 1660 (the era of civil war and Commonwealth), Parliament passed almost 2,700 acts. In contrast, in the 112 years from 1689 to 1801, Parliament passed over 13,600 acts.[18] Some of this legislation was, in effect, experiments in correcting or supplementing the machinery of government, and so introduced new ideas into English law.[19] Since neither these acts nor most of the more general eighteenth-century statutes dealing with social policy were sponsored by the government or by political parties, it is evident that the political process generating legislation in the eighteenth century differed from that in later and even to some extent in earlier eras. Indeed, this lack of association between eighteenth-century legislation and both the executive and the parties is one reason why historians had not incorporated it into their depictions of eighteenth-century England.

How then was such legislation generated and passed? In an earlier article, Joanna Innes showed how private members of Parliament, who were the sponsors of most eighteenth-century general legislation affecting social policy, formulated this legislation and ensured that Parliament and the political elite discussed it.[20] That article presented eighteenth-century legislation as seen from Parliament. Her chapter here presents

---

[17] J. Innes, 'Parliament and the shaping of eighteenth-century English social policy', *Transactions of the Royal Historical Society*, 5th series, vol. XL (1990), p. 65.

[18] S. Lambert, *Bills and Acts* (Cambridge, 1971); P. D. G. Thomas, *The House of Commons in the eighteenth century* (Oxford, 1971); J. Hoppit, J. Innes and J. Styles, 'Project report: towards a history of parliamentary legislation 1660–1800', *Parliamentary History*, vol. 13 (1994), p. 313; J. Hoppit, 'Patterns of parliamentary legislation, 1660–1800', *Historical Journal*, vol. 39 (1996), p. 109. See also J. Innes, 'The local acts of a national Parliament: Parliament's role in sanctioning local action in eighteenth-century Britain', *Parliamentary History*, vol. 17 (1998); J. Hoppit and J. Innes, 'Introduction', in J. Hoppit, ed., *Failed legislation, 1660–1800* (London and Rio Grande, 1997).

[19] Sir W. Holdsworth, *A history of English law*, vol. XI (London, 1938), pp. 323–4; P. Langford, *Public life and the propertied Englishman, 1689–1793* (Oxford, 1991), chap. 3.

[20] Innes, 'Parliament and the shaping of eighteenth-century English social policy'.

the enactment of eighteenth-century legislation as seen from the localities. Innes' chapter follows the first factory act from its bases both in measures adopted by Lancashire's justices of the peace and in campaigns of reforming societies to Sir Robert Peel's sponsorship of a bill reflecting the justices' and societies' concerns, and to that bill's enactment. As she reveals, the first factory act rested upon extended discussion of and experimentation in regulating the employment of apprentices. It therefore challenges depictions of the characteristics differentiating Hanoverian from Victorian legislation. According to one influential argument, one reason why Victorian legislation was effective and Hanoverian legislation ineffective was that Hanoverian legislation was the product of a relatively autonomic and unconsidered response to emergencies.[21] However, as Innes reveals, the first factory act was by no means a panicked response to an emergency. Her chapter is therefore an example of the ways in which depictions of eighteenth-century government which attend to the way it worked, depictions such as Beattie's, are altering historians' assessments both of the eighteenth century and of the eras to which it has been contrasted.[22]

Like Innes' chapter, Randall McGowen's examines legislation. While Innes analyzes legislation on social policy, a type of legislation which traditional accounts of the period neglect, McGowen analyzes that legislation which traditional accounts recognize and deride. McGowen's chapter examines eighteenth-century legislation on forgery, legislation which comprises a substantial part of the bloody code. McGowen has written on the statute under which most prosecutions for forgery were brought.[23] That statute, 2 George II c. 25, enacted in 1729, pertained to the forgery of monetary instruments which could be issued by private individuals. However, as McGowen states, while the vast majority of eighteenth-century prosecutions for forgery were brought under that 1729 statute, there was much more and earlier legislation decreeing that

[21] O. MacDonagh, 'The nineteenth-century revolution in government: a reappraisal', *Historical Journal*, vol. 1 (1958), p. 58. While MacDonagh's characterization of the nature of the impetus for the construction of the nineteenth-century regulatory state has been the subject of much debate, his characterization of pre-Victorian legislation has been little discussed. For some of the work defining the debate, see the essays in P. Stansky, ed., *The Victorian revolution in government* (New York, 1973), and J. Hart, 'Nineteenth-century social reform: a Tory interpretation of history', in M. W. Flinn and T. C. Smout, eds., *Essays in social history* (Oxford, 1974).

[22] For example, for an argument that the innovations of early nineteenth-century government should not be attributed, as has been supposed, to an influential class of businessmen and professionals, but instead to the same elite which dominated later eighteenth-century government, see P. Harling and P. Mandler, 'From "fiscal-military" state to laissez-faire state, 1760–1850', *Journal of British Studies*, vol. 32 (1993).

[23] R. McGowen, 'From pillory to gallows: the punishment of forgery in the age of the financial revolution', *Past and Present*, no. 165 (1999).

death be the punishment for other types of forgery. That legislation, constituting the bulk of eighteenth-century legislation on forgery and so a prime example of what reformers decried as the illogic of the bloody code, is the legislation McGowen's chapter here examines. As he shows, that legislation was neither illogical nor the automatic response of legislators in an increasingly capitalist economy to the problems of capital. It was, instead, the way in which the nation's governors and those who administered the central government's departments attempted to protect the financial instruments which the government issued as it conducted the nation's business. This legislation can therefore be presented as evidence of the later Stuart state's expansion, increasing power, and unprecedented autonomy.[24] Such legislation therefore gives substance to the forebodings of civic humanist critics of the later Stuart and Hanoverian state, who feared that the state's influence and its basis in the illusory world of financial credit would extirpate their liberty.[25]

Nonetheless, while the state presented in Beattie's work and the new depictions of law-making with which it is associated is a more effective state than that in Whig and Namierite presentations, this more effective state was constrained by its own instrument; as Nicholas Rogers' chapter shows, it was constrained by law.[26] No task was more central to the role assumed by eighteenth-century central government than the provision of the means and forces necessary for fighting its wars, and that task was highly demanding. When the state went to war, the central government had to recruit a very large number of men very quickly. For example, during the Seven Years' War, the central government had speedily to enlarge its peacetime navy of 9,797 men to a force of 81,929.[27] To do so, it used its power of impressment, the power accorded it under the common law to take civilian seamen and force them to man the navy's ships. Law therefore reinforced the power of the state; but as Rogers shows, eighteenth-century Englishmen also used the law to fend off the press. Rogers has surveyed the opposition to impressment elsewhere.[28] Here he focuses on the ways in which the law was considered to restrain the

---

[24] J. Brewer, *Sinews of power* (Cambridge, Mass., 1988); J. Brewer, 'The eighteenth-century British state: contexts and issues', in L. Stone, ed., *The imperial state at war: Britain from 1689 to 1815* (London and New York, 1994).

[25] J. G. A. Pocock, *The Machiavellian moment: Florentine political thought and the Atlantic republican tradition* (Princeton, 1975), chap. 13.

[26] For reflections on the law's constraints upon the elite, see E. P. Thompson, *Whigs and hunters: the origins of the Black Act* (New York, 1975), pp. 258–69.

[27] N. A. M. Rodger, *The wooden world: an anatomy of the Georgian navy* (London, 1986), p. 386.

[28] N. Rogers, 'Liberty road: opposition to impressment in Britain during the American War of Independence', in C. Howell and R. J. Twomey, eds., *Jack Tar in history: essays in the history of maritime life and labour* (Fredericton, New Brunswick, 1991).

press and on the ways in which it actually did constrain the press. Rogers' chapter therefore illustrates the extent to which this state, and indeed this society, was imbricated in law. As he shows, magistrates hampered the operations of the press, and the extent to which magistrates' actions deviated from those formally assigned them by law and government is one theme of the chapters in this volume. So, too, Rogers reveals the ways in which pressed men and their employers turned the criminal law against the press gangs, while using habeas corpus, parliamentary statute, and even the law of debt to release some men from the navy's holds. Clearly, sailors and their employers both knew and used the law, and the permeation of law throughout English society is another of this volume's themes.

The working of the courts

As Rogers' chapter emphasizes, the eighteenth-century English state worked through the courts. The working of the courts was therefore central to the state, a feature of eighteenth-century England which highlights the importance of Beattie's analysis of the way in which the criminal courts worked. Beattie has analyzed the institution of innovations designed to secure offenders and bring them before the courts – from the development of street lighting, to the eighteenth-century policing of the City of London, to the activities of thief-takers.[29] Similarly, he has analyzed the process of the courts, from the charges laid against an offender before a magistrate, to the indictments laid before a grand jury, to trial before a petty jury, to verdict, sentence and punishment.[30] Two chapters in this volume analyze one crucial component of this judicial system – the magistrates.

English justices of the peace were unique in early modern Europe, for it was England's idiosyncracy to lodge the powers of both judiciary and intendancy in their hands.[31] England's justices therefore wielded both administrative and judicial powers. They did so within a state which allocated responsibility for acting and even initiating action on a wide range of tasks to local governments – to county justices, borough magistrates, parish vestries, and parish officers. In theory, the action of these local governments, and in some instances even their lack of action, was regulated by law. In some cases, that regulation was effective. For example, eighteenth-century courts clearly determined which of two parishes, each

---

[29] Beattie, *Policing and punishment*, chaps. 3, 4, 5.
[30] ibid., chap. 2; Beattie, *Crime and the courts*.
[31] S. Hindle, *The state and social change in early modern England, c. 1550–1640* (Basingstoke, 2000), p. 30, and for a discussion of the imbrication of law in state and society, chap. 1.

attempting to avoid responsibility for the welfare of a poor person, was responsible for that poor person. To be effective, such a system of regulation required litigants ready and able to bring their opponents to court, as were these parishes. However, as Douglas Hay's chapter here suggests, it was a rare litigant who would enter a contest with a powerful justice. Hay has, in an earlier essay, analyzed the ways in which eighteenth-century criminal courts projected themselves as the awe-inspiring mask for the elite's rule.[32] Here he uses the heretofore unexplored records of King's Bench, the court determining criminal charges against justices and appeals against their decisions, to demonstrate that the elite, when acting as justices of the peace, were little constrained by that legal institution which according to contemporary rhetoric ensured that they did not abuse their power.

Hay's chapter focuses on a rural justice, and rural justices were the eighteenth century's icons of civic virtue and responsibility. Norma Landau has examined change in the image of that ideal rural justice.[33] Here she examines that justice's antithesis, the age's emblem of the perversion of local magistracy: the trading justices of Middlesex and Westminster. In showing that the Quarter Sessions of both Middlesex and Westminster found it necessary to create procedures supplemental to those available at common law for correcting erring justices, Landau's chapter reinforces Hay's argument as to the inadequacy of the law's control of justices. At the same time, she also suggests that, when local governors competed against each other, they might well turn to the law to restrain their opponent. Hay's and Landau's differing presentations of the extent to which justices were unrestrained by law are therefore founded on differing estimates of the cohesion of England's local elites. Quite probably, the rise and then decline of party altered the extent to which local governors throughout England thought it appropriate to use the courts against their rivals. Unlike justices elsewhere in England, the justices of metropolitan London were throughout the eighteenth century riven by a second and different competition – that for judicial business and its profits; and such competition produced justices who used the court of Quarter Sessions against their opponents. In emphasizing the extent to which contemporaries perceived the trading justices as associating business with magistracy and vilified them because of that association, Landau argues that, in some appreciable part, the trading justices' unsavoury reputation rested not on what they did but on the way in which contemporary thought categorized their activity. So, Landau's chapter, like Hay's, presents a legal

---

[32] D. Hay, 'Property, authority and the criminal law', in D. Hay *et al.*, eds., *Albion's fatal tree: crime and society in eighteenth-century England* (London, 1975).

[33] N. Landau, *The justices of the peace, 1679–1760* (Berkeley, 1984), chap. 11.

system tangentially related to the rhetoric used both to denounce and glorify it.

Whether the legal system actually worked as its rhetoric proclaimed is the central question of Peter King's chapter. King tackles a problem raised in response to John Beattie's first publication on crime, 'The pattern of crime in England, 1660–1800', an article that delineated the fluctuation in indictments for the felonious taking of property, relating those fluctuations, especially short-term fluctuations, to changes in the cost of living.[34] That article aroused such interest in the potential for understanding 'the long eighteenth century' through study of its crime that historians initiated a continuing debate as to the extent to which change in the number of indictments preferred in England's courts reflected change in the number of crimes actually committed.[35] Beattie has continued to examine change in the level of indictments, analyzing its relation to change both in structures for prosecution and in the incentives for prosecution, while arguing that short-term change in the level of indictments is a strong indication of change in the number of crimes that were actually committed.[36] In this, he has been supported by Douglas Hay, who showed how the difference in numbers and types of crime indicted in time of war from that in time of peace could be attributed to a legal system whose indictments did fluctuate in accord with fluctuations in crime.[37] Part of Hay's argument rests on the correlation of fluctuations of wartime indictments with fluctuations in the cost of living. In response, King has questioned the bases for these correlations.[38] In his chapter here, he questions the extent to which the decline in indictments that occurred during England's wars reflects decline in crime.

Meanwhile, Beattie, having begun that debate about indictments, has raised another argument emphasizing their importance. Even if change in the number of indictments did not reflect change in the crimes actually committed, change in the number of indictments had a profound effect on contemporary perceptions of levels of crime. Increase in the numbers of those indicted, especially in London, persuaded London's rulers and members of Parliament that the nation needed to take action against crime – action typified by laws increasing the penalties for criminal offences and instituting new punishments for criminal offences.[39] Beattie's argument therefore integrates what happened in England's criminal

---

[34] *Past and Present*, no. 62 (1974).

[35] That debate is summarized in Innes and Styles, 'Crime wave', pp. 208–15.

[36] Beattie, *Crime and the courts*, p. 264.

[37] D. Hay, 'War, dearth and theft in the eighteenth century: the record of the English courts', *Past and Present*, no. 95 (1982).

[38] P. King, *Crime, justice, and discretion in England, 1740–1820* (Oxford, 2000), pp. 145–52.

[39] See especially Beattie, *Policing and punishment*, pp. 45–73, and chaps. 7, 8, 9.

courts into presentation of that responsive and effective state now being portrayed by historians of Hanoverian England.

Law and society

In linking Parliament to the work of the criminal courts, Beattie has made it strikingly apparent that those courts were not located in precincts hermetically sealed from English society. Indeed, Beattie has been a pioneer in using the records of the criminal courts to illuminate structures and processes basic to English society, not only showing the relation of fluctuations in criminal indictments to fluctuations in the cost of living, but also, for example, showing the ways in which indictments of women reflect upon women's roles and opportunities in eighteenth-century England.[40] While Beattie has examined the ways in which English society affected its law courts, four chapters in this volume examine the imbrication of English law in English society.

Donna Andrew has written on the English duel – an illegal, quasi-private and lethal ritual used by members of the elite to defend their honour.[41] Here she writes about the publication of apologies in newspapers – an extra-legal and public shaming ritual used by those with some standing, however slight, to proclaim their maintenance of that standing when their standing was attacked. Like indictments, these too reflect women's position in eighteenth-century England. As in seventeenth-century New England, relatively few women issued public apologies, perhaps because, as in seventeenth-century New England, women's public voice was muted.[42] So, too, English law shaped these apologies. Andrew has found that almost two-thirds of the apologies were related to some type of legal proceeding, a finding which gives specificity to

[40] See especially, J. M. Beattie, 'The criminality of women in eighteenth-century England', *Journal of Social History*, vol. 8 (1975); Beattie, 'London crime and the making of the "bloody code"'; J. M. Beattie, 'Women, crime and inequality in eighteenth-century London', in J. Hagan and R. D. Person, eds., *Crime and Inequality* (Stanford, 1995); Beattie, *Policing and punishment*, pp. 63–72, 336–8, 356–7.

[41] D. Andrew, 'The code of honour and its critics: the opposition to duelling in England, 1700–1850', *Social History*, vol. 5 (1980).

[42] J. Kamensky, *Governing the tongue: the politics of speech in early New England* (New York, 1997), pp. 133–5, and more generally pp. 128–42. However, it does seem that there are several differences distinguishing the use of these apologies in seventeenth-century New England from that in eighteenth-century England, most especially the frequency with which legal action gave rise to such apologies. Eighteenth-century London and its metropolitan area each year generated hundreds of indictments for non-felonious offences, thousands of recognizances issued on complaint of wrongdoing, and untold numbers both of civil suits for various types of damages and of cases brought before a variety of summary courts: an amount of litigation much greater than that producing the ten to fifty apologies published each year.

Simon Roberts' contention that 'arbitration grows up in the shadow of adjudication rather than the other way round'.[43] The imbrication of law in what may otherwise appear as an unmediated and so undistorted record of minor wrongdoing is also apparent in the configuration of the offences generating these public apologies. For instance, since the common law restricted suits against defamers to those who harmed their victims' pockets,[44] it seems likely that it was this common law definition of defamation that produced apologists more likely to apologize for defamation of business than sexual conduct. That the law shaped even the extra-legal published apology suggests the extent to which law permeated this society.

Ruth Paley's chapter is evidence of the extent to which the English based their national identity on their law. As Innes' chapter demonstrates, the eighteenth-century courts were fora for debate on issues of public policy, and the press disseminated the judges' determination of these issues throughout the land.[45] No issue could be more central to English identity than the foundation of their freedom in their law, and that was the issue at the heart of *Somerset* v. *Stewart*, a case in which Lord Chief Justice Mansfield had to decide whether James Somerset, who had been brought to England as a slave, could be sent to Jamaica to be sold. Mansfield decided that Somerset could not be forcibly sent out of England, and ever since, his decision has been cited as evidence of the liberty intrinsic to England and its law. According to his nineteenth-century biographer, 'Lord Mansfield first established the grand doctrine that the air of England is too pure to be breathed by a slave.'[46] Although Mansfield insisted that his judgment was confined to the question of whether a master could send a slave out of England, an insistence corroborated by subsequent studies of his decision,[47] scholars persist in attempting to show that the decision reached beyond that narrowly defined question, a persistence which in itself is testimony to the importance of the common law to English identity. Paley uses the King's Bench records of a case that never proceeded to a final judgment, and so to legal reports

---

[43] S. Roberts, 'The study of dispute: anthropological perspectives', in J. Bossy, ed., *Disputes and settlements: law and human relations in the west* (Cambridge, 1983), p. 17.

[44] J. H. Baker, *An introduction to English legal history*, 3rd edn (London, 1990), p. 503. Those who had been defamed as committing criminal offences, unfit for their calling, or carriers of certain infectious diseases could sue without proving damage.

[45] J. Innes, 'Origins of the factory acts', in this volume, text at nn. 53–5. See also D. Hay, 'The state and the market in 1800: Lord Kenyon and Mr Waddington', *Past and Present*, no. 162 (1999), pp. 105, 158.

[46] Lord John Campbell, *The lives of the Chief Justices*, 3 vols. (1849–57; reprint Freeport, New York, 1971), vol. II, p. 418.

[47] Baker, *Introduction to English legal history*, p. 542. On Mansfield as a legal reformer, see D. Lieberman, *The province of legislation determined: legal theory in eighteenth-century Britain* (Cambridge, 1989), chap. 5.

and newspaper accounts of the judges' decision, to distinguish the judges' and therefore English law's view of *Somerset* from that both of eighteenth-century popular opinion and of the latest attempts to demonstrate that Mansfield abolished slavery in England.

Like Paley, Barbara Shapiro also demonstrates the importance of English law to English culture. Shapiro has published extensively on early modern concepts of proof.[48] In her chapter here she demonstrates that, in the later seventeenth and early eighteenth centuries, theologians imported the law's concept of 'fact' and the law's concepts of the evaluation of witnesses into their proofs of their theological contentions. As Shapiro notes, both 'fact' and 'witnessing' are constructs central to current debates in the history of early modern science, in large part because of the work of Steven Shapin and Simon Schaffer.[49] Shapin and Schaffer have drawn attention to the centrality in the scientific revolution of the establishment of a community that accepted its members' reports of their tests of the natural world as 'fact'. This nascent scientific community therefore had to decide the bases for determining who was a credible witness, a person whose report authenticated an experience as a fact. According to Shapin and Schaffer, the criteria determining scientific credibility were borrowed from current codes of conduct – codes of honour and civility, codes which therefore excluded all but the elite and their clients from scientific discourse. Shapiro's chapter is part of her argument against this contention. She argues that, from the mid-sixteenth to the early eighteenth centuries, the English reoriented their thought, in natural philosophy as well as in other spheres, so as to focus on proven natural phenomenon, and in so doing they took their concept of determination of fact from English law. English law was unique in its procedural separation of determination of law, a task it allocated to judges, from determination of fact, a task it allocated to lay juries. As Beattie has shown, members of the English petty jury, the jury which determined whether a defendant had committed the offence with which he was charged, were not members of the elite.[50] So,

[48] B. J. Shapiro, *Probability and certainty in seventeenth-century England: a study of the relationships between natural science, religion, history, law and literature* (Princeton, 1983); B. J. Shapiro, *'Beyond reasonable doubt' and 'probable cause': historical perspectives on the Anglo-American law of evidence* (Berkeley, 1991); B. J. Shapiro, *A culture of fact, England, 1550–1720* (Ithaca and London, 2000).

[49] S. Shapin and S. Schaffer, *Leviathan and the air-pump: Hobbes, Boyle and the experimental life* (Princeton, 1985); S. Shapin, *The scientific revolution* (Chicago and London, 1996).

[50] J. M. Beattie, 'London jurors in the 1690s', in J. S. Cockburn and T. A. Green, eds., *Twelve good men and true: the English criminal trial jury, 1200–1800* (Princeton, 1988). See also, all in Cockburn and Green, *Twelve good men*: P. G. Lawson, 'The composition and behaviour of Hertfordshire juries, 1573–1624'; J. S. Cockburn, 'Twelve silly men? The trial jury at Assizes, 1560–1670'; S. K. Roberts, 'Juries and the middling sort: recruitment and performance at Devon Quarter Sessions, 1649–1670'; P. J. R. King,

Shapiro argues, the permeation of English legal culture into other realms of thought, illustrated here by English theologians' appeal to the common law's standards of proof, disseminated legal culture's assumption that the ability to report and determine fact was by no means restricted to the elite, and that assumption became a foundation of English empiricism.[51]

Like Shapiro, David Lieberman examines the spread of legal thought beyond the courtroom. Lieberman has elsewhere examined eighteenth-century concepts of the respective roles of Parliament and the courts in amending law so that it addressed contemporary concerns. As he has noted, Blackstone addressed his *Commentaries*, the great classic of English legal thought, to England's legislators, for Blackstone aimed at enlightening their vision of the law which their legislation altered, usually for the worse.[52] While Blackstone's achievement has been presented as an elegant assemblage of contemporary platitudes, Lieberman here shows how much conceptual work Blackstone had to do: to convert the procedural distinction in English law between 'civil' and 'criminal' into a distinction basic to substantive law; and to convert the distinction between 'public' and 'private' into a distinction delineating the structures of English law. As he argues, since Blackstone's purpose was to present a structure making English law apprehensible to non-professionals, he regarded the categories he used to describe it and the associations he hypothesized among them as provisional. Nonetheless, even Blackstone's most vehement critics adopted these categories, making them essential to English jurisprudence. In showing that legal thought structured so as to appeal to laymen became the foundation of the legal thought of legal professionals, Lieberman's chapter demonstrates the continuous and immediate interplay of English law and English society. In so doing, his chapter provides the complement in the realm of legal thought to John Beattie's work on the activity of the courts. For Beattie has revealed the continuous interplay among what happened in England's criminal courts, its Parliament, and its society's understanding of crime and punishment.

' "Illiterate plebians, easily misled": jury composition, experience and behaviour in Essex, 1735–1815'; D. Hay, 'The class composition of the palladium of liberty: trial jurors in the eighteenth century'.

[51] Shapiro, *Culture of fact*, especially p. 218.

[52] Lieberman, *The province of legislation determined*; D. Lieberman, 'Blackstone's science of legislation', *Journal of British Studies*, vol. 27 (1988). I want to take this opportunity to thank Professor Lieberman for his interesting discussions of, and references relevant to, the questions provoked by his essay.

Part 1

Law

2 Dread of the Crown Office: the English magistracy and King's Bench, 1740–1800

Douglas Hay

High court judges and inferior magistrates

'I'll prosecute you and have you in the Kings Bench . . . I'll have no lawyers here . . . I'll have you in the King's Bench for this I'll play the Devil with you.'[1] Many justices of the peace disliked lawyers as much as John Gough, but they did not usually bellow such threats from an upper window. The men gathered in his courtyard at Perry Hall near Walsall in the autumn of 1802 were not impressed. One of them was a wealthy farmer, William Osborne, to whom Gough had irregularly and maliciously refused bail on a charge of assault a few days before; with him was his attorney. Gough's threat of a King's Bench prosecution perhaps inspired Osborne. Within a month he began a prosecution there against Gough for misdemeanour in his office.

King's Bench, one of the three central courts of the common law, was by the later eighteenth century the most important one. The dominant figure of Lord Mansfield (Chief Justice from 1756 to 1788) increased its prestige and civil business, and it had long been the main venue for state trials and constitutional argument. It was the supreme (and only) court of criminal jurisdiction in Westminster Hall. Trials on indictment in London and Middlesex came before it, but other prosecutions, arising in the provinces, also began or ended in King's Bench, argued by the greatest barristers. Some of these cases, like Osborne's prosecution of Gough, concerned justices of the peace and other magistrates who abused their office. The four judges of King's Bench were the only ones with the power to review magisterial misbehaviour, and also to punish it criminally.[2] It was here, if

My thanks to Douglas Johnson, Norma Landau, Jeanette Neeson, Ruth Paley and the Toronto Legal History Group for comments on earlier versions, and to Laird Meneley and Chris Frank for research assistance.

[1] Evidence given in Osborne's prosecution of Gough, discussed below.
[2] *Ex parte Rook* (1736) 2 Atkyns 1–2, *English Reports*, vol. XXVI, p. 398, ended any supervisory role Chancery might have exercised. Civil suits against magistrates could be brought in other common law courts (see below); habeas corpus was also obtainable in the court of Common Pleas, although rarely.

anywhere, that professional judges could control the enormous discretion of the justices of the peace and borough magistrates.

The relationship of judges to magistrates was a critically important one for government and law, arising from the peculiar (in European terms) characteristics of justice in England. The divergence of the European civilian and the English common law systems from medieval times, and the survival and entrenchment of jury trial in the latter, meant that England had very few royal judges, compared to continental jurisdictions like France. Until the nineteenth century there were only twelve common law judges: the Chief Justice and three puisne justices in each of the courts of King's Bench and Common Pleas, and the Chief Baron and three barons of the Court of Exchequer. In France, by contrast, there were 240 professional judges in the Parlement of Paris alone in the eighteenth century, and some 1,200 in all thirteen French appellate courts.[3] Their role in the criminal law was also significantly different. What juries did in England was done by judges in France, and appeals to higher benches of professional judges were mandatory in all serious cases in France but almost unknown in England. Finally, justices of the peace and borough magistrates in England carried out a great many of the duties entrusted to professional judges on the Continent, notably preliminary inquiries and committals. Yet English justices usually had no legal training. Only the most active ones were likely to have clerks learned in the law.

At county Quarter Sessions and borough Sessions English magistrates presided over an increasing proportion of jury trials. In the county of Stafford, for example, Quarter Sessions in the 1740s heard about 27 per cent of all jury trials, and the Assize judges (the common law judges on semi-annual circuit from Westminster) about 73 per cent. By the first two decades of the nineteenth century, the magistrates were hearing about 52 per cent, more than the judges. Legislation in the eighteenth century also greatly increased magistrates' jurisdiction for summary convictions, where they alone determined guilt and sentenced offenders. Moreover, since the sixteenth century they had had full responsibilities for initial bail and committal proceedings of virtually all felons who went on to jury trial. Almost all of these lay magistrates acted without pay or for relatively small fees. Paid magistrates (stipendiaries, with professional training) only appear at the end of our period, in London in 1792, and decades later in most other parts of the country. Contemporaries often observed that low justice in England was for the most part 'gratuitous': it was the creation of unpaid amateurs.

---

[3] R. C. Van Caenegem, *Judges, legislators and professors: chapters in European legal history* (Cambridge, 1987), p. 134.

There were important consequences for English criminal law, and for justice. If the law was to be enforced, the gentlemen and tradesmen who acted as county justices and borough magistrates had to be encouraged, and not deterred. Much has been written about the first – the encouragement of activity. Justices were enticed through the social status conferred by the title; by the hectoring of governments and Lord Chancellors; occasionally by financial guarantees from local elites.[4] But it was important also that they not be deterred from acting by the threat of prosecutions against them for errors they might easily make. In this chapter I argue that the great reliance of English criminal law on lay magistrates led inevitably to great tolerance by the high court judges, a tolerance for ignorant or mistaken, but also abusive and even clearly malicious, conduct.[5] The result was a well-understood but largely unmentioned equivocation central to English justice. In Westminster Hall, the seat of high law, the judges carefully constructed an inferior jurisdiction of low law in which most citizens were without remedy against insult and oppression by the magistracy.

King's Bench and lay justices: *certiorari* and criminal informations

The supervisory jurisdiction that King's Bench exercised over lay justices of the peace has been described in fulsome terms. Holdsworth argued that it is 'difficult to see how amateur justices could have applied this highly complex body of law without the constant supervision of the courts'. That supervision was effected by the prerogative writs, notably *certiorari*, and by prosecutions of magistrates, which in the case of King's Bench took the form of criminal informations for misdemeanour in their office. With the writ of *certiorari* a defendant could move all proceedings into King's Bench, where the judges could quash a summary conviction for insufficiency.[6] A prosecution on a criminal information was a charge

---

[4] For a Staffordshire example see Justice Carles of Handsworth, in Douglas Hay, 'Patronage, paternalism and welfare: masters, workers, and magistrates in eighteenth-century England', *International Labor and Working-Class History*, no. 53 (spring 1998), pp. 31–3.

[5] I use the term *magistrates* for both men in county commissions of the peace (justices of the peace), and borough justices. The judges of King's Bench and the other high courts at Westminster are sometimes referred to as justices, their form of address, but only where the context makes clear that judges, not justices of the peace or borough justices, are meant.

[6] Other writs, including habeas corpus, mandamus, and prohibition, were of lesser importance: see Douglas Hay, *Criminal cases on the crown side of King's Bench 1740–1800* (Staffordshire Record Society, forthcoming), cited below as *Crown side cases*.

brought against the magistrate himself.[7] Holdsworth suggested that the quashing of convictions brought before the court by *certiorari*, and the threat of criminal informations, made the justices careful in the use of their enormous jurisdiction, preventing 'a tyranny of the worst kind'. He quoted Squire Western as an examplar who (in Fielding's words) 'had already had two informations exhibited against him in the King's Bench, and had no curiosity to try a third'.[8] In their classic study of the justices of the peace the Webbs, less certain, quoted contradictory contemporary accounts, from the press, novels and pamphlets, to argue inconclusively that the threat of an information could be real, but that a qualified clerk was a real protection for the justice; that dishonest justices could act with relative impunity but that pettifogging attorneys and irate tradesmen made honest magistrates tremble with fear; that review on *certiorari* was costly and troublesome, but that it was not really much of a threat because it was so rarely used.[9]

It is surely crucial to ask who could use the courts, and what kinds of justices had cause to fear King's Bench. Some contemporaries drew such distinctions. A well-known Staffordshire justice, the Reverend Thomas Gisborne of Yoxall Lodge, in Needwood Forest, author of a much cited guide to gentlemanly conduct, commented on the 'tenderness' that King's Bench 'properly' had for misguided magistrates, but added that any magistrate was well aware 'that the objects whom he may be tempted to aggrieve are usually too humble, ignorant, and timid, to think of seeking redress except in very palpable and flagrant cases, and frequently too

[7] Criminal informations were abolished in 1938: Administration of Justice (Miscellaneous Provisions) Act, s. 12. For the procedure on such an information – which is to be distinguished from an information ex officio exhibited by the Attorney-General, from informations *qui tam*, and from the depositions, also called informations, taken before magistrates when they were hearing criminal cases – see Hay, *Crown side cases*. The alternative to prosecution by information in King's Bench, a prosecution on indictment, was available in King's Bench only against magistrates acting in London and Middlesex, where the court also had original jurisdiction; they could of course also be prosecuted there on information. Magistrates in all other parts of the country could be prosecuted on indictment in their own counties at Assizes and Quarter Sessions (probably a very rare proceeding, for reasons suggested below) or by criminal information in King's Bench, the method almost always used.

[8] William Holdsworth, *A history of English criminal law* (London, 1938), vol. X, pp. 249–50; Henry Fielding, *Tom Jones* (London, 1749), book 7, chap. 9. Fielding and his brother John were exposed to the threat of informations as magistrates in London, an aspect of their career discussed in unpublished work by Ruth Paley.

[9] Sidney [Baron Passfield] and Beatrice Webb, *English local government*, vol. I, *The parish and the county* (London, 1906; reprinted 1963), pp. 306, 333 (a discussion of *R. v. Spiller*, 1797), 336, 349, 389–90, 419–20.

poor to be able to undertake the task of seeking it in any'.[10] To explore that generalization (based in part on Gisborne's role in a case discussed below), and to get beyond the contradictory generalities of the Webbs and the thinly documented assertions of Holdsworth, we need to look at what King's Bench was actually doing.

The evidence can be sought in the law reports, which recorded cases significant in point of law, and also in the great mass of documentation left by the daily activity of the court. The best recent study of the justices of the peace suggests (largely on the basis of some of the reported case law) that in Kent their decisions were rarely reviewed, and that this may have been the general case, except perhaps in Westminster and Middlesex. Soundings in the archival records of the court for Kent found one instance of *certiorari*, a removal of an order of Sessions, in six years in the 1740s; there were apparently no applications for criminal informations or *certioraris* questioning summary convictions.[11] However the statistical basis of the argument needs investigation.[12] In this chapter I examine every criminal proceeding against the magistrates of one county, Staffordshire, over a period of sixty years.[13] Such cases were not numerous in Staffordshire, but neither were they unknown, and the archival record reveals some of the strategic considerations behind them.

In the last six decades of the eighteenth century in Staffordshire there were thirteen applications for criminal informations against fifteen different magistrates for misdemeanour in the execution of their office. There were also eleven proceedings on writs of *certiorari* directed to eight

[10] Thomas Gisborne, *An inquiry into the duties of men in the higher ranks and middle classes* (London, 1794), pp. 286–7. The work reached its 6th edition in 1811. Gisborne was a friend of Wilberforce and most of the eminent evangelicals (see *DNB*).

[11] Norma Landau, *The justices of the peace, 1679–1760* (Berkeley, 1984), pp. 354–5. On the case law, see below.

[12] Professor Landau used the Great Docket Book for 1743–60 (IND 1/6659) in the Public Record Office (hereafter P.R.O.) to assess the daily activity of the court. It is an index to the Crown Rolls (P.R.O., KB 28), but it is very incomplete in its coverage of cases because it records only a few of the many possible stages of process, usually only imparlances, pleas, and posteas. Thus, of thirteen attempts to get informations against Staffordshire magistrates found in my own study, the Docket Books note only two; there is similar gross underrepresentation of the numbers of *certioraris* on convictions. A six-year sample is also likely to be misleading, because of the uneven distribution of small numbers of cases; see Hay, *Crown side cases*.

[13] All the cases from 1740 to 1800 are reproduced in Hay, *Crown side cases*, parts B and E, where full references are given, and the process of the court described. The manuscript series exhaustively used in the study for the whole period 1740–1800 were P.R.O., ASSI 4, KB 1, KB 11, KB 15, KB 16, KB 20, KB 21, KB 29, KB 39 (indexes to KB 1), and the Great Docket Books (indexes to KB 28). Soundings were also made in KB 28, KB 33, and KB 36. Cases from 1800 to 1820 will be described in other publications.

different magistrates, questioning their summary convictions of sixteen defendants.[14] Over sixty years, therefore, twenty-four magistrates had their proceedings questioned in King's Bench in twenty-four separate proceedings. This does not seem a large number, given that there were perhaps 10,000 summary convictions and committal proceedings by several hundred lay magistrates in the county commission of the peace, and many other lay magistrates in the boroughs, in this period.[15] We might conclude that county and borough magistrates were for the most part administering the law well, perhaps because the formidable threat of a King's Bench information or the nuisance value of *certiorari* was effective *in terrorem*. On the other hand, so few cases might mean instead that judicial control over the justices was little but pious hope and convenient fiction, because few victims of magisterial injustice were able to go to King's Bench, as Gisborne suggested. A closer examination of the origins and outcomes of the cases, and the policy of King's Bench, is needed.

My description of judicial policy is based largely on the law reports, the stuff of the common law. The description of plaintiffs and outcomes, however, is confined to Staffordshire, and we should ask whether the county is representative. We do know that what King's Bench did with London cases was highly distinctive, for legal, social, and demographic reasons; and denunciations of justices for making a trade of their office, and for abuse of office, were common in the metropolis.[16] For most of the rest of England Staffordshire is probably broadly representative. The county had a large agricultural sector, but also burgeoning new industry; the social structure was a mix of great landed families, significant gentry, and many smallholders. There were numerous solicitors, large towns in the county (and Birmingham on its border) and growing population.

---

[14] In another case a prosecutor obtained *certiorari* directed to the justices at Quarter Sessions to remove an information he had laid against a linen draper for acting as a hatter, without being qualified under 5 Elizabeth c. 4, a proceeding designed to exacerbate costs.

[15] An estimate based on: (a) all criminal (rather than local government) cases on indictment at Staffordshire Assizes and Quarter Sessions in the period 1742–1802, including estimated totals based on decadal averages for sixteen years for which the sources are incomplete, which gives about 4,900 cases for 1740–99; a large proportion were felonies with committal proceedings; and (b) an estimate of summary convictions before magistrates, from gaol calendars, house of correction registers, and justices' correspondence in a variety of sources, which together suggest that there were as many summary convictions as there were proceedings on indictment. The principal sources are all P.R.O., ASSI series and Staffordshire Record Office (S.R.O.) Q/S series for 1742–1802.

[16] Ruth Paley's work is illuminating this aspect of the court's activity. See also Landau, *Justices*, p. 354, and 'The trading justice's trade' in this volume. As she notes, county sessions outside London and Middlesex do not appear to have disciplined justices as did the latter bench; nor have I yet found evidence of Staffordshire justices removed from the commission of the peace on complaints to the Lord Chancellor.

In 1701 it was probably the thirteenth most populous county outside London and Middlesex; in 1801, with a population of about 250,000, it was the eighth largest.

Harassing magistrates: *certiorari* and other annoyances

The writ of *certiorari* had several uses, but our concern here is with one: defendants removing summary proceedings before magistrates into King's Bench, in the hope of having a conviction quashed or the proceedings otherwise ended.[17] Some said that justices' summary convictions removed into King's Bench were usually doomed: 'there are less difficulties in penning the proceedings by action or information, than in wording a conviction [on the game laws] before a Justice, very few of which are able to stand the test when removed into the King's Bench. I scarce ever remember to have seen in my practice, a case where a conviction before a Justice hath been confirmed by the King's Bench.'[18] Certainly the high court was demanding, and some judges shared Blackstone's famous dislike of summary convictions on constitutional grounds.[19] Among the Staffordshire convictions removed by *certiorari* were three identical ones for fishing Sir John Wrottesley's pond, and all three were quashed. But none of the many hundreds (perhaps thousands) of other convictions on the game laws were removed by writ. The other Staffordshire convictions removed on *certiorari* were on the turnpike acts (three, involving four defendants), hawking and peddling without a licence (three), and stealing potatoes and turnips (one). The outcomes, including the three fishing cases, were one conviction affirmed, four quashed, two dismissed for failure of the prosecutor to respond, and three with outcomes unknown, probably because they were abandoned or compromised. The use of *certiorari* was therefore very rare, probably because it was a costly proceeding. In such cases the losing party could be put to very great expense, but the magistrate was not exposed to risk: if his conviction was quashed, only his esteem suffered, for he was not directly a party to the proceedings.

The bad justice was at risk from only three kinds of proceedings: lawsuits for civil damages, prosecutions on indictment, and criminal informations. There were undoubtedly some civil actions, in spite of barriers provided by statutory and common law protections for justices, but

---

[17] For other uses of *certiorari* see Hay, *Crown side cases*.

[18] Samuel Purlewent, *A dialogue between a lawyer and a country gentleman, upon the subject of the game laws* (4th edn, London, 1775), pp. 6–7. I discuss the case law with respect to convictions on *certiorari* in other work.

[19] William Blackstone, *Commentaries on the laws of England* (1765–9; 12th edn, London, 1793–5), vol. IV, pp. 281–2.

we still know little of their incidence.[20] The evidence about criminal indictments and criminal informations, however, is clear. The judges in
King's Bench commonly referred to prosecuting by indictment as the
'ordinary' way, since they held that prosecuting on information was an
'extraordinary' procedure, and they often refused an application for an
information by telling the prosecutor to proceed in the 'ordinary way'.[21]
But the 'ordinary' way on indictment at Quarter Sessions or Assizes was
almost unknown: it appears that not one such charge was brought against
a Staffordshire magistrate during this sixty-year period.[22] The difficulty
for a prosecutor was that the grand jury at Assizes, which had to find
the bill of indictment for a trial to result, were over 80 per cent of them
fellow-magistrates, while the bench at Quarter Sessions consisted entirely
of fellow-justices.[23] A criminal information in King's Bench was the remaining, and most public and notorious, threat to the erring magistrate.
He was said to be 'put into the Crown Office'.

Criminal informations against magistrates for misdemeanour in office

The Master of the Crown Office (properly called the King's Coroner and
Attorney), together with his secondary, clerk of the rules, examiner, calendar keeper, clerk of the grand juries, and seven clerks in court, oversaw
criminal proceedings before King's Bench and kept the records of the
Crown Side of the court. The Crown Office at the end of the eighteenth
century was on the ground floor of no. 2, King's Bench Walks, Temple,
and was open in both the law terms and vacation from 10 a.m. to 2 p.m.,
and 5 p.m. to 8 p.m.[24] The Master lent his name to the private prosecutor
of a criminal information, but to successfully 'exhibit' such an information the prosecutor had first by affidavit, and arguments of counsel, to
convince the judges of King's Bench to make a rule *nisi*. If it was granted,

[20] See Landau, *Justices*, pp. 353–4. Press reports suggest there were far fewer civil actions
than attempts to proceed by criminal information. It was necessary to choose one or the
other: see below, Osborne's proceedings against Justice John Gough; I have not found
reference to any other Staffordshire case in this period.
[21] See below.
[22] Based on an examination of all surviving indictments in undamaged rolls of Quarter
Sessions and Assizes, 1742–1802, and associated minute books and other series, about
80 per cent of the original record. For the sources, see note 15.
[23] In 1822 this fact was asserted in argument by counsel, and accepted by the judges, as
a reason for allowing proceedings by information rather than on indictment even where
the magistrates had not acted corruptly or from any improper motive, in returning a
false return to a mandamus in a poor law case. *R. v. Justices of Lancashire*, 1 Dowling
and Ryland's Mag. Cases 127.
[24] William Hands, *The solicitor's practice on the crown side of the Court of King's Bench* (London,
1803), p. iii.

the magistrate filed affidavits in defence, and made defence also by counsel. If the court thought a sufficiently strong case had been made by the prosecutor, they granted a rule absolute, giving the right to exhibit an information (the formal charge) in the name of the Master of the Crown Office. The prosecutor then had the information drawn and engrossed, prepared the case for trial at Assizes (on the *nisi prius* or civil side of Assizes, not the crown court) in the county where the cause arose, had counsel seek a guilty verdict before a petty jury (almost always a 'special' jury of gentlemen), and if successful then sought judgment and sentence back in King's Bench in Westminster Hall. It might be necessary to fight off motions for arrest of judgment, or for new trials, even after a guilty verdict.

To proceed by information was neither simple nor cheap. Costs might very well be awarded against the prosecutor. On the other hand, a successful prosecution could be embarrassing, both socially and financially, for the magistrate. Even if the court did not grant a rule absolute to the prosecutor, the judges might chastise the justice by awarding costs against him, and making adverse comments in court. But was the danger very great? Both the case law and the Staffordshire cases suggest it was not.

Procedural obstacles to prosecuting a magistrate

King's Bench erected very high barriers against such prosecutions. Some applied to all applications for informations, not only those against magistrates, but they enjoyed additional protections. In all informations, the prosecutor had to relinquish his right to sue civilly, to save a defendant in a civil action from disclosing his defence in the criminal proceedings.[25] The court also required (at least after mid-century) that the prosecutor file an exculpatory affidavit of his own innocence.[26] But for magistrates there was the added protection of notice before the plaintiff moved for a rule *nisi*. Getting both a rule *nisi* and a rule absolute was also expensive because it required co-ordination between agents and attornies in the county, with attornies and counsel in London, in order to file affidavits and make motions in the limited number of days in each law term.[27] Affidavits had to be procured in the country, forwarded to counsel for

---

[25] *R. v. Fielding* (1758, 1759) 2 Kenyon 386, *English Reports*, vol. XCVI, p. 1219; 2 Burrows 720, *English Reports*, vol. XCVII, p. 531.

[26] *R. v. Webster (and Troyte)* (1789) 3 Term Reports 388, *English Reports*, vol. C, p. 636; *R. v. Athay* (1758) 2 Burrows 653–55, *English Reports*, vol. XCVII, p. 495.

[27] There were four terms, two of fixed dates and two dated by moveable feasts: Michaelmas, Hilary, Easter and Trinity. Process in the court was tied not only to the terms, but to return days within the terms, and timing was crucial. For details see Hay, *Crown side cases*.

their opinion, the opinion communicated to the private prosecutor for his decision, then notice of the motion given to the magistrate. The prosecution could be frustrated if the defendant was vigilant, as a Lichfield magistrate apparently was in 1753. A motion could not be made in Easter term because the letter giving the justice notice was lost in the Lichfield post office. Early in June instructions to give the J.P. notice for Trinity term arrived too late, again through mysterious delays in the post. (It seems likely that the defendant had friends in the Lichfield office.) Finally, on 26 June, four days into the term, the justice was served, in person, with notice that the court would be moved for a rule on 3 July. The prosecutor's solicitor was aware that the court might object that one week's notice, only eight days before the end of term, was insufficient.[28] The prosecutor had to wait again, until Michaelmas term, to allow time for fresh notice to be given. However, no motion resulted. The defendant may have taken steps to satisfy the prosecutor, but it is also possible that the prosecutor's lawyers pointed out to him that the court would not usually accept an information against a justice more than two terms after his alleged offence.[29]

The consequences of a wholly unsuccessful complaint against a justice were serious. Costs (in what was a very expensive form of litigation) then fell on the prosecutor, and since all the persons who made affidavits against the justice were held to be prosecutors, it could be very difficult to find witnesses in the first place, and disastrous for them when proceedings failed.[30]

Judicial tenderness towards erring magistrates

More important than procedural barriers was judicial policy. By the mid-eighteenth century only intentional illegality, characterized by corruption, malice or partiality, could persuade the judges to act: in the later eighteenth century intentional illegality alone could support an indictment, but not an information in King's Bench. It appears that earlier in the century, rules for informations had been granted more readily, without a need to show evidence of corrupt motives, probably in part a reflection of the felt need to control politically aberrant J.P.s in a period of acute party conflict early in the century. Thus an information was granted against a

---

[28] He prepared an affidavit of the delays, but appears not even to have bothered to file it, for it cannot be found in KB 1, only in the prosecutor's private papers: see below.

[29] The case, *R. v. Nott*, is discussed and references given further below. For the two-term rule, see Richard Gude, *The practice of the crown side of the Court of King's Bench* (London, 1828), vol. I, p. 111, note a.

[30] Gude, *Practice of the crown side*, vol. I, p. 119.

justice who prevented a borough sessions meeting by his voluntary absence; against others who did not proceed firmly against a recusant who was 'a gentleman of fashion'; against another for charging a shilling for a warrant and committing the prisoner for non-payment.[31] In none of these cases do the reported words of the judges state a standard of corrupt or partial motives for granting a rule, although in the last clearly the magistrate had a pecuniary interest, if a very small one, in the penalty.

Lord Mansfield emphasized much narrower grounds in a series of cases not long after he became Chief Justice in 1756. Before justices were forced to defend themselves before juries, he required proof in the initial proceedings of 'partial, oppressive, corrupt, or arbitrary views': 'If their judgement is wrong, yet their heart and intention pure, God forbid that they should be punished! and he declared that he should always lean towards favouring them; unless partiality, corruption, or malice shall clearly appear.' Mansfield's language in this case in 1758 is interesting. He expressed concern about 'an arbitrary and uncontrolled power over the rights of other people' that magistrates might indulge, and appeared ready to grant a rule for an information, but then drew back. The Chief Justice was in fact balancing two interests of the government: protecting J.P.s, crucial to the administration of a system so heavily dependent upon lay justices; and yet also safeguarding the electoral interest of the government, which was often involved in licensing cases (such as this was).[32] In other cases he reiterated what became the test for even a rule *nisi*, as well as a rule absolute. A criminal information was an 'extraordinary assistance [to a prosecutor] (which they ought to dispense with caution and discretion)'; mere irregularities would never suffice.[33] Justices had the right to judge whether a matter brought before them was an offence in law, and to refuse to proceed if they thought not.[34] And in 1761 King's Bench declared that 'even where a justice of peace acts illegally . . . yet if he has acted honestly and candidly, without oppression, malice, revenge, or any bad view or ill intention whatsoever, the court will never punish him in this extraordinary course of an information; but leave the party complaining, to the ordinary legal remedy or method of prosecution, by action or by indictment'.[35]

---

[31] *R. v. Fox* (1717) 1 Strange 21, *English Reports*, vol. XCIII, p. 359; *R. v. Newton* (1721) 1 Strange 413, *English Reports*, vol. XCIII, p. 604; *R. v. Jones* (1742) 1 Wilson 7, *English Reports*, vol. XCV, p. 462.
[32] *R. v. Young and Pitts* (1758) 1 Burrows 557 at 557, 562, *English Reports*, vol. XCVII, p. 447.
[33] *R. v. Fielding* (1759) 2 Burrows 720, *English Reports*, vol. XCVII, p. 531.
[34] *R. v. Cox* (1759) 2 Burrows 785 at 788, *English Reports*, vol. XCVII, p. 562.
[35] *R. v. Palmer and Baine* (1761) 2 Burrows 1163, *English Reports*, vol. XCVII, p. 767.

The standards for determining such issues were exacting. When acting in sessions, only 'flagrant proofs of their having acted from corrupt motives' would warrant a rule for an information.[36] A number of the reported cases, and some of the unreported ones from Staffordshire, suggest the same standard was applied to the acts of single justices. The standard of corruption was met in one reported case of 1772 where a justice sat on a salvage inquiry from which he would personally benefit.[37] Mansfield reiterated throughout his long tenure (1756–88) that 'No justice of peace ought to suffer for ignorance, where the heart is right. On the other hand, when magistrates act from undue, corrupt, or indirect motives, they are always punished by this court.'[38] The language however had shifted: after 1761 the cases mention neither malice nor revenge explicitly as grounds for an information, and corruption became almost the only test.

The three puisne judges of King's Bench endorsed Mansfield's very narrow definition of corruption in 1787, and his emphasis on it as the crucial test.[39] Shortly after he left the bench there was a suggestion that perhaps it might be widened, and malice readmitted. In 1788 Mr Justice Ashhurst observed, in a case where the magistrates involved denied any interested motives, 'if they acted even from passion or opposition, that is equally corrupt as if they had acted from pecuniary considerations'.[40] Since the cases show many very passionate magistrates, in infuriated opposition to some of those who came before them, this ruling might have opened up interesting possibilities. It did not. In subsequent reported cases the definition of corruption was not widened, and the narrow test was given even more importance.[41]

The incidence of prosecution: Staffordshire

The reported cases are a good guide to the law because they constitute, taken together, the extant evidence of doctrine for us and for

---

[36] *R. v. Justices of Seaford* (1761) 1 Wm Blackstone 432, *English Reports*, vol. XCVI, p. 246.
[37] *R. v. Davis* (1772) Lofft 62, *English Reports*, vol. XCVIII, p. 534.
[38] *R. v. Cozens and another* (1780) 2 Douglas 426, *English Reports*, vol. XCIX, p. 273.
[39] *R. v. Holland and Forster* (1787) 1 Term Reports 692, *English Reports*, vol. XCIX, p. 1324 per Ashhurst: 'what the law says shall not be done, it becomes illegal to do, and is therefore the subject of an indictment, without the addition of any corrupt motives. And though the want of corruption may be an answer to an application for an information, which is made to the extraordinary jurisdiction of the court, yet it is no answer to an indictment, where the judges are bound by the strict rule of law.'
[40] *R. v. Brooke and others* (1788) 2 Term Reports 191, *English Reports*, vol. C, p. 103.
[41] I discuss the further development of the case law elsewhere.

contemporaries.[42] They are useless for assessing the numbers, origins, and outcomes of such cases before the courts, as are newspaper accounts, even when they became more common in the late eighteenth century. I have shown that in Staffordshire there were thirteen attempts to get informations against sixteen magistrates over sixty years; there were eighteen charges in all, because some of the applications were for informations against more than one J.P., and one magistrate had several cases brought against him. Only one of these Staffordshire cases entered the law reports; one other was reported in the press.[43]

The difficulties of prosecuting a justice are well illustrated in the unreported Staffordshire cases, and particularly from the detail of the affidavits. Most prosecutors alleged wrongful committal to gaol, usually because the justice had not listened to their defences or had obstinately refused to accept bail or examine them further. There was also an accusation of wrongful summary conviction because the defendant was not called; corrupt collusion with another magistrate in a game case; refusing an alehouse licence out of malice and without cause; misconduct in helping to press a man into the army. Three cases involved jurisdictional disputes with respect to poor relief, in Lichfield and Walsall.

In two instances affidavits were filed and then the case was dropped, possibly because the magistrate came to an agreement, or because costs frightened the complainant. In one of these cases, the complainant said she had come to King's Bench only because the magistrate now refused to compensate her for maliciously imprisoning her.[44] In the remaining eleven, the response of King's Bench was almost always to refuse to grant an information. A rule *nisi* was made in all of them, then discharged in eight; in a ninth case the prosecutor appears to have abandoned proceedings after the rule *nisi*. In only two cases did the court grant permission to the prosecutor to exhibit an information. In one, the poaching case, the court did so only when the two magistrates involved refused to pay costs, a compromise that had been accepted when it appeared that the evidence against them was damning. In only one case, that of the alehouse licence, did the case go so far as an order for the striking of a jury, and notice of trial, but the case did not in fact go to trial. In a third case, one in which

---

[42] The judges sometimes based decisions in part on unreported cases with which they were personally familiar, or knew from unpublished notes of their own, of counsel, or of other judges.

[43] *R. v. Corbett and Coulson* (1757) Sayer 256; *R. v. Palmer and Taylor*, reported in *Aris's Birmingham Gazette*, 24 January 1771. There were no reports of Staffordshire criminal informations in seven leading London newspapers, but there was one report of a civil suit, *Osborne v. Gough*, that followed an unsuccessful attempt to prosecute Gough by criminal information: see below.

[44] The other case was a poor rate dispute in Lichfield, possibly collusive.

a hawker had served three months in prison because the justice refused to listen to his defence (the hawker pointed out to him the exact clause of the relevant statute), the court refused to make the rule absolute, but chastised the magistrate by refusing to allow him to claim his costs from his prosecutor.

In other words, in sixty years the difficulties of bringing an information and the determination of the judges to protect magistrates meant that hardly any of them were even rebuked in King's Bench. The harshest response possible for the judges was to grant a rule absolute to allow an information to be exhibited, exposing the magistrate to the possibility of a jury trial. In only two cases (involving three justices in all) was a rule absolute made; in all the other cases the prosecution was unsuccessful. Moreover, it appears that those three justices did not in the end face trial: all the cases were discharged, possibly compromised with a financial settlement, or dropped before a jury could hear them. In only one case (against two borough justices) did King's Bench express its disapproval, by requiring the otherwise unpunished magistrates to pay their own costs (which otherwise fell on the prosecution); in one other case, the J.P. had also to pay the costs of the prosecutor.

Misbehaving magistrates

In general, the court was unmoved by accusations that justices had too hastily or too angrily committed men to gaol for one or a few weeks, or on bad warrants. Lay magistrates were likely to make such mistakes, the defendants were all rather unimportant people, as Gisborne noted, and the judges were probably convinced that there were only too many rascals willing to take advantage of an unpaid lay magistrate's ignorance. It is perhaps significant that the two Staffordshire cases in which the court actually granted an information touched on issues of sharp political and social significance to gentlemen. The malicious refusal to grant an alehouse licence was an offence that did arouse the judges of King's Bench, because licensing had strong political implications: refusal to grant a licence, or a threat to do so, was often tied to demands that the publican give his vote for a particular candidate. In the early 1760s a number of reported cases show the judges granting informations in such cases in other counties also.[45] In the Staffordshire case, however, one of the two magistrates had refused to relicense unless a cask, his property, was

[45] See *R. v. Young and Pitts* (1758), cited above, in which an information was not granted, and *R. v. Hann and Price* (1765) 3 Burrow 1716, *English Reports*, vol. XCVII, p. 1062; *R. v. Williams and Davis* (1762) 3 Burrow 1317, *English Reports*, vol. XCVII, p. 851; *R. v. Baylis and others* (1762) 3 Burrows 1318, *English Reports*, vol. XCVII, p. 851.

returned: it had been stolen from the publican's wharf. The other case in which a rule absolute was granted, the apparently corrupt collusion of two borough justices, a tanner and a maltster, to protect an offender against the penalties of the game laws, was sure to scandalize any gentleman, including those on the King's Bench. It was precisely such tradesmen as tanners and maltsters that the game laws were designed to exclude from 'society'.

The evidence from Staffordshire, then, suggests that the reported cases are a fair guide to the actual administration of the law: it was difficult to prosecute a magistrate, and very few were brought before the court. But the brief accounts in the law reports tell us little or nothing about the context of even the few cases that came to be reported. In contrast, there is a wealth of detail in the manuscript affidavits found in the records of the court. The Staffordshire affidavits show much magisterial ignorance, bad-tempered high-handedness, casual and unlawful commitments to noisome gaols and houses of correction, obstinate and (in at least one case) apparently malicious refusal to take bail. In none of these cases were the misbehaving magistrates punished: after all, they were not actuated by 'corrupt motives' or 'interest' in the narrow terms defined by the high court judges. And country magistrates clearly knew they were in little danger from King's Bench. When John Gough of Perry Hall threatened to use King's Bench against William Osborne, the aggrieved farmer who dared to bring a lawyer to his door, the magistrate himself had already had five previous allegations made against him in King's Bench for similarly questionable committals to the house of correction. Squire Gough, unlike Squire Western, clearly had not been intimidated by his experience of proceedings in the Crown Office. After all, the court of King's Bench had never yet consented to grant an information against him.

The singular case of John Gough

Gough was the defendant in one-third of the attempts to get informations against Staffordshire J.P.s. Almost half of all the complainants to King's Bench had suffered at his hands. In 1784 he was accused of committing a man to the house of correction for 'impudence' and to get revenge on the man's master: accused of not maintaining his family, he was confined under irons, locked to the floor, and treated as a felon. In another case that year Gough jailed another man under a faulty warrant, simply for charging a woman with theft. In a third case, also in 1784, he imprisoned his victim under conditions used for felons for what was a civil debt. The affidavits denounced 'the unbounded caprice of the said John Gough who has for some time past most cruelly wantonly and oppressively exercised his power and authority of a magistrate and tyrannized over many of His Majesty's subjects by committing them and releasing them at his pleasure'. The following year he jailed a woman for 'obtaining a bonnet with false pretences': her defence was that she had borrowed it for a pattern. A few months later he apparently refused to hear defence witnesses when committing several more men to custody for a brawl.[46]

Yet Gough was one of the least active justices in the county, accounting for fewer than one-half of 1 per cent of committals for trial between 1783 and 1802 (the most active J.P., the Reverend Alexander Bunn Haden, did over 23 per cent), and probably relatively few summary convictions.[47] There were many such men: in each decade between 1740 and 1800 between 40 per cent and 80 per cent of acting Staffordshire justices, depending on the decade, committed fewer than 2 per cent of those sent for trial. In contrast, a small number of justices (4 per cent to 10 per cent of them) dealt with a third or more of all committals. Gough's few recorded committals were in 1784, two years after he began acting.[48] Five of the six complaints against him in King's Bench were brought in two years, 1784 and 1785. Thereafter he did committals very seldom, although he was always available to deal with poachers on summary conviction. One reading of this history might be that Gough was precisely the sort of careless or overbearing justice who needed curbing, that such men were rare, and that the attempted prosecutions in King's Bench in 1784–5 succeeded in deterring him. But a fuller picture emerges from examining his other activities.

Gough was a wealthy, irascible eccentric, greatly interested in litigation. He or his clerk kept a notebook indexing decisions in King's Bench relevant to his work as a magistrate, or his many lawsuits.[49] He soon added to the litigation inherited from his father Walter in 1773. There were disputes with the rector, the Reverend Thomas Lane, about Gough's pew in 1776 and over services and tithes in 1778; with tenants over rents and his attorney over bills in the 1770s and 1780s; with his neighbour George Birch about warrens and trees and manor boundaries in the late 1770s and early 1780s; with the wardens of Sutton Coldfield over hunting rights in 1780–3; and again with the rector about tithes in 1793.

---

[46] The quotation is from P.R.O., KB 1/23, Trin. 24 Geo. III pt. 1, affidavit of John Inman, Richard Phillips and Samuel Bickley, 14 May 1784. For the cases against Gough see Hay, *Crown side cases*, section B.

[47] Figures based on gaol calendars for Assizes and Quarter Sessions, S.R.O. He committed only two men to the Stafford house of correction (only one-tenth of 1 per cent of the total) between 1792 and 1818, but likely more than that to the nearby Wolverhampton house of correction.

[48] P.R.O., C/193/45 and C220/9/8.

[49] Birmingham City Archives [hereafter B.C.A.], Gough deposit 203.

In the 1790s he was also involved in litigation about properties in other counties.[50]

Gough had seats at Perry Hall about 5 miles south-east of Walsall, and Old Fallings, just north of Wolverhampton; he also owned property in Gnosall, Wolverhampton, and ten other Staffordshire parishes or manors, and in Dorset and Hampshire. He died in 1828. A biographical notice of the family remarked his 'parsimony and churlishness'.[51] He hated poachers but also gentlemen pursuing game on to his land. He prosecuted the former and sued the latter, breaching the social code by which gentlemen indulged other gentlemen in their sport.[52] In 1784 he enraged many of his neighbours by luring the hounds of the Wolverhampton Hunt on to his lands, killing them, and proceeding against their owners. He violated the fundamental mores of his class by barring gentlemen from hunting over his 1,000 acres near Wolverhampton; they reciprocated. He exchanged insults in the press with his adversaries: they published a broadsheet that began 'Hic Niger est! Cavete mi Fratres',[53] 'The behaviour of a gentleman was never expected; but, in the form of a man (if such can be called the form of man) a faint shade of some single virtue might have glimmered through the foul passions of *oppressive avarice, and unsatiated revenge.*' Gough was, the author concluded, 'a wretch born in despite of nature, fostered by the blackest demons of malignity, and permitted by providence to exist as a libel upon mankind'.[54]

Gough's in-laws agreed. In late 1778 or early 1779 he had married Eleanor, the daughter of Thomas Mytton, a Shropshire country gentleman, squire of Shipton, and a cousin of Gough.[55] Gough drove a very hard bargain in negotiations for the settlement. Within a year of

---

[50] B.C.A., Gough 7423, *passim.* I discuss some of these cases elsewhere, and others below.

[51] Robert K. Dent and Joseph Hill, *Historic Staffordshire* (London, 1896), p. 260; *Aris's Birmingham Gazette* [hereafter *A.B.G.*], 25 February, 26 August 1782; *Staffs. Advertiser*, 9 February 1828. Stebbing Shaw wrote about 1799 that Perry Hall was owned by Gough, 'whose well-known *liberality* and *kindness* prohibited me giving, by personal inspection, even an external description of this old moated mansion'. Shaw, *History of Staffordshire*, vol. II, part 1 (1801), pp. 109–10. I am grateful to Douglas Johnson for bringing this and other biographical information in Shaw to my attention.

[52] B.C.A., Gough 192/1, Gough to Jesson, 27 January 1779; Gough 202/1–29; Gough 205/1–3.

[53] I thank Dr Jeremy Trevett for identifying the source: Horace, *Satires*, 1.4.85, 'Hic niger est, hunc tu Romane caveto': 'This man is black, this man, O Roman [adapted to 'my brothers'], beware of.'

[54] *A.B.G.*, 26 August 1782, 25 August 1783, 25 October, 1, 8 and 15 November 1784; William Salt Library (Stafford), broadsheets 33/12, *Answer to John Gough's advertisement in the Birmingham Gazette*; S.R.O., Q/SB 1784 Ea/70.

[55] *Victoria county history of Shropshire*, vol. X (1998), ed. C. R. J. Currie, pp. 172, 359, 370, 373, 378–9; Burke, *Landed gentry* (6th edn, 1882), vol. II, p. 1151. I thank Douglas Johnson for this information.

the marriage Gough claimed that his authority was undermined by his wife, her mother and aunt, who 'attempted to strip him of his Prerogative, as the Head of this family'. He alleged that his servants were told to spit at him: 'The oldest man living never remembered such an instance, the truth shocks every person.' He claimed to find a copy of his master key in his wife's pocket (he searched her while she was asleep), and apparently pressed her father for payment of what he owed on the portion, and for control over her fortune.[56] Her brother wrote from London threatening to horsewhip him; Gough asked for advice from the Lord Chief Justice on how to prosecute the young man. (The answer was, see a magistrate about such a simple breach of the peace.) In September Gough turned his mother-in-law and her sister out of his house. Mytton by now referred to him as 'that little wretch'.[57]

The hatred in which Gough was held raises the strong possibility that he had wealthy enemies willing to assist in prosecuting him in King's Bench; they were certainly unlikely to deter such proceedings. Several men who were disgusted by Gough's behaviour in the 1780s apparently assisted in a very expensive prosecution against him in 1802.[58] The men and women whose cases led to applications for informations in King's Bench against Gough in 1784 and 1785 were a servant, two locksmiths, a labourer, and the wife of a chapefiler.[59] None are likely to have been able to begin such expensive proceedings themselves; all prosecuted shortly after his virulent quarrels with the Wolverhampton Hunt. The last prosecution against him, in 1802, took place in the wake of a libellous quarrel with another magistrate, the Reverend Thomas Lane. It is likely that similar quarrels lay behind many other prosecutions against magistrates in King's Bench. The difficulty, expense and danger of beginning proceedings there meant that poorer people, without powerful support, could not get justice in the high court, as Gisborne observed. But if local gentry became annoyed with a justice, either because their interests were infringed or because they thought his behaviour cast a bad light on their class and office, a case was probably far more likely to be forwarded. Prosecutions of J.P.s in King's Bench, even those apparently brought solely to redress the sufferings of poor prisoners, are thus likely to be expressions of feuds between gentlemen, or between gentry and wealthy tradesmen or farmers.

---

[56] On this common problem, see Susan Staves, *Married women's separate property in England, 1660–1833* (Cambridge and London, 1990), p. 118.

[57] B.C.A., Gough 222/1–4; William Salt Library, Acc. 123/1/63. Apparently the marriage recovered to some degree. A son and two daughters were born in 1780, 1781 and 1783, when Eleanor died in childbirth. Shaw, *History of Staffordshire*, p. 188.

[58] See below, notes 68 and 72, on the involvement of Thomas and Samuel Gem.

[59] One of the many specialized metalworkers of the region; in this case, a man who makes one part of a buckle.

Two cases at the end of the century brought Gough before King's Bench again, first as a libeller, then as an oppressive justice. The first prosecutor was the rector of Handsworth, himself a J.P., the Reverend Thomas Lane. Lane had sued him for tithes in 1778, pressing the case because (in Lane's lawyer's words) Gough's 'behaviour to him has been, and continues to be, so unlike a gentleman, that he shall insist upon every thing that the law will give him'.[60] The father of Gough's bride-to-be had helped reconcile Lane and Gough, but not for long. Another J.P. was soon involved, George Birch, Lane's brother-in-law, who was in the awkward position of being jointly seized with Gough of the lordship of the manor of Perry Barr.[61] Country gentlemen were intensely territorial animals, and Birch had disputed boundaries in earlier litigation, supposedly set-tled by arbitration in 1780.[62] Moreover, Gough's seat was actually within Birch's manor of Handsworth, only a mile from the latter's house.[63] When Lane became a J.P. and began acting in the area in the late 1780s, he soon joined the battle.[64] In what appears to have been a contest for control in Perry Barr, Gough and Lane warred over cottages Gough owned there. The cottagers Gough installed had settlements, so that Lane could not evict under the poor laws; Lane removed them for en-croaching, and unroofed the cottages. Gough rebuilt and had one of his tenants sue Lane successfully. Lane then ordered some of Gough's park wall destroyed, as an encroachment on the highway, indicted him for other parts of it, and when Gough removed the case to King's Bench on *certiorari*, nonetheless managed to convict him on one count at Stafford Assizes.[65]

Meanwhile Lane called a meeting by public advertisement in 1791 to consider disorderly alehouses.[66] It was attended by Lane, his brother-in-law Birch, and Messrs Matthew Boulton and James Watt, proprietors of the well-known engineering works at Soho, 2 miles away, and the largest

---

[60] B.C.A., Gough 210/11.
[61] George Birch was the son of Thomas Birch, justice of the Court of Common Pleas between 1746 and 1757. George was lord of the manor of Handsworth and joint lord of the manor, with Gough, of Perry Barr. Birch had inherited from his uncle, the Reverend John Birch, rector of Handsworth until 1775 or 1776; Birch presented the living to Lane. By the time of the lawsuit, in 1800, Birch was married to Lane's sister Ann, and Lane was married to Birch's sister Ester. Shaw, *History of Staffordshire*, pp. 111, 113, 116.
[62] B.C.A., Gough 195.   [63] William Yates, *A map of the county of Stafford* (1775).
[64] S.R.O., Q/JC.
[65] The account of Gough's feud with Lane and Birch is based on the King's Bench pro-ceedings in Lane's prosecution of Gough on a criminal information for libel, and on the *certiorari* in the highway case (see Hay, *Crown side cases*); a broadsheet of 10 December 1794 in William Salt Library, broadsheets 3; *Glover v. Lane and others* (17 Nov. 1789) 3 TR 445, *English Reports*, vol. C, p. 669, and sources noted below.
[66] *A.B.G.*, 5 September 1791: the charge to the grand jury by the judge at summer Assizes had recommended stricter licensing.

employers in the parish. The group decided to recommend the immediate suppression of one alehouse for drunkenness and fighting, and the non-renewal of licences of five more, leaving the parched inhabitants only six pubs in a parish of 2,000 people. Popular dislike of Lane's campaign may have been the encouragement to Gough to embark on a public campaign of vilification.

He adopted the rhetoric of the paternalist squire, protector of the poor and of their amusements, and the symbolic idiom of the people. In December 1794 he published a handbill against 'a Person actuated by Malice, Revenge, and an Implacability of Disposition ... [and] the Malevolent Turpitude of an Unfeeling, Unprincipled Hard-hearted Villain'. In it he reviewed his own grievances, those of the dispossessed cottagers (without mentioning his own interest) and Lane's persecution of an alehouse keeper by removing his licence (although Gough apparently exposed the man, one of his tenants, to Lane's wrath by forcing him to post copies of Gough's handbills).[67] The following year he broadened the attack. In September a wooden effigy of Lane, placarded as 'the Devil' and 'Tom the fiddler's Son' appeared and hung in Handsworth parish for three weeks. Lane prosecuted six of Gough's tenants at January 1796 Quarter Sessions for libel, and then Gough himself at the Assizes in March. In both cases the grand jury, probably unwilling to be involved in a quarrel between two members of the bench, and perhaps somewhat amused, threw the case out of court.[68]

Thus encouraged, Gough commissioned a painting of a clerical justice and his clerk, pulling down cottages, with the devil in attendance; the title proclaimed 'HOW CAN SUCH RANCOUR DWELL IN AN HOLY BREAST'. It was fixed to the house of one of his tenants, in a prominent position near a main road in the parish, where it remained for many months. In the summer of 1800 it was remounted on the wall of another tenant's house, on the main Walsall to Birmingham turnpike, directly opposite the pub where the justices often held petty sessions. As Lane set out for Translation Quarter Sessions in July he rode by it; he saw it again when returning from the Assizes in August. The tenant explained it was Gough's idea and that he risked eviction if he took it down. Other tenants' houses in

[67] Gough's and Lane's testimonies are wildly contradictory; Lane made this claim, and added that Gough persuaded the man not to pay the fine, and be gaoled, to embarrass the magistrates. On the other hand the first extant handbill is dated after this incident, and three years after the meeting called by Lane to consider disorderly alehouses.

[68] S.R.O., Q/SR 1796, Epiphany, indictment of John Hussey *et al.*; P.R.O., ASSI 2/26, 4/7 and 5/116, Staffs. Lent 1796, indictment of Gough *et al.* Hussey turned witness for Lane in the second prosecution; another witness was Thomas Gem, perhaps a relative of a Samuel Gem, who attacked Gough in the press in 1784.

Handsworth were posted that week with handbills:

To be seen gratis near the Blue Pig Great Barr a most elegant piece of painting done by a very masterly hand, shewing in full length the following uncommon figures; The Infernal Monster with Old Nick at his back, and Clerk Solomon and other Monsters assisting him to pull down houses of great value, over the heads of several distressed families, with their helpless infants crying for mercy, attended by his Father in Law a fiddler, and his own Mother a Kitchen Maid.[69]

A mile away at Perry another of Gough's tenants displayed a signboard 'covered with indecent songs and libellous handbills' including an 'Anticipation of the Death-bed confession of a Notorious Sinner'.[70] On the ruined cottages on Perry Warren Gough again erected effigies of Lane and his clerk, pickaxes in hand, and explanatory signs. Five other houses owned by Gough in Handsworth displayed handbills, and three of them, all near public highways, displayed signs castigating Lane. When Lane met Gough in the road that week the latter shouted from his carriage and threw more handbills at him.

Lane finally prosecuted for libel on a criminal information in King's Bench. Possibly Gough's behaviour was now embarrassing the gentry, who may also have been uneasy about his appeal to the mob. It was almost certainly opposed by farmers, who probably disliked his development of the waste. Lane apparently now believed he would be able to get a verdict from a special jury at Stafford Assizes. Thomas Erskine, his counsel, convinced the judges of King's Bench to grant a rule absolute for an information in January 1801. The next stages, exhibition of the information and trial, did not follow. Perhaps Lane was ill; he died in October 1802.[71] But his initial success in King's Bench may have helped persuade William Osborne, a wealthy local farmer, to again seek a criminal information in King's Bench against Gough for misdemeanour in his office as a magistrate, the first such prosecution against him since the cases of 1784 and 1785. Osborne was rich, determined, and had Lane's example before him. He hated Gough, who had sued his father for trespassing when he had come on business to Perry Hall many years before. Like Lane, Osborne employed the celebrated Erskine to argue his case.

[69] Lane's clerk was Solomon Smith; the Blue Pig was the local inn used for petty sessions. Why Gough called Lane's father, or his wife's father, a fiddler, and Lane's mother the daughter of a fiddler and a woman who had 'employed her charms to some advantage' (a reference in the handbill cited in the following note) is obscure. The Reverend Thomas Lane was the son of Thomas Lane esquire of Bentley Hall, from a line of respected Staffordshire gentry (information from Douglas Johnson).

[70] The handbill is reproduced in my doctoral thesis (University of Warwick, 1976), and in E. P. Thompson, *Customs in common* (London, 1991), plate VI.

[71] *Staffordshire Advertiser*, 16 October 1802.

The 1802 case arose when one of Osborne's servants complained to Gough about the farmer. Osborne had given a 'smartish flogging' to his servant, a 15-year-old boy who had left the horses unattended at harvest in order to course a hare.[72] Gough wrote to Osborne to come to the Blue Pig if he wished to avoid trouble. Osborne replied that Gough was a fool and that as for his note, 'he might wipe his backside with it and kiss it'. Gough promptly issued a warrant of arrest for assault. When Osborne appeared before him, Gough reminisced with relish,

So you are come chap, ah you are a saucy fellow like your father. I had your father and you before me ten years ago I see, I have been looking over my papers and I see I had counsellors opinions and lawyers opinions upon it, and I made him pay all charges scot and lot and I'll commit you.

Osborne settled with his servant for the price of a pair of shoes, but Gough would not let Osborne go. Over a period of two days Gough ordered him held until bail and the extraordinary number of five sureties were provided, refused to accept bail of £4,000, and repeatedly refused to meet him. At that point Osborne, still under guard by the constable, brought his solicitor and sureties to Perry Hall, demanding bail from Gough at his upper window. Gough ordered Osborne, his attorney, and his sureties off his land, threatening them all with lawsuits in King's Bench, and giving notice to one of them (who rented houses and land from him) to quit. Osborne was then committed to the Wolverhampton house of correction were he spent two days with the petty thieves, disorderly servants and prostitutes held there; he was finally bailed two days later by another magistrate. When Osborne attended Quarter Sessions to face the charge of assault, none was preferred against him.

Osborne then began proceedings for a criminal information. There was clear proof of malice, but Erskine probably believed that the judges would not, in fact, grant an information, without evidence of corruption also. He started an action for civil damages, and asked King's Bench to discharge the rule for an information, a prerequisite. In the civil suit Osborne was entirely successful. A Stafford jury gave him £500 damages; he also got double costs when Gough unsuccessfully tried for a non-suit or new

[72] P.R.O., KB 1/31 Michaelmas 43 Geo. III; KB 1/32 Easter 43 Geo. III; KB 21/48 pp. 4, 13, 65, 86, 88, 98. The prosecution affidavits were sworn before Roger Williams Gem of Birmingham. One of them was by Thomas Gem the younger, gentleman, of Birmingham. A Thomas Gem was witness for Lane in the first attempt to convict Gough of libel in 1796 (see above, note 68); in the public quarrel over game in 1784, Samuel Gem was Gough's principal antagonist: *A.B.G.*, 1, 8 and 15 November 1784. The 'smartish flogging' to which Osborne admitted was described in court by his counsel, Erskine, as 'a slight blow over his smock frock – no very severe discipline' (*The Times*, 8 Nov. 1802).

trial.[73] This victory in the civil courts was the result of the unusual determination of a very wealthy victim of magisterial misbehaviour. It appears to have been a unique event in sixty years of lay justice in Staffordshire. Erskine's abandonment of the criminal proceeding in favour of a civil action also underlines the near impossibility of convicting any magistrate guilty of only malicious and oppressive behaviour.

The vulnerability of poor magistrates

Gough thus scorned the Crown Office, and this was probably true of most country gentlemen, protected by their social standing as well as by the law. This suggestion is supported by the fact that most of the Staffordshire magistrates who found themselves attacked in King's Bench in fact were not gentlemen, nor in the county commission of the peace. They were borough justices, most of them tradesmen, who by virtue of their offices as mayors or aldermen acted as magistrates. Thus seven of the thirteen Staffordshire magistrates attacked by information in King's Bench were borough justices (including a maltster, tanner, and apothecary), not landed gentlemen in the county commission, although the latter handled far more cases. Prosecutors knew that most borough justices did not have deep purses; they probably also sensed that the judges of King's Bench might view such inferior magistrates with more suspicion. To the fact that poorer justices, or those of lower social status, were in more danger of being prosecuted for misdemeanour in office, there was a corollary: they could not afford to make enemies of wealthy men who might use the court against them. As a result, the social significance of King's Bench informations cannot be assessed only on the basis of those cases that appear in the records of the court. Threats to get informations, cases which did not even result in the filing of affidavits or a rule *nisi*, may have been more common than those records suggest. And here the dangers to a poor justice, already alluded to, must be emphasized, because a mere threat to go to King's Bench would often be enough to make him change his behaviour. One Staffordshire case is a reminder of another, crucial point. The threat to go to King's Bench might be effective even when the magistrate clearly had not been acting oppressively, but had exercised his discretion in favour of an accused person.

The magistrate was John Nott, an experienced county justice who lived in Lichfield. In 1753 he hesitated to convict a 15-year-old and his aged and infirm father to the whipping and imprisonment with hard labour

[73] *A.B.G.*, 9 and 16 May, 5 December 1803; *Osborne* v. *Gough* (1803) 3 Bos & Puller 550–6, a report of Gough's subsequent, unsuccessful, attempt to have the verdict set aside on grounds of excessive damages and a defect in process.

provided by statute for their crime of burning heath (a punishment enacted by country gentlemen in Parliament because the offence destroyed
the cover for game). Nott ordered them to apologize to the landlord's
steward instead. The landlord, Lord Uxbridge, was determined to make
examples, both of heath-burners and soft-hearted magistrates, and he
prepared to get an information against Nott in King's Bench. As I have
shown, Uxbridge was unable to serve him effectively for two terms.[74] But
when he was finally served, Nott tried to appease the peer with explanations, made by his solicitor. He was prepared to carry out the punishment,
and have the old man whipped, excusing his 'Mistaken Compassion to
old Age and Poverty in Distress', although he privately wrote his solicitor that it would be 'an Act of Barbarity rather than of Correction'. His
dilemma was plain:

I should have been Well enough Pleased to have had my Conduct in this business
canvassed in ye face of my Country, but ye Expence of Controversies of this sort
is too great for a Private fortune to bear, and therefore wish it could be Stop'd
in ye first Instance, for which purpose I must earnestly intreat your Attendance
when ye Motion is made.[75]

Conclusion

Nott's case shows that a criminal information could frighten country justices, but only in the hands of rich plaintiffs, against magistrates too poor
to resist. And a paternalist justice might be subjected to attack by information as readily as an oppressive one. Meanwhile, given the cost of litigation, the usual victims of injustice – poorer women and men convicted
casually or illegally or unfairly – could not hope to prosecute a gentleman
justice without substantial legal or financial help. In short, proceedings
against justices in King's Bench were anomalies, probably often explained
by local animosities against magistrates from others of their own class.
Gentlemanly understanding, normal social courtesy, was probably the
best guarantee against a justice finding himself in the Crown Office, or
being convicted on an information. When Edward Allsopp prosecuted

[74] Above, p. 28.
[75] Lord Uxbridge was prepared to move for a rule on 3 July, but apparently relented
temporarily; Nott was again served with notice on 10 November. The case is mentioned
briefly in D. Hay *et al., Albion's fatal tree: crime and society in eighteenth-century England*
(London, 1975), pp. 243–4. The account here is from S.R.O., D603, William Cooper to
Lord Uxbridge, 3 February 1753; Nichols to Uxbridge, 22 January 1753; John Cooper
to Parry, 10 February, 4 June and 23 June 1753; U. Bourne to Parry, 27 June 1753;
Parry to Uxbridge, 28 June, 30 June and 6 November 1753; affidavit for King's Bench
of Parry, 4 July 1753; Cooper's affidavit of service, 26 June 1753; affidavit of U. Bourne,
10 November 1753.

Sir Nigel Bowyer Gresley and Dr James Falconer for maliciously refusing him an alehouse licence, a J.P. in nearby Derbyshire wrote a warm letter of recommendation for the alehouse keeper and his wife, but refused to swear an affidavit. It was not the sort of thing one gentleman did to another, presumably, at least on behalf of an alehouse keeper. We can infer as much from another aspect of the same case. One Staffordshire J.P. did actually swear an affidavit for the prosecution, supporting the character of the Allsopps, and swearing to the 'great propriety' with which they conducted their alehouse. Six weeks later, however, he changed his tune, and swore to a defence affidavit implying that Allsopp's licence had been suppressed because gross irregularities had taken place at their pub. This vacillating witness was none other than Thomas Gisborne of Yoxall Lodge, who undoubtedly felt the weight of Gresley and Falconer's displeasure until he changed his mind and supported them. Perhaps he had a bad conscience after the fact: three years later he published the comments on the relative immunity of oppressive magistrates, and their disregard for poorer men, that were quoted earlier in this chapter.[76]

I have shown that cost was not the only protection enjoyed by the oppressive magistrate against challenge by his social inferiors. The attitudes of the judges and the precedents they made meant that anything short of clear proof of a corrupt interest almost always resulted in a prosecution being ended before trial. This effective immunity from prosecution, I have argued, was a consequence of the enormous dependence on unpaid magistrates in the administration of English criminal law. The judges of King's Bench knew and stated clearly that castigating justices too often, too severely, too publicly, would be immensely destructive of their co-operation. If men named to the commission of the peace were deterred from acting, the administration of the criminal law would collapse. But I have shown that tolerance for magisterial misbehaviour was also a product of the willingness of any gentleman (and the high court judges were very great gentlemen) to credit the good faith of other men of their class. The policy imperative and the shared social outlook were mutually reinforcing: gentlemen who did a necessary and often unpleasant public duty without pay were exemplifying gentlemanly behaviour. The extremely high level of proof of malfeasance therefore required by the judges of King's Bench even to begin a prosecution, notably the insistence on proof of actual corrupt interest, effectively insulated most of the magistracy, and particularly those in the county commissions of the peace, from legal retribution. The degree to which justices behaved

---

[76] Above, note 10. Gisborne's affidavits of 9 and 27 November 1791 are filed in P.R.O., KB 1/27 Mich. 32 Geo. III bdl 59 (1791) and Hil. 32 Geo. III bdl 2 (1792).

honestly, obeyed the law, and followed the required forms, was probably largely determined by the example shown by the most competent and conscientious magistrates among their neighbours, if they cared to follow it. Perhaps good behaviour was even more tied to the wish to avoid the obloquy of neighbours, tenants and dependants, but especially of other gentry.

These generalizations must be more tentative in the case of borough magistrates. They appear to have run a somewhat greater risk of prosecutions for misbehaviour in office, almost certainly because they were not protected by either status or wealth comparable to that of most gentlemen in the county commission. It seems likely too that marginal men in the county commission, men anxious to establish their credentials as gentlemen, would be more deterred by the possible disgrace or notoriety of a prosecution, particularly if it was successful. It may be that more such men acted in some counties, and certainly their type is found in the London 'trading justice'. But in Staffordshire instances of humiliation were few; other gentlemen and magistrates would seldom carry a criticism into a public forum, let alone the courts. As a result there were very few instances of rural magistrates brought before King's Bench before 1800. The plausible inference is that most miscarriages of justice at the hands of country gentleman magistrates in the eighteenth century went unpunished and indeed unremarked except by those immediately involved.[77] Even in the rare case where a magistrate like Gough had nothing but scorn for the opinion of his fellows and contempt for his inferiors, and actually provoked criminal proceedings, he had little to dread from the Crown Office.

Yet the fact that Gough, a relatively inactive J.P. who dealt with few cases, accounts for such a large proportion of the few attempted prosecutions of magistrates in Staffordshire, raises the final question of whether those two facts are connected. Perhaps most prosecutors avoided such unstable and eccentric and unjust magistrates, and therefore few defendants suffered at their hands; perhaps the most active magistrates were unlikely to oppress those before them. Whether most magistrates administered the criminal law impartially must rest also on other evidence. Certainly there is much in Staffordshire to show (particularly with respect to the game laws) that many J.P.s were extremely anxious to please great landowners.[78] And it was not only eccentrics like Gough who were brought before the high court. Three of the six magistrates in the county commission

---

[77] An inference supported by the fact that there was significant change in the early decades of the nineteenth century, as political radicals began prosecuting country magistrates. I discuss this shift in my forthcoming book.

[78] Some of this evidence is presented in D. Hay *et al.*, *Albion's fatal tree*, pp. 236–44.

who were threatened with informations (the Reverend George Malbon in 1759, John Marsh in 1787, and James Falconer in 1791) were among the most active justices in the county, the first two accounting for between 10 per cent and 15 per cent of all committals for trial, and the last for 8–10 per cent, in the decades in which they were prosecuted.[79] Malbon was accused of organizing a mob to repossess a disputed house and illegally convicting the occupant of forceable entry. Marsh allegedly wrongfully gaoled a hawker for six months for selling toys in Wolverhampton market, and then released him after three months. Falconer was accused, in a case already noted, of corruptly and maliciously refusing to renew an alehouse licence. All three applications for an information were refused by King's Bench, although Marsh was not given costs against his prosecutor.

A King's Bench information was not therefore an entirely unknown threat in the county in the later eighteenth century, but it was extremely uncommon. No magistrate suffered a conviction; a very few probably suffered some anxiety and embarrassment before being cleared by the court or (in one case, apparently) making a monetary settlement with the prosecutor. Most were tradesmen acting as borough justices. Only six accused justices, one of them the ineffable Mr Gough, were in the county commission of the peace. Only one of them suffered the indignity of having an information actually exhibited against him in the Crown Office. None were put on trial. Thomas Gisborne's rueful observation, that most of those who suffered magisterial injustice were too poor even to think of seeking a remedy in the courts, is persuasive. Exhortations to 'men in the higher ranks' to administer the law fairly was the most that could be accomplished.[80] In the eighteenth century the high law of King's Bench effectively protected the low law of most provincial justices from being questioned, curbed, or controlled by those whom they judged. An information in the Crown Office was a threat only when wielded against them by a great magnate or by some of their peers. It almost never happened.

[79] Based on committals for trials recorded in gaol calendars at Assizes and Quarter Sessions, S.R.O.
[80] Thomas Gisborne, *An inquiry into the duties of men in the higher ranks and middle classes* (London, 1794), pp. 286–7.

3   The trading justice's trade

Norma Landau

The justices of eighteenth-century metropolitan London were a byword for corruption. In fact, they had a byword all to themselves: they were known as 'trading justices'. Like their label, their reputation was unique. Its idiosyncracy was not merely the charge that their judicial decisions were suspect, as were the profits they extracted from office. Long before the English had identified the trading justices, they had known 'basket justices' – justices who relished the fees of office, who pocketed the fines they levied when making summary convictions, and whose judicial decisions could be influenced by the gift of half a dozen chickens.[1] Unappealing as the English found such justices, their animus against the trading justice was greater still, so great that it colours these justices' portrayal to this day. According to a recent presentation, trading justices were corrupt, some so corrupt that they were 'indistinguishable from the criminals with whom they dealt'.[2] While quite striking, even this depiction pales before that presented in the eighteenth century. For to the eighteenth century, the trading justice was not merely criminal; he actually caused crime. According to one pamphleteer, trading justices connived at 'the

I want to thank Douglas Hay, Ruth Paley, Nicholas Rogers and Michael Saler for their comments on this chapter, the Duke of Northumberland for permission to read and quote from his manuscripts, and the National Endowment for the Humanities for a fellowship supporting this research. I also want to thank Harriet Jones, Sarah Millard, Susan Palmer, Louise Falcini and Richard Samways, all on the staff of the Greater London Record Office (now the London Metropolitan Archive), for their courtesy and help.

[1] J. Kent, 'Attitudes of members of the House of Commons to the regulation of "personal conduct" in late Elizabethan and early Stuart England', *Bulletin of the Institute of Historical Research*, vol. 46 (1973), pp. 52–3. In the late seventeenth century it was charged that the offer of cheap or ready labour was sufficient to influence such justices. T. Nourse, *Campania foelix* (London, 1700), pp. 264–5; E. Bohun, *The justice of peace, his calling and qualification* (London, 1693), pp. 118–20.

[2] P. Langford, *Public life and the propertied Englishman 1689–1789* (Oxford, 1991), p. 444. See also: R. Leslie-Melville, *The life and work of Sir John Fielding* (London, 1934), p. 31; Sir L. Radzinowicz, *A history of English criminal law and its administration from 1750*, vol. III (London, 1956), pp. 32–3; S. and B. Webb, *English local government from the revolution to the municipal corporations act*, vol. I, *The parish and the county* (London, 1908), pp. 326, 328.

continuance of what tends to the increase of delinquency'. According to a member of Parliament, trading justices 'frequently let felons esape, unless they could make money by convicting them'. As the *Times* stated: 'the *trade* of thieving will ever thrive, whilst there exists a *trade* of Justices'.[3] This chapter will suggest why such statements did not seem outrageous.

To do so, it will examine charges actually brought against the metropolis' justices. No metropolitan justice was ever charged in court with creating crime, although one justice, William Blackborow, was charged with threatening action against constables who took up prostitutes and reputed thieves living in the tenements he owned.[4] That charge arose in the course of Middlesex Quarter Sessions' investigation of Blackborow. For, unlike benches elsewhere in the kingdom, those of metropolitan London invented a procedure for hearing charges of magisterial misconduct, hearings they recorded in their order books.[5] As Westminster's extant order books cover just the years from 1720 to 1731, this investigation of the metropolis' trading justices focuses on Middlesex's hearings from 1716, when its series of extant order books begin,[6] to 1792, when Parliament passed a statute which ejected the trading justices from metropolitan London.[7]

Middlesex's proceedings against its justices began with an invitation to the putatively erring justice to dine with the county's justices on County Day – the day at each session on which the bench dealt with county business – and then, after dinner, to explain his actions in the incident which gave rise to the complaint.[8] On occasion, the order book records the justice's apology and promise not to repeat his error.[9] In other instances, Sessions then proceeded to build a case against the erring justice, a case

---

[3] *Letter to the Duke of Northumberland on the intended meeting of the justices* (London, 1777), pp. 22–4. *Parliamentary History*, vol. XXV, 29 June 1785, col. 908; *Universal Daily Register*, 10 October 1787, p. 3.

[4] London Metropolitan Archives [hereafter L.M.A.], MJ/OC12, 16 September 1790, pp. 77, 82–4.

[5] Metropolitan London – that part of London outside the City – was governed by the justices on three commissions of the peace, the commissions of Middlesex, Westminster and the Tower Liberty. The records of the Tower Liberty's commission are lost.

[6] It is evident that there were earlier order books which have not survived.

[7] 32 George III c. 53.

[8] Many, but not all, invitations to dine were entered in the order books. For invitations which were not so entered, but survive among the Sessions papers, see the invitations to Nathaniel Dukinfield and Henry Trent, L.M.A., MJ/SP 1748 October nos. 93, 94. There are no such invitations in the order books for the justices whom Middlesex Sessions represented to the Lord Chancellor. However, other evidence suggests that such invitations were issued. For that to Sir Samuel Gower, see MJ/SP 1751 January no. 49; for a reference to that to Henry Broadhead, see MJ/OC5, 27 April 1750, p. 199.

[9] L.M.A., MJ/OC3, 17 October 1738, p. 155 (John Troughton); MJ/OC8, 17 January 1760, p. 47 (Richard Hassell).

which Sessions would present in a 'representation' to the Lord Chancellor requesting that the erring justice be removed from the bench.[10] Sessions would appoint a committee to gather evidence about the justice's conduct. The committee either examined witnesses in the justice's presence and requested that he reply;[11] or, if he were absent – an absence usually due to his rejection of an invitation to attend – the committee sent him affidavits of the witnesses' testimony, again requesting his reply.[12] If the justice decided to attend the hearing, he could cross-examine the witnesses against him, and present witnesses in his own behalf.[13] In 1768 one justice – Ralph Hodgson – employed counsel to cross-examine the witnesses.[14]

A decade later, John Gretton attempted to have Middlesex's procedure declared illegal. When the bench investigated him, Gretton retaliated by attempting to indict the bench for conspiracy. The grand jury rejected the bill.[15] Gretton would later aver that, upon receiving his invitation to attend Middlesex's hearing, he had consulted both the then Attorney-General and a future judge, who opined that Middlesex's proceedings were 'illegal and unconstitutional', and advised him to warn Middlesex Sessions that persistence in the hearing would be countered by an action against the Sessions in King's Bench. Middlesex Sessions nonetheless voted that a

---

[10] The Lord Chancellor could use either of two procedures to remove justices from the commission. In the early eighteenth century, when commissions of the peace were reissued frequently, Lord Chancellors almost always removed justices by omitting their names from the new commission. It is also likely that these justices were prevented from acting until issue of the new commission by a writ of *supersedeas* issued by the Lord Chancellor in Chancery. By mid-century, the interval between renewals of the commission had so increased that Lord Chancellors elaborated on precedent to create a new variety of *supersedeas*, a *supersedeas* which immediately removed the justice from the commission. (N. Landau, *The justices of the peace, 1679–1760* (Berkeley, 1984), pp. 128–32; N. Landau and L. Glassey, 'The commission of the peace in the eighteenth century: a new source', *Bulletin of the Institute of Historical Research*, vol. 45 (1972), pp. 259–60.) Of the justices both represented and removed after 1738, all but Broadhead were removed by *supersedeas* (Public Record Office [hereafter P.R.O.], C234/24).

In addition to the justices whom Lord Chancellors superseded on representations from the Middlesex bench, Lord Chancellors also superseded the following Middlesex justices: John Rotheram in 1719 (C231/9, p. 474); Simon Michel and Ambrose Godfrey in 1741; John Green in 1748; Samuel Waddington in 1767; Sir Thomas Frederick in 1768; and Thomas Miller in 1778 (C234/24). Rotheram was soon restored to the commission (L.M.A., MJ/SBB807, list of justices present; WJP/L10), as was Miller (MJP/L/13, MJP/L/10a).

[11] L.M.A., MJ/OC2, 13 January 1724[5], p. 135v.

[12] L.M.A., MJ/OC5, 18 January 1749[50], p. 189v; 27 April 1750, p. 199; MJ/OC4, 30 April 1735, p. 30.

[13] L.M.A., MJ/OC4, 13 April 1738, p. 108.

[14] L.M.A., MJ/OC8, 8 September 1768, p. 87.

[15] *Morning Post*, 21 February 1778, cited in R. Paley, 'The Middlesex justices act of 1792: its origins and effects' (University of Reading, Ph.D. thesis, 1983), p. 211.

representation be made against Gretton to the Lord Chancellor, who removed Gretton from the bench forthwith.[16] Middlesex's proceedings were extra-legal, but they were nonetheless considered quite acceptable. According to Middlesex's Lord Lieutenant, Sessions had 'authority' to consider charges against a justice, and to reach a decision as to whether the justice's conduct warranted removal from the commission. Indeed, the Lord Chancellor himself might refer a complaint made to him to the Middlesex bench for further investigation.[17]

In distinguishing conduct which merited removal from that meriting mere postprandial reprimand, Middlesex's bench distinguished justices who acted illegally from those whose conduct was legal but nonetheless distasteful. In so doing, Middlesex's bench challenged modern depictions of the trading justice, for the bench's actions suggest that, despite the trading justices' noisome reputation, what defined the trading justice was not illegal activity. Instead Middlesex's hearings indicate that what contemporaries found troubling in the trading justices was their devotion to judicial business. It was this commitment, contemporaries believed, which produced justices who created crime.

Justices represented to the Lord Chancellor

The tales of the justices whom Middlesex Sessions represented to the Lord Chancellor do indeed demonstrate that some Middlesex justices did act so as to undermine or attack the law they administered. At the same time, the tales suggest that illegal activity was not the defining characteristic of trading magistracy. For, as these tales reveal, Middlesex Sessions represented to the Lord Chancellor justices who acted illegally, and the Lord Chancellor removed these justices from the bench.

Between 1716 and 1792 Middlesex's bench submitted representations against fifteen justices, of whom Lord Chancellors removed twelve.[18] The behaviour of three of those removed was so bizarre that, whether legal or not, it undermined English justice. The case of John Sherratt is perhaps the most extraordinary. Sherratt was represented and removed within six months of his appointment. He had been twice a bankrupt, was once again

---

[16] P.R.O., H.O. 42/34, fos. 104–7, Gretton's memorial; C234/24, 25 March 1778. L.M.A., MJ/OC10a, 13 March 1778, pp. 203–4, 209.

[17] Alnwick Castle, Alnwick MSS Syon Y IV 6a, Box 2, Envelope 9, 'To the author of a Letter published in the *London Evening Post* Tuesday April the 5th'.

[18] This count includes among those removed: Cornelius Martin, who died before the representation against him was presented to the Lord Chancellor (L.M.A., MJ/OC10a, 13 March 1778, p. 202); and William Blackborow, against whom Middlesex Sessions voted a representation and then decided to suspend proceedings on condition that he not act (MJ/OC12, 15 Sept. 1790, p. 91; 28 Oct. 1790, pp. 100–1).

in debt, and to protect himself from arrest had had his name inserted in the list of servants to the Envoy from Bavaria.[19] Clearly, a man who was the servant of the diplomatic representative of another government, and so both that government's tool and exempt from England's laws, could not claim to act for English justice.

Justice Charles Whinyates' error was to flaunt, before the watch, his use of his office to extort complementary service from brothels and prostitutes, while at the same time ordering the watch to take up 'honest people going about their Lawfull occasions' and threatening to commit a constable who took up the disorderly. The constables and watch jointly submitted a report to the bench stating that Whinyates had so frequently 'threatened' the watch that the constables feared they 'would quit their Imployments'.[20]

However, the justices themselves probably considered the conduct of Thomas Robe even more outrageous. In Robe's eyes, Middlesex Sessions was the offender, for the Sessions had opposed him when he had brought a suit in King's Bench to increase the profits of his office as clerk of the market of the King's Household, and had financed this attack upon him by use of £119 18s. of the funds collected by various county rates.[21] Robe thereupon commenced a campaign against collection of the county rates, to which Middlesex Sessions responded in 1735 by presenting a representation demanding his removal,[22] to which Robe replied by instigating a petition to the House of Commons against Sessions' collection of the rates. On 10 June 1737 the House of Commons voted that the petition was 'frivolous, vexatious, scandalous, and malicious', and that Robe, as its 'Contriver, Promoter, and Prosecutor', should be taken into custody by the sergeant-at-arms.[23] Five days later, Hardwicke, the newly appointed Lord Chancellor, removed Robe from Middlesex's bench.[24]

It may be that the behaviour of Robe, Whinyates and Sherratt was legal simply because neither the law nor Parliament had ever imagined that a justice would act in this manner. In contrast, eight of the nine remaining

[19] L.M.A., MJ/OC8, 6 April 1769, pp. 97–8. P.R.O., C234/24, 19 July 1769.
[20] L.M.A., MJ/OC2, 16 January 1724[5], pp. 138, 140; MJP/L3.
[21] L.M.A., MJ/OC3, 23 and 24 February 1726[7], pp. 86–8; 14 January 1730[1], pp. 272–3; 29 April 1731, p. 279; 13 January 1731[2], p. 299v. For Robe, see Webb and Webb, *Parish and the county*, pp. 560–1, n. 3.
[22] L.M.A., MJ/OC4, 27 February 1734[5], pp. 26–7; 17 April 1735, pp. 29–30; 23 May 1735, pp. 36–7.
[23] *A report ... from the committee of the House of Commons to whom the petition ... of the churchwardens ... and inhabitants of the several parishes ... and also the petition of His Majesty's justices of the peace ... for Middlesex, were referred* (London, 1737), p. 96, reproduced in S. Lambert, ed., *House of Commons sessional papers of the eighteenth century*, vol. XV (Wilmington, Del., 1975).
[24] P.R.O., C234/24, 15 June 1737.

justices represented to and removed by the Lord Chancellor had committed clearly illegal acts as justices of the peace. Francis Jennison, alone among these eight justices, did not commit his offence as part of an attempt to enrich himself. Jennison's offence was alteration of a warrant that recorded the committal of his brother to gaol, and 'abuse of his authority' as justice in discharging his brother from gaol without taking bail. That Jennison's brother was arrested in the course of Sessions' campaign against London's crime, a campaign ordered by the Secretary of State, probably increased the gravity of Jennison's offence.[25]

The illegal acts of the seven other justices arose from their pursuit of judicial profits. Three justices were charged (among other charges) with demanding bribes. William Blackborow demanded a guinea, on top of the three guineas paid to his clerks, for ensuring that a publican got his licence; John Gretton demanded five guineas for a licence for a puppet show, a licence that was in itself illegal. Sir William Moore was more creative. He was himself in custody for debt, and when a man appeared before him on a warrant Moore had issued for bigamy, Moore offered 'to make the matter easy' for the bigamist, if the bigamist stood bail for Moore.[26]

One of these three justices, John Gretton, had also acted illegally by extorting fees greater than he had a right to demand, and fees which he had no right to demand.[27] Three other justices also acted illegally when taking fees. Cornelius Martin demanded that those he convicted pay him a fee 'for the conviction' and pocketed some of the fines he had levied using his powers of summary jurisdiction.[28] Thomas Cotton profited from informations under the Gin Act of 1736, exacting £1 7s., and sometimes more, from informers. As Middlesex's representation noted, Cotton's practice encouraged suspicion among a rioting populace that convictions under the act 'might be owing to the large fees those Convictions produced'.[29] Henry Broadhead's cupidity was even more outrageous.

---

[25] L.M.A., MJ/OC3, 5 December 1728, pp. 164–7.

[26] For Blackborow, L.M.A., MJ/OC12, 16 September 1790, pp. 77, 81, 84, 85–6; MJ/SP 1790 September no. 61, pp. 14, 17–18. For Gretton, MJ/OC10a, 13 March 1778, pp. 207–8; for Moore, MJ/OC1, February 1720[1], pp. 114–15.

[27] L.M.A., MJ/OC10a, January and 13 March 1778, pp. 189–93, 204–6.

[28] L.M.A., MJ/OC10a, January 1778, pp. 195–7; 19 February, pp. 201–2.

[29] L.M.A., MJ/OC4, 13 April 1738, pp. 107–8. Bodleian Library, Rawlinson MSS D918, fo. 151, those omitted, 1738. P. Clark, 'The "mother gin" controversy in the early eighteenth century', *Transactions of the Royal Historical Society*, 5th series, vol. XXXVIII (1988), pp. 78–82. L. Davison, "Experiments in the social regulation of industry: gin legislation, 1729–1751", in L. Davison *et al.*, eds., *Stilling the grumbling hive: the response to social and economic problems in England, 1689–1750* (Stroud and New York, 1992), pp. 36–40.

Broadhead elaborated on a fee allowed by Sessions – that of a shilling for a warrant.[30] Accordingly, he refused to examine defendants until the prosecutor paid his shilling. He refused to examine even if, without a warrant, the defendant stood before him, even if that defendant was accused of felony. Indeed, he refused to act without his shilling even if the defendant before him confessed to felony. Issue of a warrant gave Broadhead the right, sanctioned by Sessions, to levy another fee – for discharge of the warrant, cost again one shilling. Broadhead's avidity to collect his shilling could free a felon: if the prisoner was obviously guilty, even of felony, and yet still able to pay his shilling, Broadhead might discharge him – taking his shilling.[31]

Compared to his successors, William Booth – the subject of the first representation in Middlesex's extant records – had committed a relatively trivial offence. Like many of his successors, Booth had extracted more money than was appropriate from people who appeared before him. Unlike his successors, he was charged with only one instance of such extortion. Booth had ordered that Richard Manley and his wife, Elizabeth, either produce sureties in the next quarter of an hour or go to gaol. He had obstructed the Manleys' search for sureties, written and charged for four separate documents committing them, and then, when they produced sureties, demanded 400 per cent of the usual fee for discharge and bound them in twice as many recognizances – taking twice the usual fees – as was necessary. It may be that Booth had erred in coupling extortion to an affront to status. The representation against him reveals that he had imprisoned Richard Manley, Esq., on a complaint made by a former servant, who – as Booth knew – had been charged with beating Elizabeth Manley.[32] Indeed, it is possible that the man he imprisoned in 1719 was the Richard Manley who was appointed a justice of Middlesex and Westminster in 1729.[33]

It may also be that the Lord Chancellor decided that Booth should be removed because his actions appeared both deliberate and malicious. In contrast, conduct which could be interpreted as a mere mistake in judgment did not merit removal, as Samuel Newton's case reveals. In 1723 Middlesex Sessions ordered its chairman to attend the Lord Chancellor with the information that Samuel Newton had discharged from gaol a

[30] L.M.A., MJ/OC1, January 1720[1], p. 111.
[31] L.M.A., MJ/OC6, 27 April 1750, p. 199; British Library [hereafter B.L.], Add. MSS 35603, fo. 300, Broadhead's petition. Broadhead's pursuit of fees should not be attributed to straitened circumstances. When he died, the *Whitehall Evening Post* reported that he left an estate of £3,000 a year (M. C. Battestin with R. R. Battestin, *Henry Fielding: a life* (London, 1989), p. 675, n. 110).
[32] L.M.A., MJ/OC1, October 1719, pp. 84v–85.
[33] P.R.O., C234/25, 17 December 1729. L.M.A., MJP/CP114.

man accused of robbery on the highway, and so an alleged felon. Newton remained on the commission. A year later Middlesex bench delivered a representation against Newton for: discharging another alleged felon; superseding a warrant against a woman alleged to be an accessary to a felony and delaying three days before binding her in recognizance to attend Sessions; and granting a licence to sell ale to a house refused a licence by another justice.[34] There is no evidence that Newton was removed from the commission.[35] It is quite clear that Sir Henry Dutton Colt was not removed from Middlesex's bench despite its representation against him in 1725 for bailing Lawrence St Loe, Esq. St Loe had been committed to Newgate as the ringleader of the riots in the New Mint. He was also a former justice of both Middlesex and Westminster, which may explain why Colt had bailed him even though in so doing he violated a resolution of Middlesex Sessions against bailing prisoners committed by other justices.[36] Henceforth, Middlesex's bench would reprimand but not represent justices who could be considered merely to have made one or two errors in judgment – who bailed a prisoner committed by another,[37] or bailed an alleged felon,[38] or did not ensure the appearance in court of the prisoner he was bailing by insisting that those standing bail were persons of substance.[39]

Similarly, in 1751 the Middlesex bench discovered that failure of a justice to ensure that his tenant kept a respectable public house was insufficient cause for his removal from the commission. Sir Samuel Gower, knight, owned a house in Goodmans Fields Wells where plays were performed to draw customers, who stayed and drank, and then proceeded to nearby brothels. The bench had urged Gower, without effect, to suppress playhouse and brothels; but he had instead signed a 'permissive licence' granting the playhouse the right to sell alcoholic beverages.[40] Shortly

[34] L.M.A., MJ/OC2, 28 August 1723, p. 84; 3 December 1724, pp. 129–30; MJ/OC3, 23 February 1724[5], pp. 2v–3.

[35] It is possible that he died before 1727, when the next commission was issued. For the list of those removed from that commission, see L.M.A., MJP/L3.

[36] L.M.A., MJ/OC2, 13 and 16 January 1724[5], pp. 135, 139; MJP/CP104. P.R.O., C234/25, 6 June 1721.

[37] L.M.A., MJ/OC3, 24 and 25 February 1726[7], pp. 87, 90 (Simon Michel); 6 June 1728, p. 136, and 17 October 1728, p.155 (John Troughton); 12 October 1732, p. 315 (John Nicol); MJ/SP 1748 October no. 93, and December no. 67 (Henry Trent); MJ/SP 1748 October no. 94 (Nathaniel Dukinfield); MJ/OC6, 29 April, 3 June 1756, pp. 93v, 98 (Joseph St Lawrence); MJ/OC12, 12 August 1790, pp. 86, 88–9, and 16 September 1790, p. 91 (Charles Triquet).

[38] L.M.A., MJ/OC3, 12 April 1727 (Ralph Harwood); MJ/OC5, 10 April, 15 May 1746, pp. 89, 94 (Thomas Jones).

[39] L.M.A., MJ/OC3, 28 August 1725, p. 29 (Sir Henry Dutton Colt).

[40] L.M.A., MJ/OC5, 13 September 1750, pp. 207v–8; 17 January 1750[1], p. 216v; 28 February 1750[1], pp. 221–2.

before they represented Gower to the Lord Chancellor, Middlesex's justices had launched a campaign to close unlicensed playhouses, and they had also resolved that no justice sign a 'permissive licence', a direction to the excise commissioners issued in the interval between annual licensing sessions to grant a licence to sell liquor until the next licensing session.[41] Nonetheless, it seems that the Lord Chancellor did not consider activity which was distasteful but not illegal reason sufficient to remove a justice from the bench. It was not illegal to rent one's property to people who then used it for improper purposes. (Indeed Gower claimed that his tenant ran a respectable establishment.[42]) Nor was it illegal for a Middlesex justice to act in defiance of a resolution of Middlesex Sessions. Gower remained a justice of Middlesex.

It seems likely that during the course of the eighteenth century the standards which a charge against a justice had to meet if that charge were to result in his removal were set higher: the evidence against him presented in a manner more attuned to legal niceties; and the charge against him more akin to those recognized in law.[43] When in 1764 Sir John Fielding and William Kelynge requested that the Lord Chancellor remove three justices from Westminster's bench, the Lord Chancellor seems to have requested evidence of their 'dishonour' which met a legal standard of proof. So, Fielding and Kelynge submitted a memorial stating that the 'drunken, Scandalous, infamous, Cruel, Oppressive and fraudulent Behaviour' of Richard Manley had resulted in his discharge from the navy and was therefore a 'matter of Record in the Admiralty Books'; that the fraud of Benjamin Cox had been exhibited by Westminster's annoyance jury, who had broken his grocer's scales, a 'fact' which was 'a Matter of Record in the Burgesses Court'; and that evidence of the 'scandalous practices' of Samuel Waddington – practices which included exercising his office of justice of the peace in alehouses, borrowing but not repaying money from gaolers and constables, and 'encouraging litigious Suits among the poor' – was 'founded on Our own knowledge'.[44] However, the Lord Chancellor considered such evidence, or the charges, or both, insufficient for removal. All three justices remained on Westminster's

---

[41] L.M.A., MJ/OC5, 12 July 1750, pp. 205v–7; 7 December 1749, p. 186.

[42] L.M.A., MJ/SP 1751 April no. 72, Gower's reply.

[43] See D. Hay, 'Dread of the Crown Office', in this volume on similar increase in the difficulty of bringing a successful prosecution against a justice.

[44] P.R.O., SP44/138, pp. 182–3, Fielding and Kelynge to Earl of Halifax, 11 January 1764; p. 181, Earl of Halifax to Lord Chancellor, 12 January 1764. B.L., microfilm 298, Alnwick MSS 37, fo. 18, Fielding to Duke of Northumberland, 15 Jan. 1764. The Richard Manley referred to here is not the same person as the Richard Manley mentioned in the text associated with note 33 above.

commission.[45] According to the Duke of Northumberland, Lord Lieutenant and custos of Middlesex and Westminster from 1763 to 1786, removal of a justice 'is such a degradation and carries with it such an imputation of bad morals' that it 'should therefore not be done but in consequence of some formal and regular proceeding'. Nor should justices be removed for 'errors and irregularities of proceeding without proof of some blameable intention unless where enormous repetitions of them appear'.[46] By the early nineteenth century the Lord Chancellor had 'laid it down as a rule' that he would never remove a justice 'until he had been convicted of some offence by the verdict of a Court of Record'.[47]

Increasing commitment to the concept that removal should follow only upon clear, partial and malicious violation of the law in the exercise of judicial powers may explain some anomalies associated with the representation against Ralph Hodgson – the remaining justice removed by the Lord Chancellor on a representation from the Middlesex bench. Hodgson was a justice in Shadwell, where he also ran a registry office for the employment of coalheavers. By 1768 his office was competing with another, and the coalheavers were on strike and rioting against his competition. On St Patrick's Day Hodgson had marched at the head of a parade of several hundred coalheavers, a shamrock in his hat, advertising his determination to protect his men. A month later the coalheavers attacked and fired upon the house of his competitor's agent, battle ensued, and several people were killed. In response to a petition from those involved in the coal trade, Middlesex Sessions represented Hodgson to the Lord Chancellor as 'an accessary to the outrages and disorders'. However, Sessions' record of the representation is unique: it is the only representation accompanied by a notation that some justices 'did not vote in this matter'. Eight justices abstained: John Hawkins (chairman), Thomas Lane (former chairman), Saunders Welch (the only justice other than Sir John Fielding in receipt of a salary for his judicial services to the government),

[45] cf. Leslie-Melville, *John Fielding*, pp. 144–5, and A. Babington, *A house in Bow Street* (London, 1969), p. 136. Waddington was superseded in 1767, shortly after an information was brought against him in King's Bench for abusing his powers of summary conviction. (P.R.O., C234/24; KB1/16, Part VI, Crown Side Affidavits, Hilary 7 George III, no. 1; KB1/17 (Part II) unlabelled bundle, affidavit of Samuel Waddington *et al.*, 10 February 1767. I want to thank John Styles for the reference to these affidavits and Tim Wales for locating and copying them.) Manley and Cox remained justices until they died (C234/25, 20 Jan. 1769).
[46] Alnwick Castle, Alnwick MSS Syon Y IV 6a, Box 2, Envelope 9, 'To the author of a Letter published in the *London Evening Post* Tuesday April the 5th'.
[47] Hansard, *Parliamentary Debates*, n.s. vol. XVIII (1828), 7 February 1828, cols. 162–3, Brougham citing Eldon.

and five other justices, all of the division in which Hodgson acted.[48] The Lord Chancellor's action was similarly anomalous. Rather than removing Hodgson on receipt of the representation in early September, he waited until the end of December, shortly after Hodgson's continued presence on Middlesex's commission was instanced in the House of Commons as an example of governmental malfeasance.[49]

As even the proceedings against Hodgson indicate, by mid-century removal of a justice from the commission was increasingly seen as a disinterested legal judgment that the justice had violated or undermined the law. Accordingly, even the format Middlesex Sessions had invented merely to investigate a justice's actions came to be perceived as invidious. Middlesex Sessions began its investigation by inviting the justice to dine with his judicial colleagues on County Day. When Sir John Fielding received such an invitation in 1764, he moved a resolution that, if a justice had a complaint to make against another justice, the complaining justice should ask the other justice to explain his actions before raising the matter in Sessions, so that the matter could be 'Adjusted and Reconciled in a friendly manner' without giving rise to a dinner invitation. The resolution was later rescinded and later still reinstated.[50] Nonetheless, Middlesex did not abandon investigation of complaints against its justices. Middlesex justices still made complaints about the judicial conduct of their colleagues, complaints which the bench demanded that the alleged offender answer. However, if the complaint was insufficient to launch proceedings that could culminate in a representation, and if the offender's response was satisfactory, no mention whatsoever was made of either complaint or hearing in the court's order books.[51] More serious allegations did enter the order books and so the historical record. In 1777 Middlesex Sessions established a committee on judicial misconduct to investigate such complaints. The committee promptly investigated the conduct of three justices, two of whom Middlesex Sessions represented to the Lord Chancellor, and in 1790 investigated two more justices, one of whom Sessions represented.[52]

---

[48] L.M.A., MJ/OC8, 19 May and 8 September 1768, pp. 79–80, 84, 85–7. M. D. George, 'The London coal-heavers: attempts to regulate waterside labour in the eighteenth and nineteenth centuries', *Economic Journal*, Supplement (May 1927), pp. 231–9; P. Linebaugh, 'Tyburn: a study of crime and the labouring poor in London during the first half of the eighteenth century' (Warwick University Ph.D. thesis, 1975), pp. 510–28.

[49] *Sir Henry Cavendish's debates of the House of Commons*, drawn up by J. Wright (London, 1841), vol. I, p. 102, 12 December 1768. P.R.O., C234/24, 26 December 1768.

[50] L.M.A., MJ/OC8, 4 May 1764, p. 23v.

[51] L.M.A., MJ/SP 1776 April, nos. 36, 38 (Cornelius Martin).

[52] L.M.A., MJ/OC10a, December 1777, p. 171; MJ/OC12, 8 July 1790, p. 69. One document (MJ/SP 1780 misc. no. 69) refers to a committee on judicial misconduct which met in 1780. However, as Sessions' order book does not record its meetings for February

Middlesex's representations prove that a few of its justices acted illegally. At the same time, they raise doubt as to whether illegal activity was the essence of trading magistracy, for it is unlikely that the activities of the dozen justices both represented and removed were sufficient to besmirch the entire metropolitan bench, a bench that at any one time was comprised of well over 100 active justices. Indeed, most of the dozen had not acted long enough to establish themselves as the epitome of the Middlesex justice. Sir William Moore, Charles Whinyates, Francis Jennison and John Sherratt were represented within a year or less after their appointment to the commission; William Booth within one to four years of his appointment; John Gretton less than two years and Cornelius Martin less than three years after each obtained his *dedimus* – the document which allowed the justice to act once appointed to the commission. While Henry Broadhead had obtained his *dedimus* over a decade before he was represented, his removal too suggests that judicial notoriety evoked relatively speedy retaliation from Middlesex's bench. Broadhead did not act in matters demanding that he hear charges against alleged defendants until 1747, just three years before he was represented to the Lord Chancellor.[53]

Perhaps, then, the activities of these dozen justices epitomize the illegal activities of a far larger number of justices who were not represented. While it definitely cannot be claimed that every justice who acted illegally was eventually removed from the commission,[54] it is likely that a surprisingly large proportion of those who so acted were indeed represented. For, as examination of the justices whom Middlesex Sessions investigated but did not represent will make evident, metropolitan justices had considerable incentive to bring charges against their colleagues. Should the reputation of the metropolitan bench then be attributed to the justices of the two commissions for which records of hearings have not survived – the justices of Westminster and the Tower Liberty? Like Middlesex's bench, Westminster's did investigate charges against its members and represent miscreant justices to the Lord Chancellor,[55] and the Lord Chancellors'

through October 1780, it is not possible to determine whether such a committee met in 1780 or whether the reference refers to the committee on the application of the vagrancy laws, whose work resulted in a representation (never sent to the Lord Chancellor) against two Westminster justices in January 1780.

[53] See L.M.A., MJ/SBB. I want to thank Tim Wales for tracking Broadhead's recognizances in these sessions books.

[54] See the suspicions raised about Sir Samuel Gower in R. Paley, 'Thief-takers in London in the age of the McDaniel gang, c. 1745–1754', in D. Hay and F. Snyder, eds., *Policing and prosecution in Britain 1750–1850* (Oxford, 1989), pp. 314–15, 330.

[55] L.M.A., WJ/OC1, 4 February 1720[1], 12 April 1721, p. 10 (Sir William Moore); *London Evening Post*, 14–16 July 1778 (Robert Elliot, John King), cited in Paley, 'Middlesex justices act', p. 211.

removal of Westminster's justices does not suggest that these justices were more nefarious than those of Middlesex. From 1716 to 1792 the Lord Chancellor used his *supersedeas* to remove only one Westminster justice, George Garnon, who was not also so removed from Middlesex's commission.[56] While the disappearance of the Tower Liberty's records renders it impossible to determine whether its bench investigated its justices, that a Lord Chancellor never found it necessary to supersede any justice on this small bench suggests that the illegal activities of these justices were not the source of the trading justices' reputation.

Since justices whom Middlesex Sessions represented to the Lord Chancellor were justices who repeatedly acted in knowing defiance of the law or in a manner contemporaries construed as a flagrant attack on English justice, since it is likely that a surprisingly large proportion of such justices were so represented, and since the Lord Chancellor removed these few justices from the bench relatively soon after they exhibited this pattern of activity, it seems likely that what defined the trading justice was not illegal activity. Evidently, what defined the trading justice was activity the eighteenth century found distasteful but not necessarily illegal. Middlesex Sessions' dinner guests – justices whom Sessions reprimanded but did not represent – were justices who both continued on the bench and quite clearly acted in a manner Sessions considered reprehensible. Their activity therefore seems to be that which characterized trading magistracy.

Justices who were dinner guests

That judicial activity which elicited an invitation to dine with Middlesex Sessions is epitomized by that which produced an invitation to Sessions' most renowned guest – to Sir John Fielding, the blind beak of Bow Street, the progenitor of modern magistracy, and according to some observers, the metropolis' premier trading justice.[57] Fielding was invited to dine because an alleged felon committed to New Prison by justices acting in the east end had been examined, not by those justices and not at the time and place specified in the order of commitment, but by the justices at Bow Street. According to the dinner invitation, Bow Street's action had inconvenienced the witness and obstructed the committing justices' proceedings.[58] Bow Street's actions had also stolen the east end's business: to Bow Street now went the fees and other spoils of further proceedings. Like almost all the other judicial dinner guests, Fielding was invited to dinner because he had sought judicial business.

[56] P.R.O., C234/24, 27 December 1763.
[57] Leslie-Melville, *John Fielding*, pp. 91–2, 257, 261; Battestin, *Henry Fielding*, pp. 475, 561.
[58] L.M.A., MJ/OC8, 3 May 1764, p. 23.

Middlesex Sessions considered such pursuit suspect. When Justice William Blackborow was subjected to Sessions' investigation on complaint of Justice Charles Triquet, Blackborow retaliated by bringing charges against Triquet, among them the allegation that Triquet employed a clerk to stand outside his office door, advertising his services.[59] There were other ways for justices to find customers. Blackborow was said to have granted warrants on credit.[60] Sessions invited justices to dine for issuing warrants for the apprehension of people living some distance from them, warrants which demanded that those apprehended appear before the justice who issued the warrant and forbidding appearance before any other justice; and issue of such warrants was instanced as an abuse of office in representations to the Lord Chancellor.[61]

On the other hand, if a justice acted in a case initiated before another justice, his action too might be considered inappropriate. Nathaniel Dukinfield, J.P., offended by intervening in a case initiated before another justice. Dukinfield had discharged Sarah Frasier, who had been taken into custody for assault on Eleanor Stone. Dukinfield explained that he had issued a warrant against Stone at Frasier's request, and then each complainant had withdrawn her charge against the other.[62] Similarly, in 1777 Edward Bindloss complained that Jonathan Durden was a judicial interloper. Durden had, according to Bindloss, threatened to send a prosecutor to Bridewell unless the prosecutor allowed Durden to determine his case, even though the prosecutor had initiated the case before Bindloss and wanted Bindloss to determine it. On another occasion, against the prosecutor's wishes, Durden had a defendant taken on Bindloss' warrant brought before him and then told the contending parties that in going to Bindloss they had gone 'to a Man who knew nothing about the matter and if the[y] went to Fools they could not expect good Usage'.[63] Clearly, Bindloss and Durden, like many of their colleagues, were engaged in a contest for business.

In 1787 the parish officers of Mile End Old Town told Sessions that their justices were 'striving and contending against each other for business, with all the eagerness and jealousies attendant upon jarring

[59] L.M.A., MJ/OC12, 12 August 1790, p. 88.
[60] E. W. Bayley, *Londiniana*, 4 vols. (London, 1829), vol. IV, p. 287.
[61] L.M.A., MJ/OC1, 9 September 1720, p. 107 (Thomas Boteler and Nathaniel Blackerby); February 1720[1], pp. 114–15 (Sir William Moore); MJ/OC10a, January 1778, pp. 193–4 (John Gretton). Middlesex's clerk kept a copy of a letter summoning Thomas Railton to dine along with Boteler and Blackerby (MJ/SP 1720 Sept. no. 35), but its order book does not note that he was so invited.
[62] L.M.A., MJ/SP 1748 October no. 94, draft of Waller to Dukinfield, 10 October 1748; no. 95, Dukinfield to Waller, 12 October 1748.
[63] L.M.A., MJ/OC10a, December 1777, pp. 166–9.

interests'.[64] In 1794 Brentford, outside metropolitan London, discovered the local excitement attendant upon such rivalry. Two trading justices, John Spiller and Nathaniel Bland, had each moved to Brentford to escape the restrictions imposed by Parliament in 1792 on metropolitan trading magistracy. The competition between the two inflamed a riot and resulted in the indictment of Bland's clerk for assault.[65] In 1731 competition between contending justices was even keener: that judicial contest culminated in the armed attack of one justice upon another. The struggle began when Justice John Webster superseded a warrant. Justice Thomas DeVeil nonetheless took action on the matter, refusing to honour Webster's supersession of the warrant. Webster thereupon summoned DeVeil to a room over a coffeehouse in Leicester Fields, had his confederate bar the door, drew his sword and stabbed DeVeil.[66] As one would therefore expect, justices were also disturbed when a colleague discharged a prisoner whom another justice had committed. Simon Michel, John Troughton, John Nicol, Henry Trent and Joseph St Lawrence each received an invitation to dinner to answer such charges.[67]

There was good reason for justices to poach their colleagues' business: fees. Justices could levy a fee for every legal document they issued or signed. So, in 1790 Charles Triquet complained to the committee on judicial conduct that William Blackborow had offered the Keeper of New Prison's servant sixpence per copy for copies of the warrants committing bailable prisoners. Blackborow, it was alleged, found that the copy provided the information requisite for bailing the prisoners, which he did – for a fee. Blackborow replied that he had offered sixpence because Triquet had offered fourpence.[68] As such avidity to acquire judicial business indicates, the amount of work available to an enterprising metropolitan justice could generate a substantial income. While throughout England justices conducted judicial business, in metropolitan London, justice was a business. In metropolitan London, and possibly in metropolitan London alone, justices acquired premises devoted solely to magistracy.[69]

[64] quoted in Webb and Webb, *The parish and the county*, p. 562.

[65] P.R.O., H.O. 42/21, fo. 102, 'Applications ... under the new police act', 13 July 1792; fos. 428–9, 'List of the present acting justices' [1792]; H.O. 42/26, fo. 69, Middlesex justices 'under particular circumstances', 10 July 1793; H.O. 42/31, fo. 110, from Bland, 6 June 1794. L.M.A., MJ/SP 1794 October no. 26, affidavit of William Turner, clerk to Bland, 6 June 1794. *Times*, 9 April 1792, p. 3; 4 June 1794, p. 3.

[66] Westminster's bench petitioned for and obtained Webster's removal from Middlesex's bench. DeVeil had been acting on his commission as a justice of Westminster, and Webster was a member of Middlesex's commission but not Westminster's. L.M.A., WJ/SBB889, back page; WJ/OC2, 5 April 1731, pp. 100–1. *Gentleman's Magazine*, vol. 1 (1731), pp. 125, 307.

[67] See note 37 above.   [68] L.M.A., MJ/OC12, 16 September 1790, pp. 76, 78.

[69] Two of the trading justices' offices became stipendiaries' offices. P.R.O., H.O. 42/21, fos. 163–5, Reeves to Dundas, 28 July 1792; fos. 251–5, Same to Same, 1 August 1792;

The justices christened their places of business a 'public office'.[70] To the public, the justice's office was 'his Worship's Justice Shop'.[71]

The justice's shop generated profit – not only for the magistrate and his clerk, but also for those who serviced the judicial machinery set in motion by the magistrate's action. For instance, William Berry, Justice Blackborow's clerk, began his career in law enforcement when, 'having no other Employment', he spent his days attending Blackborow's office, where he subsisted on the fees he earned by serving warrants.[72] Similarly, informers flocked to the office of a justice willing to convict those against whom they informed, and so win the informer his statutorily mandated share of the fine. Constables too could profit from association with a compliant justice. Middlesex Sessions found that a few justices had authorized large numbers of inappropriately large payments to constables for apprehending and passing vagrants. In some cases, Sessions either wrote a monitory letter to the justice or requested that he explain his actions.[73] In other cases, Sessions invited the justice to dinner.[74] Even if a justice did not act so as to attract an inordinate proportion of the metropolis' informers and constables, that his office was so clearly a place of business meant that contemporaries associated the busy justice with justices who acted illegally: both profited from judicial business.

Alnwick Castle, Alnwick MSS Syon Y IV 6a, Box 2, Envelope 7, David Wilmot, Public Office, Curtain Rd, Shoreditch, 24 January 1775.

[70] L.M.A., MJ/SP 1786 April no. 11, letter to John Staples at the Public Office, Whitechapel; 1797, Box 6, folder Oct.–Nov. appeals, convictions by John Spiller at Public-Office, New Brentford; MJ/OC10a, 13 March 1786, p. 203.

[71] *Universal Daily Register*, 19 October 1789, p. 3. See also: *Middlesex Journal*, 24 August 1769, quoted in J. Brewer, 'The Wilkites and the law, 1763–74', in J. Brewer and J. Styles, eds., *An ungovernable people: the English and their law in the seventeenth and eighteenth centuries* (New Brunswick, New Jersey, 1980), p. 145; *Old England*, 15 July 1749, quoted in Battestin, *Henry Fielding*, p. 475; S. and B. Webb, *English local government from the revolution to the municipal corporations act*, vol. III, *The manor and the borough. Part two* (London, 1908), p. 666; B.L., Add. MSS 35601, fos. 261v, 262, 'A true account of some justices' [1743].

[72] L.M.A., MJ/OC12, 12 August 1790, pp. 88–9.

[73] L.M.A., MJ/OC5, 12 October, 7 December 1749, p. 185v; MJ/OC6, 24 February 1757 p. 109; MJ/OC7, 6 December 1759, p. 45, and 17 January 1760, p. 47; MJ/OC12, 15 April, 8 July 1790, pp. 45, 67, and January 1795, pp. 405–7.

[74] L.M.A., MJ/OC7, 22 May 1760, p. 56 (Benjamin Cox); MJ/OC8, 11 May 1769, p. 98v (John Spinnage). In 1780 Middlesex Sessions voted to represent two Westminster justices – James Fielding and William Hyde – because they had authorized such payments. (Middlesex Sessions administered the vagrant funds for both Middlesex and Westminster.) When the two justices promised to mend their ways, Sessions suspended its proceedings against them. A year later, both justices were raised to the Middlesex commission, a promotion due in Hyde's case to his service as a justice during the Gordon riots (MJ/OC10a, 13 Jan. 1780, pp. 379–84; MJ/SP 1780 April no. 13; MJP/L10a. Alnwick Castle, Alnwick MSS Syon Y IV 6a, Box 2, Envelope 10, William Hyde to Duke of Northumberland, 29 Dec. 1780. P.R.O., 30/8/147, fos. 179–80, William Hyde to William Pitt, Nov. 1795). *The Times* considered Hyde a trading justice (9 April 1792, p. 3).

As metropolitan magistracy was a business, its practitioners attempted to regulate its business practices. One of the major goals of such regulation was the limitation of competition. Early in the reign of George I, Middlesex and Westminster Sessions passed identical resolutions inhibiting judicial interloping. A justice was not to: bail those committed by or discharge those taken on another justice's warrant without consulting that justice; hear informations against those living out of their petty sessional division; license alehouses in areas out of their petty sessional division; authorize the rates of a parish other than his own; or authorize payments of poor relief to people living in a parish other than his own.[75] The Sessions' resolutions attempted to ensure fair dealing among judicial entrepreneurs.

For judicial entrepreneurs who nonetheless faced unfair competition the metropolitan benches created another remedy: dinner invitations, hearings and representations. It may well be that the competitive entrepreneurial environment of metropolitan London is sufficient explanation for the metropolitan benches' invention of a procedure to hear complaints against their members. Elsewhere, complaints against justices were made directly to the Lord Chancellor.[76] In metropolitan London, and in metropolitan London alone, the justices' Sessions heard such complaints. Indeed, because metropolitan magistracy was a competitive business, it is likely that Middlesex Sessions heard complaints, brought by their competitors, against a remarkably large proportion of its justices who acted both frequently and illegally. According to John Gretton, charges were brought against him because his conduct of his office diminished the fees accruing to justices in a nearby office.[77]

While the conduct of justice as a business may well have produced the self-regulation of the metropolitan bench, that same entrepreneurial conduct explains the most serious charge against the trading justices – the charge that they fostered crime. After all, since justices were judicial entrepreneurs, then surely – or so contemporaries believed – it was to be expected that they would try to increase judicial business. There were only two ways to do that: steal customers from one's colleagues, and justices did do that; or foster an environment in which more people needed the justice's services more frequently. Contemporaries put it bluntly: trading justices caused crime and dissension because they

[75] L.M.A., MJ/OC1, 6 December 1716, pp. 13–14; WJ/OC1, 5 January 1720[1], p. 8; WJ/OC2, 6 October 1725, pp. 24–7. B.L., 7754 c. 13(14), *Middlesex Sessions, order of Sessions,* 6 December 1729.
[76] B.L., Add. MSS 35604, fo. 331, draft from Hardwicke to Sir Jacob Astley, 14 August 1756.
[77] P.R.O., H.O. 42/34, fos. 104–7, Gretton's memorial.

profited from crime and dissension. Their rhetoric elaborated upon this suspicion. What would it profit a justice if brothels and gaming houses were suppressed – as by law they should be – and the justice could not then be bribed to ignore their presence?[78] Would it not be prudent in a justice to save petty offenders from condign punishment so that they could mature into felons hung on the evidence of a thief-taker, a thief-taker who shared his reward with the justice?[79] Surely, it was the justices themselves who were to blame for the frequency with which the London poor brought charges against each other, for the justice took a fee whenever he acted on such charges. As the *Middlesex Journal*'s comment on a trading justice noted: 'The more quarrelling and drinking, the better his trade.'[80] To contemporaries, the opportunities for profitable misuse of office were so clear and tempting that they created a veritable tradition of ironic remark. From at least the days when Henry Fielding sat in Bow Street, commentators had wryly noted that the metropolis' chief magistrate was situated in the district most renowned for its houses of illicit pleasure, a juxtaposition of magistrate and potential sources of illicit magisterial profit which reinforced the Fieldings' image as London's leading trading justices.[81] So, too, there was an easily recognized and readily understood rhetoric associating the trading justice with crime: the *Times* found two simple clauses – 'the *trade* of thieving will ever thrive, whilst there exists a *trade* of Justices' – sufficient to convey the argument without further

[78] B.L., Add. MSS 35601, fo. 261, 'A true account of some justices' [1743]; P.R.O., H.O. 42/29, fo. 524, from Alexander Cumming, 28 April 1794. *Parliamentary Papers* [hereafter *P.P.*], *Second report from the committee on . . . the police of the metropolis*, 1817 (484) VII, p. 422. *Old England*, 15 July 1749, quoted in Battestin, *Henry Fielding*, p. 475. *Gentleman's Magazine*, vol. 27 (1757), p. 454. *Universal Daily Register*, 28 March 1788, p. 3; 19 October 1789, p. 3; 2 November 1789, p. 2.

[79] B.L., Add. MSS 35601, fo. 260, 'A true account of some justices' [1743]. *Letter to the Duke of Northumberland*, pp. 22–4. *Universal Daily Register*, 10 October 1787, p. 3. *Parliamentary History*, vol. XX, 5 March 1781, col. 1322; vol. XXV, 29 June 1785, cols. 902, 908.

[80] *Middlesex Journal*, 24 August 1769, quoted in Brewer, 'The Wilkites and the law', in Brewer and Styles, eds., *An ungovernable people*, p. 145. See also: *Universal Daily Register*, 29 July 1786, p. 2; P.R.O., H.O. 42/26, fo. 28, *The Diary*, 3 July 1793; *Legis speculum de pace. A method proposed for the better regulation of justices in . . . Middlesex* (London, 1759), pp. 3–4; *Gentleman's Magazine*, vol. 39 (1769), p. 539; Radzinowicz, *English criminal law*, vol. III, p. 37, n. 19, quoting J. Fielding, *Extracts from the penal laws*, (1768), p. 5; *The Senator*, vol. 14 (1796), debate of 19 February 1796; *P.P.*, *Report from the committee on the state of the police of the metropolis*, 1816 (510) V, p. 140; *P.P.* (1817) VII, p. 422; *Calendar of state papers domestic, Anne*, vol. II, p. 373, petition of Simon Fanshaw, 4 December 1703; B.L., Add. MSS 33932, fos. 28–9, 77–9; Add. MSS 35601, fo. 266, Anthony Wroth to Hardwick, January 1743[4].

[81] Battestin, *Henry Fielding*, p. 475 quoting *Old England*, 15 July 1749; Leslie-Melville, *John Fielding*, pp. 91–2; *Legis speculum*, pp. 4–5; *Universal Daily Register*, 14 October 1788, p. 3; and see references in note 78 above.

elaboration.[82] The argument's logic was inexorable: metropolitan magistracy was a business; businessmen seek profits; metropolitan magistrates therefore fostered conditions in which their trade would flourish. The rhetoric was persuasive.

The trading justice's activities

Indeed, metropolitan magistracy's reputation became so malodorous that Parliament decided that a salaried magistracy was preferable to the voluntary unsalaried service of metropolitan London's current justices, and Parliament made this decision even though it considered voluntary magistracy a bastion of liberty and salaried magistracy an extension of the power of the state.[83] In 1792 Parliament passed an act establishing salaried magistrates, the stipendiaries, in metropolitan London. In decreeing that fees for judicial services could be levied only at the seven offices appointed for the stipendiaries and at Bow Street, the act extirpated trading magistracy in metropolitan London. Henceforth, the justices of metropolitan London would be the stipendiary magistrates, three to each office, none of whom would profit from fees since all were paid a salary by the state, as were the housekeeper, two clerks and six constables attached to each office.[84] Fittingly, the act which pronounced the end of trading magistracy also testified to the belief that metropolitan magistracy was a very profitable enterprise, even when conducted by those who could not profit from it. According to the act, the annual cost of the new public offices and their staffs would amount to £14,000, and both act and Parliament assumed that all or almost all that sum would be funded by the fees paid at the public offices.[85] As the stipendiaries inherited the trading justices' business but not their reputation, they provide a standard against which to measure their predecessors. Does the stipendiaries' record validate contemporary opinion of the trading justices? What was gained, and what lost when entrepreneurial justice disappeared?

---

[82] *Universal Daily Register*, 10 October 1787, p. 3; and see references in note 79 above.

[83] D. Philips, '"A new engine of power and authority": the institutionalization of law-enforcement in England 1780–1830', in V. A. C. Gatrell *et al.*, eds., *Crime and the law: the social history of crime in western Europe since 1500* (London, 1980), pp. 167–9.

[84] 32 George III c. 53. Fees could be levied at Quarter Sessions and licensing sessions. A justice's clerk could also take fees when enforcing the payment of taxes or acting under local acts. For the act, see Paley, 'The Middlesex justices act', chap. 7.

[85] *Twenty-Eighth report from the select committee on finance, etc: police* (1798), pp. 10–11, reproduced in Lambert, ed., *House of Commons sessional papers*, vol. CXII. *Legis speculum* (1759), p. 8 estimated that the fees taken by metropolitan London's trading justices amounted to £12,000 *per annum*. See also *Parliamentary History*, vol. XXIX (1792), col. 1180, and P.R.O., H.O. 42/43, fo.148, from Samuel Tolfrey, 1798.

What was lost, and lost immediately was money – the government's money. On average, the cost of the stipendiaries and their offices was £16,000 a year, and on average their offices took in £2,605 a year in fees. Clearly, metropolitan magistracy was by no means as profitable as contemporaries assumed.[86]

Similarly, the 1792 act's effect on crime was not quite what rhetoric had led its supporters to expect. When pressed, the government would claim that some varieties of serious crime had been reduced, a reduction which one of the act's proponents attributed not to the stipendiaries, but instead to a clause in the 1792 act which increased justices' powers to sweep the streets of suspected thieves. However, the act's opponents and even some of its supporters claimed that it had effected no reduction whatsoever in London's crime.[87]

Nonetheless, the replacement of unsalaried justices by stipendiaries did alter the conduct of judicial business, an alteration that validates two of the less sensational charges made against the trading justices. One of these charges is that trading justices profited from abuse of their powers of summary conviction, and did so through collusion with the informers who laid informations at their office. They did so in two ways. First, it was alleged that trading justices pocketed fines levied on informations – either keeping the portion of the fine which should have been paid to the parish in which the offence was committed,[88] or graciously reducing the fine, so that the offender paid only that portion due the informer, which the informer then split with the justice.[89] George Reid was prosecuted in King's Bench for pocketing fines,[90] but comparison of the stipendaries' record to that of their predecessors suggests that he was not the only justice to do so. Justices were supposed to return a record of the fines

---

[86] *Twenty-Eighth report . . . on finance*, p. 11.
[87] *The Times*, 22 June 1793, p. 1; 20 February 1796, p. 2. Radzinowicz, *English criminal law*, vol. III, pp. 133, 135. Scottish Record Office [hereafter Scot.R.O.], GD51/1/290, 'Burton, The good effects of the Police bill'. The number of defendants indicted for felonies and trespasses at the Old Bailey and at Middlesex Sessions did diminish shortly after the stipendiaries assumed office. (Paley, 'The Middlesex justices act', p. 393; M. Feeley and D. Little, 'The vanishing female: the decline of women in the criminal process', *Law and Society Review*, vol. 25 (1991), pp. 775–6.) However, as Britain also went to war with France shortly after the stipendiaries assumed office, I cannot distinguish a decline in indictments attributable to the stipendiaries from that due to the war (for which see P. King, 'War as a judicial resource', in this volume).
[88] L.M.A., MJ/OC12, 12 August 1790, p. 86 (Charles Triquet).
[89] P.R.O., H.O. 42/26, fo. 28, *The Diary*, 3 July 1793. L.M.A., MJ/OC10a, January 1778, pp. 195–7 (Cornelius Martin).
[90] *Universal Daily Register*, 6 November 1788, p. 3; P.R.O., H.O. 42/21, fo. 102, 'Applications . . . under the new police act', 13 July 1792; fos. 428–9, 'List of the present acting justices'; H.O. 42/26, fo. 69, Middlesex justices 'under particular circumstances', 10 July 1793.

they levied to Sessions, and fines which were not reported, and so not recorded, were obviously more easy to pocket than recorded fines. According to Middlesex Sessions' record of summary convictions, 114 fines were levied in the three months from 9 November 1793 to 3 February 1794, including 89 made by the stipendiaries. In contrast, in the days of their predecessors – from 29 October 1773 to 13 December 1786 – 1,375 convictions were reported, a suspiciously low average of just 26 convictions every three months.[91]

Comparison of the offences for which the stipendiaries levied fines with the offences fined by their predecessors also substantiates the other allegation about trading justices' collusion with informers – that the trading justices convicted in order to profit from the fine, and did so on flimsy or manufactured evidence. Trading justices and informers were satirized as feeding off two sets of laws – those regulating the sale of bread, and those regulating signs on coaches or hired vehicles.[92] The record of fines returned to Middlesex Sessions does indeed indicate that the stipendiaries' predecessors were inordinately interested in fining violations of the laws regulating the sale of bread. Of the 1,375 convictions recorded from 29 October 1773 to 13 December 1786, 479 (39 per cent) were for offences relating to the sale of bread. In contrast, there are only four convictions, all made by stipendiaries, for offences relating to the sale of bread among the 114 convictions of 9 November 1793 to 3 February 1794. By 1817 there was a marked increase in stipendiaries' convictions for such offences, and these too suggest that some of the trading justices' convictions were based on evidence manufactured by informers. When in 1817 the stipendiaries at the Southwark office convicted a large number of bakers for selling underweight bread, the government learned that the convictions should be attributed to a conspiracy between the office's police and local informers, who 'plucked' the bread so that its weight when produced at the stipendiary's office was less than that at which it was sold.[93]

The stipendiaries' experience also substantiates the allegation that the laws regulating signs on hired vehicles were being exploited by informers. In 1816 a stipendiary told Parliament that enforcement of these laws

---

[91] L.M.A., MSJ/CC1, MSJ/CC3. The surviving notebooks in which Sessions' clerks entered record of the summary convictions returned to Quarter Sessions cover the period from 29 October 1773 to 3 February 1794 only. I want to thank Erika Quinn for entering the information in these books into a database.

[92] B.L., Add. MSS 33932, fos. 36–7.

[93] *P.P.* (1817) VII, p. 426. P.R.O., H.O. 42/163, Stanley Mailer to Sidmouth, 18 April 1817; for the prosecution of a justice for making convictions on the evidence of a 'plucked' loaf, see KB1/17 (Part II), unlabelled bundle, affidavit of William Vigurs *et al.* on complaint against Thomas Miller Esq., 7 February 1767.

oppressed the poor,[94] and stipendiaries rarely convicted under these laws. Between November 1793 and February 1794 they did not make any such convictions. Convictions under these laws also do not feature prominently in the returns to Middlesex Sessions for 29 October 1773 to 13 December 1786, and the vast majority of the fifty convictions relating to carts and coaches there returned are so laconic that it is not possible to determine whether the offender's offence was failure to post the requisite sign. However, one justice's statement of his convictions is quite specific. Humphrey Jackson, who makes his first appearance in Middlesex's record of summary convictions in November 1785, made twelve such convictions in the next thirteen months, during which time he also returned record of 121 other convictions – 3 for selling or firing fireworks, 88 for offences relating to the sale of bread, and 30 for selling products such as hair powder without a stamp or without posting the requisite sign before the vendor's place of business. (Jackson had been a chemist, keeping a shop in St Botolph Aldgate; it may be that the thirty convictions for sale of goods were aimed at rival chemists.[95]) When the 1792 act establishing the stipendiaries awarded their offices a monopoly of the fees levied in metropolitan London, Jackson moved to Enfield, whence in 1794 the Home Secretary received a petition from the other resident justices alleging that Jackson was colluding with informers, using the law about signs to extort money from the owner of a stage coach.[96] Similarly, when two trading justices decamped to Brentford after the 1792 act prohibited their trade in metropolitan London, the owners of Brentford's coaches had to appeal to Middlesex Sessions against improper convictions, and Brentford's inhabitants, declaring that these justices had 'directly encouraged and indirectly supported a set of Informers that have harassed his Majesty's subjects', petitioned for a stipendiary's office to be established in their town.[97]

According to their proponents, stipendiaries also provided relief from a second of their predecessors' practices – that of unnecessarily entangling the populace in the toils of the law. In 1793 a clerk at a stipendiaries' office produced an extended description of such activity, activity which he boasted the appointment of stipendiaries had eradicated.[98]

[94] *P.P.* (1816) V, p. 133.
[95] Alnwick Castle, Alnwick MSS Syon Y IV 6a, Box 1, Envelope 5, undated list [1769].
[96] P.R.O., H.O. 42/29, fo. 334, George W. Prescott *et al.*, 5 April 1794; fos. 336–9, petition of Ann Newton, 5 April 1794.
[97] For the appeals: L.M.A., MJ/SP 1794 January nos. 45a–f, 46a–j, 48, 50; April nos. 26–7, 29, 30; June no. 25; July no. 24a; October no. 4b; WJ/SP 1797; MJ/SP 1797, box 6, October folder. For the petition: University of Nottingham Library, PwF 10519, cited in Paley, 'Middlesex justices act', p. 261.
[98] P.R.O., H.O. 42/26, fo. 28, *The Diary*, 3 July 1793. See also the references in note 80 above.

Then for Warrants, Summonses, etc. it had come to such a pitch, that it almost bore the similitude that had a canine animal brought a Shilling in his mouth, with a label, specifying his complaint, a Warrant was readily granted, and instantly executed upon any of the human species; and on being brought before such magistrate, let the complaint be never so frivolous, Bail was instantly required, not with the smallest view of the ends of Justice, but to bring grist to the mill, and there it did not end, for the Runners (by whose direction I need not say) were sure to whisper in the ear of the Defendant, to take out what is called a Cross Warrant, which, from the sudden impulse of revenge was generally approved of, when the same process immediately took place, and of course the same pecuniary emoluments rolled into the pockets of the Magistrate, etc as it did from the Complainant; leaving, at length, Prosecutor and Defendant to regret their folly, and such as could not procure Bail were committed. Hence, the prisons were crouded [*sic*], the Recognizance List swelled, and the County put to an enormous expence for Bread and common necessaries.

Comparison of the stipendiaries' record to that of their predecessors does indicate that the clerk had identified a hallmark of the trading justices' practice. As his lampoon predicts, the 'Recognizance List' – the list of bonds, taken by justices out of Sessions, requiring those bound to attend Sessions – suffered an immediate and precipitous decline when the metropolis' voluntary justices were replaced by stipendiaries. In 1791, the year before the institution of stipendiaries, 7,322 recognizances were returned to Middlesex and Westminster Sessions. In 1793, the year after the institution of stipendiaries, only 2,752 recognizances were so returned, and the stipendiaries' adherence to judicial practices which entangled fewer people in the law became a hallmark of their practice. A quarter-century after the stipendiaries were instituted, in the years 1817 through 1820, the average number of recognizances returned annually to these Sessions was only 4,109, just over half of the number so returned in the last days of the trading justices.[99] Similarly, and as the lampoon predicted, the advent of stipendiaries would produce a notable decline in the number of recognizances exacted by defendants of those who had lodged complaints against them. Of the 318 recognizances returned to Middlesex and Westminster Sessions in April 1797, only two were counter-recognizances to another two recognizances in these rolls. In contrast, of 415 recognizances returned to Middlesex and Westminster Sessions in January 1756, fifty-two were either the original recognizance

[99] L.M.A., MJ/SBB, WJ/SBB, for 1791, 1793, 1817–20. It is unlikely that this decrease in the issue of recognizances caused the decrease in the number of advertisements of apology noted in D. Andrew, 'The press and public apologies', in this volume. Disputes generating such advertisements infrequently generated recognizances. Of fifty-three such advertisements published in the *Daily Advertiser* in 1751 and 1771, just three – including two for cases in which the grand jury found a bill of indictment – are associated with recognizances returned to Middlesex Sessions. I wish to thank Professor Andrew for sending me copies of these apologies.

in a dispute which generated a counter-recognizance in the same roll, or that counter-recognizance.[100] Clearly, the stipendiaries' predecessors issued recognizances in matters for which stipendiaries considered such issue unnecessary.

Such abstemiousness in the creation of legal obligations was what Parliament had intended in establishing the stipendiaries. When in 1796 Parliament debated the renewal of the 1792 act, Burton – its sponsor – instanced the decrease in the number of recognizances as evidence of the stipendiaries' value. So, too, he instanced a similar decrease in the number of defendants who each year were, first, committed to gaol because neither they nor their acquaintance had wealth sufficient to stand surety in a recognizance for the defendant's appearance in court, and then discharged from gaol when the plaintiff neglected to present his plaint to the grand jury.[101] The stipendiaries' restraint meant that those advocating the establishment of stipendiaries in areas bordering London could argue that the 1792 act had 'contributed to quell a spirit of litigation among the lower classes', a spirit of litigation which had 'detained' justices and juries 'in Sessions to try petty Assaults and Brawls fostered by the Authority which ought to have suppressed them'.[102] As a stipendiary explained to Parliament in 1817, one of his functions was 'to keep the people from spending their money in law'.[103]

Seen from the viewpoint of a plaintiff bent on achieving legal and condign retribution for his plaint, the stipendiaries' restraint might seem a failure to deliver justice, a withdrawal from the poor. Denigration of the trading justice had been associated with derision of his clientele.[104]

> If Termagent [sic] should chance to take
> offence, and feel herself offended on pretence
> that Neighbour Boothby did upon her Spit
> straitways apply's for Justice Sapseul's write [sic].

---

[100] L.M.A., MJ/SR 3048, 3611; WJ/SR 3047, 3610. These counts include neither recognizances to answer indictments found at an earlier session nor recognizances to prosecute indictments. Almost all the recognizances generating counter-recognizances in 1756 were in the Westminster roll. However, samplings in Middlesex's recognizances for 1702 and 1788 indicate that a significant proportion of plaintiffs who had their defendants bound in recognizance were, in their turn, so bound.

[101] The Senator, vol. 14 (1796), debate of 19 February 1796. The Times, 20 February 1796, p. 2. See also: P.R.O., H.O. 42/25, fo. 644, from C.T. Kerby; fo. 319, from Mr Gliddon, 2 May 1793.

[102] Scot.R.O., GD51/9/1260/2 [from Samuel Tolfrey]. P.R.O., H.O. 42/45, fo. 251, from Tolfrey. See also Scot.R.O., GD51/17/4 [P. Colquhoun], 'Letters . . . on the subject of police', p. 2.

[103] P.P. (1817) VII, p. 402. B. Lambert, The history and survey of London and its environs, 4 vols. (London, 1806), vol. III, pp. 523–4.

[104] B.L., Add. MSS 33932, fo. 76. P.R.O., H.O. 42/26, fo. 28, The Diary, 3 July 1793.

It may be that Parliament, which considered the metropolitan justice the poor's 'principal Court',[105] had intended that the stipendiaries act so as to diminish the poor's unfortunate tendency to make use of the magistrate and of the law of crime and misdemeanour which he administered. However, whatever Parliament's intentions, the poor's demand for magisterial services was such that the stipendiaries were soon serving at least some of their needs. Use of the law administered by the justices of the peace cost much less than resort to the civil courts, and the stipendiaries – like their predecessors – faced plaintiffs who expected redress in matters scarcely related to the law of crime and misdemeanour.[106] These plaintiffs reveal a feature of the trading justice's trade slighted in eighteenth-century discussion: the trading justice had a trade because there was considerable demand for his services. Indeed a justice could convert an office in which each transaction yielded but a miniscule fee into a business only if a very large number of people were willing to pay for his services.

Whether the stipendiaries provided service to the poor similar to that provided by the trading justice cannot now be determined. In driving the trading justice from metropolitan London, Parliament extirpated the pursuit of profit, and so entrepreneurial justice, from common law magistracy. Whether providers of services who are not rewarded by the services' recipients will be as responsive to those recipients' demands as providers directly paid by those recipients remains an unanswered question. Nonetheless, it seems likely that the trading justice served a clientele who insisted on using their magistrates in ways which the eighteenth-century elite, and we today, unaccustomed to entrepreneurial magistracy, find surprising. As one bemused stipendiary observed, 'the lower orders of the people will actually pawn their clothes to take out warrants'.[107]

---

[105] *The Times*, 17 March 1792, p. 2.

[106] T. De Veil, Knt., *Observations on the practice of a justice of the peace: intended for such gentlemen as design to act for Middlesex or Westminster* (London, 1747), pp. 3–4, 12–14, 16. *P.P.* (1816) V, pp. 130–1. J. Davis, 'A poor man's system of justice: the London police courts in the second half of the nineteenth century', *Historical Journal*, vol. 27 (1984), pp. 309–35. My assessment of the stipendiaries is also influenced by S. Auerbach, 'A domestic and paternal tribunal: police court magistrates and the poor in London, 1870–1914', which I heard at the April 2000 meeting of the Pacific Coast Conference on British Studies.

[107] *P.P.* (1816) V, p. 61 (Thomas Evance); see also p. 131 (William Fielding).

4   Impressment and the law in eighteenth-century Britain

Nicholas Rogers

In September 1744 the press gang of the *Royal Sovereign* was informed that a deserter was hiding in the Fountain tavern off Rag Fair, in the heart of the seafaring quarter of London's east end.[1] Led by the flamboyant and braggart Hamilton Montgomery, the ship's mate who sported a 'lac'd hat', the gang entered the pub and commandeered 'a man in a sailor's habit' who happened to be singing a sea shanty. A scuffle ensued in which the landlord, one Robert Wallis, was wounded and a ganger was pummelled to the ground by a group of local curriers who had come to the seaman's rescue. The seaman was eventually taken, but the gang swore revenge for the affray. They returned the following morning, threatening 'to have the landlord's blood, cut his Head off, chop him to pieces, & be the Death of him'. They ransacked the house while searching for Wallis, ran their cutlasses through the bedding in an attempt to find their quarry, and sword-whipped the local headborough who had attempted to raise a posse against them. When one of their men was arrested and taken to Clerkenwell prison, the press gang collected reinforcements and secured his rescue, admonishing the turnkey for 'taking in a King's man'. 'Damn your Blood, you rascall', they swore at the turnkey, 'if ever you take in another we will cut you all to pieces, and pull down your Gaol to the Ground'. Only the intervention of the Tower guard prevented an escalation of insult and violence, and it was only after a two-hour standoff at another tavern that the gang finally surrendered to the civil authorities. Montgomery and his gang were charged with threatening the life of the landlord, with assaulting the headborough and rescuing a ganger from prison. At the Middlesex Quarter Sessions they were lucky to get away with the relatively small fines imposed upon them: 6s. 8d. apiece for the rescue; 2s. each on two accounts of assault. Had the Admiralty not made discreet settlements out of court to both the landlord and headborough for the injuries and damages they had incurred, had the presiding justice

---

[1] For the depositions on this case, and the Admiralty Solicitor's report, see Public Record Office [hereafter P.R.O.], Adm. 1/3675/343–75.

not looked leniently on their transgressions, noting that the 'Admiralty needed their service at this time', they might well have felt the full rigour of the law.

Anyone familiar with the popular folklore of impressment would not find this episode unusual. The rough way in which press gangs recruited for the Royal Navy has long been commemorated in print and ballad, supplemented in the press by often harrowing accounts of the affrays that ensued. Yet the episode is also noteworthy for the light it sheds on the legal actions that civilians could take in curtailing the excesses of naval impressment. How the law was used in this manner, how it was deployed as a political strategy of containment as well as a means of evading impressment, is the subject of this chapter.

Historians have seldom looked at impressment in quite this way. Certainly they have addressed the legal status of impressment, even the degree to which press gangs operated within the law. But such inquiries have generally served as a prelude to the problem of manning the Royal Navy, foreclosing rather than opening a discussion of how the law was mobilized in the controversies surrounding impressment.[2] In practice naval impressment was a very contentious issue in the eighteenth century, involving a good deal of give-and-take among the interested parties about what was 'legal' and what was 'just'. The troubled relationship between these two concepts has been usefully explored in the context of the popular struggles surrounding the rights of subsistence and customary perquisites in Georgian Britain. It applies equally to naval recruitment, where the legality of impressment was hedged by operational constraints and inconsistencies, and where the gulf between what was legal and what was popularly considered just was often very wide.

Opposition to naval impressment has sometimes been attributed to the self-interest of merchants or to the 'frothy talk' of hypocritical politicians.[3] It struck deeper roots than such statements suggest. Levellers protested against impressment in the mid-seventeenth century. A remonstrance to the Commons in 1646 asked 'what difference there is between binding a man to an oar, as a galley-slave in Turkey or Algiers, and pressing of men to serve in your war'. The *Agreement of the people* the following year denounced impressment as a violation of English freedom; every 'man's conscience', it asserted, had 'to be satisfied in the justice of that

---

[2] Stephen F. Gradish, *The manning of the British navy during the Seven Years' War* (London, 1980), chap. 3; N. A. M. Rodger, *The wooden world: an anatomy of the Georgian navy* (London, 1986), chap. 5. Rodger notes the litigious circumstances in which impressment was sometimes carried out, (pp. 169–70), but like Gradish's, his treatment of the law regarding impressment is very summary.

[3] Christopher Lloyd, *The British seaman 1200–1860. A social survey* (London, 1985), p. 151.

cause wherein he hazards his own life or may destroy other's'.[4] Similar complaints were echoed in the eighteenth century in popular tracts such as *The sailor's advocate*, one that ran through seven editions in fifty years. Impressment was not only seen as a violation of the 'native liberty' of Englishmen,[5] it was contrary to Magna Carta. Clause 39 of the Great Charter declared that 'No free man [freeman] shall be arrested or [and] imprisoned or disseised or exiled or in any way victimised, neither will we attack him or send anyone to attack him, except by the lawful judgment of his peers or [and] by the law of the land.'[6] This principle was reaffirmed in the Petition of Right and the Bill of Rights, or so it was claimed.[7] After 1688 it was commonly believed that the prerogative powers on which impressment had been based had been irrevocably contained, if not nullifed. One owner of a Greenland whaler, angered by the forcible recruitment of several of his seamen during the off-season, told Captain Fergusson that impressment was contrary to the 'revolution['s] principal topick', that is, freedom from arbitrary government. Should Fergusson 'persist in his tyrannie', he threatened, 'it will be necessary to complain to the house of Co'mons who its hopt will not suffer these Laws to be trampled upon'.[8] In this specific instance the owner was referring to the statutory exemptions for Greenlanders,[9] but behind this concession lay the larger issue of whether the impressment of seamen was contrary to the immanent spirit of liberty that animated English law and manifested itself on such momentous occasions as the 'Glorious Revolution'.

The Whig version of history provided opponents of impressment with clear evidence of its anti-libertarian character; the campaign to abolish slavery provided them with rhetorical grist for the mill. If slavery was a

---

[4] Christopher Hill, *Liberty against the law* (London, 1996), pp. 166, 168. For further seventeenth-century protests against impressment, see Bernard Capp, *Cromwell's navy: the fleet and the English revolution, 1648–1660* (Oxford, 1989), p. 272.

[5] [James Oglethorpe,] *The sailor's advocate* (London, 1728), p. 10.

[6] Cited; ibid., pp. 4–5, and in [Lieut. John Mackenzie,] *Considerations on the impress service* (London, 1786), in J. S. Bromley, ed., *The manning of the Royal Navy* (Navy Records Society, vol. CXIX, London, 1976), pp. 130, 139. Magna Carta was also cited by John Wilkes, for example, in a debate in the Court of Aldermen on impressment, October 1770. See *Middlesex Journal*, 13–16 October 1770. For the original Latin version of the clause, see William Stubbs, *Select charters* (Oxford, 1880), p. 300. For a translation, see *English historical documents*, vol. III, *1189–1327* (London, 1975), p. 320. The brackets reveal there was room for interpretation, as '*liber homo*' could mean free man or the more juridical freeman, and '*vel*' could mean either 'or' or 'and'.

[7] See the arguments of Granville Sharp and James Oglethorpe, outlined in John A. Woods, 'The City of London and impressment, 1776–1777', *Proceedings of the Leeds Philosophical and Literary Society*, vol. VII (1956–9), pp. 122–5.

[8] P.R.O., Adm. 1/1783 (Fergusson) 3 February 1756. For an earlier statement that impressment was contrary to the Bill of Rights as well as Magna Carta, see *Mist's Weekly Journal*, 18 May 1728.

[9] 13 George II c. 28.

blight upon British libertarian traditions, was not impressment; especially when those called upon to defend British freedoms by force of arms were denied the right of personal protection?[10] If slaveholders had no right to deport their slaves from Britain, as the *Somerset* case appeared to establish, could seamen be forcibly set afloat to do the king's business? Impressment was a 'badge of slavery' incompatible with a 'free people', argued the *General Evening Post*. Custom and usage were poor arguments in its favour.[11] 'People may talk of negro slavery and the whip', remarked a gunner a few years later, 'but let them look nearer home and see a poor sailor arrived from a long voyage exulting in the pleasure of being among his dearest friends and relations. Behold him just entering the door, when a press gang seizes him like a felon' and sends him off to a man of war, where, 'if he complains he is likely to be seized up and flogged with the cat'.[12] Harsh treatment, chains and verminous holds aboard tenders only added to the ignominies of the British sailor. The fact that impressed seamen were locked down in hatches aboard tenders and confined in cramped fever-ridden conditions for days on end was sometimes compared to the deplorable stacking of slaves during the middle passage.[13]

In view of the general hostility to the principle of impressment, it is not surprising that pro-government politicians trod warily in its defence. Confronting opposition outrage in 1740, Sir Robert Walpole admitted that impressment was unpopular and of dubious legality. Yet without a voluntary and workable register, he added, it was the state's sole safeguard for its defence. 'To assert the empire of the sea' and to protect 'our dominions of the greatest value', he went on, 'we must not only have ships, but sailors; sailors ready to obey our call and rush out on sudden expeditions'. Such imperatives should not be 'impeded by an ill-timed regard for the case of particular persons [sailors], or a popular affectation of tenderness for liberty'.[14]

Politicians were seldom as blunt as Walpole. They usually appealed to patriotic or imperial sentiments to assuage the opposition to impressment. They left it to the judges to clarify the law. The critical decision was rendered by the Recorder of Bristol, Mr Sergeant Foster, at the Bristol

[10] This argument can be found in the *Sailor's advocate*, p. 3; it also crops up in the petitions from the fleet during the naval mutiny of 1797. See P.R.O., Adm. 1/5125, cited in J. R. Hutchinson, *The press gang afloat and ashore* (London, 1913), p. 17.

[11] *General Evening Post*, 15–18 May 1790. For Somerset's case and public opinion about it, see R. Paley, 'After Somerset', in this volume.

[12] Christopher Lloyd, *Nation and the navy* (London, 1954), pp. 131–2. See also *Newcastle Courant*, 31 July 1790, where it is suggested that seamen should organize petitions against impressment in much the same way as abolitionists were organizing them against the slave trade.

[13] *English Chronicle and Universal Evening Post*, 22–4 July 1790.

[14] *Cobbett's parliamentary history*, vol. VII (1739–41), pp. 428–9.

Assizes in August 1743. The case in question involved Alexander Broad-foot, a seaman of the merchant ship, the *Bremen Factor*, who had resisted impressment in the King Road by firing a blunderbuss at the press gang, killing one of its members on the spot. Foster was called upon to direct the jury as to whether Broadfoot should be found guilty of murder or manslaughter, a matter which essentially turned on the legality of the press warrant and the rights of resistance to unlawful impressment. But he also took the opportunity to expatiate broadly on the legality of impressment, recognizing its 'very great and national importance'.[15]

Foster argued that naval impressment took precedence over private rights in matters of national security; it was 'a prerogative inherent in the Crown, grounded upon common-law, and recognized by many Acts of Parliament'. In defining impressment in this braided manner, Foster made it impossible for opponents to argue that impressment was an anachronistic royal prerogative incompatible with 'revolution principles'. The right of naval impressment was not based on feudal law, which pertained principally to the military obligations of great tenants (the Cinque Ports excepted). Rather it inhered in the bonds of allegiance which every subject owed the sovereign in 'cases of extreme necessity' such as invasion or insurrection. Foster admitted that it was unfortunate that these obligations of personal service now fell to one occupational class of men; but he did not think that such obligations were illegal because they had not been positively recognized in statute law, as some critics had implied.[16] In Foster's view there was plenty of evidence of commissions to impress from the medieval era onwards. None of this practice was incompatible with statute law, nor with the Augustan press acts which quite explicitly set up privy searches for seamen.[17] Furthermore, the statutory exemptions from impressment, which had grown apace since 1700, tacitly acknowledged the right of the crown to impress seamen and those 'who used the sea'. The right to impress did not rest on these statutory regulations, Foster insisted, but upon a royal prerogative 'grounded in immemorial usage'.[18] The various acts which exempted certain classes of mariners from

---

[15] *Rex* v. *Broadfoot*, 2 Salk. 31, *English Reports*, vol. CLXVIII, p. 78. See also P.R.O., Adm. 1/3675/236–40. Broadfoot was found guilty of manslaughter but not murder and burnt in the hand.

[16] Newcastle seamen in 1793 emphasized that impressment, while 'countenanced by Precedent and supposed to have been a Part of the common Law', had 'never been sanctioned by the authority of Parliament'. *Newcastle Chronicle*, 2 February 1793. This was contested in the *Newcastle Courant*, 2 February 1793, 'Judge Forster' being cited as the ultimate authority.

[17] 4 Anne c. 19; 4 & 5 Anne c. 6. These 1705 and 1706 acts for the 'speedier manning' of the fleet were clearly intended to be supplementary to the routine acts of impressing. Or so Foster argued. *Rex* v. *Broadfoot*, 2 Salk. 31, *English Reports*, vol. CLXVIII, pp. 87–8.

[18] ibid., p. 84.

impressment served only to confirm the seeming symmetry of custom, prerogative and statute law.

Foster's judgment concerning the legal complexities of impressment was broadly endorsed by King's Bench in 1776 in *Rex* v. *Tubbs*.[19] In seeking to determine whether John Tubbs, a City of London waterman, was exempt from the press, Lord Mansfield and his fellow judges all concurred that impressment was a vestigial prerogative power of the crown, founded on 'immemorial usage', recognized but not authorized by an act of Parliament. This unanimity of judicial opinion made it extremely difficult, if not impossible, to challenge the general principle of impressment in the eighteenth century.

Opposition politicians within the City of London certainly tried. During the American war, anti-ministerial aldermen, encouraged by reformers such as Granville Sharp, hoped to exploit suits designed to protect City freemen from impressment into a general campaign against the practice.[20] Yet in all of these cases the Admiralty's lawyers proved adept at sidestepping general principles. All that the City could achieve from these suits was a recognition that their own constables were immune from impressment. The Admiralty refused to concede that freemen were exempt from the press, having been advised that freeholders (and logically freemen) were not exempt from impressment.[21] No judge was prepared to clarify the law further, despite the fact that voters had been exempted from certain press acts in the reign of Queen Anne.[22] Nor were the City's legal counsel keen to muster a general challenge to impressment. Although they were well-known reformers, lawyers John Glynn, John Dunning and Alexander Wedderburn basically endorsed Foster's judgment of 1743. Impressment was 'founded on that Universal Principle of Laws, that private interest must give way to public Safety, being well established by antient and continued Usage, [and] frequently recognised and regulated by the Legislature'.[23] Consequently they advised the City to concentrate upon procedural infractions in impressment, upon ensuring in particular that regulating officers did not exceed their authority in taking up men in streets and taverns.

---

[19] *Rex* v. *Tubbs*, Foster 155, *English Reports*, vol. CLXVIII, pp. 1215–20.

[20] On these cases, see John Sainsbury, *Disaffected patriots: London supporters of revolutionary America, 1769–1782* (Kingston and Montreal, 1987), pp. 134–9; Woods, 'City of London and impressment', pp. 114–21.

[21] P.R.O., Adm. 7/299, no. 64.

[22] And were to be so again. See 18 George III c. 53, and 19 George III c. 10, an abstract of which can be found in the *Annual Register*, vol. XXII (1779), p. 254.

[23] *Annual Register*, vol. XVII (1770), p. 232; also printed in *Middlesex Journal*, 22–4 November 1770; *Felix Farley's Bristol Journal*, 1 December 1770.

Nonetheless there were a few points in the judgments upon impressment that opponents could exploit. Both Foster and Mansfield had emphasized that impressment could only be vindicated as a measure intended to protect the safety of the state.[24] In time of war there could hardly be any disagreement of what this meant, but it was not unusual for the Admiralty to issue press warrants prior to formal declarations of war; in effect, to put Britain on a war footing for months, even a year, before war was formally proclaimed. Moreover, naval mobilizations were sometimes little more than modes of diplomatic bullying, designed to impress upon other nations the seriousness of British objectives. In its disputes with the declining imperial power of Spain, for instance, Britain issued press warrants to assert territorial claims over the Falkland Islands in 1770 and trading rights in Nootka Sound twenty years later. In 1787 Britain also mobilized its navy to prevent the French fleet from assisting the Patriots (the opponents of the Prince of Orange) in the Netherlands.[25] Britons might reasonably have been forgiven for wondering how an obscure island in the South Atlantic and the future of the sea-otter trade impinged on the safety of the state, or whether the internal struggles of a neighbouring European power necessitated such a show of force. Newspapers and politicians publicly aired such views. One radical complained that seamen had to tolerate impressment 'merely because a minister of the country may perhaps from motives of corruption, or views of ambition, chuse [sic] to enter into a war, and by an unjust exercise of power, *force* these honest fellows to become the instruments either of his villainy, or his vengeance'.[26]

Understandably, resistance to impressment in the 'phoney wars' was often high; proportionate to the number of seamen borne, higher than in more serious engagements.[27] Magistrates were correspondingly reluctant to back press warrants in their jurisdictions, feeling that the navy's manning requirements might well be fulfilled by encouraging volunteers through generous bounties, or by sweeping the streets of vagrants,

---

[24] *Rex v. Tubbs*, Foster 155, *English Reports*, vol. XCVIII, p. 1218; *Rex v. Broadfoot*, 2 Salk. 31, *English Reports*, vol. CLXVIII, p. 79.

[25] On this episode, see Simon Schama, *Patriots and liberators. Revolution in the Netherlands, 1780–1813* (London, 1977), pp. 121–9.

[26] *Newcastle Chronicle*, 24 November 1792. For complaints about the 'supposed necessity' of impressment, see the speech of the Duke of Richmond in the Lords, 11 February 1771, cited in *Berrow's Worcester Journal*, 21 February 1771. For newspaper comment, see *The Whisperer*, XXXVI (20 Oct. 1770), p. 124; *Felix Farley's Bristol Journal*, 8 December 1770, 15 May 1790; *London Evening Post*, 12–14 November 1776.

[27] These conclusions are based on an inventory of over 500 impressment affrays and riots for the period 1739–1805. I plan to publish these results in the near future.

however defined. The City of London magistrates strenuously advocated this policy during the Falklands crisis of 1770–1. The Lord Mayor, Sir Thomas Sainsbury, did so again in 1787, suggesting to Lord Howe and to members of the Privy Council that press warrants were questionably legal in the circumstances of this European conflict, which did not directly involve Britain or imperil its territories. The Privy Council did not take kindly to this intervention. Lord Chancellor Thurlow retorted that 'his Lordship might be a very good tradesman, but he was not a politician; that he (as Lord Chancellor) was to judge of the necessity, and as to the warrants, he pronounced them *legal*.[28]

Magistrates thus found themselves unable to challenge the necessity of impressment, but they were able to constrain its operation. Under a press warrant, the civil power was enjoined to assist the press gangs in their task. Indeed, it was customary for the regulating officers to seek an audience with mayors and magistrates to get their endorsement. From the Admiralty's point of view this was a politic course of action. The co-operation of magistrates was important in any disturbance that might flow from impressing seamen, especially in larger ports where the constables and beadles outnumbered the press gang on duty. Furthermore, mayors in larger ports often had intimate contact with shippers and merchants, and gentlemanly agreements with them over impressment were likely to smooth the day-to-day operations of the regulating officer. No captain wished to be mired in litigious proceedings with merchants, especially over the quotas of men who were protected from the press, either by statute or Admiralty licence.

Whether magistrates were obliged to back press warrants or not was a contentious issue. The Admiralty sought legal advice on just this question in 1757, because the regulating officer at Gravesend, Captain Howard Hutchinson, had been given the run-around by the mayor when he had asked for his assistance. The Admiralty's legal counsel advised that civil co-operation was customary but not essential to press-gang operations.[29] He also thought there was no law that expressly mandated a magistrate to back warrants, even though the language of the warrant 'required' the civil power to 'aid and assist' impressment.[30] The Admiralty Solicitor agreed with this judgment, but some magistrates continued to believe that their consent was necessary. The Greenock justices of the peace argued this in 1760, when Captain Gentil was besieged by an angry mob while searching for deserters in this Clydeside port. In their view his search was irregular, and they committed him to gaol for trespass and

[28] *Whitehall Evening Post*, 9–11 October 1787.   [29] P.R.O., Adm. 7/298, no. 99.
[30] See *Rex v. Broadfoot*, 2 Salk. 31, *English Reports*, vol. CLXVIII, pp. 77–8.

assault.[31] This legal uncertainty put regulating captains in a difficult position. Faced with an unco-operative mayor or justice of the peace, press captains would often appeal to the Admiralty to put pressure on him to comply; perhaps by advising him that Admiralty protections would be withdrawn, or that Admiralty convoys of merchant vessels would be hard to come by. This tactic normally brought mayors to their senses, although sometimes further threats were necessary. In 1755 the Lords of the Admiralty had to threaten the mayor of King's Lynn with a general press of the town, that is, one that ignored protections, before he agreed to back warrants.[32]

Local magistrates sometimes dragged their feet in backing warrants, if only to placate merchants who wanted a little time to protect their most experienced or skilful seamen from the press. They were unlikely to defy the Admiralty in a blatantly confrontational way. The only exception to this rule were the aldermen of the City of London. In the Wilkesite era of the 1770s, in particular, they refused to back press warrants and strove to make the City a press-free zone. Although some pro-ministerial aldermen agreed to back warrants, and although the City's legal counsel thought this a good idea, since it would allow magistrates to better regulate impressment in the city,[33] radical aldermen felt such an endorsement would undermine their political objections to the press. As far as they were concerned, press warrants were analogous to general warrants and as reprehensibly unconstitutional.[34] Whenever they sat as presiding magistrates at Guildhall, they ordered the constables and beadles to bring all impressed men before them, discharging them on the slightest pretext. At the same time, gangs were officially discouraged from operating within the City precincts by the Court of Aldermen. When one gang defiantly paraded past the Council House with drums beating and fifes playing, the Lord Mayor committed its members to the Compter for disturbing the peace.[35]

---

[31] P.R.O., Adm. 1/3678/98–9. In 1787 press warrants executed in Edinburgh and Leith were said to have been 'irregular' because they were not endorsed by the magistrates. *Ipswich Journal*, 6 October 1787.

[32] P.R.O., Adm. 1/1486 (Baird) 1 & 4 March 1755, Adm. 1/3677/32.

[33] *Annual Register*, vol. XIII (1770), p. 232.

[34] See 'Constitutional queries' in the *London Evening Post*, 27–9 November 1770. Later in the century, a serjeant-at-law said that press warrants, 'however ... tollerated from necessity' were 'always obnoxious, as being derogatory to the liberty of the Subject and repugnant to the principles of a free Government'. P.R.O., Adm. 1/2309 (Hyde Parker), 2 September 1791, enclosure from Thomas Anthony Minchin, dated 31 August 1791. For aldermen discharging impressed men during the Falkland Islands crisis, see *Middlesex Journal*, 30 October–1 November, 1–3 November 1770.

[35] *Middlesex Journal*, 19–21, 29–31 January 1771. Faced with magisterial hostility, the Admiralty sought to ensure that its gangs were properly mustered and regulated and

This policy of legal obstruction reached a crisis in 1777, when three lieutenants were restrained from impressing men within the City. Two of them were later charged with assault for continuing to press men in Lime Street ward. When their captain, James Kirke, expostulated with the Lord Mayor about the City's lack of co-operation with the war effort, he was told that the navy's mode of impressment was considered by the Court of Aldermen to be 'insupportable in law'.[36] On precisely what grounds Captain Kirke was unable to determine. The Lord Mayor, Sir Thomas Hallifax, refused to be pinned down and declined to render a written statement of the aldermen's decision without consulting the Recorder. Eventually the lieutenants were discharged because the witnesses for the prosecution failed to appear in court.[37]

The City's opposition to impressment was fuelled by radical ideology and pro-American sentiment. If its politicians failed to challenge the constitutionality of impressment, their vigilance against the gangs did have some basis in law. As the City's counsel had recognized, process was critical. Justice Foster may have defended the legality of impressment in *Rex* v. *Broadfoot*, but he also presided over a case in which a press warrant had been improperly executed. Warrants had to be properly dated and endorsed by the regulating officer on duty, who had to be present when boats were boarded or pubs entered in the search for eligible seamen. In 1798 the impressment of five apprentices from a collier in Shields harbour was considered legally dubious because the lieutenant in charge had supervised the search from the shore.[38] Lawyers representing clients who resisted impressment were quick to pick up on these matters, even to the point of demanding evidence that the signatures of the Lords of the Admiralty on the press warrant were authentic.[39] If there was an irregularity, then it was commonly thought that resistance to impressment was legitimate. Neither Sergeant Foster nor any other judge actually said this, but this was how their judgments were represented in the newspapers.[40]

---

insisted that lieutenants accompany them. One lieutenant was dismissed from the service on account of his absence. See *The Hawke papers. A selection 1743–1771*, ed. Ruddock F. Mackay (Navy Records Society, Aldershot, 1990), docs. 470, 473–4.

[36] *General Evening Post*, 23–5 January 1777. See also Sainsbury, *Disaffected patriots*, pp. 134–8; Woods, 'City of London and impressment', pp. 116–17.

[37] *General Evening Post*, 16–18 January 1777.   [38] P.R.O., Adm. 7/304, no. 406.

[39] P.R.O., Adm. 1/3680/238, Admiralty Solicitor Sedden to Lords of the Admiralty, 24 July 1777, reporting on a case involving a charge of common assault against one of the press captains at Portsmouth.

[40] In 1740 Thomas Corbet compiled a list of precedents about impressment because of the widespread feeling that resistance to impressment was lawful. See Lloyd, *British seaman*, p. 152.

Magistrates, too, wanted evidence that due process had been observed. In 1778 Alderman John Sawbridge upbraided a press gang for failing to show its warrant when it attempted to impress a grocer's assistant on Ludgate Hill, even though the warrant was in order and had been backed by the Lord Mayor.[41] Nine years later magistrates in Edinburgh and Leith imprisoned the press gangs because no regulating officer led them in a massive round-up of seamen and shipwrights.[42] Ordinary citizens could also be assertive in demanding that press officers show their warrant to impress, not only because they wanted due process to be observed by gangs who sometimes had a reputation for lawlessness, but also because men were not above impersonating gangs to exploit the unwary.[43] In the summer of 1790, for example, when a disturbance broke out over the impressment of a man near Whitehall, several bystanders insisted upon the lieutenant 'showing his authority'. When he failed to deliver, he was chased through the streets and only escaped the fury of the mob through the intervention of some soldiers in St James' Park.[44]

Executing proper warrants was the first legal step that press gangs had to observe. They also had to be careful not to use undue force in securing men for the navy. Judges sometimes took a very dim view of gangs firing in pursuit of recruits. In 1742 the gang of HMS *Russell* fired at several seamen who were evading impressment aboard a Jamaicaman in Bristol's King Road, shattering the knee of one of them. In presiding over this case at the Bristol Assizes, Justice Denison observed 'that although a regard was due to the King's Ships, yet that great care ought to be taken by the officers in the execution of their Duty, so as to not injure the rest of the King's subjects ... [H]e knew of no Authority that a man of war's crew had of firing balls upon mariners belonging to merchant ships in order to oblige them to bring to, and that there was no evidence to prove the assertion.'[45] He therefore instructed the jury to disregard much of the testimony for the defendants, Lieutenant Roots and William Ferrier, with the result that the jury awarded 120 guineas to the injured man.

Trials like this one made officers wary of firing across the bows of merchant ships to force them to heave to, unless there was clear evidence that putative recruits aboard the vessel openly resisted impressment, either by ignoring the signals to be searched or by verbal acts of defiance.

---

[41] P.R.O., Adm. 1/3680/345–7.   [42] *Ipswich Journal*, 6 October 1787.
[43] On lawless gangs, see *London Evening Post*, 13–15 May 1755; *Monthy Review*, vol. 57 (Dec. 1777), p. 491; *Hawke papers*, docs. 470, 473. On phoney gangs, see *London Evening Post*, 17–19 July 1739, *Middlesex Journal*, 4–6 October 1770; *Newcastle Journal*, 24 November–1 December 1770; *Whitehall Evening Post*, 11–13 October 1787.
[44] *English Chronicle*, 24–6 August 1790.   [45] P.R.O., Adm. 1/3675/45–6, 88–90.

Admiralty Solicitors were scrupulous in collecting such evidence, especially in situations where resisting seamen had been killed and coroner's inquests had indicted officers for murder. Understandably, regulating captains sometimes went out of their way to placate local inhabitants in situations where the violence of the gangs had been fatal. In the summer of 1777, for example, the press tender in the River Avon fired on several men from the *Friendship* who had gone ashore for the purpose of obtaining a pilot from Pill, killing one seaman and wounding two others. Captain Hamilton had their wounds dressed by a surgeon at the Admiralty's expense and arranged for the burial of the dead man at a nearby parish. He was 'apprehensive of a tumult', he told the Admiralty, if 'the body had been brought to Bristol'.[46] He also helped organize a coroner's inquest aboard another tender, sensing that his co-operation might improve the chances of the master of the tender charged with murder.[47] Meanwhile, the Admiralty collected evidence that the *Friendship*'s crew had exchanged hostile words with the press tender further down the estuary, bolstering the argument that the gang had genuinely believed the men were evading impressment rather than seeking help to navigate the vessel to port.

Like those afloat, impressments ashore also had to be executed with restraint and due process. As a clerical justice from South Shields declared in 1803, the press gangs had 'no authority for dragging Men from their Houses in a forcible manner'.[48] Nor were they supposed to kidnap sailors from the benches and booths of quayside pubs, even though a 'hot press' left little time for formalities. Press gangs were supposed to inform landlords of their intention to search their houses and if requested, to show their warrants. Moreover, they could not simply break down the doors of houses where seamen were harboured. If rooms were locked, they had to obtain search warrants and have them executed by officers of the peace. Such regulations were known to publicans, who sometimes exploited their infractions in court. In 1755 the former seaman and publican James Shambrooke successfully resisted a search of his house by insisting on such formalities. The local justice, George Rooke, niggled by his knowledge, conspired with the gang to take up his son and brother in revenge, detaining them aboard a man of war for five days. But Shambrooke retaliated by successfully suing the constable and press officer for trespass, assault and false imprisonment.[49]

---

[46] P.R.O., Adm. 1/1903 (Hamilton), 17 August 1777.
[47] P.R.O., Adm. 1/3680/244, 303.   [48] P.R.O., Adm. 1/2141 M42.
[49] P.R.O., Adm. 1/3677/40, 135. See also, Adm. 1/3689, 23 September, 10 October 1803, the case of John Barbary, a publican of Flushing, Cornwall.

Justices of the peace may have bridled at the way in which ordinary citizens used the law against the press gang, but there were occasions when they followed suit. In 1779 Captain Alms, irritated by the way in which the fishermen of Brighton were using protections to evade the press, ordered a general raid on the village with the help of a troop of soldiers from nearby Lewes. When it was known that the village was about to receive a visit from the press gang, the inhabitants locked their doors and refused to co-operate with the search. So, too, did the resident magistrate, Mr Warden. He was requested to be present 'to force open the Doors of such Houses I should think proper to search', Alms reported. 'But to my great Disappointment, he flatly refus'd to grant me that Order, or even send the Constables with me, Unless I would give upon Oath that there was Men secreted in any particular House. This I could not do, And therefore in Course of staying Ten Hours, I was under the Necessity of quitting the Town without being able to get only one Man.'[50] His only consolation was that he was able to round up a gang of smugglers during the raid.

Captain Alms approached the legal technicalities of impressing seamen with a certain equanimity. Others let their exasperation get the better of them. Regulating captains were not necessarily superannuated officers hoping for a quiet time. They were often young men on the make, ready to cut a figure in a navy and anxious to assume command of a ship.[51] As gentlemen they sometimes had a low tolerance of petty officers and officious landlords, not to mention fishermen who knew the law. When one oysterman refused to take some sick men to hospital without a ticket of leave, the captain called him a 'saucy son of a bitch' and clapped him in irons. 'You should have kept a better tongue in your head', the captain is alleged to have told him.[52] Naval officers were sometimes outraged if their own gentility was called into question. When one customs officer from Sheerness had the temerity to consider his commission equivalent to that of a naval captain, he was threatened with a flogging and forcibly detained aboard a man of war for over five months.[53]

Naval honour could be brittle; naval ambition careless of legal niceties. Admiralty solicitors were routinely confronted with lieutenants who denied constables their authority, denounced them as 'scurvy fellows', or

---

[50] P.R.O., Adm. 1/1446 (Alms), 24 July 1779.
[51] Rodger, *Wooden world*, p. 166; cf. Gradish, *Manning*, p. 56. On the predominately genteel or professional background of the naval officer, see Michael A. Lewis, *The navy in transition 1814–1864. A social survey* (London, 1965), p. 22.
[52] P.R.O., Adm. 1/3676/129–30.   [53] P.R.O., Adm. 1/3678/256–7.

bucked the proprieties of search-and-entering because they suspected landlords were hiding deserters. In 1744 a lieutenant ordered his men to break down a 'Hundred doors', if necessary, while searching for deserters in a Bermondsey pub. When the landlord remonstrated with him, he hit him so hard that he coughed blood for days.[54] A similar incident occurred at Greenhithe, Kent, in 1803. On this occasion the landlord told the lieutenant he could search no further than the tap-room, having only a 'common press warrant' in his possession. The lieutenant replied 'he would go where he pleased, and his men should follow him, and break open every door in the house if he thought proper'. He promptly drew his sword and knocked the landlord down, whereupon the gang moved in and 'beat him dreadfully about the head with the butt end of their pistols'.[55] No Admiralty solicitor was about to condone this behaviour, nor the assault upon a landlord's wife, who thought the officer more of an 'Irish bog-trotting fellow' than a gentleman because he had tried to silence her by thrusting his cane in her mouth.[56] If they were sued, such officers were advised to settle out of court or suffer the consequences.

The Admiralty would not, however, leave regulating officers and their press gangs at the total mercy of the civilian courts. It had no wish to encourage resistance to impressment or undermine naval morale by refusing to defend its men. It recognized that suits against the press gang could be vexatious, the culmination perhaps of deteriorating relations between the gang and portside communities. It also knew that it was sometimes difficult to determine who was responsible for the many tavern brawls and street affrays that accompanied impressment. Consequently the Admiralty was routinely involved in defending or funding the legal suits of regulating officers and their men, even where their legal culpability was not incontestable. In 1787 the Admiralty took up the case of a lieutenant who had become embroiled with a militant publican and his cronies, even though the Admiralty's counsel thought that the lieutenant's visit to this house, a rendezvous for volunteers, to be 'improper' and probably provocative.[57] Seven years later, the Admiralty agreed to pay the legal costs of Captain Thomas Affleck, who had refused to release James Townsend on the grounds that he was a sea apprentice of less than three years' standing. In fact Affleck had defied a writ of habeas corpus to produce Townsend, shipping him off to the East Indies instead.[58] Although the Admiralty Solicitor admonished Affleck for flouting the jurisdiction of

[54] P.R.O., Adm. 1/3675/35; Adm. 1/3680/390–5.
[55] *Johnson's British Gazette*, 17 April 1803.
[56] P.R.O., Adm. 1/3675/191–6, 11 March 1743.   [57] P.R.O., Adm. 7/301, no. 251.
[58] P.R.O., Adm. 1/3683, 13 July 1795; Adm. 1/3684, 17 August 1796.

the courts and warned him that any future help would be dependent upon his compliance with the law, he probably sympathized with the captain's complaint that the so-called apprentice had exploited the law to evade service.

The Admiralty would finance the suits of its officers where their opponents were suspected of manipulating the law, or where they appeared vexatiously litigious or aggressively hostile to impressment.[59] It would also try to protect its men from humiliating public punishments. In 1770 it was reported that a lieutenant who had falsely impressed an officer of the Lord Mayor had been pilloried, fined £500 and sentenced to imprisonment for seven years, but there is no evidence that this was more than wishful thinking on the part of City radicals.[60] In fact, those cases where press gangs were likely to bear the brunt of local anger were frequently removed to another jurisdiction.[61] In 1762 the Admiralty Solicitor was distressed that he had been unable to prevent a case involving Lieutenant Runsiman from being tried in the local courts. According to the depositions, Runsiman had impressed a young sailor named Benjamin Bell who had been wounded at Quiberon Bay and subsequently exempted from the press. Bell, however, spent his spare time alerting other sailors to the gang's approach, and Runsiman thought he would teach him a lesson by detaining him on the tender until he could find a substitute, taking him up when he was without his protection on his person. In a strict sense, Runsiman operated within the law; but the locals in King's Lynn thought his actions vindictive and successfully charged Runsiman and two gangers for assaulting Bell's father in the course of their dealings with the young man. The lieutenant and his men were fined 1s. each and spent two weeks in gaol, impairing the impress service in the process. The Admiralty Solicitor, Samuel Sedden, had hoped that the justices would have allowed the Admiralty time to remove the case to King's Bench. He regretted that the navy had been unable to avoid the 'disgrace of an immediate commitment'.[62]

---

[59] P.R.O., Adm. 1/3681/194, 200. This case concerned John Brassett, a publican in St Katherine's, London, who sued a lieutenant and midshipman for false arrest. The officers searched his pub for men but did not break down any of the doors that were shut. Brassett assaulted the lieutenant and verbally abused him, for which, as a former seaman, he was impressed. The Admiralty Solicitor said Brassett had been on shore too many years for this action to stick. In view of the circumstances, however, he recommended that the Admiralty pay Brassett's costs and damages of £146 17s. 8d. and also Lieutenant Wilkinson's costs of £5 11s. 3d.

[60] *Middlesex Journal*, 1–3 November 1770.

[61] Captains sometimes requested such action to punish their assailants, fearing they would not get their just deserts before sympathetic juries. See P.R.O., Adm. 1/3683, 13 September 1790.

[62] P.R.O., Adm. 1/3678/244–7.

The most sensitive cases where local passions might influence the law were clearly those where gangers had killed someone. If the death occurred as the result of a tavern brawl outside the line of duty, gangers could expect no help from the Admiralty.[63] If it occurred in the course of an impressment affray, especially where a coroner's inquest had indicted a gangsman for murder, then the Admiralty would organize a defence and muster evidence. Often the Admiralty tried to remove the case to another jurisdiction, hoping thereby to insulate the defending seamen from popular judgment. If the incident occurred in any place definable as the high seas, this would mean the High Court of Admiralty. In 1795, in a case involving the death of a fisherman resisting impressment in Poole Harbour, the Admiralty removed the case to the Admiralty court in London on the grounds that Brownsea Castle was outside the shire jurisdiction, much to the consternation of the corporation, which tried to reindict the officers at the Dorchester Assizes.[64]

More frequently, cases were removed from the Assizes to the Court of King's Bench to await special verdicts. This happened to fifteen gangsmen prosecuted for the murder of an Ipswich publican, and to a midshipman who had attempted to recruit men from a fishing smack off the Devonshire coast and had fired at its master out of frustration.[65] In both instances the judges upheld the Admiralty's defence that the men had acted in the course of duty, reducing the charge to manslaughter. Where a ganger was successfully indicted for murder at a county assize, and this was rare, the Admiralty Solicitor moved quickly to obtain a respite of the sentence until his majesty's pleasure was known.[66] No government wanted gangsmen hanging from the gallows. That would be extremely damaging to naval morale and to the legitimacy of impressment. But no government wanted the press gangs to think they were above the law either.

Thus far I have argued that while impressment remained an unpopular method of naval recruitment in the eighteenth century, it proved extremely difficult, if not impossible to challenge its legality. What opponents could do was to ensure that impressment was executed with due process: to check that press warrants were properly executed; to invigilate

---

[63] See the case reported in P.R.O., Adm. 7/300, no. 194.

[64] The corporation of Poole was outraged when the Admiralty pulled this stunt in a case involving the death of a fisherman who had resisted impressment in Poole Harbour. It tried unsuccessfully to have the two lieutenants and the midshipman of the gang tried again at the Dorchester Assizes. See P.R.O., Adm. 1/3683, 28 February, 7 March, 15, 28 July 1795; 1/3684, 15 March 1786.

[65] *Gentleman's Magazine*, vol. 49 (1779), p. 323, vol. 50 (1780), pp. 72–4; P.R.O., Adm. 1/3680/317–22.

[66] P.R.O., Adm. 1/3677/188–94, 1/3681/270.

the operations of the press gangs, whose search for men had to take into account the laws respecting the property and privacy of individuals and the jurisdictions of civil officers. On this terrain, there were opportunities for curbing the excesses of the gangs, and indeed, for holding them at arm's length. Precisely who was able to avail themselves of this regulatory space is something we must now contemplate. It has some bearing upon the larger historical question of who was able to use the law in the eighteenth century, and how successfully.

Most of the litigants who crop up in the papers of the Admiralty Solicitor were men of property: merchants, ship-owners, masters demanding the return of runaway apprentices, publicans seeking damages that resulted from tavern brawls, or perhaps demanding the release of a seaman-debtor to the civil authorities. These were middling people with enough credit or personalty and enough time to bring an action against the impress service. Seamen, as mates, masters, or apprentices, were often the subject of litigation but rarely the litigants themselves. There were, of course, exceptions. John Alexander, the owner of an oyster-boat on the Medway, successfully sued the captain who confined him in irons for refusing to take sick prisoners to Rochester without proper authorization.[67] George Duncan, a seaman-turned-smuggler who had sailed on several West Indian voyages, had enough money to hire an attorney to obtain his release from the service on the somewhat improbable grounds that he was a Middlesex freeholder.[68] Another exception to the rule was John Nicholson, a Greenlander who was working in the coal trade during the off-season when he was impressed and carried aboard HMS *Eurydice*.[69] He threatened to sue the Admiralty for the losses incurred by his confinement of over one year. These included £40 wages for his next Greenland voyage and £17 for his release and costs. Nicholson had an attorney write to the Admiralty demanding his release and impressing upon their Lordships the 'serious inconvenience' his detention had been to such 'a poor Man'. The Admiralty Solicitor took the threat of prosecution seriously. Recognizing that Nicholson's impressment was contrary to statute, he advised the captain and lieutenant of the *Eurydice* to settle out of court 'as no Defence could be made for them'.

Nicholson's was a clear-cut case of unlawful detainment and it is probable that an attorney would find it in his interest to pursue it with a good prospect of being paid. Not all cases would have been so simple, and a local attorney must have sometimes wondered whether the cost of prosecution, which could easily amount to £20 or five to six months' wartime

---

[67] P.R.O., Adm. 1/3676/129–30. He asked for £500 in damages and received £300.
[68] P.R.O., Adm. 7/300, no. 207.   [69] P.R.O., Adm. 1/3283, 7 January 1795.

wages for an able seaman,[70] was enough of an incentive. Unless seamen had powerful friends in port, litigation through the courts was usually something of a luxury. The best most seafarers could hope for was to exploit the law to evade impressment, not to confront it directly.

The prospects for evading impressment by manipulating its legal regulations were not bad. In order to reconcile the imperatives of trade with those of war, the Admiralty routinely came to some arrangement with local portside employers about the number of men who could be kept (anachronistically) in 'reserved occupations'. The number of protections that the Admiralty and Navy Office issued in 1757 amounted to about 17,250; together with those seafaring occupations protected by statute (10,761) and by other maritime agencies (nearly 20,000), the total number of seafarers annually exempted from impressment approached 50,000.[71] Whatever the economic benefits that accrued from this concession – and the Admiralty made a tidy sum in protection fees – it opened the door to the eighteenth-century equivalent of 'draft-dodging'. As early as 1734 Admiral Norris was told that 'there was not three seamen in Deal but what were protected, and that as soon as a man can but get three half-crowns or ten shillings to give to any freeman of Sandwich, he gets ... a protection'.[72] This sort of practice so troubled the navy that after 1740 it insisted that protections carry an exact description of its holder – including height, hair-colouring, tattoos and facial scars. This curbed the trade in protections, but it certainly did not eliminate it. In 1755 Captain Patrick Baird complained that a master carpenter in King's Lynn had only used half of his sixteen protections, ensuring 'that room is left to foist in ... any person they wish to protect'.[73] This kind of scam troubled the regulating officers, as did the prospect of protected sailors straggling along the quayside at the time of a hot press. In Liverpool the regulating captain attempted to ensure that the seamen and ship's carpenters who were protected remained near their dock during recruiting drives. Otherwise, he complained in 1777, the press gangs would never know who was a legitimate quarry, leaving themselves very vulnerable to altercations in the street and to mob intervention.[74]

The Admiralty could put the squeeze on portside communities who made a trade in protections by refusing to issue any under its own

[70] On seamen's wages, see Jonathan Press, *The merchant seamen of Bristol 1747–1789* (Local Historical Association, Bristol, 1976), pp. 6–8; Ralph Davis, *The rise of the English shipping industry* (Newton Abbot, 1962), pp. 136–40.

[71] Gradish, *Manning*, pp. 66–7.

[72] Daniel A. Baugh, ed., *Naval administration 1715–1750* (Navy Records Society, vol. CXX, London, 1977), p. 112.

[73] P.R.O., Adm. 1/1486 (Baird), 12 April 1755.

[74] P.R.O., Adm. 1/2672 (Worth), 15 April 1777.

authority. When William Hurry's dockyard workers rioted against the press at the resumption of war against Napoleon in 1803, the regulating captain advised the Admiralty to withhold protections to the yard 'till their people behave properly'.[75] Even so, the Admiralty had to contend with those protections that were issued by other departments, and, more importantly, with those that were guaranteed by statute. Foreigners were exempt from impressment. So, too, were the masters and first mates of shipping vessels and sea apprentices in the first three years of their indenture.[76] All of these concessions were open to abuse. Sailors sometimes impersonated foreigners; especially after American Independence, when seamen could plausibly claim they were citizens of the new republic. Others pretended, usually with their employer's connivance, that they were first mates or masters of ships. Captain John Bover of Newcastle complained that many Tyneside masters 'would swear a man was a mate to keep him out of the navy, tho' in reality he was not before; and by way of a *salvo* to their Conscience, have let him act as such for 3 or 4 days, and then turn him before the Mast again'.[77] What was true on Tyneside was also true further south. Captain Patrick Baird reported from King's Lynn that a local merchant and known enemy of the press gang had tricked him out of four seamen by producing fake evidence of their ratings. The one designated as the master of the vessel, he complained, 'was never capable of any trust above a Cook'.[78]

The same strategy of evasion pertained to apprentices. In Anne's reign Parliament had passed legislation designed to curb the abuse of sea apprenticeships by enacting that anyone who had prior experience of the sea could not then be bound to a master mariner.[79] The qualification was often ignored. Captain Napier believed that the Edinburgh shipmasters used 'every Stratagem' to keep their seamen at arm's length from the gangs, including the large-scale indenturing of their crews.[80] Lieutenant Scott revealed that on Tyne and Tees a shopkeeper named John Moreson provided false indentures on demand to any merchant who wanted them for his crews, thereby depriving the navy of 'many young men'.[81] Not that all of the so-called apprentices were necessarily young. Captain Thomas

[75] P.R.O., Adm. 1/2141 M26.

[76] 2 & 3 Anne c. 6; 13 George II c. 17. For a useful summary of statutory protections, see Rodger, *Wooden world*, p. 177.

[77] P.R.O., Adm. 1/1503 (Bover), 20 January 1782.

[78] P.R.O., Adm. 1/1486 (Baird), 26 April, 6 May 1755.

[79] Under 4 Anne c. 19, clause 17. The exemption for apprentices of less than three years' standing was in 2 & 3 Anne c. 6, s.17. For legal opinion about these statutes, see P.R.O., Adm. 7/299, no. 165.

[80] P.R.O., Adm. 1/2220 (Napier), 22 February 1777.

[81] P.R.O., Adm. 1/3684, 20 June 1795.

Affleck was disgruntled with James Townsend because he was too old and too worldly to merit exemption as an inexperienced apprentice. He thought that Townsend, a former chimney sweeper aged 28 or 29 years, was 'a great *rogue* & capable of almost *anything*'. There was 'every reason to think among his various employments', he advised the Admiralty, 'that he has been at sea at different times'.[82] The only trouble was Affleck knew he couldn't prove it, as Townsend had been away from his Norfolk birthplace (South Repps) for years and now had 'connections & mates' who would swear anything. Consequently Affleck decided to send him aboard HMS *Stately*, beyond the reach of the law. It was illegal, but in the captain's opinion it was the rough justice Townsend deserved.

One of the ways in which seamen might avoid Townsend's fate was by having themselves sued for debt. No one could order the arrest of a seaman in the Royal Navy for small debts, save conceivably in the Channel Islands, but under a 1758 statute, a civil suit was possible if the debt was £20 or more.[83] The concession was sufficient to cause trouble for the navy. When Jonathan Kelly, a seafarer and publican in Liverpool was impressed in August 1778 upon his return from a voyage, a local wholesale brewer sued him for a debt of £20 5s. and threatened the regulating officer with a suit if he was not released.[84] His case may well have been genuine, but in others it was dubiously so. James Dowell, a mate impressed in Newcastle while off duty, was immediately served with a writ for a debt of £20; but 'upon particular inquiries' the regulating officer discovered 'this had been done by the advice of some attorney or another, at the suit of his Mother; & merely to screen him from the King's service'.[85] At Dover, writs for fictitious debts abounded, and when a notorious smuggler from Eyemouth was sued for debt upon his impressment, the regulating officer in the Firth of Forth feared the custom would soon spread further north. 'If such a precedent were once allowed', Captain Napier wrote to the Admiralty, 'every Man who is impressed would cause his friends [to] rear up debts against him and procure the judges warrant for taking him ashore'.[86] Napier was not alone in fearing that a flood of debt actions would undermine impressment. Captain Gordon complained of the same practice in Bristol, while at Plymouth it was discovered that local publicans routinely made seamen take out bonds of £20 in order to secure their credit, a custom that placed the navy in this busy port at

[82] P.R.O., Adm. 1/3884, 13 July 1795.
[83] 31 George II c. 10, clause 27. The people of the Channel Islands believed that the £20 or over qualification did not apply to them; that, in effect, all debtors could be taken out of the navy at the demand of their creditors. See P.R.O., Adm. 1/3681/54.
[84] P.R.O., Adm. 1/3680/408, 420.
[85] P.R.O., Adm. 1/1498 (Bover), 22 March 1778.
[86] P.R.O., Adm. 1/2220 (Napier), 22 April 1777; for Dover, see Adm. 1/3681/82.

the virtual mercy of the crimp.[87] In fact the recovery of seamen's debt was a sufficiently grave problem for the Admiralty Solicitor to suggest a counter-strategy. Confronted with reports that bailiffs had been busily demanding the delivery of indebted sailors at the Nore, one of the other major stations of the navy, he wondered whether the Admiralty could claim that the Nore was 'upon the High sea' and therefore beyond civil jurisdiction. Perhaps 'a judicial determination' of this issue, he submitted to their lordships, would cut down the traffic in debtors and insulate the navy from the importunities of the civil courts.[88]

Admiralty officials were clearly worried that legal actions initiated in the civil courts would compromise its manning operations. While the Admiralty never openly defied the law, it certainly attempted to work it to its advantage. In some instances it shied away from testing the eligibility of impressment in the courts on the grounds that 'legal definitions would hamper rather than facilitate the service'. This was so on the question of whether keelmen were technically liable to impressment, a matter which had never been formally contested by Newcastle's Hostmen but one that could potentially disrupt Tyneside recruitment in a major way.[89] In other contexts, however, the Admiralty was not prepared to give any ground on matters that might widen the existing loopholes in the law. At various times in the eighteenth century, for example, discharged sailors had been allowed to set up in trade without fulfilling the normal apprenticeship requirements, a concession designed to minimize the social dislocations of demobilization in the aftermath of war.[90] Yet at the same time, men with adequate sea experience were legally bonded to the state until their fifties. Which law prevailed, statute or prerogative? Admiralty counsel said the latter,[91] even though local regulating officers often gave some discretionary licence to sailors who had clearly settled into land-based trades. They would only insist on a strict reading of the law where dual occupations might seriously undermine the search for men. This was the case at Perth, where Alexander Wedderburn reported that it was 'common practice' for young men, who had served apprenticeships as weavers, shoemakers, or other trades, to go to sea, 'where they continue shorter or longer as they find it answer'.[92]

[87] P.R.O., Adm. 1/1835 (Gordon), 23 July 1760; Adm. 7/299, no. 145. A crimp was an agent who entrapped men for the armed service; often a landlord who used his credit to ensnare men into the army or navy.
[88] P.R.O., Adm. 1/3680/256; Adm. 1/2220 (Napier), memorial to Napier, 20 June 1777.
[89] P.R.O., Adm. 7/299, no. 165.
[90] In 1713 and 1749, for example, under 12 Anne c. 13 and 22 George II c. 44.
[91] P.R.O., Adm. 7/300, no. 183. The opinion of F. C. Cust in 1779.
[92] P.R.O., Adm. 1/1783 (Fergusson), 19 July 1756.

The degree to which regulating captains exercised their discretion was also dependent upon the overall manning imperatives of the navy. In periods when volunteers were flush, shore captains might turn a blind eye to minor infractions of the regulations governing impressment. In periods when the manning requirements of the Royal Navy assumed new levels of urgency, they were encouraged to be officious: to impress all apprentices who did not carry indentures; to follow up on debtors and try to reimpress them once they were discharged from gaol.[93] In the mid-1790s, when the government had to institute quota acts to tap the manpower of the nation, the Admiralty conducted a legal review of statutory protections to ensure that it had not been too liberal in its interpretation of them. It scrutinized the legal exemptions in the coal trade, for example,[94] and decided that the employment of juvenile workers under the system known as 'colting' was not a formal apprenticeship, making 'colts' vulnerable to impressment.[95] The Admiralty was also advised that those able-bodied men impressed for being 'idle and disorderly' under the 1795 vagrancy act could only be discharged for criminal, not civil, causes, making it impossible for them to be arrested for debt.[96] When this policy of discretionary vigilance failed to bring in enough men, the Admiralty would ignore all protections, departmental or statutory, and take up just about every seaman or riverside worker from the quayside. In the summer of 1779, when Britain faced the combined forces of America, France, Spain and Holland, the navy literally took up everyone: even those with statutory exemptions. Only after the manning crisis had passed did it seek a parliamentary indemnity for its actions.[97]

In the last analysis the Admiralty could be quite ruthless in the way it understood and applied the laws and regulations pertaining to impressment. On balance it had the power and resources to act first and take questions afterwards. Potential grievers had to have money and influence on their side if they were to stand a good chance of redress. And any action taken against arbitrary or illegal impressment had to be taken quickly;

---

[93] Regulating officers were also officious about statutory protections. For example, Greenlandmen (whale fishermen) could work as colliers (sailing coal ships) in the off-season, but they could be impressed if they were found doing other types of work. See P.R.O., Adm. 1/714, Temple West, 16 February 1755; Adm. 2/522/56, 27 February 1758, cited by Gradish, *Manning*, p. 68n.

[94] In the 1790s, for example, the Admiralty reviewed the exemptions granted mates and apprentices in the coal trade. See P.R.O., Adm. 7/302, no. 283, and Adm. 7/304, no. 399.

[95] P.R.O., Adm. 1/3684, 15 January 1796.

[96] The relevant act was 35 George III c. 34. For legal advice about the discharge of 'vagrants' for criminal but not civil cases, see P.R.O., Adm. 1/3684, 30 March 1796.

[97] On this incident, see Nicholas Rogers, 'Liberty road: opposition to impressment in Britain during the American War of Independence', in *Jack Tar in history*, ed. Colin Howell and Richard Twomey (Fredericton, N.B., 1991), pp. 72–4.

otherwise the press gang would whisk men away to the tenders and on to the men of war at the Nore or Spithead, where captains could make life difficult for those who came to claim them with writs of arrest or habeas corpus.[98] This necessarily placed poor men at a great disadvantage. Few seafaring families were in a position to mobilize a petition or suit against impressment without outside help; and much of this help emerged within a structure of employer or political paternalism. Members of Parliament of port constituencies would sometimes intervene on behalf of their seamen, or, as in the case of the Brighton fishermen, prominent patrons such as the Duke of Newcastle.[99] A more likely source of aid, however, was the ship-owner or master who wanted a particular apprentice or protected seaman before the mast and was prepared doggedly to pursue the Admiralty through the courts to get him. The Hurry family of Yarmouth – merchants, ship-owners, Dissenters, reformers – seems to have been noticeably litigious on this score.[100] But the more independent or surly the seaman, the less likely it would be that such protection would be offered. If such a seaman could not mobilize a few friends to have him arrested for debt, probably the cheapest way legally to evade the service, he would have to resist the gang in other ways. That included direct physical confrontation. With over 500 reported impressment affrays in the period 1740–1805, that would seem to be the more typical recourse of the beleaguered tar.

What should we conclude, then, about the accessibility of the law in the eighteenth century from the experience of impressment? It is clear that one cannot regard seamen, or putative seamen, as legally illiterate subjects, simple victims of a recruiting system whose legal intricacies they did not understand. Edward Thurlow remarked in 1777, on the issue of whether freeholders were exempt from the law, that if the Admiralty ever conceded this exemption, sailors would readily exploit it. 'There is no knowing a Freeholder by sight', he noted, 'and if claiming

---

[98] For a case of a naval captain threatening to throw a writ of habeas corpus and its bearer into the sea, see P.R.O., Adm. 1/3684, 11 November 1796. For other captains refusing writs, see Adm. 1/3680/138 and 139.

[99] Baugh, *British naval administration*, p. 203; for other examples see William L. Clements Library, Townshend papers 297/3/2, 21, 23, and Peter Marshall, *Bristol and the American War of Independence* (Local History Association, Bristol, 1977), pp. 15–17.

[100] See P.R.O., Adm. 1/3681/27–8, 64; Adm. 1/3684, 11 November 1796; Douglas Hay, 'Prosecution and power: malicious prosecution in the English courts, 1750–1850', in Douglas Hay and Francis Snyder, eds., *Policing and prosecution in Britain 1750–1850* (Oxford, 1989), pp. 365–6; Ian R. Christie, 'Great Yarmouth and the Yorkshire Reform Movement 1782–1784', in *Myth and reality in late-eighteenth-century politics* (London, 1970), pp. 284n., 294; James E. Bradley, *Religion, revolution and English radicalism* (Cambridge, 1990), pp. 239–40, 404, 411.

that character, or even shewing deeds is sufficient, few sailors will be without it.'[101] Thurlow was in no doubt that seamen would work the system if they could, and we know that some became adept at evading impressment by exploiting the laws regarding debt, or volunteering for the militia or sea fencibles in order to exclude themselves, or by purchasing fake protections, or having themselves 'reclassified' as mates or masters.

We also know, from the lengthier reports concerning impressment affrays and from the often quite public confrontations between naval officers and the civil power, that seamen would have gleaned a rudimentary knowledge of the procedures that were designed to ensure that press gangs operated within the law and upheld the peace of the neighbourhood. Whether press warrants were properly endorsed, whether regulating captains sought the co-operation of the magistrates and constables in making thorough searches of quayside pubs and taverns, were not matters exclusive to middling shopkeepers and those above them. The critical issue is not whether seamen lacked the knowledge to use the law, but whether they had the money and social networks to use that knowledge in instances where they were improperly impressed. It is here that the notion of the law as an accessible use-right needs to be qualified. Although seamen could in theory apply for a habeas corpus if they were improperly impressed (and their exemption would have to be quite explicit), time, influence and money were on the Admiralty side. By and large seamen could only seek legal redress with the help of social superiors, and that usually meant some endorsement of or investment in the structures of patron–client relations through which the law was exercised. In the picaresque world of maritime labour, full of young men in their twenties who were impatient of the proprieties of rank and place, only a minority could avail themselves of the kinds of protection and aid that made legal redress a success.

[101] P.R.O., Adm. 7/300, no. 207.

Part 2

Crime

5   War as a judicial resource. Press gangs and prosecution rates, 1740–1830

Peter King

The paradoxical relationship between war and crime was well understood by the propertied classes of eighteenth-century England. 'The appearance of war is a present safety to the public', *The Times* announced in the early 1790s. 'Press gangs are better magistrates than the Middlesex justices.'[1] In eighteenth-century England, which usually succeeded in exporting its military conflicts, war meant peace and peace meant problems for those responsible for the protection of property.

As historical work on the eighteenth century's nearest equivalent to a recorded crime index (i.e. property crime indictment rates) began in earnest in the 1970s, the intimate relationship between war/peace transitions and recorded crime gradually emerged as an important theme – most notably in the work of John Beattie and Douglas Hay but also in a number of other county studies.[2] A distinctive and fairly consistent pattern emerged from this research. In virtually every area studied the outbreak of war led to a reduction in indictments while the coming of

Part of the work for this article was funded by the ESRC as part of its Crime and Social Order initiative (Award number L210252020). Thanks are also due to Cris Gostlow, research assistant, for her work on inputting and processing the data; to John Styles and Roger Ekirch for unpublished references; and to all those with whom I have discussed the ideas about crime rates and criminal justice touched on here, among whom the foremost has, of course, been John Beattie himself.

[1] *The Times*, 3 November 1790.
[2] J. Beattie, 'The pattern of crime in England 1660–1800', *Past and Present*, no. 62 (1974), pp. 93–5; J. Beattie, 'The criminality of women in eighteenth-century England', *Journal of Social History*, vol. 8 (1975), p. 103; J. Beattie, 'Crime and the courts in Surrey 1736–53', in J. Cockburn, ed., *Crime in England, 1550–1800* (London, 1977), pp. 159–61; D. Hay, 'Crime, authority and the criminal law. Staffordshire, 1750–1800' (University of Warwick, Ph.D. thesis, 1975), pp. 31–41; D. Hay, 'War, dearth and theft in the eighteenth century: the record of the English courts', *Past and Present*, no. 95 (1982), p. 157; J. Beattie, *Crime and the courts in England, 1660–1800* (Princeton, 1986), pp. 213–35; S. Pole, 'Crime, society and law-enforcement in Hanoverian Somerset' (University of Cambridge, Ph.D. thesis, 1983), pp. 137–44; R. Williams, 'Crime and the rural community in eighteenth-century Berkshire, 1740–1789' (University of Reading, Ph.D. thesis, 1985), pp. 255–9; G. Morgan and P. Rushton, *Rogues, thieves and the rule of law. The problem of law-enforcement in north-east England, 1718–1800* (London, 1998), pp. 63–4; P. King, *Crime, justice and discretion in England, 1740–1820* (Oxford, 2000), pp. 153–68.

peace increased them. On average peacetime indictment rates were over a third higher than wartime ones – a pattern only broken in a few years of either peacetime recruitment (e.g. 1770–1) or exceptionally bad wartime harvests (e.g. 1740–1, 1800–1).[3]

In attempting to explain this pattern historians have briefly explored some of the potential effects of mobilization and armed forces recruitment, but they have mainly focused on the impact of demobilization. Building on contemporary accounts, which frequently made explicit links between demobilization and rising crime, they have linked rising peacetime indictment rates to flooded post-war labour markets, to the moral panics which post-war periods often experienced and to a number of other factors.[4] In doing so, however, they have largely ignored two important dimensions of the relationship between changing indictment rates and the effects of war/peace transitions – the age-specific nature of war/peace changes in recorded crime, and the role of press gangs (and of enlistment more generally) as an alternative to prosecution in cases involving young males. Through an analysis of these two dimensions this chapter will explore the extent to which the impressment of young male offenders created an alternative judicial resource which proved very valuable to the authorities, and will argue that the use of pre-trial enlistment as an alternative to indictment may well have had a very important impact on patterns of recorded crime.

War, peace and the age structure of offenders

What impact did war have on the age structure of indicted property offenders in the English courts? Although systematic information on the ages of all indicted offenders is not available until the 1830s,[5] the gaol calendars of a few counties do include sufficient information to enable comparisons to be made both between genders and between wartime and peacetime periods. The gaol calendars of the three contrasting

[3] This pattern can be seen in Surrey, Sussex, Staffordshire, Somerset, Essex and Berkshire and in the parliamentary statistics on the Home Circuit gathered in the 1810s (see citations in footnote 2).

[4] Beattie, *Crime and the courts*, pp. 213–35; Hay, 'War, dearth and theft', pp. 124–58; N. Rogers, 'Confronting the crime wave: the debate over social reform and regulation, 1749–1753', in L. Davison *et al.*, eds., *Stilling the grumbling hive: the response to social and economic problems in England, 1689–1750* (Stroud and New York, 1992), p. 83; *Observer*, 22 January 1815; P. King, 'Newspaper reporting, prosecution practice and perceptions of urban crime: the Colchester crime wave of 1765', *Continuity and Change*, vol. 2 (1987), pp. 423–54; D. Hay and N. Rogers, *Eighteenth-century English society: shuttles and swords* (Oxford, 1997), p. 159.

[5] V. Gatrell and T. Hadden, 'Criminal statistics and their interpretation', in E. A. Wrigley, ed., *Nineteenth-century society: essays in the use of quantitative methods for the study of social data* (Cambridge, 1972), p. 342.

jurisdictions studied here – the rapidly industrializing county of Lancashire, the large and long-established port and borough of Bristol, and the predominantly rural and declining proto-industrial county of Gloucestershire – all provide data on a sample of both Quarter Sessions and Assizes accused.[6] As might be expected from the fact that army and navy recruitment was confined entirely to males, the proportion of indicted offenders who were female tended to be considerably higher in wartime than in peacetime. In Lancashire, for example, 32 per cent of property offenders were female between 1801 and 1805, compared to 18 per cent in the peacetime period 1820–2. Similarly, in Gloucestershire the figures were 18 per cent immediately before the outbreak of the French wars (1789–93), 23 percent between 1806 and 1811 and 11 per cent by the post-demobilization period 1817–18. Only in Bristol where sample sizes were very small was this pattern not observable.[7] Given that demobilized soldiers and sailors increased the male population by as much as 5 or 6 per cent at the end of some eighteenth-century wars, and that that increase was concentrated in the age groups most vulnerable to prosecution,[8] these figures are not particularly surprising. More important, however, was the gendered nature of changes in the age structure of offenders observable between peacetime and wartime periods.

Extensive previous research on two peacetime data sets drawn from London just before the outbreak of the French wars and from the Home Circuit Assizes in the mid-1780s[9] has shown that the age structure of property offenders followed a fairly consistent pattern. Starting from a

---

[6] The calendars do not, however, survive consistently in any of these three jurisdictions for these early periods. In most jurisdictions and in most years calendars are not available for all six Quarter Sessions and Assizes hearings. In some areas very patchy survival produces rather small sample sizes particularly for the pre-1793 period. Therefore, it is not possible to create data on the absolute numbers indicted in any particular jurisdiction. However, the sources do allow the proportion of offenders who belonged to a particular age group to be compared across time and between regions. Bristol Borough court was almost unique in having both Assizes and Quarter Sessions jurisdictions. The analysis has been confined to property offenders because they have been the focus of historical debate on recorded crime rates.

[7] The records sampled were: Lancashire, Assizes gaol calendars, and quarterly prison calendars in the recognizance rolls – Lancashire Record Office [hereafter R.O.], QSB/1 and QJC, 1801–1805, 1820–22; Gloucestershire, gaol calendars – Gloucestershire R.O. QSG/2, 1789–93, 1806–11, 1820–2; Bristol, Sessions bundles, gaol calendars – City of Bristol R.O., 1786–92, 1794–1805, 1820–2. Only offenders awaiting trial have been included in these samples, those imprisoned post-trial being an untypical sample of those originally accused. The early Lancashire sample does include a brief peacetime period but is mainly centred on a major mobilization and wartime period.

[8] Hay, 'War, dearth and theft', p. 139, calculated that demobilizations increased the number of men in England who were heads of families (or might be) by 20 to 30 per cent.

[9] P. King, 'Decision-makers and decision-making in the English criminal law, 1750–1800', *Historical Journal*, vol. 27 (1984), p. 36; King, *Crime, justice and discretion*, pp. 169–75 for

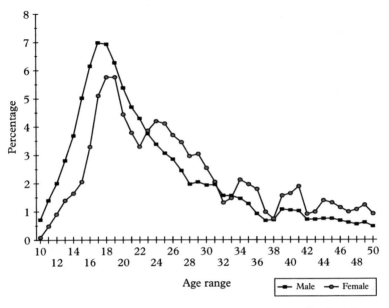

1 Age structure of male and female property offenders, Lancashire,
1820–1822.

very low point in the early teens, it rose sharply to a major peak in the
late teens and early twenties. About half of all offenders were aged 16 to
25. More than a third were between 18 and 23. This broad pattern was
followed by both males and females. There were minor differences between the sexes. In London, for example, the female age structure rose
at a slightly later age and to a rather less pronounced peak. However,
for both sexes the more mobile period between the usual age at leaving
home (mid-teens) and the most frequent age at marriage (some ten years
later) was the key period when both males and females were most vulnerable to prosecution for theft. The peacetime pattern found in London
in the early 1790s (and indeed in the early 1820s) is remarkably similar
to that found in the Lancashire data for the period following the end of
the Napoleonic Wars (see fig. 1). Both male and female age structures
peaked in the late teens and once again females peaked a year or so later
than males and reached a slightly less pronounced high point.[10]

the Home Circuit data. For London, see P. King, 'Female offenders, work and life-
cycle change in late eighteenth-century London', *Continuity and Change*, vol. 11 (1996),
pp. 54–5.

[10] King, 'Female offenders', p. 65; King, *Crime, justice and discretion*, pp. 169–207; P. King
and J. Noel, 'The origins of "the problem of juvenile delinquency": the growth of juvenile

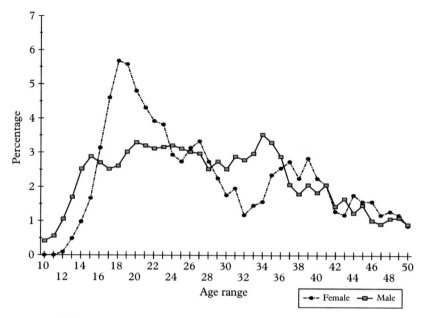

2 Age structure of male and female property offenders, Lancashire, 1801–1805.

In wartime, by contrast, the Lancashire data indicates that male and female property offenders had entirely different age structures (fig. 2). The female accused followed broadly the same pattern as that found in peacetime Lancashire (and indeed in peacetime London or the Home Counties), reaching a high point in the late teens.[11] The male age structure did nothing of the kind. The huge peacetime peak of male offenders aged 15 to 25 was simply not there in times of war (see fig. 3). In peacetime Lancashire the predominant group indicted for property crimes were young adult males aged 15 to 25. In wartime as the proportion of the accused who were males declined considerably and as the 15 to 25 age group ceased to make a significantly greater contribution than those aged 25 to 40, young adult males became simply another subgroup – significant but by no means dominant or central.

prosecutions in London in the late eighteenth and early nineteenth centuries', *Criminal Justice History*, vol. 14 (1993), pp. 26–7.

[11] Around 6 per cent of all female offenders were aged 18. To be more precise, since a three-age-group moving average is being used, a 6 per cent mark or just under at the 18-year-old point on figure 2 means that around 18 per cent of all female offenders were aged either 17, 18 or 19.

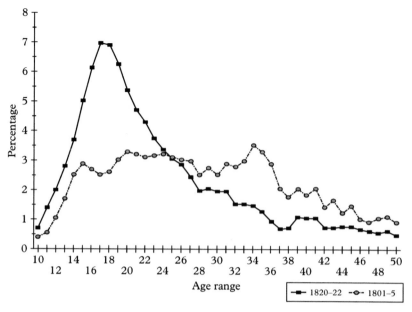

3 Age structure of male property offenders, Lancashire, 1801–1805 and 1820–1822.

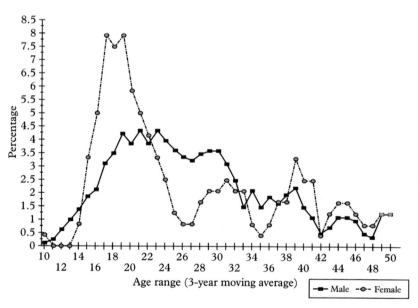

4 Ages of male and female property offenders, Gloucestershire, 1806–1811.

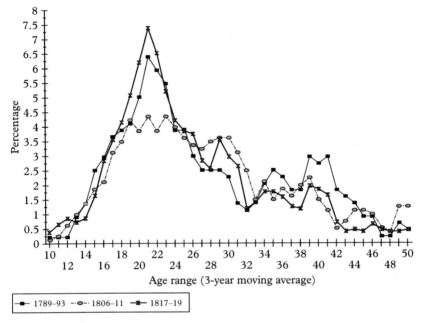

5 Ages of male property offenders, Gloucestershire, 1789–1793, 1806–1811 and 1817–1818.

The Lancashire data is not without its problems[12] and in particular no ages appear to have been recorded in the Lancashire records before 1801–2, but in Gloucestershire limited evidence from the previous peacetime period (1789–93) is also available. It is therefore interesting to note that the Gloucestershire data in figures 4 and 5 shows a very similar pattern of war/peace changes to that found in early nineteenth-century Lancashire. The wartime data for the years 1806 to 1811 in figure 4 shows the usual huge female peak between the ages of 15 and 24 and the same absence of such a peak for the male accused. The comparison of male age structures only in figure 5 shows that the male peacetime peak in the late teens and early twenties seen in both 1789–93 and 1817–18 is simply not there in the wartime period 1806–11.[13]

Although the Bristol data involves much smaller samples making meaningful comparisons between male and female age structures impossible, the male age structures can be roughly compared (see fig. 6). Once again,

---

[12] Quarter Sessions level cases for which age information is available in the early period do not appear to have as full a geographical coverage as they do by the 1820s.

[13] Bedfordshire and south-east England saw similar contrasts. King, *Crime, justice and discretion*, pp. 187–8.

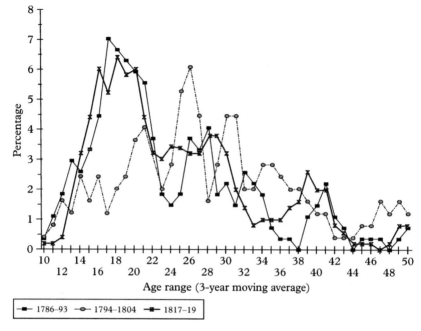

6 Ages of male property offenders, Bristol, 1786–1793, 1794–1804 and
1817–1819.

the two peacetime periods 1786–93 and 1817–19 contain a dominant
peak in the late teens and early twenties while in the wartime period 1794–
1804 no such peak exists. The patterns found in figures 1 to 6 reflect, of
course, a wide variety of factors, most of which cannot be discussed in
detail here. The age structure of male and female accused differed in a
number of minor ways both between regions and across time. Equally,
as I have analyzed in detail elsewhere, the proportion of the accused who
were juveniles was increasing very rapidly in urban areas by 1820, but not
yet in rural ones.[14] However, despite this diversity, the war/peace patterns
in figures 1 to 6 are remarkably consistent. In Lancashire, Gloucestershire
and Bristol the wartime male age structures stand out as entirely different from all others. Male and female peacetime age structures and female
wartime ones rose to a high peak in the later teens and early twenties. Male
wartime ones did not. War clearly removed many if not most young adult
males from the clutches of major courts.

[14] P. King, 'The rise of juvenile delinquency in England, 1780–1840: changing patterns of
perception and prosecution', *Past and Present*, no. 160 (1998), pp. 119–31.

The limited information available on the armed forces suggests that 16- to 25-year-olds dominated recruitment in wartime at least as much as they dominated the ranks of indicted offenders in peacetime. About 80 per cent of ordinary seamen and more than half of all able seamen between 1764 and 1782 were aged 16 to 25, and this age group was also the dominant one amongst the quota men raised in the 1790s.[15] The exceptional, almost aberrant, age structure of indicted male offenders in wartime may well have been mainly a function of the mobilization process, and this analysis of war/peace changes in the ages of offenders suggests that in emphasizing the impact and importance of demobilization historians may not yet be giving sufficient weight to its opposite. It was probably mobilization rather than demobilization that created the key distortion – a unique collapse in the proportion of young adult males among recorded offenders. The mobilization process therefore requires further investigation.

There are a number of ways in which the massive mobilizations which most eighteenth-century wars involved[16] may have affected both indictment levels and the age structure of indicted offenders. First, as John Beattie has pointed out, by drawing off some of the surplus labour force, mobilization may have improved the employment prospects and wages of those who remained, making it less necessary for them to have recourse to theft in difficult times.[17] Secondly, the demands of war may have stimulated economic activity and employment opportunities, thus having the same effect (although in some areas the interruption of international trade may have had the opposite result). However, the extent to which the impact of these changes was age-specific remains unclear. Better employment prospects would have affected almost all age groups and perhaps both genders (to some degree at least). Thus it is difficult to see how these changes can explain the huge relative impact that the coming of war had on the appropriation habits of young males alone.

More importantly, of course, as some contemporaries observed, impressment and voluntary enlistment mainly affected young, unmarried men living on the margins of society. Wartime recruitment removed many of those perceived by the propertied to be vagrants, idle, undesirable or unemployable – indeed these were the principal targets of much

---

[15] N. A. M. Rodger, *The wooden world: an anatomy of the Georgian navy* (London, 1986), pp. 360–1; C. Emsley, ed., *North Riding naval recruits. The quota acts and the quota men, 1795–7* (North Yorkshire Record Office, publication no. 18, 1978), p. 19. Nicholas Rogers has helpfully pointed out, however, that N. Rodger's figures do not allow for the large number of cases where ages are not known, which may inflate the younger cohort.

[16] For the impact of war on the proportion of adult males in the armed forces, Hay and Rogers, *Eighteenth-century English society*, p. 228.

[17] Beattie, *Crime and the courts*, pp. 229–31.

of the legislation aimed at encouraging enlistment.[18] By sweeping large numbers of marginalized young men into the armed forces, mobilization clearly removed some of those most likely to commit crimes, and indictment rates and the age structure of male offenders were undoubtedly affected by this. However, there is considerable evidence that many male offenders were enlisted after they had committed crimes but before they were formally indicted, that is, that pre-trial enlistment was frequently used as an alternative to prosecution during periods of rapid mobilization.

Leon Radzinowicz argued in the late 1960s that this practice was extensively used and that 'robberies were daily compounded before the magistrates, on condition that the thief would be handed over to the tender'. However, as John Beattie has pointed out, little evidence has yet been provided about the extent and nature of this practice.[19] By using a diverse range of sources to analyze the ways that both victims and magistrates used recruitment into the armed forces as an alternative to indictment, and by looking at the reasons why this was such an attractive option to both groups, the rest of this chapter aims to fill that gap. It will argue that war created a separate set of judicial opportunities and resources for those who wished to avoid the expensive, time-consuming and generally unrewarding process of indicting offenders in the major courts. Press gangs made better magistrates than the Middlesex justices not only because they removed potential offenders before they could commit crimes, but also because they channelled acknowledged offenders informally into the forces rather than leaving them to be indicted in the major courts.

The nature and extent of pre-trial enlistment

Although the use of pre-trial enlistment as an alternative to indictment created few formal records and has therefore been largely ignored by historians, the fragments available from letters, diaries, magistrates notebooks, newspapers, petty sessions records, parliamentary papers, criminal autobiographies, and gaol or house of correction calendars suggest that both victims and magistrates made widespread use of the armed forces in this way.

In some cases victims acted without any formal reference to the local magistracy, in others the imposition of impressment as an informal sanction involved both parties. Victims' pre-trial behaviour is notoriously

---

[18] P. Colquhoun, *A treatise on the police of the metropolis* (4th edn, 1797), pp. 92–3. Sir L. Radzinowicz, *A history of English criminal law and its administration from 1750* (London, 1968), vol. IV, pp. 87–96.

[19] Radzinowicz, *History of English criminal law*, vol. IV, p. 96; Beattie, *Crime and the courts*, p. 221.

difficult to analyze, but a number of victims clearly ensured that in wartime young male offenders were either taken directly to a local recruiting party with very little choice, or coerced into agreeing to enlist by the threat of a prosecution. The Williamson letters, for example, contain this account of the transactions that ensued when their Irish footman overpowered a rather timid young highwayman who had threatened the footman's master and mistress with a faggot shaped like a pistol and then demanded their money.[20]

There is a house; we brought him into it with his hands tied behind him. A great crowd gathered. He cried and kneeled and begged for mercy, and not to send him to Newgate, said he was but 18, never attempted such a thing before; his father died but three months ago; his mother – she cooks at certain days for judges in Sergeant's Inn – would break her heart; and was indeed horribly frightened, and so forth. What account he gave of himself proves true enough, and that he had been prentice to a pastry cook. In short, I delivered him to the captors, not resolving to carry him before the justice. So my bold fellows walked him down to Westminster. There, late at night, they let him send for his mother and friends. I interfered not; so far I pitied him, as did my wife. So the next day, order was taken to deliver him to a press gang. He is, I was assured, put aboard a man-of-war. The hack horse is restored to the owner.

The diary of Suffolk merchant James Oakes records a similar scenario in 1796.[21]

This morning I provd the Boy Wm Pentuney guilty of stealing several Shillings. I had some time suspected him of these petty Thefts & by markg Money, wch being missd & found upon him, brot the fact clearly to his Charge. I immediately sent for his Mother & his Uncle Prigg and instead of presenting him mean, if possible, sending him to Sea.

A rather different type of source, *The authentic narrative of the celebrated Miss Fanny Davis ... modern Amazon,* who was sentenced to death at the Essex Assizes in the 1780s, professed to record a similar story from the mouth of Fanny herself. Having been caught with two male accomplices committing a burglary in the house of a nobleman, whose mistress she had previously been, Fanny was released by the victim. However, 'the King at this time much wanting men, my Lord caused the two thieves to be impressed by the constables'.[22]

---

[20] F. Manning, ed., *The Williamson letters, 1748–1765* (Bedfordshire Historical Record Society, 1953), pp. 76–7 (my thanks to John Styles for this reference).

[21] J. Fiske, ed., *The Oakes diaries. Business, politics and the family in Bury St Edmunds, 1778–1827,* vol. I, *Introduction: James Oakes diary, 1778–1800* (Suffolk Record Society, 1990), p. 321.

[22] Anon., *An authentic narrative of the most remarkable adventures and curious intrigues exhibited in the life of Fanny Davis, the celebrated modern Amazon, who received sentence of death at the last Chelmsford Assizes* (London, 1786), p. 22.

While individual victims not infrequently managed to get offenders put into the armed forces without formal reference to the local magistracy, it was often the summary courts themselves that substituted enlistment for indictment. This practice was openly discussed by witnesses before the 1819 parliamentary committee on the criminal laws. The evidence of a London professional man, Dr Lushington, for example, told a similar story to that recorded in Oakes' diary. Having suspected a servant of regularly taking money from his purse, Lushington secretly marked his money and obtained a confession. Although, unlike Oakes, Lushington involved a magistrate, the outcome was very similar. 'I then took him before the sitting Magistrate at Guildhall', he recalled, 'and finding that if I prosecuted him at all, it must be for the capital offence, I declined to do so, and had him sent on board the tender.' The London hardware man, Frederick Thornhill, told the committee a parallel story about his father's past treatment of an employee who had systematically stolen from him. 'Being taken into custody, he was brought up and examined before the sitting alderman, by whose consent, at the intercession of my father (who refused to prosecute as the offence was capital) he was sent on board the navy.'[23] The witnesses chosen to appear before the 1819 committee were carefully selected to illustrate the negative impact of the capital code on victims' willingness to formally indict property offenders. However, a range of other sources suggest that the evidence they provided about the informal use of pre-trial enlistment was by no means untypical. In 1762, for example, the *London Chronicle* reported that two offenders caught stealing from their master's warehouse 'were carried before the Lord Mayor, who upon examination offered them the choice of going on board a tender or standing trial and they wisely chose the former'.[24] During the following decade the private papers of the anti-slavery campaigner Granville Sharp record that when he caught a young pickpocket robbing him of his handkerchief, he took him before the Lord Mayor's court and forced him to enlist in the navy.[25]

More importantly, the scattered summary court records that survive in the City of London archives provide (for brief periods at least) much more systematic evidence of this practice. For example, the only summary court minute book that survives for 1777 – that for the Guildhall Justicing Room, 15 August to 29 September – indicates that while seven suspected male property offenders were impressed in this period, only four were definitely sent on for formal indictment (many were simply

[23] 'Report from the select committee on criminal laws', *Parliamentary Papers* (1819) VIII, pp. 116, 106.

[24] *London Chronicle*, 13 July 1762.

[25] J. Woods, 'The City of London and impressment, 1776–1777', *Proceedings of the Leeds Philosophical Society*, vol. VIII, Part II, p. 112.

discharged or warned). The minute books rarely describe the accused's offence in detail but four of the seven impressed property offenders were accused of pickpocketing; one was a boy who had confessed to stealing 10 guineas and a banknote; the other two were accused of stealing a watch but, since the victim 'could not recollect the name or number', the evidence was weak and the decision that they be 'sent on board the tender' may therefore have been a compromise.[26] Although a brief sampling of the same records at the beginning of the next war in 1794 has also revealed that more than one suspected felon was 'enlisted as a soldier', it is difficult to ascertain whether the 1777 pattern was typical of wartime practice because the only years for which either of the main eighteenth-century London summary courts have left full records are located in the peacetime period 1785–90.[27] However, the large-scale, if brief, mobilization that occurred during the international crisis that developed between late September and early November 1787 does provide another very useful opportunity to examine the summary courts' use of impressment against property offenders.

In late September 1787 the unstable situation in the Dutch United Provinces, where the patriotic movement was challenging Orangist control, seemed likely to ignite into a full-scale European conflict. 'The alarm of war is spread abroad', *The Times* reported. 'Europe presents a singular scene at this time – Every country is on the eve of being involved in a war ... France, Spain and the democratic party in Holland, against the Stadtholder – with the aristocratic party, England and Prussia.'[28] By the end of the month the Prussians had invaded the Netherlands, the French were reported to be 'making the greatest preparations of war in all their ports', while the British were rapidly mobilizing the navy and sending out press warrants to all ports.[29] A hot press ensued and although the City authorities remained extremely ambivalent about the legality of press warrants in general, their attitude to the impressment of offenders was clear.[30]

26 City of London Record Office [hereafter C.L.R.O.], GJR/M5.

27 C.L.R.O., GJR/M52; and for the full years MJR/M2–65.

28 E. H. Kossmann, *The Low Countries, 1780–1940* (Oxford, 1978), pp. 34–47; O. Hufton, *Europe: privilege and protest 1730–1789* (Brighton, 1980), pp. 293–8; I. Christie, *Wars and revolutions: Britain, 1760–1815* (London, 1982), pp. 194–5; *The Times*, 21–2 September 1787.

29 *The Times*, 22, 24, 25, 26 September and 1, 2, 3, 6 October 1787; *London Chronicle*, 20–2, 22–5, 27–9 September and 29 September–2 October 1787.

30 On the hot press, *The Times*, 2, 5, 6 October 1787. On the City authorities' ambivalence, *The Times*, 27 September and 4 October 1787. *London Chronicle*, 6–9, 9–11 October 1787; *The World*, 6 October 1787. The Lord Mayor's refusal to accept Pitt's arguments that press warrants were legal reflected a long tradition of opposition to impressment in the City. Woods, 'The City'; N. Rogers, *Crowds, culture and politics in Georgian Britain* (Oxford, 1998), pp. 85–121; N. Rogers, 'Impressment and the law', in this volume.

Between 1 October and 6 November a wide range of cases recorded in the London Mansion House Justice Room minute books ended in impressment. About a dozen involved offenders accused of being disorderly or vagabonds, of assault, of breaking windows, of leaving their children chargeable to the parish or of gambling in the streets. A further ten involved property offenders. On 24 October alone three men charged with felony by different prosecutors were 'sent to the Rendezvous'. Others were accused of pilfering wool and other commodities on the quays or of stealing loaves of bread. Since only a dozen male property offenders were committed for trial by the court during this period,[31] the decision to impress rather than indict these ten offenders may have nearly halved male indictment levels for property offences. However, not all of those who were impressed after being accused of property offences would necessarily have been indicted in more peaceful times. Some might have been either summarily imprisoned in Bridewell – a practice not infrequently resorted to by the City magistrates – or dealt with informally in other ways.

There can be no doubt, however, that a very considerable number of indictable property offenders were enlisted in both 1777 and 1787. The London newspapers rarely reported summary court proceedings in this period, but two reports of London summary trials published in *The World* on 28 September 1787 made the court's policies, and their gendered nature, clear. After reporting that a 17-year-old servant girl, who had stolen from her master, had been committed to the Wood Street compter, the paper went on to describe the fate of 'One Oakley' who, having been charged before the Lord Mayor's court with robbing his employers, 'was sent to serve his majesty . . . being a stout young man, and his first offence'.

The year 1787 was a year of very high indictment rates and great anxiety about property crime, and when *The Times* reported on 12 September 1787 (just before the international situation deteriorated) that the Old Bailey sessions that were about to commence would be 'as heavy as any sessions for many years past', they confirmed this pattern. However, when the same paper reported on the court's next meeting, on 30 October, it stressed that the Old Bailey sessions were 'the shortest we remember for some years'. It was also clear about the role of impressment in this rapid decline in recorded crime. 'We must give some credit to the press gangs', *The Times* observed, 'for having provided our vagrants with better employment than robbing and stealing'.[32] While the impressment of

---

[31] C.L.R.O., MJR/M33–4. Some offenders were remanded but the final resolution of the case is unknown.
[32] *The Times*, 30 October 1787.

'disorderly persons, vagrants and such as have no visible means of liveli-hood'[33] was undoubtedly an important factor behind this temporary de-cline in Old Bailey business, the summary court records suggest strongly that another mechanism (less visible perhaps to contemporaries, but no less potent) was also in operation. Even if only half of the property of-fenders impressed by the City's summary courts in 1777 and 1787 would have been indicted if they had not been impressed, in both cases recorded crime rates as measured by the index historians usually use – indictments – would have ended up at least 30 per cent and possibly over 50 per cent lower than they otherwise would have been. Moreover, the overall effect of pre-trial enlistment was almost certainly much greater than this for two reasons. First, as the private papers of men like Oakes and Williamson show, many other offenders who might otherwise have been indicted were put into the armed forces without ever being taken to a summary hearing. Second, some of those who were committed to gaol to await trial were later allowed to avoid formal indictment by agreeing to enlist. In every wartime period, and in the final quarter of 1787, the Essex gaol records contain references to property offenders avoiding formal trial by being 'sent on board his majesties tender' or 'discharged by entering on board one of his majesties' ships'.[34]

If the many other summary courts of Middlesex, Westminster and London followed the same policies as the one City court for which records survive, and if the two additional processes we have just analyzed also si-phoned off even a small minority of potentially indictable property offend-ers before they could be formally charged before a grand jury, pre-trial enlistment may well have accounted for the remarkable fall in indict-ment rates that occurred in both 1777 and at the late October Old Bailey sessions in 1787. The City of London summary court records therefore suggest that the anecdotal evidence of the prevalence of pre-trial en-listment provided by parliamentary committee witnesses, by occasional newspaper reports of summary trials, and by the more scattered evidence of provincial gaol calendars and summary court records I have analyzed elsewhere,[35] have to be taken very seriously. If these pre-trial enlistment strategies were pursued over long periods by victims and magistrates, then most of the differences between peacetime and wartime indictment levels may well be explained by these policies alone.

[33] *London Chronicle*, 27–9 September 1787, records warrants being issued for taking up these specific groups 'and pressing them into his Majesty's land service'. The papers also recorded planned attacks by press gangs on the haunts of notorious groups of London offenders. *London Chronicle*, 29 September–2 October 1787; *The World*, 2 and 5 October 1787.
[34] Essex Record Office [hereafter E.R.O.], Q/SBb 294/18, 218/5, 287/7, 361/.
[35] King, *Crime, justice and discretion*, pp. 91–2.

The process of pre-trial enlistment was multilayered. The accused and their families or friends, as well as the victims, witnesses and committing magistrates all had roles to play. In a number of cases there is a strong indication that the offender maintained a considerable element of choice between pre-trial enlistment and public trial. It is clear that both before and after being taken to a magistrate many offenders (or their parents) took due account of the possibility of pre-trial enlistment in deciding which would be their best post-detection strategy. For major offenders, such as the highway robber described in the Williamson letters, enlistment was clearly a better option than facing a public trial for an offence that frequently led convicts to the gallows. Not all offenders were successful in obtaining this outcome. In 1815 the *Observer* reported that 'a young man' accused of stealing a very considerable quantity of plate from his master 'asked to be permitted to enter the army or navy'. 'To this, however, the prosecutor would not consent in consequence of what he had suffered in his property' and the Guildhall magistrates therefore committed him for trial.[36]

Those accused of minor thefts and non-capital larcenies, for which the maximum sentence was transportation and the most likely one was often imprisonment and/or a whipping, did not necessarily see pre-trial enlistment as such an attractive option. In 1770, for example, Thomas Randall, a 14-year-old Essex boy accused of stealing rabbits, was examined several times during the time he was awaiting trial in the Barking House of Correction so that 'the father might send him to sea'. He stubbornly 'refused to go' and was eventually convicted and sentenced to be whipped at the following Quarter Sessions.[37] However, if the victim and the petty sessions bench were in agreement, most physically able male offenders would have found the pressure to enlist very difficult to resist, given the magistrates' wide discretionary powers. After 1744, for example, if a J.P. could find a way of labelling the offender as a vagrant, the latter could be imprisoned until the next Quarter Sessions, when, to quote Burn, 'if such person, being a male, is above 12 years of age, the Court may, before he is discharged by the house of correction, send him to be employed in his Majesty's Service by sea or land'.[38] Faced with this prospect, some of those most vulnerable to such policies took drastic physical action to avoid enlistment. John Clare's autobiographical writings record that gypsies, who were specifically defined by statute as rogues and vagabonds, 'disabled the finger of every male child in wartime ... to keep them from being sent for a soldier for any petty thefts they might

[36] *Observer*, 1 October 1815.   [37] E.R.O., Q/SBb 263/8.
[38] R. Burn, *The justice of the peace and parish officer* (19th edn, 1797), vol. IV, p. 269, *sub* Vagrants.

commit, which would invariably be the case if they had been able men when taken before a magistrate', and in 1779 a large group of gypsies who were known to 'get their bread by plundering the poor farmers of their livestock . . . having some intimation given them of their being likely to be pressed cut off the first joint of their forefinger to avoid serving the King'. In 1763 the *Ipswich Journal* reported that 'before the war was ended' the locally notorious house-breaker James Knight 'was ordered to be taken by the constable to be sent for a soldier, or to sea'. However, while the constable was taking him away his wife cut him so desperately in one leg that she prevented his enlistment.[39]

Pre-trial enlistment was also used against property offenders who had committed non-indictable forms of appropriation. Peter Munsche uncovered a number of examples of the informal use of impressment by game preservers anxious to rid themselves of notorious poachers, and occasionally even wood or vegetable thieves found themselves in a similar position.[40] Thus for a broad spectrum of property offenders, but more especially for those accused of indictable property crimes, there is considerable evidence that war, and the possibility of impressment or semi-compulsory enlistment, created a parallel sanctioning system, an alternative judicial resource for both victims and magistrates. For a number of reasons the eighteenth century and the early years of the nineteenth century provided particularly fruitful conditions in which that system could establish itself. First, unlike the century that followed, England spent about half of the years between 1700 and 1815 actively engaged in fighting wars abroad. In every wartime period and in a number of other years such as 1771, 1787 and 1790, when brief mobilizations occurred but the anticipated full-scale conflict did not materialize, recruitment into the armed forces was taking place on a very significant scale. At some point during every war between 1700 and 1815 at least 8 per cent of the male population aged between 15 and 59 found themselves in the armed forces. In the early nineteenth century the figure was 15 per cent.[41]

Secondly, although halting steps were made towards conscription through the various militia acts,[42] recruitment remained both unsystematic and highly problematic. Despite widespread campaigns to attract

---

[39] E. Robinson, ed., *John Clare's autobiographical writings* (Oxford, 1986), p. 71; *Ipswich Journal*, 31 December 1763 and 20 March 1779.

[40] P. Munsche, *Gentlemen and poachers: the English game laws, 1671–1831* (Cambridge, 1981), pp. 88–9. Kent Archives Office, PS/SE1, 26 March 1709 for a wood stealer 'listed for a soldier'.

[41] Hay and Rogers, *Eighteenth-century English society*, p. 228.

[42] P. Langford, *A polite and commercial people: England 1727–83* (Oxford, 1989), pp. 334–5; J. Western, *The English militia in the eighteenth century* (London, 1965).

voluntary recruits, both the army and the navy were often chronically short of manpower and therefore evolved various coercive or semi-coercive means of obtaining men. A growing body of parliamentary legislation and government orders put increasing pressure on the local authorities at both county and parish levels to supply the armed forces with more recruits than they could easily get their hands on. This forced both magistrates and parish officers to use a variety of expedients in order to fulfil their various obligations or quotas. In 1758, for example, the Sussex overseer and churchwarden, Thomas Turner, and a fellow-parishioner went round the local alehouses 'to see if there were any disorderly fellows, that we might have them into the sitting tomorrow in order to send them to sea'. On this occasion they 'found none we thought proper to send',[43] but many local constables may often have deemed it very much in their interests to do so. In 1770, for example, those who responded to the Admiralty orders sent to the Essex Quarter Sessions by both arresting 'seamen and seafaring men . . . found lurking in these parts' and carrying them to Harwich, were offered 20 shillings per head and 6 pence a mile travel allowance.[44] By 1795, when the quota acts began to impose heavy fines on any parish that failed to find their 'quota' of recruits, another act (which enabled county benches to levy 'able-bodied and idle persons' for the navy) ensured not only that parish constables received 20 shillings per recruit, but also that any citizen giving information leading to an enlistment would get a 10 shilling payout.[45] Both the formal rewards received direct from the authorities and the more informal financial encouragements that were offered by recruiting groups, who themselves were rewarded according to the number of recruits they generated,[46] meant that a victim of crime (and those who had helped to detect and arrest the offender) could turn a potentially expensive situation – the prospect of having to mount a formal prosecution at their own expense – into a potentially lucrative one. The Williamsons' servants did not march their captive highwaymen off to the press gang simply in order to help the English navy meets its manpower requirements. They almost certainly expected to make a considerable profit from the transaction.

Thirdly, in the eighteenth century both magistrates and victims shared deep traditions about the use of informal sanctions in cases involving theft. Magistrates frequently resolved cases informally, acting as mediators aiming to produce an outcome acceptable to both victim and

---

[43] D. Vaisey, ed., *The diary of Thomas Turner, 1754–65* (Oxford, 1985), p. 144.

[44] E.R.O., Q/SBb 263/1, 340/60, 60a.

[45] Emsley, *North Riding naval recruits*, pp. 9–11; Radzinowicz, *History of English criminal law*, vol. IV, pp. 90–1.

[46] Rodger, *Wooden world*, p. 166.

accused.[47] Given their wide powers in relation to vagrants, unruly apprentices and servants, and the disorderly poor – precisely the groups which recruitment policies and impressment acts mainly targeted – the magistracy could and did use their discretion to shape criminal justice policy in ways that made informal pre-trial enlistment a potentially important plank of penal policy in the eighteenth century. The gradual movement towards stricter statutory control over, and greater lawyerly involvement in, summary court proceedings which occurred during the nineteenth century meant that the eighteenth and early nineteenth centuries were almost certainly the high point of magisterial discretionary power in this arena.

Finally, as I have shown, the data available on the gender and age structure of property offenders in peacetime suggests that the nature of those accused of such crimes was particularly conducive to the development of widespread pre-trial enlistment practices. Most of the offenders who were brought before the magistrates were adolescent or young adult males whose physical fitness was sufficient to meet the fairly basic requirements of the armed forces. If the victim was willing to agree, and if (as was usually the case) the accused was in too weak a position to resist effectively, the committing magistrates would have been able to consider pre-trial enlistment as a potential option in the majority of the property crime cases that came before them.

The combination of these four factors made pre-trial enlistment a potentially powerful force in shaping the ways offenders were dealt with in wartime and therefore in shaping the short-term changes in indictment levels so much studied by eighteenth-century historians. The extent to which that potential was fulfilled is only partly recoverable and, given the piecemeal nature of the surviving evidence on pre-trial procedures, the data presented here inevitably raises as many questions as it answers. It is conceivable, for example, that pre-trial enlistment may have been less prevalent at the beginning of the eighteenth century than it was at the end of it. John Beattie's recent work on male and female London indictment rates around 1700 has certainly raised this as a possibility. It is also possible that pre-trial enlistment was much more important in southern England than it was elsewhere until naval impressment expanded into northern areas after 1750, and that its impact outside the London area and the larger ports was generally more limited.[48] However, the sources that would enable us to test such an assumption have yet to be uncovered.

[47] King, *Crime, justice and discretion*, pp. 82–110.
[48] J. Beattie, 'Crime and inequality in eighteenth-century London', in J. Hagan and R. Peterson, eds., *Crime and inequality* (Stanford, 1995), pp. 135–6; Rogers, *Crowds, culture*, pp. 90–1.

Equally, the data presented in figures 1 to 6 on the period from the 1780s to the 1820s is also open to a number of different interpretations. Several factors have to be taken into account in any attempt to explain why male and female peacetime age structures, and female wartime ones, rose to such a high peak in the late teens and twenties, while male wartime ones did not. Demobilization clearly had an impact. So did the role of wartime recruitment in siphoning off many young men before they committed crimes.[49] However it is clear that a considerable proportion of the eighteenth-century population believed that press gangs did indeed make for better justice. They therefore mobilized impressment and enlistment policies either directly, or with the help of a magistrate, as a separate resource that could help them find more suitable ways of dealing with property offenders than those offered by the formal courts. Since the absolute numbers involved were very small in comparison to the large numbers being recruited, this did not, of course, mean that a substantial proportion of recruits were untried criminals,[50] but it may have had an important impact on short-term changes in recorded crime. In order to understand the war/peace rhythms of property crime indictment rates in the eighteenth and early nineteenth centuries the powerful potential of pre-trial enlistment to depress those rates needs to be given much greater weight. In a period such as this, when only a tiny proportion of property offenders were ever formally indicted,[51] the changing prosecution strategies of victims and magistrates, and the role of press gangs within those strategies in wartime, may well have been the key determinants of indictment levels at certain points. War was a judicial resource in eighteenth-century England and press gangs may therefore have had as important a role in shaping recorded crime rates as the peacetime property appropriation practices of poverty-stricken soldiers or sailors.

[49] Briefly discussed in C. Emsley, 'The social impact of the French wars', in H. Dickinson, ed., *Britain and the French Revolution, 1789–1815* (London, 1989), p. 216.

[50] Rodger, *Wooden world*, p. 170; Emsley, *North Riding naval recruits*, pp. 8–12; S. Conway, 'The recruitment of criminals into the British army, 1775–81', *Bulletin of the Institute of Historical Research*, vol. 108 (1985), pp. 46–58.

[51] King, *Crime, justice and discretion*, pp. 132–4.

6   Making the 'bloody code'? Forgery legislation in eighteenth-century England

Randall McGowen

The proponents of legal reform in early nineteenth-century Britain developed a critique of the existing criminal law whose appeal was as much emotional as it was intellectual. The prominent place of the gallows in English justice struck them as morally repugnant. They resorted to a highly charged language in which to express their revulsion. William Wilberforce, in 1819, bemoaned the fact that the nation had been saddled with what he called 'that code of blood'. He meant by this phrase the many statutes that imposed the death penalty for a staggering range of offences. The law, he said, breathed a vindictive spirit. It was at odds with the humane sentiments that represented the true feelings of the English people. So long as the code continued to exist, it would cause anguish to the benevolent, while brutalizing the less civilized portions of the community. The operation of justice, the reformers argued, was perverted by this steady reliance upon death. Piecemeal change would not remedy an institution so fatally flawed. Nothing less than a fundamental transformation of the law would rescue the reputation of the nation.[1]

The advocates of change justified their portrait of the law by appealing to a variety of arguments. They offered examples of the inconsistencies between various capital statutes, and they pointed to the seemingly trivial nature of the offences, as proof of the ills that afflicted the code. There was, however, one 'great fact', which more than any other, exposed at one and the same time the ridiculous and yet also brutal character of this code. It was the large number of crimes made capital in what appeared to be an endless succession of statutes passed during the preceding 100 years. 'A century has passed away', the Evangelical reformer, Thomas Fowell Buxton, told the Commons in 1821, 'marked by nothing so extraordinary in our legislation, as the rapid growth of criminal laws.' Opponents of the code gave much place to the counting of statutes that imposed death.

I would like to thank John Beattie, Peter King, Joanna Innes and Norma Landau for their assistance with this chapter.

[1] *Parliamentary Debates* [hereafter *P.D.*], vol. XXXIX, pp. 82, 808–9.

They presented the total as a figure that spoke for itself. Quantity became a measure of the quality of the legislation, a sure guide to the character of the entire code. 'For two hundred and fifty years', Sir James Mackintosh explained, 'the House had proceeded, year after year, to heap one capital felony upon another.' A petition from the City of London in 1819 declared 'that upwards two hundred crimes very different in their degrees of enormity are equally subject to the punishment of death'. Claiming even greater precision, Buxton, in the same year, announced that he held in his hand 'a list of those offences, which at this moment are capital, in number 223'.[2]

The scale of this legislative activity was supposed to give contemporaries pause. The casualness with which Parliament passed capital statutes earned unflattering remark. One of the few 'inconveniences' that accompanied the triumph of parliamentary government in 1688, Mackintosh told the Commons, was 'the unhappy facility afforded to legislation'. 'Every member of Parliament', he explained, 'has had it in his power to indulge his whims and caprices on that subject'. The criminal laws 'were but the mushroom growth of modern wantonness of legislation'. The result, Buxton added, was the passage of 156 capital statutes since 1715. 'It is a fact', he concluded, 'and a melancholy fact, that there are persons living in this kingdom, at whose birth the criminal code contained less than sixty crimes, and who, in the short space permitted to the life of man, have seen that number quadrupled.'[3] As these passages suggest, the tabulation of the number of capital statutes was no pedantic exercise. It was meant to reinforce a particular interpretation of the criminal law. In one of the more frequently cited summaries, Blackstone characterized the 'multitude of sanguinary laws' as 'a bad symptom of the distemper of any state'. They were, he wrote, 'absurd and impolitic', and implied 'a kind of quackery in government'.[4]

The argument that the criminal law constituted a 'bloody code' became a standard trope of the reform movement. It lost little of its power in its constant repetition. The phrase implied that the makers of the law were insensitive to the value of human life. It hinted at something even darker, a nation with a bloodthirsty disposition, one that delighted in the periodic slaughter at the gallows. Sanguinary laws, the reformers claimed, were the

---

[2] *P.D.*, n.s. vol. V, p. 902; *P.D.*, n.s. vol. IX, p. 400. Sir Leon Radzinowicz begins his massive study, *A history of English criminal law and its administration from 1750* (New York, 1948), with the question of 'the exact number of statutes imposing capital punishment without benefit of clergy' (vol. I, pp. 3–8). See also Douglas Hay, 'Property, authority, and the criminal law', in D. Hay *et al.*, eds., *Albion's fatal tree: crime and society in eighteenth-century England* (New York, 1975), pp. 18–19.

[3] *P.D.*, vol. XXXIX, pp. 787, 808–10; *P.D.*, n.s. vol. IX, p. 405.

[4] William Blackstone, *Commentaries on the laws of England* (Chicago, 1979; reprint of first edition, 1765–9), vol. IV, pp. 17–18.

hallmark of tyrannical regimes and barbaric ages. They were immoral and inhumane, as well as ill-suited to a civilized country. Even an opponent of sweeping reform of the law found himself forced to acknowledge the steady advance of this conclusion. The code, Robert Peel conceded in 1830, might lead other nations to misunderstand the sensibility of the English people. It had, he admitted, become a source of acute embarrassment. 'The multiplication', he granted, 'of this threat in the laws of England has brought on them and the nation a character of harshness and cruelty which evidence of a mild administration of them will not entirely remove'. Peel's fears proved justified; the reformers' polemic fixed in the minds of contemporaries, as well as the work of later scholars, an image of the eighteenth-century legal code.[5] This code appeared to be monolithic, the same in content and origin throughout its vast extent. At the very least, the legislators who created it were accused of inattention to the dictates of reason; at worst they stood condemned of basic inhumanity, since they were so ready to sacrifice the lives of the poor to protect all forms of property. 'It is significant', Radzinowicz writes, 'that practically all capital offences were created more or less as a matter of course by a placid and uninterested Parliament.'[6] So compelling was this portrait of the law that for many years scholars uncritically accepted that the 'bloody code' offered a key to understanding the eighteenth century.

In this chapter I want to examine the validity of these conclusions about the 'bloody code'. I will do so by considering the 'brute fact' that loomed so large in the debates, the great number of capital statutes, the majority of them created in the eighteenth century.[7] In particular, I will investigate the category that produced the most legislative activity, that of forgery. The crime might well seem the quintessential offence of the long eighteenth century. Judges, with tedious regularity, intoned against the danger presented by the crime. Legal aids devoted many pages to listing the vast number of different statutes that dealt with the subject. Scarcely a session of Parliament passed without some act dealing with it. By some estimates forgery accounted for a third of the capital legislation of the period.[8] Peel, in 1830, reported that of some 120 statutes dealing

---

[5] *P.D.*, n.s. vol. XXIII, p. 1181; Peel's summary became Radzinowicz's conclusion, *History of English criminal law*, vol. I, p. 35.

[6] Radzinowicz, *History of English criminal law*, vol. I, p. 35.

[7] The phrase is used by David Lieberman, *The province of legislation determined* (Cambridge, 1989), pp. 28, 13–17.

[8] Thomas Dogherty, *The crown circuit assistant* (London, 1787), pp. 360–2; see the preface, written by Capel Loftt, to John Jebb's *Thoughts on the construction and polity of prisons* (London, 1786), pp. 37–92. 'I believe', Blackstone noted, 'through the number of these general and special provisions, there is now hardly a case possible to conceive, wherein forgery, that tends to defraud, whether in the name of a real or fictitious person, is not made a capital crime.' *Commentaries*, vol. IV, p. 247.

with forgery, 61 inflicted the death penalty. Even this count, he admitted, was imperfect, since each measure usually 'comprehended five distinct offences', such as the making or uttering of forged instruments.[9]

Historians confronted by this mass of forgery legislation have seldom stopped to investigate in detail the content of these measures. They have seen their occurrence as a natural consequence of the increasing use of paper instruments in an ever expanding financial economy. Most often they assume the homogeneity of such legislation, the more easily to enlist the frequency of these measures in support of their theories about the character of the capital code. 'As the decades passed', writes Douglas Hay, 'the maturing trade, commerce, and industry of England spawned more laws to protect particular kinds of property.' 'New forms of economic activity and commercial organization', argues John Langbein, in an essay otherwise at odds with Hay's, 'gave rise to new issues of definition.'[10] Despite recent criticism of such sweeping generalizations about the character and shape of the 'bloody code', the astounding number of capital statutes seems to weigh in the balance against such revisionism.[11]

A close examination of the legislative history of forgery will call these conclusions into question, even as it presents us with new paradoxes to resolve. The focus upon the simple number of statutes, I will argue, not only misleads us about the nature of the 'bloody code', it also obscures

---

[9] *P.D.*, n.s. vol. XXIII, p. 1179. Peel, like so many other participants in the debates over the criminal laws, relied upon the evidence gathered by the Select Committee on the Criminal Law of 1824. This committee was appointed on the motion of the criminal law reformer, Stephen Lushington, and much of the work was carried out by Anthony Hammond, a proponent of the rationalization of the law. It focused upon forgery for investigation because the crime had become a flashpoint for the heated debates over the capital code. Though the report seems to present a dry and exhaustive catalogue of forgery legislation, this presentation succeeded in emphasizing familiar reform themes. Hammond made no effort to explain why the legislation had been passed. Instead, he demonstrated how difficult it was to get a clear picture of how the law stood. The evidence all went to enforce one conclusion, that the law with respect to forgery was ill-drawn; it was a tangle of contradictory measures, of doing and undoing, without rhyme or reason. He discovered the staggering number of 382 measures dealing with forgery, down to 1822. He presented these acts in such a way as to reinforce the sense that the issue belonged to arcane legal scholarship, and that it was absurd that on the basis of such technicalities, human lives stood in peril. Radzinowicz, *History of English criminal law*, vol. I, p. 576; *Parliamentary Papers* [hereafter *P.P.*] (1824) (205) IV.

[10] Hay, 'Property, authority', p. 21; John Langbein, 'Albion's fatal flaws', *Past and Present*, no. 98 (1983), pp. 115–19; Joanna Innes and John Styles, 'The crime wave: recent writing on crime and criminal justice in eighteenth-century England', in A. Wilson, ed., *Rethinking social history: English society 1570–1920 and its interpretation* (Manchester, 1993), p. 246.

[11] Innes and Styles, 'Crime wave', pp. 240–50; John Beattie, 'London crime and the making of the "bloody code", 1689–1718', in L. Davison *et al.*, eds., *Stilling the grumbling hive: the response to social and economic problems in England, 1689–1750* (Stroud and New York, 1992), pp. 49–71; Langbein, 'Albion's fatal flaws', pp. 115–19.

other interesting issues raised by these measures. Forgery legislation was not all of a piece. For instance, while some forgeries were punished capitally, others earned a fine or the pillory. The vast bulk of forgery statutes dealt with a relatively narrow range of instruments. These measures had no particular connection to the changing forms of 'economic activity'. On the other hand, they do seem to express a particular logic, to possess a certain coherence; they do not seem to be random or haphazard creations. Perhaps most disconcerting is the fact that this sustained legislative activity appears to be unconnected with the actual occurrence of the crime. Only a handful of prosecutions were carried out under the terms of these statutes. The picture presented by this contradictory history ill-accords with the expectations raised by the phrase, the 'bloody code'.

Yet in this chapter I want to do something more than offer another caveat about the unreliability of sweeping generalizations concerning eighteenth-century criminal justice. I want to suggest that all this legislative activity, apparently so narrow and inconsequential, really does have a story to tell us. If the passage of the overwhelming majority of forgery statutes was mechanical, it was not without meaning. This story, however, concerns the security of the fiscal-military state and the distinction drawn between threats to the public, as opposed to the private, financial integrity of the nation. Much of the support for this interpretation comes from a careful analysis of the content of forgery legislation as well as attention paid to the chronology of its passage. Forgery became a capital crime in the 1690s. The government, during this period, assigned the death penalty as a punishment for the counterfeiting of a small range of symbolically charged instruments which represented the revolution in state finance. It would be several decades before Parliament, in 1729, extended a similar protection to 'private' paper. Treasury bureaucrats, the custodians of the new finance, oversaw both the regular reenactment as well as the gradual extension of the capital provisions in succeeding decades. In doing so, they were motivated by a concern for the vulnerability of a state whose strength seemed peculiarly dependent on the integrity of its system of finance. The large volume of capital legislation testifies to the intensity of this concern.

If the history of forgery appears to be a story of the late seventeenth and eighteenth centuries, this was scarcely because earlier periods had no knowledge of the crime. Forgery at common law, Blackstone wrote, was 'the fraudulent making or alteration of a writing to the prejudice of another man's right'. It could be punished with 'fine, imprisonment, and pillory'.[12] The crucial, early statute dealing with the offence was an

---

[12] Blackstone, *Commentaries*, vol. IV, p. 245.

Elizabethan act of 1563. In that year Parliament passed a general measure which took as its subject 'forging and publishing false and untrue characters, evidences, deeds and writings'. 'Evil people', it complained, were tempted by the light punishment to commit various frauds. The statute acknowledged the increased importance of written documents, even as it expressed concern about their vulnerability. It sought, first and foremost, to protect legal records and documents concerned with the ownership and transfer of land, but it covered commercial instruments as well. It was a broad act, a bold effort on the part of government to confront new forms of deceit. It proposed as a penalty that upon conviction the offender should pay double costs and damages. The act also ordered that the transgressor should be 'set upon the pillory in some open market town or other open place'. This punishment was intended both to shame the criminal and publicize his guilt. For a second offence, an individual was made liable to death.[13] The statute proved remarkably flexible and durable. Judges co-operated in extending its terms to cover the new forms of commercial paper that multiplied in the century and a half after its passage. Most forgeries of private paper, down to 1729, were prosecuted under its terms.

Subsequent to the Elizabethan measure, forgery attracted little attention until the end of the seventeenth century. The 1824 parliamentary committee that investigated the criminal laws counted only eleven acts mentioning the crime before 1688, and most of these offences were treated as misdemeanours. The dramatic increase both in the number of forgery statutes and the severity of the punishment followed the Revolution; the reigns of William III and Anne saw the passage of twenty-nine acts dealing with the crime. The pace of legislation quickened over the following decades. Fifty-four acts during the reigns of George I and George II dealt with forgery, and that total was overshadowed by the 278 enacted during the sixty years of George III's reign.[14] Not all of this legislation treated the particular instance of forgery as felony, nor did it uniformly impose the death penalty. Still, these numbers suggest two conclusions: that the last years of the seventeenth century saw a remarkable change in the attitude towards the crime, and that the concern with the

[13] 5 Elizabeth c. 14; John Guy, *Tudor England* (Oxford, 1990), pp. 327–9; G. R. Elton, *The parliament of England, 1559–1581* (Cambridge, 1986), pp. 96–7, 107, 277–9; Adam Fox, 'Custom, memory and the authority of writing', in P. Griffiths *et al.*, eds., *The experience of authority in early modern England* (New York, 1996), pp. 89–92. For a failed effort to pass forgery legislation, see David Dean, *Law-making and society in late Elizabethan England* (Cambridge, 1996), pp. 72–3.
[14] *P.P.* (1824) (205) IV. There are good reasons for thinking that Hammond's statistics do not represent all instances where forgery was mentioned in legislation. It was difficult to 'count' forgery statutes precisely because penal clauses were often deeply buried within long measures primarily concerned with other matters. Many of these acts simply reenacted earlier legislation.

crime, at least as measured by legislative activity, remained high well into the nineteenth century.

When we look closely at the forgery legislation passed shortly after 1688, what is most striking is its political rather than commercial character. The financial crisis of the state, rather than any threat to commercial instruments, produced the heightened anxiety about forgery. The issue arose because of changes introduced in public finance. The wars inaugurated by William and his ministers confronted England with unparalleled challenges. Charles Davenant traced the problem to the altered nature of war in the late seventeenth century. 'For war', he wrote, 'is quite changed from what it was in the time of our forefathers, when in a hasty expedition, and a pitched field, the matter was decided by courage; but now the whole art of war is in a manner reduced to money; and now-a-days, that prince who, can best find money to feed, cloath, and pay his army, not he that has the most valiant troops, is surest of success and conquest.'[15] By 1693 the king's ministers desperately sought new sources of funding. They did so in a charged political environment, where politicians were deeply divided over the consequences of various forms of taxation and faced mounting suspicion of new financial interests. The political stakes of the controversy were high, involving both the legitimacy and the practical survival of the new regime. Politicians were acutely aware of the challenges to its authority. The debate over war finance was fierce; it provides the necessary background to understand the penalty imposed for a select class of forgeries.[16]

In this difficult situation the government pursued a number of different strategies, some of them suggested by 'projectors', for raising revenue. They looked to Dutch models for inspiration. In 1694 they created the 'Million Lottery' and offered annuities on generous terms. That year also saw the creation of the Bank of England. Parliament heatedly debated new excises and duties. While there was some discussion of the idea of a general excise, politicians backed away from the scheme because it was thought likely to provoke unrest. Even as M.P.s wrestled with these proposals, authors like Davenant cautioned that it was important to discover a form of taxation that would not weigh unduly upon the nation, one that would not impoverish the poor or burden too heavily the land.[17]

---

[15] *The political and commercial works of Charles D'avenant* (London, 1771), vol. I, p. 16; Craig Rose, *England in the 1690s* (Oxford, 1999), pp. 132–7.

[16] Bruce Carruthers, *City of capital: politics and markets in the English financial revolution* (Princeton, 1996), especially chap. 8.

[17] John Brewer, *The sinews of power: war, money and the English state, 1688–1783* (New York, 1989), pp. 143–54; J. V. Beckett, 'Land tax or excise: the levying of taxation in seventeenth- and eighteenth-century England', *English Historical Review*, vol. 100 (1985), pp. 298–9.

In the midst of this controversy the government considered several duties on selected goods. In December 1693 it secured an excise on salt. A proposal for a duty on leather, however, faced considerable opposition and was voted down. During the spring of 1694 a bill was discussed for imposing a duty on fine paper. The plan seems to have been proposed by James Isaakson and John Kynvin, men who later occupied positions in the revenue office. In the context of such sensitivity to the public perception of taxes, the measure had much to recommend it. It would fall more heavily upon the rich than the poor, and it would tap the wealth of the urban professional and commercial classes more than the landed interest. The Commons ordered the Solicitor General to prepare a bill on 7 April, and it was presented to the House on 11 April. Its preamble announced the special circumstances that required its passage. 'Great and present expense in the necessary defence of your realm' demanded extraordinary fiscal measures. The act called for the creation of commissioners to oversee the collection of the duty, and among their responsibilities was the provision of marks or stamps to signify the payment of the levy. It further stipulated that any person guilty of forging such a mark or stamp to defraud their majesties would suffer death without benefit of clergy. The measure was limited to four years, but it was renewed in 1698, when duties were doubled; eventually it became a regular feature of eighteenth-century revenue. Initially the legislation produced consternation, especially within the legal community. 'The act for taxing paper and parchment', one contemporary noted, 'by reason of its intricate penning hath caused much busle with us and the Judges are now consulting to put out some explanatory rules.' It was 'much exclaimed against'. Paper-makers and stationers petitioned Parliament, complaining that it would discourage English manufacturing and throw hundreds out of work. The protests were futile. The measure soon proved its value; by 1697, Narcissus Luttrell reported, it had raised over £55,000.[18]

[18] *House of Commons Journals* [hereafter *C.J.*], vol. XI, pp. 153, 157; 5 William & Mary c. 21, s. 11; Edward Hughes, 'The English stamp duties, 1664–1764', *English Historical Review*, vol. 56 (1941), pp. 234–64; Brewer, *Sinews of power*, pp. 114–22; P. G. M. Dickson, *The financial revolution in England* (London, 1967), pp. 52–3; D. W. Jones, *War and economy in the age of William III and Marlborough* (Oxford, 1988), pp. 95–126; Henry Horwitz, *Parliament, policy and politics in the reign of William III* (Newark, Del., 1977), pp. 111, 128–31, 150, 166–7; J. Keith Horsefield, *British monetary experiments, 1650–1710* (Cambridge, Mass., 1960), p. 124; Henry Roseveare, *The financial revolution, 1660–1760* (London, 1991), pp. 48–9; *The Portledge papers* (London, 1928), p. 180; Narcissus Luttrell, *A brief historical relation of state affairs* (Oxford, 1857), vol. III, pp. 308, 311, 319, 323, 334, vol. IV, p. 256; J. A. Heraud, *A digest of the stamp laws* (London, 1801), p. 19. When Thomas Neale secured his act for creating a lottery, 5 William & Mary c. 7, one section declared that forgery of a ticket was a felony.

What remains to be explained is why the death penalty came to be affixed to this measure. The most obvious parallel was to coining. The stamp employed the royal seal or insignia. Thus its abuse could be seen as an assault upon majesty. Forgery of a stamp, like coining, as Blackstone said of the latter crime, infringed 'the king's prerogative' and involved 'assuming one of the attributes of the sovereign'. 'Besides', he wrote of coining, 'as all money which bears the stamp of the kingdom is sent into the world upon public faith ... whoever falsifies this is an offender against the state, by contributing to render that public faith suspected.' The analogy to coining would have been particularly acute in the 1690s, when the government was preoccupied with the threat of coining and clipping. Parliament passed several measures increasing the penalties for abuses of the coin, and a regular procession of coiners died on the gallows during these years.[19] This sense of urgency was no doubt sharpened by the mounting financial crisis that gripped the government. There were high expectations of the paper duty yield. Any threat to these returns would imperil the confidence necessary to sustain government borrowing. 'For the further security', Davenant wrote, 'the laws likewise inflict severe punishments upon those who defraud him in his stores, treasure, or revenue, counting such public robbers more criminal than petty and common thieves.'[20]

From the first, however, paper, and the stamp affixed to it, carried a heavier load of significance. Even as the stamp represented an effort to make the paper economy bear some of the cost of the war, the mark itself helped to lend legitimacy to the instrument, thus becoming one of the tokens of its authenticity. The stamp sought not only to benefit from the spread of paper, whether as financial instrument or newspaper, but to regulate it as well. Forgery subverted this effort. The crime was all the more disturbing because it was recognized early on that the perpetrators would come from the ranks of the respectable. Shopkeepers, merchants, lawyers and even government administrators were among the people who possessed the skill to commit the crime and were in a position to do so. These various considerations suggest that there was a symbolic dimension to this offence that seemed to contemporaries to demand a more severe penalty. There was much suspicion of the paper economy associated with the changes in war finance. Paper instruments stood opposed to the solidity and authority of the land. Paper was a metonymy for the new

---

[19] Blackstone, *Commentaries*, vol. IV, p. 88; *cf.* Luttrell, *Brief historical relation*, vol. III, pp. 255, 276, 299; Rose, *England in the 1690s*, pp. 137–41. One projector proposed a scheme for the government to issue bills of credit to cover short-term debt. He suggested that counterfeiting the bills should be treated the same as coining. *A proposal for the more easie advancing the crown any fixed sum of money* (London, 1695), pp. 1–2.

[20] *Works of D'avenant*, vol. III, p. 6.

economy, centred upon London, which transformed the real wealth of the country into debt and transferred income from the landed to new classes. The stamp was not only an attempt to tap the wealth of these classes, it was a measure to assert control over an undisciplined dimension of the economy.[21]

The preoccupation with forgery connected with government finance continued into 1696 when the government, faced with the greatest financial crisis of the war, searched for new expedients to carry the nation through the troubles. Mordecai Abbot, cashier of the customs, offered a plan to create Exchequer bills that would circulate in small denominations, and so ease the liquidity problem. Amidst debate over the measure for creating a National Land Bank as a rival to the Bank of England, an amendment to the measure authorized the Exchequer to issue such bills. At the same time it was made a capital offence to counterfeit these notes. No doubt concern about the extent of the crisis, and a deep uneasiness about how precarious the entire venture was, help to explain the seriousness of the penalty. Charles Montagu, Chancellor of the Exchequer, expressed doubts about the success of this manoeuvre, but also felt that he had no other recourse. 'Tis the most difficult thing', he wrote, 'yt was ever brought about.' Not the least of his worries was the rumour that advocates of the Land Bank sought to undermine the bills in order to advance their own scheme. In May he added that 'the Exchequer Bills do as well as could be expected from so new a thing, under great opposition, but Wee are almost at the end of our Tedder in them'.[22] The uneasiness mounted when the ministers discovered a scheme by several revenue cashiers to alter Exchequer bills in order to defraud the government of interest due. The crime so disturbed the government that the King himself 'declared he will sitt in the treasury, and hear the villainy of these matters'. Although the crime had every appearance of being a simple fraud, officials were so sensitive that they scented a conspiracy. Luttrell reported the rumour that 'greater persons have been concerned with them to destroy the credit of the nation'.[23]

[21] J. G. A. Pocock, *Virtue, commerce, and history: essays on political thought and history, chiefly in the eighteenth century* (Cambridge, 1985), pp. 103–23.

[22] 7 & 8 William III c. 31; *C.J.*, vol. XI, p. 673; Dickson, *Financial revolution*, pp. 52–3, 365–9; Horwitz, *Parliament, policy*, pp. 176–7; P. G. M. Dickson, 'War finance, 1689–1714', in J. S. Bromley, ed., *The new Cambridge modern history*, vol. VI (Cambridge, 1970), pp. 287–93. It is no doubt a reflection of the mounting concern with the crime that forgery of the seals of both the proposed Land Bank and the Bank of England were declared to be felony.

[23] The discovery of a conspiracy to forge stamps in 1697 hinted at a Jacobite plot to undermine the credit of the government. One of the participants, a non-juring parson, denied any criminal intent. He had only meant, he said, 'to prejudice King William's government'. Luttrell, *Brief historical relation*, vol. IV, pp. 201, 248, 265, 282, 292–6, 302, 305, 328; Dickson, *Financial revolution*, p. 369.

The next flurry of capital statutes dealing with forgery came in 1710–11, during a period of renewed financial uncertainty. The build-up of debt, along with agricultural distress and stalemate on the battlefield, meant trouble for government accounts. The sense of peril found expression in a Commons resolution that⌈whoever design'd by endeavours to lessen the publick credit, especially at a time when the kingdom is threatened with an invasion, is guilty of a high crime and misdemeanour, and an enemy to her majestie and the kingdom'.[24]⌋First Godolphin and then Harley wrestled with the mounting problems. By 1711 Harley faced mounting arrears of navy, victualling and transport debentures, without any established funds devoted to their repayment. He also had to cope with a residue of mistrust of the new ministry. Among the various fiscal measures proposed, acts dealing with stamps for insurance policies and marks upon hides, and culminating in a long statute concerning stamps on such items as playing cards and dice, all imposed death for the forging of these stamps or marks. This legislation was not casually created. These were government acts drawn with the advice of bureaucrats and the crown's legal advisors.[25]

It is worth taking a moment to consider the scope of forgery legislation down to 1715. There is little evidence of a more general panic about forgery. Parliament did not hasten to apply the ultimate penalty to all of the instances of the crime that came up for consideration. The acts did not touch the private instruments that constituted the bulk of commercial transactions. Nor did they all impose the death penalty. In 1703 and 1706 Parliament passed measures for the better registration of deeds in Yorkshire. It did so because of complaints about moneylenders, whose shady practices with regard to loans raised on estates had 'ruined' many families. The statutes specifically invoked the Elizabethan forgery act when mentioning the penalty for forging any 'memorial or certificate' covered by the new legislation.[26] Other revenue measures imposed a variety of lesser penalties, usually fines, for tampering with official marks. Acts which generated far more money, such as those that dealt with salt or malt, wine or spirits, levied fines for frauds in connection with records or certificates. This tended to be true of regulations concerning the customs as well. A statute which addressed the frauds of 'Scotch men' in trade with the American plantations established a £500 fine for counterfeiting a

---

[24] Luttrell, *Brief historical relation*, vol. VI, p. 281.

[25] Dickson, *Financial revolution*, pp. 361–3; David Macpherson, *Annals of commerce* (London, 1805), vol. III, pp. 18–23; B. W. Hill, *Robert Harley* (New Haven, 1988), pp. 134–45.

[26] 2 & 3 Anne c. 4, s. 19; 5 Anne c. 18, s. 8; for a similar act for Middlesex, see 7 Anne c. 20, s. 15. Neither the act for the better payment of the inland bill of exchange, 9 & 10 William III c. 17, nor the parallel measure to provide a like remedy for promissory notes, 3 & 4 Anne c. 9, raised the problem of forgery.

permit. An act imposing a duty on silk warned that any who 'should alter, counterfeit, or misapply' the 'seals or marks now used ... at the custom house', for each offence should forfeit £500 and stand in the pillory for two hours. More interesting still, a measure concerning navy pay set fines for those who impersonated seamen or forged certificates to secure pay.[27] This pattern suggests that the legislators who made particular forgeries capital possessed a narrow view of what instances they intended to cover, that they had in view the protection of instruments that represented new public finance.

This conclusion is reinforced by a surprising comparison between the treatment of the stamp duty on paper and the instruments of the Bank of England. The act creating the Bank in 1694 made no specific provision for protection of the notes it issued. Such a proposal was discussed at the time, but it was withdrawn, perhaps because the development of the Bank itself was so controversial a measure.[28] Yet within a year of its creation, the directors of the Bank debated the alarming discovery of several forged notes. The four men responsible for the episode were fined and sentenced to stand in the pillory. Still, the directors were not content with this outcome. They ordered their subordinates to undertake a series of measures, largely administrative, to deal with the challenge. They required, for instance, that no more printed notes be issued for the time being. By December 1695 they were considering special directions for how their notes might be printed and the use of a 'peculiar sort of paper' as ways of making their instruments more secure. Evidently some of the directors doubted that these measures were adequate. When Parliament took up consideration of a Bank bill in 1697, the directors recommended adding a chapter dealing with the forgery of its notes. The court also ordered that the deputy governor and five other directors attend the Commons, 'from time to time', to observe the passage of the measure. Finally, they suggested consulting the Attorney-General for advice in drawing up its provisions.[29]

The actual discussion in Parliament took place at a time of great fiscal uncertainty, when petitions like that from Colchester flooded in from all over the country, calling for some way to 'be found out to enable the Bank of England to pay their bills, as formerly they have done'. Thus the Bank's own concerns for the security of their issue coincided with public anxiety that their circulation be protected. In February the Commons addressed a series of resolutions, one in particular complaining of 'late frauds and

---

[27] 7 & 8 William III c. 22; 9 & 10 William III c. 43, s. 5; 9 & 10 William III c. 41, s. 3.
[28] *C.J.*, vol. XI, p. 162.
[29] Bank of England, *Court of Directors*, B, pp. 60–4, 84–5; W. Marston Acres, *The Bank of England from within* (Oxford, 1931), vol. I, pp. 58–9.

cheats' and calling for greater care to be taken to prevent them. Much of the subsequent statute, which was extensively debated before its passage, dealt with the organization of the Bank and the revenues to be devoted to paying off its loans. It was a long act, and only in section 36 did it address the problem of forgery. There it announced that any forgery of the seal of the Bank, or of sealed Bank bills, 'or of any Bank note of any sort whatsoever', was made felony without benefit of clergy.[30] The point here is that the Bank did not automatically secure special treatment of its paper; rather it took the peculiar circumstances of financial crisis touching the state for the security of Bank notes to be presented as a public rather than simply a private concern.

This episode established a pattern with respect to the Bank and forgery that would be repeated on other occasions over the next century. Although Parliament had accepted the argument that Bank paper was a public matter, in other respects the Bank's legislative history is distinct. The number of statutes dealing with Bank forgeries was small compared to the flood of legislation arising from the revenue. The former were invariably a response to a specific instance of forgery, most often in the form of legal doubts expressed by the judges during the prosecution of a case. The Bank measures were crafted by its solicitors, at the order of the directors, and they were carried through Parliament with the careful attention of its 'friends'. For instance, in the wake of a clever alteration of a Bank note perpetrated by Francis Kite in 1724, the directors advised 'the governor to endeavour to get a clause inserted in the bill' then under consideration in the Commons concerning the reduction of Bank funds. The section strengthened the language which made any alteration of its notes punishable by death.[31] In 1764 the numerous frauds committed by the stock broker, John Rice, led to legislation clarifying the law with respect to the forgery of powers of attorney. Similarly, the discovery of forged stock transfers in 1792 caused the Bank to lobby for a new bill to punish capitally company employees found guilty of such offences.[32]

The 1697 Bank statute produced a gradual transformation in the way 'public' corporations, at least those with a significant stake in the nation's financial health, were regarded. It was no doubt by analogy to the Bank that the South Sea Company, in 1711, secured in its charter a clause making the forgery of its seal capital. By 1719 the protection was broadened to include its receipts or the warrants for its dividends. In the same year

---

[30] Bank of England, *Court of Directors*, B, pp. 207–8; *C.J.*, vol. XI, pp. 688, 698, 721–2; 8 & 9 William III c. 20.

[31] Bank of England, *Court of Directors*, K, p. 92. For a summary of the cases that led to this statute, see Acres, *Bank of England*, vol. I, pp. 120–6.

[32] Acres, *Bank of England*, vol. I, pp. 177–8, 186–7, 252–3.

the forgery of the seals, or of any policy, bill, bond, or obligation issued by the two assurance companies became capital.[33] The calamity of the South Sea Bubble, with the revelations that followed of sordid transactions among those dealing in stocks, resulted in a significant expansion of the law regarding the forgery of stock-related instruments. Although the impetus came from the discovery of several crimes against the South Sea Company, the statute that followed sought to reach any of those who dealt in the stocks of the public companies, especially lawyers and stock brokers. 'Whereas of late divers frauds and abuses have been committed', the preamble read, 'by forging and counterfeiting the hands of some of the proprietors of the shares and of the capital stock and funds' of corporations 'established by act ... of Parliament', forging hands of people entitled to annuities or dividends was declared to be capital. In the wake of another forgery, a measure of 1725 announced that the counterfeiting of East India or South Sea bonds was punishable by death.[34] These measures did not, by any means, cover all forms of paper employed by these corporations. The legislation tended to arise out of individual episodes, and to reflect an immediate alarm, especially with regard to the abuses of those who dealt with the paper that represented the debts of the nation.

The surprising point is how little of the paper circulation of the country was touched by these measures. The vast majority of forgeries prosecuted at the Old Bailey during these years concerned the promissory notes, bills of exchange, and bonds of private individuals or those new creatures, the bankers. They continued to be prosecuted as misdemeanours under the terms of the Elizabethan statute. William Hawkins, in 1724, acknowledged the distinction in his treatment of the crime. He dealt with 'offences by counterfeiters of Bank-notes, Exchequer-bills, Stamps, South Sea bonds, Lottery orders' in one chapter, and all other species of forgery in a later section dealing with misdemeanours.[35] Despite the flurry of parliamentary activity over the previous forty years, most paper instruments continued to be treated as distinct from the public paper that had aroused the protective instincts of government officials. The bulk of the mercantile and financial community continued, with no apparent distress, to employ a statute whose primary penalty consisted of a fine, the pillory, and, occasionally, a term in prison.

This situation changed dramatically in 1729, when a sweeping statute transformed the treatment of the forgery of 'private' instruments. The

[33] 9 Anne c. 21, s. 57; 6 George I c. 11, s. 50; 6 George I c. 18, s. 13.
[34] 8 George I c. 22, s. 1; 12 George I c. 32, s. 9; Dickson, *Financial revolution*, pp. 463–4.
[35] William Hawkins, *A treatise of the pleas of the crown* (New York, 1972), chap. 58, 'Of offences by counterfeiters of bank-notes, exchequer-bills, stamps, South-Sea bonds, lottery-orders', chap. 70, 'Of forgery', pp. 123–4, 182–7.

previous year a well-connected banker and speculator had perpetrated forgeries worth thousands of pounds upon several members of Parliament. The government acted decisively; within months the Lord Chancellor introduced in the Lords a brief measure whose purpose was to make a wide range of offences capital. This act followed the lines of the Elizabethan statute; it was general and inclusive, seeking to encompass all paper instruments that might be said to represent money, in addition to deeds and wills. In this way it stood in sharp contrast to the specificity of the forgery measures since 1688. The act, carefully crafted by the crown's legal advisors, in effect redefined the meaning and significance of private finance, as well as its relationship to public credit. In other words, it punished the forgery of private instruments capitally, less because of the injury done to individuals, than out of a fear about the threat posed by such frauds to the entire interconnected structure of public and private finance. The extraordinary instance of forgery in 1728 had focused an awareness of the public consequences of private credit that arose out of the debate surrounding the collapse of the South Sea Bubble. This new sensitivity was most marked among the judges, who solemnly referred to the relationship as they sentenced offenders to death in subsequent years. As was the case with the sixteenth-century statute, judicial interpretation gave this act great flexibility. The twelve judges were regularly asked to rule upon its application; they uniformly supported its intent. Just as consistently the crown turned aside appeals, leaving the condemned, in cases of forgery, to suffer at the gallows.[36]

The 1729 act became the century's most important piece of forgery legislation. With this statute, as judicial review soon made clear, eighteenth-century England possessed a potent weapon against forgery. 'The statute of Elizabeth', Edward East explained, 'has now fallen into disuse since the passing of the statute 2 George II c. 25, which extends to all deeds and wills, upon which the prosecution is easier and the punishment is capital in the first instance.' In 1734, following a dispute arising from a forgery prosecution, a statute added the word 'alter' to the list of actions subject to the death penalty. And in 1736, after a brief lapse, the measure was made permanent, because, in the words of the act, it had been 'found useful and beneficial to the public'.[37]

Despite the passage of this 'useful' measure, the tide of forgery legislation did not ebb. Indeed, what is most striking about the statistics derived

---

[36] 2 George II c. 25. For a fuller discussion of the circumstances surrounding the passage of this measure, see my article, 'From pillory to gallows: the punishment of forgery in the age of the financial revolution', *Past and Present*, no. 165 (1999), pp. 107–40.

[37] Edward Hyde East, *Pleas of the crown* (London, 1972), vol. II, p. 919; 7 George II c. 24; 9 George II c. 18.

from the 1824 report is that the pace accelerated after 1760. Before this date one or two statutes a year might be passed. There were several years when no measure dealing with the crime was enacted. But in 1763 five acts with provisions touching forgery became law, four in 1765, and four again in 1769. Even more dramatic increases followed; there were seven measures in 1783, and ten in 1785. The character of this legislation remained unchanged; only the volume increased. Of course in part this increase was simply the consequence of revenue legislation coming up for consideration on a more regular basis. In some instances, as a new commodity became subject to a duty, forging the stamp or mark representing payment became a crime. For instance, in the last years of the century legislation made it a capital crime to forge the stamp for the duty on hats or for a clerkship for attornies. Few of these measures attracted much attention. The penalty, again, could vary widely. Forging a customs permit for selling tea was punished with transportation for ten years. In 1786 there were ten statutes passed which imposed some penalty for forgery. Not one of these measures was new. Parliament voted to renew duties on such items as paper, hair powder, starch, and wine. The measures were long, complicated, and dull. Peel, in a discussion of the law with respect to forgery in 1830, offered the example of the Land Tax as an illustration of the familiar process. 'In that Act', he related, 'there were 200 separate clauses, although only one of them related to forgery, but then that clause, the 194th section, overruled and referred to the whole of the other clauses, and expressly declared, that the penalty affixed to the crime of forgery attached to forging the documents referred to in the preceding clauses.'[38] Legal authors emphasized the extent to which the punishment had become a matter of routine. In acts that raised different loans, W. O. Russell noted, 'common clauses have usually been inserted, in substance nearly the same, by which it is made a capital offence to forge certificates, debentures, receipts, etc'.[39]

Much of this activity, the frequent reenactment of fiscal legislation as well as the gradual expansion of penal sanctions, simply testified to the growth of government bureaucracy, especially in its revenue branches, that was a product of the wars of William III and Anne. These offices required and soon secured a high level of professional skill. 'A new duty', one author wrote, 'requires the constant application of men of the best judgment, integrity and industry who are not loaded with

---

[38] *P.D.*, n.s. vol. XXIII, pp. 1177–9.

[39] W. O. Russell, *A treatise on crimes and misdemeanors* (London, 1819), vol. II, p. 1529. 'The stamp laws', Chitty wrote, 'being so intricate ... [were] consequently some times misunderstood, even at the head office.' J. Chitty, *A practical treatise on the stamp laws* (London, 1829), p. v.

greater concerns but have time and leisure as well to contrive proper methods, as also for the exact levying thereof.' The administrators responsible for managing these duties frequently served long terms, and they often moved from one office to another as needed. William Bridges, 'first secretary to the new Stamp Office in 1694 ... was still in the same post thirty years later'. When Harley launched the new Leather Office in 1711, he turned to George Townshend, who had served on the Excise Board since 1699, for help.[40] These officials, with long experience and a departmental perspective, assumed increasing responsibility for fiscal legislation. In 1734 William Pulteney pointed out that it was skilled civil servants who drew up money bills. 'The Treasury', one source noted, 'seldom gave itself much trouble about the formation of bills of revenue but left it generally to the respective public boards to frame them.' Although the normal rule was for the punishment section of statutes to be left blank, to be filled in during committee discussion, this does not seem to have been true in these cases. Peel, in 1830, reported that each department brought in, 'with very little consideration, an Act to punish forgeries applicable to their own business'. By the early nineteenth century the number of such statutes was staggering. The Customs alone, Peel suggested, had '360 acts connected with that department'.[41] The portrait we get is of nervous administrators with a highly developed sense of departmental interest and jealous of any threat to the collection of their respective duties. They may also have been ready to magnify any instance of forgery into a threat to the security of the nation.

It would, however, be a mistake to assume that the death penalty was attached to forgery simply out of habit or in measures that were never subject to discussion. Capital provisions sometimes appeared in acts that attracted a great deal of scrutiny by Parliament. For instance, Hardwicke's Marriage Act made it capital to forge entries in marriage registers. Here, no doubt, the act simply fell into line with other statutes meant to secure the integrity of legal records. Still, the statute was drawn up with care, and it is unlikely that there was anything casual about the choice of

---

[40] Quoted in Edward Hughes, *Studies in administration and finance, 1558–1825* (Manchester, 1934), p. 198. In recognition of the increased responsibilities connected with their office, 'the Commissioners of the Stamp Office got a raise of £100 a year after the imposition of new stamp duties by Parliament in 1712'. Geoffrey Holmes, *Augustan England: professions, state and society, 1680–1730* (London, 1982), pp. 243–5, 258; Brewer, *Sinews of power*, pp. 64–85.

[41] Dickson, *Financial revolution*, p. 20; Hughes, *Studies in administration*, pp. 232–5; *P.D.*, n.s. vol. XXIII, pp. 1177–9. The best discussion of stamp duties and their administration remains that of J. E. D. Binney, *British public finance and administration, 1774–92* (Oxford, 1958), pp. 41–5.

punishment.[42] In 1807 the act for the abolition of the slave trade made it capital to forge certificates in order to secure a bounty for slaves taken in war. While the motive was the familiar one of protecting the revenue, the chapter occurred in a statute that was the focus of intense debate.[43] A statute of 1773 dealing with the retailing of spiritous liquors also announced that it was intended to address doubts arising with respect to the status of excise stamps. It reenacted the death penalty for the counterfeiting of stamps connected with the commodities named in earlier legislation.[44] The point here is that there were a number of occasions when politicians gave the issue of forgery serious consideration, and when they deliberately applied the death penalty to the crime. Bureaucrats may have been responsible for the bulk of forgery statutes, but upon those occasions when the measures came in for careful attention, Parliament endorsed the punishment.

When East came to summarize the law with respect to forgery in the early nineteenth century, he pointed to the central concern that continued to govern much of the legislation that dealt with the crime. 'Stamps denoting payment of certain duties are required by various acts of parliament to be affixed on a multiplicity of written and printed documents.' 'For the purpose of protecting the revenue from fraud in counterfeiting, uttering, or vending the same', he explained, the offences had been made capital. East wrote in 1803; the principle he described operated as powerfully after that date as before. In 1806 Parliament revised the law touching certain excise stamps. Forgery of these instruments had been punishable by a £500 fine. The statute of that year made forgery of them felony.[45] Indeed, the power of this logic, or the strength of this reflex, was such that it continued to operate even after forgery became the subject of heated controversy in the early nineteenth century. In 1830 Parliament had passed an act consolidating the law of forgery, restricting it to a narrow range of instruments, and a statute of 1832 narrowed the application of the death penalty to 'cases of forgery of wills, or powers of attorney to transfer stock or receive dividends'. Yet so powerful was the bureaucratic reflex to make the forgery of particular instruments capital, that another act of 1832, a measure creating exchequer bills to raise funds for the West Indies, imposed the death penalty for the forgery of certificates in connection with the bills. Similarly, 'a statute was passed to enable the Commissioners for the Reduction of the National Debt to

[42] 26 George II c. 33, s. 16; Philip Yorke, *The life and correspondence of Philip Yorke, Earl of Hardwicke* (New York, 1977), vol. II, pp. 60–6.
[43] 47 George III c. 36, s. 12.   [44] East, *Pleas*, vol. II, pp. 988–9; 13 George III c. 56.
[45] East, *Pleas*, vol. II, pp. 886–7; *P.D.*, vol. XL, p. 1529.

grant life annuities, in which is a clause making it a capital felony to forge the name of any person to a transfer of an annuity, or to a power of attorney authorizing the transfer'. 'It may be remarked', the commissioners on the criminal law noted with considerable sarcasm in 1834, 'that it is not easy to discover why the forgery of the certificate of the Exchequer Bill Commissioners, or the receipt of the cashier of the Bank should be made capital felonies by the 2 & 3 William IV c. 125, when the forgery of the Exchequer Bill itself is by the 2 & 3 William IV c. 123, only punishable with transportation for life.' To the law reformers these were all instances of the inconsistency and illogic that marked the capital code and that cried out for reform. Yet this relentless activity, not without its own rationale, offers evidence not so much of the senselessness of the process as of the power of the convictions at stake.[46]

Perhaps the most surprising aspect of this flood of forgery legislation is that it had little to do with the actual occurrence of the crime, at least as measured by the number of prosecutions. With the notable exception of the Bank statutes and, above all, of the 1729 act, the vast number of measures dealing with the crime went unused. There were, between 1715 and 1800, as few as thirty trials at the Old Bailey involving the forgery of stamps, lottery tickets, legal records or the signatures of particular government officials. By contrast, there were over 500 trials for forgeries of private instruments (including Bank of England notes). A handful of the former cases were prosecuted by the Stamp Office. These rare prosecutions seem to have been selected to make a signal example of some notorious offender. So, for instance, two men were indicted in 1724 for selling dice with counterfeit stamps on them. In 1735, Joshua Dean, a calico printer, was charged with the forgery of a stamp in imitation of the sixpence stamp for paper. He was clearly a large dealer, distributing his wares in Manchester, Newcastle and Chester. Dean was sentenced to death.[47] Yet so rare were these cases that when the Solicitor General prosecuted Holland Palmer for uttering 1,000 forged stamps in 1784, he announced that it was 'the first of the kind'. It was, he said, a trial 'of infinite importance to the public', for the 'public good is so materially interested in this case'.[48] Two other trials hint that the authorities were particularly sensitive to instances where revenue officers committed frauds. In 1757 William Adams, an examiner of certificates,

---

[46] *First report of the commissioners on criminal law*, *P.P.* (1834) (537) XXVI, pp. 29–30; 11 George IV and 1 William IV c. 66; 2 & 3 William IV c. 123; 2 & 3 William IV c. 125.

[47] *Old Bailey Sessions Papers* [hereafter *O.B.S.P.*], 8–10 July 1724, cases of John Merry and Anthony Walraven; *O.B.S.P.*, 11–17 September 1735, case of Joshua Dean.

[48] *O.B.S.P.*, 8 December 1784.

was prosecuted for making a counterfeit entry for twenty pipes of wine, thereby defrauding the revenue of £252. He was found guilty and condemned to death. Even more sensational was the case of James Gibson, who was charged with forging a writing 'purporting to be an office copy of the accountant general's certificate of paying into the Bank the sum of £437 13s. 7d.' Gibson was well educated, had been articled to an eminent attorney, admitted to practice at the courts at Westminster, and had been taken on as partner to the deputy solicitor of the Treasury. His death was offered as a warning to others against betraying offices of trust.[49]

These cases were so rare that they could scarcely have sustained the legislative obsession with forgery suggested by the simple number of acts. What, then, did all of this legislative activity amount to? In 1830, as the Commons debated consolidation of the criminal law, Peel offered a scheme for thinking about forgery. There were, he argued, two categories of acts, 'those relating to public and general affairs, and those relating to official and departmental [affairs]'. Under the former he included 'all documents relating to the public funds and to negotiable securities – to bills of exchange and promissory notes, and all documents connected with the transfer of property – all papers relating to marriage settlements and testamentary bequests, and registers in public offices'. The latter category took in 'all documents connected with the Navy and the Army, the Customs, the Excise, the Post-office, and Greenwich or Chelsea Hospitals – every act relating to which contained some enactments on the subject of forgery'.[50] What this scheme exposed was a concern about forgery that saw it as a danger, in part to public finance, but especially to the state. It portrayed society as dependent upon the security of certain types of paper. Though the inclusion of the capital sanction in revenue legislation became little more than a bureaucratic reflex, it continued to speak of deeper currents of unease. So great was the apprehension that it imagined a threat even where little evidence of a risk existed. This perception arose initially in the context of the late seventeenth-century wars against France, yet it was sustained throughout the century. The unlooked-for triumphs of the English state were largely recognized to be dependent on its credit. This strength depended in turn upon belief and trust in its word as symbolized by the paper it issued. Though they were not the largest source of revenue, the stamp duties were the offspring of revolutionary finance, and the stamp itself said as much. The stamp upon paper symbolized the state, even as it spoke of the dependence

[49] *The Newgate calendar* (London, 1793), vol. V, pp. 229–32.
[50] *P.D.*, n.s. vol. XXIII, p. 1178.

of the English state upon paper, and upon the revenues that sustained confidence in that paper.[51]

If this is, at least in part, the story told by the legislative history of forgery in the eighteenth century, does it have anything to tell us about the 'bloody code'? The most obvious lesson, again one that revisionists have been telling us for some time, is that the century's criminal legislation contains many different tales, with themes quite other than those suggested by the phrase 'sanguinary laws'. Even a category of laws seemingly as unproblematic as that of forgery offers a complicated narrative. In the case of forgery we begin with a paradox, one that demonstrates how unreliable simple numbers are as a guide to the meaning of the criminal code. The vast bulk of this legislation resulted in very few prosecutions, while the 1729 statute, so different from the other acts, produced some of the most sensational trials of the century. This measure, which loomed so much larger in the practical experience of courts and public, represented an extension by analogy from principles asserted in the far more voluminous legislation touching the revenue. We misread the relationship if we look to that peculiar act to explain all the other measures. Similarly, we misunderstand the significance of the great number of forgery statutes if we look for their meaning in the rhetoric of the reformers who used both the large number and the seeming triviality of the acts to advance their own cause. In one sense the repeated occurrence of forgery legislation was prosaic; all this activity amounted to very little. Forgery produced a narrow range of legislation, more significant for its obsessive character than for its scope. Yet in another sense it alerts us, as I have shown, to a disquiet that ran through the governing classes. The danger was largely imaginary, but no less important for all that.

When we ask, 'who made the bloody code', the glib answer is, of course, that it was invented by the advocates of reform of the criminal law. They were the ones who argued that one spirit informed the criminal code, that it was all of a piece, that it traced its origin to one impulse or testified to one attribute. They took this varied mass of legislation and distilled out of it one meaning, which cast all other ways of seeing the laws in the shadows. The law to them was casual, irrational and brutal. They employed this portrait to brilliant polemical effect. The image sustained an overwhelmingly negative judgment on the existing system of justice. The

---

[51] The most famous subsequent struggle over the stamp duties came in the context of the debate over colonial taxation in 1764. Here, too, pressing financial considerations became wrapped up with questions of political legitimacy. P. D. G. Thomas, *British politics and the stamp act crisis* (Oxford, 1975), pp. 74–100; E. S. and H. M. Morgan, *The stamp act crisis* (Chapel Hill, 1953), pp. 62–3; C. A. Weslager, *The stamp act congress* (Newark, Del., 1976), pp. 31–48; Nancy Koehn, *The power of commerce: economy and governance in the first British empire* (Ithaca, 1994), pp. 71–8.

critics were no doubt sincere in their revulsion against the 'bloody code'. And it was because they understood it in just this way that they abhorred it and felt compelled to fight for its overthrow. The reformers' character-ization of the law was dramatic; it was meant to induce conversion to a new image of justice.

Effective as this description was in debate, there is no reason to take it as a good guide to the purposes of those who passed criminal legislation in the eighteenth century. The reformers' accusations obscure as much as they reveal, and they deflect us from other questions of interest. The point here is not to conjure away the major place given to the gallows in eighteenth-century justice. Rather it is to complicate its meanings. It is worth making the obvious point, that legislators did not set out to create the 'bloody code'. They enacted penal statutes for a variety of reasons, sometimes in the heat of the moment, inspired by some flagrant instance of a crime, other times coolly, in a calculated fashion, to contribute a weapon to justice in the struggle with crime. At still other moments, it was not an actual episode, but a more general fear, that inspired a measure. In the case of forgery, it was the symbolism of the stamp and its relation to the state that was important. The criminal law arose in piecemeal fashion. Few legislators took a view of the whole. Support for one statute or opposition to another did not yet presume disenchantment with the entire system.[52] Some authors felt qualms about the frequency with which death was prescribed; others believed that the serious consequences of some offences demanded the gallows. The phrase, the 'bloody code', evoked powerful emotions in the debates over the criminal law in the early nineteenth century. The time is long since past when historians should uncritically use this term to characterize either the spirit or intent of eighteenth-century criminal legislation.

[52] When one legal scholar came to write of criminal legislation in 1775, he complained of the 'obsolete statutes' that continued in force, but praised many of the measures passed during the reign of George II. John Raynor, *Readings on statutes: chiefly those affecting the administration of public justice in criminal cases passed during the reign of George II* (London, 1775), p. 169.

7 Mapping criminal law: Blackstone and the categories of English jurisprudence

David Lieberman

The map of English law

John Beattie's contributions to the historical study of crime and criminal justice have been so formative and so distinguished that it seems almost presumptuous for someone not engaged in this specific field of inquiry to attempt any characterization of his achievement. Still, for the purposes of this chapter it is useful to observe some of the important general lessons of his researches for understanding legal change in eighteenth-century England. Beattie himself concluded his magisterial account of *Crime and the courts in England* by emphasizing the prominence of this particular theme. During the period 1660–1800 'significant changes' occurred throughout England's system of criminal justice – 'in the criminal law, in criminal procedure, in prisons, and in punishment' – and cumulatively these 'transformed the system of judicial administration'.[1] Interpreting this transformation required not only the historical recovery of patterns of crime and their prosecution, but even more a reconstruction of the technical administrative structures and legal processes through which the criminal law was enforced. The transformation of criminal justice, as charted by Beattie, did not occur without public debate and controversy; and on infrequent occasion, as in the case of the 1718 Transportation Act, it depended critically on parliamentary intervention. But in contrast to the more immediately visible statutory law reforms of the Victorian era, legal change in the eighteenth century rarely involved any direct or sweeping dismantling of historical practices and forms. Instead,

Earlier versions of this chapter were presented at the 1997 meeting of the North American Conference on British Studies and at the Legal History workshop of the Buchmann Faculty of Law, Tel Aviv University. I am grateful to the participants at these occasions for their comments and questions. I also have received valuable guidance from several friends and colleagues: Lindsay Farmer, Claire Finkelstein, James Gordley, Ron Harris, Sanford Kadish, Norma Landau, Thomas Green and Robert Post. Much my greatest debts are owed to James Oldham and to Michael Lobban: both supplied detailed comments on an earlier draft, and both generously alerted me to important source material I otherwise would have neglected.
[1] J. M. Beattie, *Crime and the courts in England 1660–1800* (Princeton, 1986), p. 619.

institutional change outwardly preserved inherited routines by operating through the piecemeal adaptation and adjustment of existing institutional routines and legal understandings. The criminal law of 1800, in its trans-formed state, remained a system of clergyable and non-clergyable of-fences; treasons and felonies; grand and petty larcenies; praemunire and misprisions.

My concern in this chapter is to explore some of the distinctive ways in which eighteenth-century common lawyers attempted to identify and delineate criminal law as a discrete and specific component of the legal order, distinguishing the legal category of 'criminal' from that of 'civil' and, in this setting, the related distinction between 'public' and 'private'. The discussion will attend principally to the analysis of these topics as presented by Blackstone in his mid-century *Commentaries on the laws of England*, taking up Blackstone not only as a singularly elegant and influ-ential treatment of these issues, but also as a convenient point of entry for examining some of the alternative and rival approaches adopted by his near contemporaries. As I shall show, this was an episode in the history of English jurisprudence that contained key elements of transformation. In presenting England's criminal law, Blackstone chose not to highlight settled procedural distinctions and arcane terms, but instead invoked a distinctive kind of legal wrong he identified as 'public' in nature. Nonethe-less, this conceptual 'transformation' fully conformed to the kind of legal change Beattie has taught us to identify for this period. Blackstone's in-novative map of criminal law did not rely upon the explicit introduction of novel terms and fresh categories. Rather, it involved a selective ra-tionalization and adaptation of a messy and technical body of inherited materials.

Recent scholarship on the history of crime and criminal justice help-fully reminds us of some of the challenges facing any juristic effort to provide a clear definition of England's criminal law. The terms *crime* and *criminal law*, while enjoying wide linguistic currency, were not part of the technical vocabulary of the law, which instead recognized other general categories such as felony and trespass, as well as the intricate procedu-ral routines by which specific injuries were prosecuted at specific courts.[2] The practical operation of the law, moreover, undermined any easy appli-cation of the modern categories of 'criminal' or 'civil' in the classification of legal disputes. In a system in which the initiative and most of the costs of all prosecutions fell to private parties (including penal cases formally indicted by the crown and its officers), decisions about what kind of suit

---

[2] See G. R. Elton, 'Introduction: crime and the historian', in J. S. Cockburn, ed., *Crime in England, 1550–1800* (Princeton, 1977), p. 2.

to initiate and before which tribunal naturally turned on considerations of costs and access. As Beattie and other historians have shown, the high rate at which seemingly criminal indictments for assault, riot or other non-felonious offences actually ended in a private settlement between prosecutor and defendant indicates that the aim of such prosecutions was not the state's punishment of a delinquent, but an out-of-court payment of compensation to the prosecuting party. Beattie captured the ambiguity of such common cases by characterizing them as 'quasi-civil settlements'; while Norma Landau similarly maintains that these indictments 'were, in essence, civil suits'.[3]

And yet, for all the proper allowance that must be given to the technical and complicating contours of eighteenth-century English law, it would be equally misleading to suppose that the jurisprudence of that era simply lacked any more general or abstract conception of an area of law that might properly be distinguished as 'criminal'. Already in the medieval period, English law was explicitly differentiating between civil and criminal materials. And as is immediately disclosed by the titles of such works as Lord Kames' 'History of the criminal law' (1758) and William Eden's *Principles of penal law* (1771), eighteenth-century jurists certainly supposed there existed a general category of law that might serve as the object of their scholarly attention.[4] The adopted terminology, admittedly, was by no means uniform, nor necessarily very precise. William Hawkins' widely consulted and frequently reissued *A treatise of the pleas of the Crown* of 1716 became, in the alternative language of its late-century editor, 'this admired treatise of criminal law'.[5] And contributors to the increasingly lively eighteenth-century debate over the principles governing the severity and application of criminal sanctions shifted readily among such phrases as 'penal law', 'penal jurisdiction', 'criminal code', 'the penal or criminal laws', or more idiosyncratically, 'executive justice'.[6]

This terminological range and variation makes plain that legal commentators did not lack resources for labelling what Richard Wooddeson more carefully described as that 'part of the civil institutions' of the state

---

[3] Beattie, *Crime and the courts*, p. 457, and Norma Landau, 'Indictment for fun and profit: a prosecutor's reward at eighteenth-century Quarter Sessions', *Law and History Review*, vol. 17 (1999), p. 508.

[4] Henry Home, Lord Kames, 'History of the criminal law', in *Historical law-tracts*, 2 vols. (Edinburgh, 1758), vol. I, pp. 1–90; William Eden, *Principles of penal law* (1771; 3rd edn, London, 1775).

[5] William Hawkins, *A treatise of the pleas of the Crown* (1716; 6th edn, by Thomas Leach, 2 vols., Dublin, 1788), 'Preface to the present edition', vol. I, n.p.

[6] See Eden, *Principles of penal law*, p. 3; Richard Wooddeson, *A systematical view of the laws of England*, 3 vols. (London, 1792–3), vol. II, p. 544; Martin Madan, *Thoughts on executive justice, with respect to our criminal laws* (London, 1785), pp. 7, 19–20.

'which defines the several species of crimes, limits their punishments, and prescribes the mode of prosecution'.[7] What the varied usage in most contexts did not require was any special effort to establish a boundary that fixed the criminal law as a distinct component of the larger legal order; nor to identify those characteristic features that served to identify this part as specifically *criminal* law; nor to indicate how this classification related to the older and established categories of the common law (such as felonies and trespasses). It is on these matters that the project of Blackstone's *Commentaries* proves especially helpful. Blackstone, at the outset of his four-volume survey, expressly presented the work 'as a general map of the law', concerned to mark 'out the shape of the country, its connexions and boundaries, its greater divisions and principal cities'.[8] And in concluding the final volume, he returned to the same theme (if not to the earlier cartographic metaphor). 'It hath been the endeavour of these commentaries', he emphasized, 'to examine [the law's] solid foundations, to mark out its extensive plan, to explain the use and distribution of its parts, and from the harmonious concurrence of these several parts to demonstrate the elegant proportion of the whole.'[9]

Blackstone's, of course, was by no means an unprecedented attempt in the canon of English legal letters to fashion an orderly map of English law (though the immediate success of the *Commentaries*, along with its numerous later editions and abridgments, meant that it came to overshadow all of its near contemporary rivals). What did distinguish the *Commentaries* was the special circumstances of its composition. Unlike the vast bulk of English legal literature before the nineteenth century, the *Commentaries* was a product of the university lecture hall. Blackstone, a Fellow of All Souls and unsuccessful candidate for Oxford's Regius Professorship of Civil [Roman] Law, in 1753 began offering private lectures on English Law at Oxford. Five years later he was elected to the recently established Vinerian Professor of English Law at Oxford. This appointment made him the first professor of English law at an English university. Several years later, between 1765 and 1769, Blackstone's lectures appeared in published form as the *Commentaries*.[10]

[7] Wooddeson, *Systematical view*, vol. II, p. 544.
[8] William Blackstone, *Commentaries on the laws of England* (1765–9; 11th edn, 4 vols., Dublin, 1788), vol. I, p. 35.
[9] ibid., vol. IV, p. 433.
[10] For background on the creation of the Vinerian Chair and the circumstances of Blackstone's election, see J. L. Barton, 'Legal studies', in L. S. Sutherland and L. G. Mitchell, eds., *The history of the University of Oxford: the eighteenth century* (Oxford, 1986), pp. 600–5, and Lucy Sutherland, 'William Blackstone and the legal chairs at Oxford', in Rene Wellek and Alvaro Ribeiro, eds., *Evidence in literary scholarship: essays in memory of James Marshall Osborn* (Oxford, 1979), pp. 229–40.

The *Commentaries'* exceptional origins had a pervasive impact on the work.[11] In the first place, it involved two distinct audiences for English legal learning. In addition to seeking to instruct those beginning students destined for professional careers in the law, Blackstone also aimed his jurisprudence at 'such other gentleman' who merely sought 'some general acquaintance' with the English legal system. To reach both groups, he 'made it his first endeavour to mark out a plan of the Laws of England so comprehensive as that every Title might be reduced under some or other of its general Heads', and yet 'at the same time so contracted that the Gentleman might with tolerable application contemplate and understand the Whole'.[12]

The realization of this objective, as Blackstone and his contemporaries well appreciated, placed great priority on matters of legal arrangement, organization and classification. In order to supply such a comprehensive overview of the English legal system, it was necessary to bring a vast – and notoriously, labyrinthine – body of abstruse, highly technical, and irregular legal materials into a manageable, synoptic order. But the challenge went beyond matters of pedagogic communication. Order and organization further involved a settled project of institutional legitimation. English law, according to a familiar complaint, simply lacked much by way of system or coherent organization, particularly as compared with Roman law, which hitherto dominated university law studies and which set the relevant standard for juristic elegance. 'It has been thought impracticable to bring the Laws of England into a Method', explained one of Blackstone's eighteenth-century precursors, 'and therefore a Prejudice has been taken up against the study of our Laws, even by Men of Parts and Learning.'[13] On this basis, English law could not become an object of rational learning, and instead had to be mastered through the practical, craft-like techniques of legal apprenticeship. Blackstone, like earlier generations of common lawyers, was confident of the law's credentials as a rational system. In presenting the virtues of English law, he accordingly

---

[11] In characterizing Blackstone's project in the next few paragraphs, I draw on important discussions by S. F. C. Milsom, 'The nature of Blackstone's achievement', *Oxford Journal of Legal Studies*, vol. 1 (1981), pp. 1–12; John W. Cairns, 'Blackstone, an English institutist: legal literature and the rise of the nation state', *Oxford Journal of Legal Studies*, vol. 4 (1984), pp. 318–60; Michael Lobban, 'Blackstone and the science of law', *Historical Journal*, vol. 30 (1987), pp. 311–35; Alan Watson, 'The structure of Blackstone's *Commentaries*', *Yale Law Journal*, vol. 97 (1988), pp. 795–821. For a valuable examination of the broader context of contemporary legal writing in England, see Michael Lobban, 'The English legal treatise and English law in the eighteenth century', *Iuris Scripta Historica*, vol. 13 (1997), pp. 69–88.

[12] William Blackstone, *An analysis of the laws of England* (Oxford, 1771), p. iv.

[13] Thomas Wood, *An institute of the laws of England, or the laws of England in their natural order, according to common use* (1720; 4th edn, London, 1728), p. i.

and frequently emphasized its achievement as a true system: a body of legal materials that displayed order, balance, consistency, coherence.

Unfortunately, as Blackstone glibly acknowledged in his outline preview of the *Commentaries*, the 1756 *Analysis of the laws of England*, the established canon of English legal letters had done little to vindicate the project of 'reducing our laws to a System'. There he critically detailed the limitations of such antiquated, though illustrious, predecessors as 'Glanvil and Bracton, Britton and the author of Fleta'; moved on to consider the more recent efforts of jurists such as Bacon, Coke and Finch (Coke's famous four-part *Institutes* being found 'as deficient in Method as they are rich in Matter'); and finally embraced as his leading model, Matthew Hale's posthumously published *Analysis of the law* as 'the most natural and scientifical' of 'all the Schemes hitherto made public for digesting the Laws of England'.[14]

Blackstone has often appeared, particularly in his political and constitutional doctrines, a distinctively insular voice of whiggish English pieties. Nonetheless, his basic project to produce 'a general map of the law' made him a participant in a broad genre of early modern law writing, in which jurists composed systematic statements of national law, often, as in Blackstone's case, producing these synthetic texts as part of the introduction of courses in native law at the European universities.[15] The archetype for this legal literature was Justinian's *Institutes*, the most famous introductory law book in the western canon, and frequently, the early modern instructional texts echoed this title. Thus, in the case of Scottish law, George Mackenzie's influential survey of 1684 appeared as the *Institutions of the law of Scotland*; and in the case of English law, Thomas Wood's 1720 *An institute of the laws of England*.

Justinian's *Institutes* served as a model in two ways. First, it provided an *aspirational* model: the example of a concise, ordered, single-volume presentation of the basic structure of an entire legal order. Second, it provided something of a *methodological* model. Following an early declaration that 'the whole of the law' under examination 'relates either to persons, or to things, or to actions' (Book I, Title ii), it then proceeded through the space of four roughly balanced books to expound the major categories and concepts of Roman private law: the law of persons (in Book I); of things or property (in Book II); of succession, contracts and quasi-contracts (in Book III); and of non-contractual obligations (in Book IV). This juridical structure and set of categories were readily exploited in the early modern institutes of national law.

[14] Blackstone, *Analysis*, pp. v–viii.
[15] See Klaus Luig, 'The institutes of national law in the seventeenth and eighteenth centuries', *Juridical Review*, vol. 17 (1972), pp. 193–226.

Of course, there was much in the classical law of ancient Rome which ill-served early modern European law, especially English law. Much of the Roman law of persons was dominated by the institution of chattel slavery (a legal category whose absence in the eighteenth-century law English jurists took pride in highlighting).[16] The Roman law of property knew nothing of 'the feudal system' or 'military tenures', which common lawyers routinely understood to be the organizing elements of English real property.[17] And since these rights of real property proved 'the most important, the most extensive, and the most difficult' components of English law, this legal material enjoyed central prominence in legal pedagogy and literature.[18] The effort of the Roman law scholar, John Cowell, in the early seventeenth century, literally to set out the whole of English law according to all the titles of Justinian's *Institutes* had been strongly condemned by common lawyers (a repudiation made easier by the standard linking of Roman law and continental absolutism as the political antipode to common law and English liberty).[19]

Nevertheless, even in England, the general, organizing structures of Roman law enjoyed evident and acknowledged prestige and influence. Matthew Hale thus organized his *Analysis of the law* by first covering the law of persons before moving on to present the 'rights of things'. The adopted order, he explained, conformed 'to the usual method of civilians', even though 'that must not be the method of a young Student of the common law ... [who] must begin his study here at the *Jura Rerum*'.[20] Richard Wooddeson, Blackstone's successor as the third Vinerian Professor, likewise explained that his own Oxford University lectures, published in 1792 as *A systematical view of the laws of England*, were organized according to 'the same three-fold division' utilized by 'the *Institutes* of Justinian'; this arrangement appearing 'the most clear and analytically just'.[21]

Criminal vs. civil

Given this background, it is possible to read the *Commentaries* as the product of a set of critical decisions over the presentation and ordering

---

[16] See Blackstone, *Commentaries*, vol. I, pp. 122–3, and the further discussion in James Oldham, *The Mansfield manuscripts and the growth of English law in the eighteenth century*, 2 vols. (Chapel Hill, 1992), vol. II, pp. 1221–44.

[17] See Blackstone, *Commentaries*, vol. II, pp. 44–58, and John Dalrymple, *An essay towards a general history of feudal property in Great Britain* (1757; 2nd edn, London, 1758).

[18] Francis Stoughton Sullivan, *An historical treatise on the feudal law, and the constitution and laws of England* (London, 1772), p. 18.

[19] For details of this example, see the discussion in J. P. Sommerville, *Politics and ideology in England, 1603–1640* (London, 1986), pp. 121–7.

[20] Matthew Hale, *The analysis of the law* (London, 1716), p. 55.

[21] Richard Wooddeson, *Elements of jurisprudence, treated of in the preliminary part of a course of lectures on the laws of England* (London, 1783), p. 111.

of English law. Easily rejected was the crude expedient of earlier legal primers and law dictionaries, which simply presented English law through an alphabetical listing of major topics and titles. More substantial was the decision not to elaborate the law in terms of the procedural machinery of English justice and legal process. The common law, after all, was a casuistical system of jurisprudence, generated by the network of royal courts and their officers. The vast body of English legal literature, since the twelfth century, had been learning about cases and the methods of processing cases: reports of cases; formularies of writs; commentary on pleadings and forms of action; and digests and abridgments which summarized this learning for more modern practitioners. The *Commentaries* necessarily covered a great deal of this procedural system in its survey of English law; indeed, Blackstone treated it with rare elegance and lucidity. But by the eighteenth century the system of writs and forms of action had become so cumbersome and technical as to render this structure an unlikely vehicle for the kind of ordered and balanced survey Blackstone sought to supply.

Nor was the programme all that much better served if the scheme of classification shifted from the procedural machinery of English law to a more substantive ordering of legal materials in terms, chiefly, of the organization of magistrates and tribunals. According to this ordering structure, the basic parts of the law were identified in terms of the specific institutions in which claims of legal right were presented and resolved. This approach (which also appeared regularly in the legal literature and which, again, received coverage in the *Commentaries*) considerably simplified the classification of law, but only to a degree. Thomas Wood's *Institute*, for example, offered one such version of this ordering of English law, which itself comprised a simplification of a typology in Coke's *Institutes*:

There is another Division of our Laws as into the Prerogative or Crown Law; the Law and Custom of Parliament; the Law of Nature; the Common Law; the Statute Law; reasonable Customs; the Law of Arms, War and Chivalry; Ecclesiastical or Canon Law in Courts in certain Cases; Civil Law in certain Courts and Cases; Forest Law; the Law of Marque and Reprisal; the Law of Merchants; the Laws and Customs of the Isle of Jersey, Guernsey, and Isle of Man; the Law and Privileges of the Stannaries.[22]

Blackstone, following Hale's example, pursued a far more abstract and analytical classificatory scheme. He defined the positive law of an organized political community as 'a rule of civil conduct commanding what is right and prohibiting what is wrong'; he then devoted his first two volumes of the *Commentaries* to the system of rights in English law, and the next

[22] Wood, *Institute of the laws of England*, p. 10.

two volumes to the system of wrongs and their remedies.[23] The titles of the first two books (much less their contents) directly echoed the leading titles of the first two books of Justinian's *Institutes*: 'Of the Rights of Persons' (*jura personarum*) and 'Of the Rights of Things' (*jura rerum*). The former treated constitutional arrangements as well as individual rights, and the latter was dominated by the summary of law of real property.

The titles of the latter two volumes 'on wrongs' (that is, volumes III and IV of the *Commentaries*) conformed much less tightly to the Justinian model, although the general ordering of materials sustained the Roman *Institutes'* basic distribution of law as relating to either persons, things or actions. Here Blackstone's terminology, however, did not replicate classical titles. Thus, he wrote of 'rights and wrongs', rather than the more Latinate 'right' and 'injury' (*jus* and *injuria*). Presumably, by this time, the phrase 'rights and wrongs' had become such a standard terminological trope that Blackstone deployed it, preferring 'wrongs' to the older English legal category of 'trespasses' and to the available alternative generic term of 'offences'.

The two volumes on wrongs covered what Blackstone also described as 'remedial law'; and here he surveyed much of the complex, technical apparatus for processing cases which formed so much of the traditional juristic learning of the common law. Nonetheless, the books were ordered on a different basis. Volume III treated 'private wrongs' in contradistinction to volume IV's coverage of 'public wrongs'. And this division between private and public wrongs marked the distinction between civil injuries (on the one hand) and crimes and misdemeanours (on the other). As he explained at the outset of the final volume,

in the beginning of the preceding volume wrongs were divided into two species; the one private and the other public. Private wrongs, which are frequently termed civil injuries, were the subject of that entire book: we are now therefore, lastly, to proceed to the consideration of public wrongs, or crimes and misdemeanours.[24]

Unifying all this material under the generic label of 'wrongs' enabled Blackstone to maintain the overall symmetry of the four volumes (again: two volumes on rights and two on wrongs), while the classification of wrongs into two main species enabled him to capture a familiar juristic distinction between civil and criminal. In this rendering, what distinguished the category of 'civil injuries' was their private character. These offences, exemplified in injuries caused to personal property, 'are a privation of the civil rights which belong to individuals, considered merely as individuals'. In contrast, crimes and misdemeanours 'are a breach and

---

[23] Blackstone, *Commentaries*, vol. I, p. 44, and see vol. III, p. 1.
[24] ibid., vol. IV, p. 1, and see vol. II, p. 2.

violation of the public rights and duties, due to the whole community, considered as a community, in its social aggregate capacity'. Thus, such exemplary instances of crime as 'treason, murder, and robbery' were properly identified as public wrongs, since these offences 'strike at the very being of society, which cannot possibly subsist where actions of this sort are suffered to escape with impunity'.[25]

This qualitative difference in kinds of wrong, in turn for Blackstone, grounded a secondary distinction between kinds of legal remedies and sanctions. In the case of private wrongs, the restoration of the violated property right or 'a civil satisfaction in damages' properly served to 'atone' for 'an injury to private property'. But in the contrasting case of wrongs that were 'public' in nature, the law's concern was to protect the public by preventing such acts through the instrument of punishment.[26]

In so distinguishing civil from criminal and compensation from punishment, Blackstone navigated a set of distinctions which were commonplace in English jurisprudence. The categories themselves were Roman in origin, and in the medieval period they figured prominently in canonist materials which drew on the Roman law sources. As David Seipp has explained in a valuable treatment of the early common law, already in Glanvil in the late twelfth century and in Bracton in the thirteenth century, English lawyers were utilizing these terms of classification.[27] Some of this trend reflects a more general 'Romanizing' pattern within medieval English jurisprudence, for which Bracton is the famous (though controversial) benchmark. At the same time, as Seipp proposes, a more direct, political dynamic likely was also at work. The great institutional struggle of the twelfth century between the royal courts and the ecclesiastical courts concerning jurisdiction over clergy in England was resolved through a compromise in which (roughly) the royal courts gained authority over clergy in civil suits, while in criminal causes clergy were entitled to appear before a church court. The political conflict facilitated the adoption of the canonist categories of civil and criminal into English law; the terms of its resolution gave incentive to the common lawyers to enlarge the sphere of civil suits, since it was here that the royal courts enjoyed authority over accused clerical offenders.[28]

---

[25] ibid., vol. IV, p. 5, and see vol. I, p. 122, for Blackstone's first presentation of the division between public and private wrongs.

[26] ibid., vol. IV, pp. 6–7, 11–12.

[27] David J. Seipp, 'Distinction between crime and tort in the early common law', *Boston University Law Review*, vol. 76 (1996), pp. 59–87. See also Seipp's more general treatment of these medieval materials in 'Bracton, the year books, and the "Transformation of elementary ideas" in the early common law', *Law and History Review*, vol. 7 (1989), pp. 175–217.

[28] Seipp, 'Distinction between crime and tort', pp. 80–3.

Significantly, however, Blackstone's handling of the categories differed in critical respects from this earlier jurisprudence. Originally, the distinction between criminal and civil was utilized to classify procedural options available at common law to those seeking redress against alleged injuries and wrongs. The categories served to classify types of pleas and forms of action, according to whether the injured party sought *compensation* (a civil plea) or *vengeance* and punishment against the wrongdoer (a criminal plea). The very same injury could stimulate either a criminal or a civil proceeding (for example, an 'appeal of felony' as opposed to a 'writ of trespass'); and the very same injury could stimulate a proceeding initiated by a private party or by a royal official (for example, an 'appeal of felony' as opposed to an 'indictment of felony').[29]

In the early modern literature of the common law, the terminology was again deployed for the purposes of classifying procedural forms. Thus, Coke in his *Institutes* invoked the medieval jurists to support his account of how the common law writs and forms of action were distinguishable as 'some be criminall and some be civill or common'; and he relied on earlier authority in further classifying the civil branch of actions into the subcategories of 'reall, personall, and mixt'.[30] The eighteenth-century surveys of English law retained the same scheme. 'Actions are either Criminal or Civil', Thomas Wood explained. 'Civil are either Real, Personal or Mix'd.'[31] Of course, at this point in time the actual system of common law writs and remedies to which this classification was applied differed dramatically from the legal order observed by Glanvil and Bracton. By the end of the Tudor period, the original structure of common law process had been transformed by the introduction of a newer and more flexible family of actions named 'trespass on the case' (or 'trespass on the special case'). And common law practice now relied overwhelmingly on these more modern forms, such as 'ejectment' (for disputes involving real property); 'trover' (for disputes involving personal property); and *assumpsit* (for disputes involving agreements and contracts).[32]

Blackstone, in a well-chosen metaphor, likened the resulting 'system of remedial law' to 'an old Gothic castle' whose 'magnificent and venerable'

---

[29] Seipp sets out the details of these specific procedural forms in ibid., pp. 61–78.

[30] Edward Coke, *Institutes of the laws of England* (1628–44; 4 parts, London, 1817), part 2, p. 40, and part 1, p. 284b.

[31] Wood, *Institute of the laws of England*, p. 534. See also Blackstone, *Commentaries*, vol. III, p. 117, and Wooddeson, *Systematical view*, vol. III, pp. 1–2.

[32] This historical transformation of the common law system is summarized in J. H. Baker, *Introduction to English legal history* (London, 1979), pp. 49–61. For an important and more detailed recent exploration, see D. J. Ibbetson, *Historical introduction to the law of obligations* (Oxford, 1999), pp. 95–151. (Ejectment was derived from the earlier form of 'trespass *vi et armis*', rather than the later form of 'trespass on the case'.)

original quarters had been 'neglected', and whose 'inferior apartments' had been successfully remodelled 'for a modern inhabitant'. Yet, as he properly acknowledged, the mass of legal 'fictions and circuities' through which this modernization occurred, left the law 'winding and difficult'.[33] Eighteenth-century surveys obviously struggled to manage the cumulative, technical complexity. The antiquated legal forms contained in the first subcategory of civil actions, 'real' actions, could be sketchily treated as a result of their now being 'much out of Use'.[34] Yet they still demanded some discussion, if only to the extent required for making sense of their modern replacements. The historically fashioned cluster of legal forms under the action of trespass likewise defied easy summary. When, for example, Wooddeson in his *Systematical view* reached the uneven class of legal suits and claims that were 'denominated' by common law to be 'actions of trespass on the case', he simply gave up any pretence of being able to provide a satisfactory definition or comprehensive survey of 'these anomalous suits'.[35]

These specific taxonomic complexities all concerned the discussion and organization of legal materials within the 'civil' branch of common law process. But the same patterns of historical development and adaptation likewise complicated efforts to distinguish between civil and criminal. The term 'trespass' itself remained ambiguous. It still appeared in a generic, though increasingly antiquated, form as a synonym for misdeeds or wrongs (including criminal misdeeds and wrongs), as well as being used more technically to identify the large family of (non-criminal) common law writs.[36] Furthermore, the earliest trespass writs of the medieval period concerned alleged wrongs committed 'with force and arms and against the king's peace' (*vi et armis et contra pacem regis*). This formula denoted a jurisdictional claim, indicating why the alleged wrong should be heard by a royal court; and these actions of trespass from the start were identified as civil pleas. Nonetheless, the classification meant that the types of misconduct covered under the category of civil actions included kinds of wrongdoing that might as readily be labelled criminal. Thus, Blackstone, immediately following his rehearsal of the established classification of civil actions into 'personal, real, and mixed', went on to describe a quite different and alternative ordering of 'civil injuries',

---

[33] Blackstone, *Commentaries*, vol. III, pp. 267–8.

[34] Wood, *Institute of the laws of England*, p. 534.

[35] Wooddeson, *Systematical view*, vol. III, pp. 167, 217.

[36] Thus, for example, the opening of the entry 'Trespass' in Giles Jacob's law dictionary: 'Is any Transgressing of the Law under Treason, Felony, or Misprision of either: But it is most commonly used for that Wrong or Damage which is done by one private man to another.' See Giles Jacob, *New law dictionary* (London, 1729), *sub* 'Trespass (*Transgressio*)'.

between those committed '*without force* and violence' (such as 'breach of contract') and those 'coupled *with force* and violence' (such as 'batteries'). The 'latter species', he reported, 'savour something of a criminal kind, being always attended with some violation of the peace'; and this distinction between 'injuries with and without force', he further explained, would be found 'to run through all the variety' of civil injuries.

Further terminological messiness resulted from the impacts of parliamentary statutes on the common law system. One common function of both medieval and early modern legislation was to specify new, and usually more severe penalties for those convicted of existing offences; or to create new kinds of offences by specifying penalties or remedies for previously unsanctioned forms of conduct. The term 'penal statutes' was applied to label one typical version of this legislation: 'such acts of parliament' that inflicted 'a forfeiture' as the penalty 'for transgressing the provisions therein contained'.[37] Often parliamentary legislation operated in a manner that chiefly affected the ordering of legal materials *within* the civil or criminal branches of the law. The 1278 Statute of Gloucester, that specified 'treble damages' in certain cases involving 'an action of waste', shifted what previously had been a 'real' form of civil action into the subcategory of a 'mixed' kind of action.[38] Statutes specifying new forms of treason or removing benefit of clergy from certain types of offences altered legal matter within the criminal branch.[39]

At the same time, however, the legislative materials also worked to introduce further terminological complexity to an already burdened domain. Some of the confusion was the result of the frequently lamented vagaries of parliamentary draftsmanship, where it was evident that the statutory language failed to honour the technical niceties of English law.[40]

---

[37] See Blackstone, *Commentaries*, vol. III, p. 161, and vol. I, p. 88.

[38] In 'real' actions, the plaintiff pursued what was solely a claim of real property. In the case of an 'action of waste', the Statute of Gloucester's treble damages added a monetary claim against the injury to supplement the real property claim, and thereby created a 'mixed' kind of action. The statute furnished a standard illustration of this kind of change to the common law forms; see Blackstone, *Commentaries*, vol. III, p. 118, and Wooddeson, *Systematical view*, vol. III, p. 31.

[39] Thus Coke, in introducing the third part of his *Institutes* on 'pleas of the crowne and criminall causes', explained that 'most of them' were created 'by act of parliament'; Coke, *Institutes*, part 3, 'Proeme', n.p.

[40] The common law courts developed specific rules for the interpretation and application of this class of 'penal' laws, in response in part to the perceived defects in legislative drafting; see Blackstone, *Commentaries*, vol. I, p. 88. See also the specific problems in the language of several statutes noted in the judicial rulings in the case of *Atcheson* v. *Everitt* (1775), 1 Cowp. 382, *English Reports*, vol. XCVIII, pp. 1147–8, and in the case of *R.* v. *Clark* (1777), 2 Cowp. 610, *English Reports*, vol. XCVII, pp. 1267–8. (I am indebted to James Oldham and to Michael Lobban for drawing my attention to this and other case law material.)

But, additional complications arose from the practice of referring to a class of statutes as 'penal acts' or 'penal laws' in a setting where the range of meaning ascribed to the term 'penal' was itself unsettled. Some legal writers reserved the term 'penal' to refer to this specific kind of legislative enactment, and to the common law suits that were authorized by these statutes. The brief title on 'Penal laws' in Giles Jacob's popular *New law dictionary*, for example, was exclusively devoted to the 'Penal Statutes' enacted 'upon many and various occasions to punish and deter Offenders'.[41] And under this specific usage, penal law might readily support forms of action and suits at common law that were classified as civil, as in the situations where a statutory penalty provided the legal foundation for an 'action of debt' or an action of 'trespass on the case'.[42] Here penal law and penal causes were linked to 'civil' matters; and, as a result, needed to be distinguished from criminal law and criminal causes. 'Penal actions were never yet put under the head of criminal law or crimes', insisted Lord Chief Justice Mansfield, by which he meant that a civil action brought in support of a claim to a statutory penalty did not turn the action into a 'criminal cause'.[43]

Unfortunately, however, this narrow and technical common law usage of 'penal' law was easily at odds with more general linguistic practice that tended to join 'penal' and 'criminal' as two parts of a unified field of legal ordering. The term, *'penal'*, Jeremy Bentham noted in 1789, 'is wont, in certain circumstances, to receive the name of *criminal*'.[44] This alternative (and now more familiar) usage commonly figured in the eighteenth-century debate over the reform of capital statutes, where the discussion of penalties was firmly directed at the matter of crime and punishment. Thus, when William Eden presented to his readers the *Principles of penal law*, his subject matter was explicitly 'the right of punishment and the different classes of punishment' in connection with 'the several species of crimes, their definitions and gradations'.[45]

All this terminological complication reinforces the level of challenge Blackstone faced in seeking to bring order and division to English legal practices. Volume III and volume IV of the *Commentaries*, of course, fully detailed those procedural differences that formed the centrepiece of the common law's established approach to the distinction between the criminal and civil branches of the law. Blackstone's important innovation,

[41] Jacob, *New law dictionary*, *sub* 'Penal laws'.
[42] Such actions '*grounded on a particular act of parliament*' are helpfully surveyed in Wooddeson, *Systematical view*, vol. III, pp. 192, 214–16.
[43] See *Atcheson* v. *Everitt* (1775), 1 Cowp. 382, *English Reports*, vol. XCVII, p. 1147.
[44] Jeremy Bentham, *An introduction to the principles of morals and legislation* (1789), ed. J. H. Burns and H. L. A. Hart (London, 1970), p. 299.
[45] Eden, *Principles of penal law*, p. 83.

however, was the attempt to fashion out of these materials an alternative foundation for the familiar categories. His typology of England's remedial law did not in the first instance invoke procedural options. Instead, he suggested a substantive difference in areas of law, distinguished according to qualitatively different kinds of wrongs. Some kinds of wrongs were 'public' in nature; these kinds of wrong demanded 'punishment' by the community; and these kinds of wrongs comprised 'crimes and misdemeanours'.

Pleas of the crown

As I shall show, serious difficulties attended this attempt to map a boundary between private and public wrongs in English law. Nonetheless, the project was greatly facilitated by yet another important technical legal category that Blackstone deployed to identify 'public wrongs': pleas of the crown. Public wrongs, he explained, included the law which 'forms in every country the code of criminal law; or, as it is more usually denominated with us in England, the doctrine of the *pleas of the crown*'.[46] 'Pleas of the crown' referred to those actions at common law in which the crown appeared formally as the party prosecuting the individual charged with the offence in question.[47] And it was this identification of criminal law with pleas of the crown, rather than Blackstone's category of 'public wrongs', that represented standard common law usage in the seventeenth and eighteenth centuries. Coke, for example, introduced his subject matter in the third part of his *Institutes*, by explaining that 'we are to treat *de malo*, viz. of high treason and other pleas of the crowne, and criminall causes'. Thomas Wood similarly titled the relevant section of his own *Institute*, 'Of crimes and misdemeanours, or of the pleas of the crown'.[48]

This general identification of English criminal law with 'the doctrine of the pleas of the crown' (or 'crown law') was made possible as a result of the earlier historical development in which these pleas replaced the larger number of older procedural options for the prosecution of crime. The process in which the institutions of the state wrested control of the punishment of crime from the practices of private vengeance formed the organizing theme of eighteenth-century accounts of the historical development of the criminal law. In these treatments, the public

[46] Blackstone, *Commentaries*, vol. IV, p. 2, and see vol. I, p. 268.
[47] This was the process that usually began with an indictment, which was then considered by a grand jury, before proceeding on to trial involving a petty jury. For an account of the procedures, see J. H. Baker, 'Criminal courts and procedure at common law 1550–1800', in Cockburn, *Crime in England*, pp. 15–48.
[48] Coke, *Institutes*, part 3, 'Proeme' (n.p.); Wood, *Institute of the laws of England*, p. 339.

administration of punishment for the acknowledged purposes of collective welfare formed a basic indicator of societal progress and refinement.[49] And, as Blackstone perceived, since the most serious forms of crime were now virtually always prosecuted through a plea of the crown, this legal form further clarified what was 'public' about the class of public wrongs. The crown was the proper prosecutor of these wrongs since 'the king, in whom centers the majesty of the whole community, is supposed by the law to be the person injured by every infraction of the public rights belonging to that community'.[50]

In fact, as English jurists acknowledged, the category of pleas of the crown could not quite serve to stabilize the boundaries of criminal law itself. In one respect, the crown law was too large: it ranged over areas of law which plainly did not involve crimes or criminal causes. Thus, for example, in his famous treatise on *The history of the pleas of the crown*, Matthew Hale distinguished the criminal and the civil pleas, the latter of which concerned 'franchises and liberties'.[51] In another (more familiar) respect, the crown law was too narrow: it did not contain all the law governing criminal causes in England. Thus, Hale in his *Analysis of the law* only arrived at the pleas of the crown following a series of divisions which made plain the number of criminal offences which did not fall under the 'conuzance' of the courts of common law: crimes under the 'conuzance' of the ecclesiastical courts (adultery, fornication, incest); those under the 'conuzance' of the Admiral's Court (piracy); and those under the 'conuzance' of the Constable and Marshal's Court (usurpation of coats of arms).[52]

Even more serious for Blackstone's classification was the survival in eighteenth-century law of the older criminal pleas, the common law 'appeals of felony', in which 'a private subject' prosecuted another 'for some heinous crime; demanding punishment on account of the particular injury suffered, rather than for the offence against the public'. Blackstone, inevitably, placed 'this private process for the punishment of public crimes' within the English law of 'public wrongs', notwithstanding

---

[49] Among the most elaborate and best-known rehearsals of this historical theme was Kames' essay on the 'History of the criminal law'. For similar contemporary discussions, see Eden, *Principles of penal law*, pp. 2–3; Robert Chambers, *A course of lectures on the English law* (1767–73), ed. Thomas M. Curley, 2 vols. (Oxford, 1986), vol. I, pp. 305–26; and Wooddeson, *Systematical view*, vol. III, pp. 564–6.

[50] *Commentaries*, vol. IV, p. 2. Although the crown, as a matter of legal form, prosecuted these offences, in practice the processes of criminal justice still depended on the initiative of private parties; see Beattie, *Crime and the courts*, pp. 35–41.

[51] Matthew Hale, *Historia placitorum coronae: the history of the pleas of the crown* (1726; 2 vols., London, 1736), vol. I, 'Proemium', n.p. (Hale did not in fact complete this projected section on 'franchises and liberties'.)

[52] Hale, *Analysis of the law*, pp. 98–9.

the anomalous features. He discussed the procedure 'very briefly', emphasizing its rare appearance in the operations of current law.[53] The 'appeal of felony' may have posed a rather unthreatening exception to Blackstone's classificatory scheme, given its plain status as an antiquated vestige of an earlier era of English criminal justice.[54] Other complications, however, could not be marginalized in this fashion. Much more common and contemporary was a form of action, termed *qui tam*, which undermined the terms of Blackstone's categories by purposefully inviting the collaboration of private parties and the government in the prosecution of particular offences. *Qui tam* actions were supported by numerous parliamentary statutes that provided the opportunity for the prosecution of particular offences either by the crown or by a private party; and which, in the latter case, specified a monetary penalty that was divided between the crown for 'some public use' and the private 'informer or prosecutor'.[55]

Both the appeals of felony and *qui tam* actions disclosed some of the difficulties in preserving the boundary between 'private' and 'public' wrongs. Still, even in the absence of such procedural hybrids, the *Commentaries*' map for the criminal law faced a more systematic and analytical challenge. Many of the most familiar kinds of *public* wrongs treated in volume IV, such as murder or assault, involved just as much a wrong done to a particular 'private' individual by another 'private' individual as did the kinds of offences identified as *private* wrongs in volume III. Blackstone, of course, was well aware of the difficulty. His solution was to allow that 'every public offence is also a private wrong, and somewhat more; it affects the individual, and it likewise affects the community'. The provision of punishment rather than compensation was, in this sense, a decision to allow 'the private wrong' to become 'swallowed up in the public'.[56] In these comments, Blackstone recognized the many cases in which the division of civil injuries and public crimes was less a distinction between two kinds of wrongs than it was a juridical characterization of two separate elements of the same conduct. But this refinement concerning the private dimensions of public wrongs still left unexplored the public dimensions of those wrongs which the law treated as private. If the public, 'considered . . . in its

---

[53] Blackstone, *Commentaries*, vol. IV, pp. 312–13.

[54] Blackstone's account, moreover, constituted something of a premature obituary for a procedure that remained good law and did not lack for judicial defenders. Chief Justice Holt, in a 1699 decision, praised the appeal of felony as 'a Nobel prosecution, and a true badge of English liberties'. The statement proved embarrassing for those, like Blackstone, who sought to marginalize the legal form; see Wooddeson, *Systematical view*, vol. III, p. 566.

[55] See Blackstone, *Commentaries*, vol. III, pp. 161–2, and vol. IV, p. 308. (I am indebted to James Oldham for first drawing my attention to these *qui tam* actions.)

[56] ibid., vol. IV, p. 6.

social aggregate capacity', had an interest in the prevention of wrongs like murder and assault, in what sense did it lack an interest in the prevention of violations of civil rights and personal property?[57]

The relevant complications tended to surface in those cases where English law treated an offence as either a civil injury or a crime. The offence of libel, the *Commentaries* explained, allowed 'as in many other cases, two remedies': as a *'public* offence' by indictment, or as a civil injury 'by action'.[58] The difference turned on the now familiar question of which procedure was utilized, one of which led to punishment and one of which led to compensation. Blackstone, however, again sought to rationalize the difference in terms of the qualitative distinction in kinds of wrongs. What made the personal injury to reputation in libel a public wrong was the 'tendency' of 'every libel' to lead 'to a breach of the peace, by provoking the person libeled to break it'.[59] But, this rationalization would equally serve to transform perhaps every private injury into a public wrong: each of these civil injuries potentially might likewise provoke the victim into a line of retaliatory conduct which would threaten the public peace.

Public vs. private

The public–private distinction has become such an important and even notorious object of scrutiny in the critique of liberal legal and political theory that one might readily pursue, in the manner undertaken by Duncan Kennedy, a far more ambitious criticism of the inadequacies and instabilities of the *Commentaries'* programme of classification.[60] In utilizing this terminology, Blackstone, once more, sought to adapt and stabilize a cluttered inheritance of legal categories and concepts. The ultimate legal source for this terminology was classical Roman law, where public law referred (roughly) to what concerned 'the welfare of the Roman state', and private law referred to what concerned 'the advantage of the individual citizen'.[61] By the eighteenth century a version of these Roman categories was equally familiar in the natural law tradition associated with Grotius and his successors, where so much of the analysis of rights and

[57] ibid., vol. IV, p. 5. Blackstone's own presentation of the positive rules governing the transmission of private property drew attention to these considerations of public convenience; see ibid., vol. II, pp. 1–15.
[58] ibid., vol. III, p. 125.   [59] ibid., vol. III, pp. 125–6, and see vol. IV, p. 150.
[60] Duncan Kennedy, 'The structure of Blackstone's *Commentaries'*, *Buffalo Law Review*, vol. 5 (1979), pp. 209–382. The wider critical discussion in political theory of the 'liberal conception of public and private' is usefully surveyed in the contributions by Anthony S. Walton, Eugene Kamenka and Carole Pateman to Stanley I. Benn and Gerald F. Gaus, eds., *Public and private in social life* (London and Canberra, 1983).
[61] See *The Institutes of Justinian*, trans. J. B. Moyle (Oxford, 1913), book 1, title 1, p. 3.

obligations was examined in terms of the transformations wrought by the introduction of public authority and positive law.[62] The generality of this terminology probably eased its utilization in English law, where it was applied in a range of classificatory settings. Acts of Parliament, for example, earlier classified as either 'general' and 'special', came additionally to be distinguished as 'public' and 'private'.[63]

Eighteenth-century English law utilized the terms 'private' and 'public' with a frequency and range sufficient to frustrate any precise or simple definition.[64] Nonetheless, the term was routinely given at least two distinctive meanings, both of which figured in Blackstone's conceptualization of 'public' wrongs. 'Public' could refer to the institutions and agents of state authority. Thus, for example, Thomas Wood, in discussing cases of 'Justifiable Homicide' in English law, distinguished between those 'of a Publick' and those of a 'Private Nature'. *Public* justifiable homicide occurred in the legitimate operation of governmental authority: as 'when judgment of Death is given by one that hath jurisdiction in the Cause'. In contrast, *private* forms of justifiable homicide occurred 'in defence of One's person, house or goods; as when a woman kills one that attempts to ravish her'.[65] In addition and more loosely, the term 'public' was used to denote situations of collective benefit or interest, where the benefit derived or the harm avoided was not to be assigned or limited to any particular individuals. Thus, Wood, in treating the common law of 'nuisances', identified as 'Publick' those nuisances that affected 'the whole

---

[62] Early modern treatments of natural law and natural right tended to utilize the categories of 'nature' and 'civil society' to mark this distinction between pre-political and political forms of human society. The phrase 'civil society' and its derivatives (civil authority, civil law, etc.) was derived from the Latin *civitas*', which Locke, for example, took to signify 'any Independent Community' and for which he proposed 'Commonwealth' as the generic English equivalent. Nonetheless, it was common, more loosely, to associate this 'civil' state with the term 'public' and its linguistic derivatives. Thus, in treating the aims of 'political society' and of the 'Supream Power of any Common-wealth', Locke emphasized the 'Peace, Safety, and publick good of the People'. See John Locke, *Two treatises of government* (1690), ed. Peter Laslett (Cambridge, 1964), pp. 371, 373.

[63] Blackstone utilized and explained the terminology at *Commentaries*, vol. I, pp. 85–6. However, the nomenclature represented a rather forced rationalization of a distinction that was chiefly sustained by procedural forms in the processes of parliamentary law-making; see Sheila Lambert, *Bills and acts: legislative procedure in eighteenth-century England* (Cambridge, 1971), pp. 84–109.

[64] Here the range of legal usage conformed to the patterns of more general linguistic usage. Samuel Johnson's *Dictionary* supplied five meanings for 'publick' in its adjectival form, including the meanings noticed above. Two valuable discussions of the wider linguistic practice are J. A. W. Gunn, *Beyond liberty and property* (Kingston and Montreal, 1983), chap. 7, and John Brewer, 'This, that and the other: public, social and private in the seventeenth and eighteenth centuries', in Dario Castiglione and Lesley Sharpe, eds., *Shifting the boundaries: transformation of the languages of public and private in the eighteenth century* (Exeter, 1995), pp. 1–21.

[65] Wood, *Institute of the laws of England*, pp. 360–1.

Kingdom', in contrast to 'Private' nuisances which injured 'a particular Person, as to his house, mill, etc'.[66]

Blackstone, in his category of public wrongs, plainly drew on a well-established stock of linguistic usage. Crimes and misdemeanours were 'public' in the sense of matters of state action, since in the case of these wrongs the law gave the crown distinctive prosecutorial responsibilities. And crimes and misdemeanours were 'public' in the wider sense of matters of collective concern, since these were the wrongs that harmed 'the whole community, considered as a community, in its social aggregate capacity'.[67] There was little novelty to either claim as a substantive point about how English law generally handled criminal offences. Blackstone's readers did not need the *Commentaries* to instruct them that the law legitimately punished crimes for the sake of the collective welfare of the community (and not for personal vengeance); and that the routine prosecution of these offences involved the mobilization of government authority in a manner that plainly differed from other legal suits. What was innovative about Blackstone's map here was the attempt to unify these legal practices in terms of a distinctive kind of wrong, and to attach the label 'public' to it.

Blackstone's immediate successor to the Vinerian professorship, Robert Chambers, in his Oxford lectures of 1767–73, embraced this terminology more ambitiously, and presented a revised classificatory scheme that utilized 'public' and 'private' categories to arrange the whole of English law. In this classification, 'public law' referred to 'that law of government by which the supreme power in a state regulates its own conduct and that of its subordinate officers', which in England covered the rules governing the arrangement of the constitution and the operation of royal government. 'Private law' comprised the law 'by which the particular rights of the subject are protected'. Between these two juxtaposed branches of the law, Chambers introduced a distinct and separate category of 'Criminal Law', which contained features of both public and private law. Criminal law treated offences (such as 'murder, robbery and mayhem') that simultaneously comprised 'a private injury' to 'him whose natural and civil rights are thereby invaded' as well as a 'public crime' against 'the peace and good order of the commonwealth'.[68]

Chambers' tripartite arrangement neatly avoided the challenges Blackstone encountered in seeking to secure a clear boundary between public and private kinds of wrongs since it explicitly situated criminal law as a mediating category that combined public and private elements. At the same time, his lectures (which he struggled to compose and declined

---

[66] ibid., p. 443.   [67] Blackstone, *Commentaries*, vol. IV, p. 5.
[68] Chambers, *Course of lectures on the English law*, vol. I, pp. 89–91, 122.

to publish) relied on an avowedly Roman conception of 'public law' that remained generally foreign to English orthodoxies. When in 1803, for example, the Scottish jurist, John Millar, deployed the categories of 'public' and 'private' law, in a manner that echoed Chambers and the classical Roman usage, to distinguish 'that part' of the law 'which regulates the powers of the state' from the part 'which regulates the conduct of the several members' of the political community, he promptly acknowledged that the adopted terminology did not represent 'the common acceptation'.[69] Millar's observation was reflective of the important elements within English jurisprudence that served to resist any sharp boundary between a discrete body of public law relating to the state and another discrete body of private law relating to the conduct among the individual members of the kingdom.[70]

Instead, English law regularly characterized the structures of political life in terms of the categories and doctrines of private jurisprudence.[71] The franchise, government office and even the kingship thus were conceptualized as various forms of personal property or estate, held (respectively) by the parliamentary elector, the magistrate and the monarch himself. The common law jury epitomized the democratic elements in English governance as much as did the House of Commons; specific legal forms, such as of the writs of habeas corpus and *quo warranto*, were as foundational to the system of public liberty as was the mixed constitution. 'By a constitutional policy', Burke enthused in the *Reflections on the revolution in France*, 'we receive, we hold, we transmit our government and our privileges, in the same manner in which we enjoy and transmit our property and our lives.'[72]

Blackstone, himself, cogently sustained this understanding of the permeability and continuity between public and private legal realms in his organization of the first volume of the *Commentaries*, which included discussion of the law concerning the central bodies of government: crown,

---

[69] John Millar, *An historical view of English government* (1803; 4 vols., London, 1818), vol. IV, p. 285.

[70] This theme provides an organizing thesis for J. W. F. Allison's recent study of 'English public law', which maintains that, notwithstanding occasional usage, 'The old English authorities generally ignored, rejected, or rendered insignificant the distinction between public and private law' (*A continental distinction in the common law* (Oxford, 1996), p. 8). See also the helpful article by Alice Erh-Soon Tay and Eugene Kamenka, 'Public law – private law', in Benn and Gaus, *Public and private in social life*, pp. 67–92.

[71] In what immediately follows here, I draw on material that I explore more fully in 'The mixed constitution and the common law', in *The Cambridge history of eighteenth-century political thought*, ed. Mark Goldie and Robert Wokler (Cambridge University Press, forthcoming), especially part 5.

[72] Edmund Burke, *Reflections on the revolution in France* (1790), ed. Conor Cruise O'Brien (Harmondsworth, 1969), p. 120. (Burke linked this 'constitutional policy' to Coke 'and the great men who follow him to Blackstone'; see pp. 117–18.)

Parliament, and courts of justice. Given this material, it became common for later writers to treat the book as Blackstone's account of 'constitutional law'. However, as I have shown, Blackstone's own title for the volume was, 'the Rights of Persons'; he began the book with a chapter-length survey of 'the three great and primary rights' of English subjects – 'personal security, personal liberty, and private property'. The kingdom's political arrangements (such as 'limitation of the king's prerogative' and 'the constitution, powers and privileges of Parliament') were introduced next as part of a larger network of 'auxiliary subordinate rights' designed to protect the basic 'primary rights' of the individual subject.[73] And finally Blackstone went on to survey, in ample detail, 'the rights and duties of persons' who exercised 'supreme' magistracy (King and Parliament); the 'rights of persons' exercising 'subordinate' magistracy (sheriffs, constables, etc.); the rights associated with particular social ranks and stations (clergy, nobility, military, etc.); the rights 'in private oeconomical relations' (master–servant, husband–wife, etc.); and the rights of 'artificial persons' (corporations). In elaborating this hierarchical system of 'rights of persons', Blackstone did at one point contrast 'public relations' between 'magistrates and people' from 'private oeconomical' relations within a domestic household. Nonetheless, the overall approach served to erode the kind of organizing boundary between state and society, and between public and private spheres, that featured in later treatments of English constitutional law.[74]

Blackstone's readiness thus to combine a classification of the 'rights of persons' which united government structures and private conditions (on the one hand) with a classification of legal 'wrongs' which separated public crimes and private injuries (on the other) largely followed from the *Commentaries'* basic didactic and expository purposes. The point was to develop a structure for introducing the legal order to a non-professional audience, and this required as much literary skills, partial borrowings and selective innovations as it did pristine categories and rigid classifications. Blackstone, however, in displaying his map did not emphasize the heuristic and provisional nature of this exercise. For all his express debts to Matthew Hale's *Analysis of the law* for the arrangement of the *Commentaries*, he declined to follow his mentor in conceding any final failure 'to reduce the Laws of England' to 'an exact Logical Method'.[75] Instead, as in the division of private and public wrongs, Blackstone's

[73] Blackstone, *Commentaries*, vol. I, pp. 136–9.
[74] ibid., p. 422. For the contrasting, later approaches to constitutional law, see the criticisms of Blackstone offered by A. V. Dicey in *Law of the constitution* (1885), 9th edn (London, 1948), pp. 7–8.
[75] Hale, *Analysis of the law*, 'Author's preface', n.p.

language suggested some firmer, more essentialist foundation to his adopted categories. And this left the *Commentaries* especially vulnerable to attack for its methods of classification and arrangement.

The criticism of Blackstone's methods began within a decade of the appearance of the *Commentaries*, when an unknown jurist, who earlier had attended the Vinerian lectures at Oxford, anonymously published *A fragment on government* in 1776. Included among the multitude of crippling defects Jeremy Bentham there identified for censure was what he termed Blackstone's 'technical arrangement' of English law: 'a sink', as Bentham put it, that 'will swallow any garbage that is thrown into it'.[76] The details of Bentham's attack, and the later critical reactions to Blackstone's more specific efforts to classify and delimit criminal law, cannot be pursued here. But, there is one particular feature of Bentham's response to Blackstone that deserves brief notice. This is the extent to which Bentham, for all his dismissive repudiation of the *Commentaries*' classificatory scheme, in his own jurisprudence fully sustained the Blackstonean project to systematize analytically the law; and did so in a way that relied extensively on the ordering logic of public vs. private, civil vs. criminal.[77] Later English jurisprudence likewise routinely returned, often without acknowledgement, to the well-rehearsed distinctions and categories that Blackstone's celebrated *Commentaries* placed firmly in the foreground of the map of law. In the 1820s, for example, John Austin embarked on another comprehensive analysis of the organizing concepts and categories of positive law, as part of his duties as professor of jurisprudence at the new London University. Drawing once more on the materials and arrangement of classical Roman law, Austin soon found himself in a painfully familiar set of conceptual tangles. 'In order to determine the place which should be assigned to the *Criminal Law*', he casually reported in his commentary on the Roman institutional arrangements, 'it would be necessary to settle the import of an extremely perplexing distinction: namely, the distinction between *Public* Law and *Private* (or Civil) Law.'[78]

---

[76] Jeremy Bentham, *A fragment on government* (1776), in *A comment on the Commentaries and A fragment on government*, ed. J. H. Burns and H. L. A. Hart (London, 1977), p. 416.

[77] I explore the manner in which Bentham's early theory of legislation was developed through a critical and protracted engagement with Blackstone's *Commentaries* in my *Province of legislation determined: legal theory in eighteenth-century Britain* (Cambridge, 1989), chap. 13. See also the illuminating discussion by J. H. Burns in 'Bentham and Blackstone: a lifetime's dialectic', *Utilitas*, vol. 1 (1989), pp. 22–40.

[78] John Austin, *Lectures on jurisprudence* (1861; 2 vols., London, 1885), vol. II, p. 928. Subsequent efforts in this area of English jurisprudence, both during and after Austin's era, are critically examined by Lindsay Farmer in 'The obsession with definition: the nature of crime and critical legal theory', *Social and Legal Studies*, vol. 5 (1996), pp. 57–73, and in 'Reconstructing the English codification debate: the criminal law commissioners, 1833–45', *Law and History Review*, vol. 18 (2000), pp. 397–425.

Part 3

Society

8   After *Somerset*: Mansfield, slavery and the law in England, 1772–1830

Ruth Paley

The *Somerset* case

In June 1772 Lord Mansfield freed a single slave and made legal history. From that day onwards there was no slavery in England. Or was there? Just what Lord Mansfield achieved that day remains a matter for speculation and controversy. This chapter seeks to re-examine the immediate aftermath of *Somerset* in the light of fresh evidence, in order to determine just what effect it had upon the legal status of slaves in England until slavery was abolished throughout the British Empire in the early 1830s.

The case of James Somerset is well known. He was brought as a slave from the Americas to England, ran away, was recaptured and then imprisoned on a ship bound for the West Indies. In response to a writ of habeas corpus, the captain returned that Somerset was a slave who had absconded from his master's service and refused to return, and that he had been delivered over in order to be returned to Jamaica, where he would be sold. Lord Mansfield declared the return unlawful, stating that 'Slavery is so odious that it must be construed strictly' and derive from positive law, and that 'No Master was ever allowed here to send his servant abroad because he absented himself from his service or for any other cause.'[1]

It was once widely accepted that *Somerset* had ended slavery in England; the American courts, in particular, interpreted *Somerset* to mean that slavery was prohibited under the common law unless there was specific legislative authority to the contrary. Later scholars have tended to be more doubtful. Yet the case still provokes controversy. The most recent accounts include an authoritative discussion of the legal background,

---

I am indebted to Donna Andrew, Seymour Drescher, Douglas Hay and participants in the London Legal History and Legal History in the Making seminars for comments on an earlier version of this chapter.
[1] For a discussion of the wording of Mansfield's judgment, see James Oldham, 'New light on Mansfield and slavery', *Journal of British Studies*, vol. 27 (1988), pp. 56–8. The most commonly accepted version of the judgment appears in *Somerset v. Stewart*, 1 Lofft 1–19, *English Reports*, vol. XCVIII, p. 499.

emphasizing the extreme care with which Mansfield phrased his decision and its consequent limitations,[2] and a discussion of the effects of the decision which claims that it did both de facto and de jure abolish slavery in England.[3] Some of the difficulties associated with later interpretations of *Somerset* can be resolved only by an examination of subsequent English cases, especially those that considered a wider range of issues. Unfortunately, relevant cases in the English courts are rare, and both their archival documentation and the accounts in the law reports are sparse. However, there are also a few well-documented unreported cases, hitherto virtually unknown to historians. Perhaps the most significant of these is the case of Little Ephraim Robin John and Ancona Robin Robin John, a consideration of which will form the core of this chapter.

On 18 September 1773, Thomas Jones received a letter from these two young Africans, informing him of their imprisonment as slaves on board the *Brickdale*, at Bristol. They knew Jones from his visits to their home in Africa and now sought his help to secure their freedom. Their case offers striking parallels to that of James Somerset: they were held on an English ship in English waters in order to be returned against their will to slavery in Virginia. If *Somerset* had established either that slavery did not exist in England, or that slaves could not be forcibly expelled, then their detention was manifestly illegal. Yet Henry Lippincott, the owner of the *Brickdale*, and William Jones, the agent for their supposed owner, refused to free them, unles they were compensated for their value as slaves.

Thomas Jones sought a habeas corpus to free them, but his application revealed a number of striking differences to *Somerset*. In *Somerset*, although the lawyers argued about the legality of slavery as an institution in its own right, the evidence they presented contained a very narrow set of facts,[4] thus enabling Mansfield (already on record as suggesting that such questions 'should never be discussed or settled . . . for I would have all Masters think them free, and all Negroes think they were not, because then they would both behave better'[5]) to avoid the wider issues. In recounting the tale of the Robin John brothers, however, Thomas Jones raised substantive issues of law, issues that Mansfield had avoided in *Somerset*. Moreover they were issues that posed a significant threat to the conduct of the slave trade: for Thomas Jones made it all too clear that he believed the two Africans to be free men.

---

[2] Oldham, 'New light', pp. 45–68.
[3] William R. Cotter, 'The *Somerset* case and the abolition of slavery in England', *History*, vol. 79 (1994), pp. 31–56.
[4] See below under 'Legal issues'.
[5] *R. v. Stapylton*, quoted in James Oldham, ed., *The Mansfield manuscripts and the growth of English law in the eighteenth century*, 2 vols. (Chapel Hill, 1992), vol. II, p. 1223.

Enslavement at Calabar

By 1773 the Robin John brothers had been slaves for nearly six years. Their home was Old Town, Old Calabar, in the Bight of Biafra. The dominant tribe, the Efiks, played an important role as middlemen in the slave trade, capturing or buying slaves from the hinterland for sale to European traders; their weekly slave fair was one of the most important in the region. The profits turned the Efik rulers into 'commercial barons . . . [who] controlled the wealth of the region . . . [thus gaining] political and economic control of both the coast and the hinterland'. Their power was visible and savage. They were conspicuous consumers, flaunting their wealth with European goods and large numbers of household slaves. They also practised conspicuous waste, especially of the lives of their own slaves, many of whom were sacrificed at funeral and other rites: when King Duke Ephraim II died in July 1786, fifty of his slaves were ceremonially beheaded, nine were buried (possibly alive) with him, and a further six were killed in his honour by other parts of the community.[6] The rulers of Calabar were vociferous in their opposition to the eventual abolition of the slave trade by the British government and active in ensuring its clandestine continuance.[7]

For most of the eighteenth century Old Town (*Obutong*) dominated both the slave trade and the region. However, by the 1760s the power of the Old Town elite was increasingly challenged by its rival, New Town, founded some time after 1748, and later to be known (after its dominant lineage group) as Duke Town (*Atakpa*).[8] In 1767 a dispute between them disrupted trade, and the captains of several British slave ships offered to mediate.[9] About 300 men of Old Town, including Amboe Robin John, Little Ephraim Robin John and Ancona Robin Robin John, set out to negotiate with men from New Town in the supposedly neutral surroundings offered by the British ships. The resultant massacre is well known. Amboe Robin John was overpowered by the British and delivered to the men of New Town, who instantly beheaded him. The British then opened

---

[6] Daryll Forde, ed., *Efik traders of Old Calabar* (London, 1956, reprinted 1968), p. 153.

[7] Ekei Essien Oku, *The kings and chiefs of Old Calabar (1785–1925)* (Calabar, Glad Tidings Press, 1989), pp. xii–xv; A. J. H. Latham, 'The pre-colonial economy: the lower Cross region', in Monday B. Abasiattai, ed., *A history of the Cross River region of Nigeria* (Enugu, 1990), pp. 70–89; A. J. H. Latham, *Old Calabar, 1600–1891: the impact of the international economy upon a traditional society* (Oxford, 1973), pp. 20–1.

[8] Forde, *Efik traders*, pp. 1–4, 119.

[9] The *Indian Queen, Duke of York, Nancy* and *Concord*, all of Bristol, *Hector* of Liverpool and an unnamed ship from London. Information about the Bristol ships is given in David Richardson, ed., *Bristol, Africa and the eighteenth-century slave trade to America*, 4 vols. (Bristol Records Society, 1991–6), vol. III, pp. 209–10, 213, 200.

fire on the remaining Old Town men; those who escaped the gunfire were killed as they reached the shore.

A few did survive: Little Ephraim Robin John and Ancona Robin Robin John were amongst them. But their survival was a problem in itself. Although the captains had just actively participated in mass murder, they were, it seems, reluctant to 'be called to an account for having violated the Acts of Parliament for regulating the Trade to Africa', which quite specifically stated that 'No commander or master of any ship trading to Africa shall by fraud, force or violence or by any other indirect practice whatsoever take on board or carry away from the coast of Africa any negro or native of the said country or commit or suffer to be committed any violence to the natives to the prejudice of the said trade.' Accordingly they sought 'to give the Transaction some sort of Colour or Appearance of a fair Trade'. Captain John Lewis, who held several survivors (including Little Ephraim Robin John and his brother), therefore agreed to give the headmen of New Town goods valued at 100 coppers for each of his prisoners. Whether this was an appropriate price is unclear.[10]

The brothers were taken to Dominica and sold. They ran away 'to go home to their own country again, but were deceived and sold to a gentleman ... of Virginia'. Five years later, they were spotted by two of their countrymen, crewmen on the British ship *Greyhound* and, by their own account, managed to persuade the captain, Terence O'Neill, 'to carry them to Bristol, and from thence to their own Home'. O'Neill himself claimed that they had stowed away. Although he took them to Bristol he tried to dissuade them from contacting their friend, Thomas Jones, then handed them over to William Jones, the agent acting for their supposed Virginian owner. It was William Jones who had had them imprisoned in irons on board the *Brickdale*.

The legal issues

Case law on the subject of slavery in England before *Somerset* was confused and uncertain. The precedents were not only badly reported but contradictory. Many of them simply recorded *dicta:* that is, remarks that did not form part of a judgment. Such remarks are certainly informative, and clearly played a part in influencing the legal discourse; nevertheless they were without precedential value. Put in very simplistic terms, the legal issue was not only about whether slavery could exist in England, but whether if it did exist it turned slaves into chattels or merely into

---

[10] 23 George II c. 31, s. 29; Public Record Office [hereafter P.R.O.], KB 1/19, Mich. 1773, affdt. William Floyd, 5 October 1773; Latham, *Old Calabar*, p. 23.

servants 'whose freedom was restricted but not annihilated'.[11] *Somerset* had offered an opportunity to settle the issue – which was precisely why Mansfield had tried to keep it out of court. The case only came to judgment once it became apparent that it had ceased to be a simple dispute between the two nominal parties, but had been transformed into a test case between the West India interest on one side and Granville Sharp and the abolitionists on the other.

The legal issues in *Somerset* were clear. No one, as far as we know, ever denied that, according to the laws in force in Africa and Virginia, James Somerset was a slave,[12] even though he had been baptized, which was popularly believed to act as a form of manumission.[13] The rhetoric of the lawyers on both sides concentrated on whether the laws of England recognized slavery at all. This was an issue that went to the heart of imperial relationships. Could colonial laws be different to those of England? Could the common law evolve in different directions in different jurisdictions? Were the English courts bound to uphold local law even if it conflicted with the laws of England?[14]

But also at issue was a much narrower question. Could a master forcibly send his slave abroad? There was a simple answer to this question: the deportation of subjects and residents of the kingdom (sentences of transportation apart) was specifically forbidden under a statute of 1679.[15] Mansfield chose to make his decision on this basis alone. This was certainly an advancement of slave rights, imposing limitations on the powers of slave owners and implying that the law recognized slaves as servants rather than chattel goods. But it was an extremely limited advancement, *not* an outright declaration that slavery did not exist in England.

Superficially, the case of the Robin John brothers raised very similar legal issues. The very language of Thomas Jones' affidavit mimics that of *Somerset*: the men were imprisoned 'in order to be conveyed out of this Kingdom to Virginia against their consent and in order to be made Slaves of at Virginia'.[16] In later years Mansfield was at pains to emphasize the limitations of *Somerset*, but he never retreated from the core of the ruling: that 'the Master had no right to compel the Slave to go into a foreign

---

[11] For a fuller discussion of the state of the law, see William M. Wiecek, '*Somerset*: Lord Mansfield and the legitimacy of slavery in the Anglo-American world', *University of Chicago Law Review*, vol. 42 (1974), pp. 86–101.
[12] No affidavits in support of the application survive.
[13] Guildhall, baptismal register, St Andrew Holborn, 12 February 1771.
[14] This issue was not finally resolved until 1865, when the Colonial Laws Validity Act (28 Victoria c. 63) was passed.
[15] 31 Charles II c. 2, s. 12 (1679).
[16] P.R.O., KB 1/19, Mich. 1773, affdt. Thomas Jones, 18 September 1773.

country'.[17] Certainly those responsible for detaining the brothers thought they were in the wrong. Why otherwise would they have responded as they did when served with the writ of habeas corpus? The two Africans were brought ashore but instead of being sent to London they were 'arrested on an Action ... at the Suit of Terence O'Neill (the Master of the Vessel who brought them from Virginia to England ...) for a pretended Debt for their said passage to England'.[18] Debt was clearly thought to provide a rather better excuse for imprisonment than slavery; presumably those responsible had overlooked a basic premise of medieval law – that only a free man could contract a debt.[19]

But this case was *not* a rerun of *Somerset*. How could the 1679 act apply? The brothers were not subjects of the crown and it is difficult to argue that passage on an English ship made them residents of the kingdom. More importantly, the case raised much wider issues. How could free men become slaves? In many of the colonies such issues were simplified by the clear association between race and slavery. Any individual with a black skin could be assumed to be a slave unless able to prove otherwise. For the judges in England, matters were less clear cut (though one doubts whether they would have had quite so much difficulty if the case had involved enslaved white Europeans). In *Somerset* the unresolved issue was whether the laws of England could uphold the laws of Africa and Virginia by recognizing that an individual regarded as a slave in those societies was also a slave in England; in this case it was specifically stated that the individuals concerned were *not* regarded as slaves in Africa. And if the enslavement of even one African was open to challenge in an English court, then what protection could there be in the future for traders who bought slaves by the hundred and had never before felt the necessity to inquire into their individual circumstances?

As has already been seen, the two Africans came from a society in which slavery was endemic. Efiks did kidnap free people and sell them into slavery, although this seems to have been comparatively unusual, since there was a plentiful supply of those who had been legitimately enslaved. In Calabar as in other parts of Africa slavery existed within a clear and sophisticated cultural framework that justified the enslavement of previously free people. Enslavement was used to exact revenge, and to punish debtors and criminals. It could also result from being on the losing side in battle, and in its simplest form can be seen as a form of ransom or deportation for prisoners of war. Furthermore, Efik society recognized

---

[17] Thomas Hutchinson, *The diary and letters of his excellency Thomas Hutchinson, Esq.*, 2 vols. (Boston, 1884–6), vol. II, p. 277.

[18] P.R.O., KB 1/19, Mich. 1773, affdt. Thomas Jones, 21 October 1773.

[19] I am indebted to Michael Lobban for drawing my attention to this point.

different degrees of enslavement: some slaves were also chattels who could be bought, sold (and sacrificed) at the whim of the master; some were not and the masters' rights over them (including rights of sale) were limited; for others enslavement was both voluntary and partial and resulted from what Europeans would have seen as entry into a patronage network. Slaves in Calabar could own property and achieve relatively high social and economic status; some were entitled to automatic manumission under certain circumstances.[20]

Arguably, therefore, the enslavement of Little Ephraim Robin John and his companions was justified in Efik terms. Strikingly, all the evidence that we have of the reaction of their friends and relatives in Calabar suggests that their enslavement was not disputed.[21] Yet it would be a brave man who would argue the merits and intricacies of African tribal law in an English court, especially when those most knowledgeable about the laws and customs of Calabar (the two slaves at the centre of the case) explicitly stated

that when we first went on board Captain Bevan's ship, we were free people, and no ways subject to the people of New Town; nor had they any right or power over us; nor were we conquered in fight or battle, or taken prisoners by them; nor had they any right to sell us ... we had not done anything to forfeit our liberty; or had the people of New Town any right or power over us; nor had the English captains (as we understood and verily believe) any right to assist the people of New Town, if they and the people of Old Town had been actually engaged in fight or battle, whilst the English captains were present. But there was not any war between the people of New Town and the people of Old Town, but only a quarrel or dispute about trade, which never occasioned any fighting.[22]

Enslavement by war was regarded as legitimate in Africa, and as supporters of the slavery cause regularly pointed out, it saved the lives of men who would otherwise have been killed. In this case – judging by the fate of Amboe Robin John – enslavement had indeed saved the brothers from summary execution. Yet it is clear that European concepts of war and nationhood were very different to those of the Efiks, who unashamedly described unprovoked attacks on neighbouring villages as 'war'. The Robin John brothers had not only been tricked into an ambush, they had not been enslaved by Africans at all. The mere fact of making payments for them did not establish a right of ownership. The evidence allows

---

[20] Forde, *Efik traders*, *passim*; Oku, *Kings and chiefs*, *passim*; Latham, 'Pre-colonial economy', *passim*; Latham, *Old Calabar, passim*.

[21] P.R.O., KB 1/19, Mich. 1773, affdt. Thomas Jones, 15 November 1773 and attached letters.

[22] Thomas Clarkson, *The substance of the evidence of sundry persons on the slave trade collected in the course of a tour made in the autumn of the year 1788* (London, 1789), pp. 6–11. I am indebted to James Walvin for guiding me to this reference.

for two (not necessarily distinct) arguments. Firstly, that the enslavement was open to challenge under African laws and therefore could not be condoned by an English court. Secondly, that it was carried out forcibly by Englishmen in English ships in contravention of English law, and was therefore open to challenge in an English court. Mansfield himself indicated that the case revolved around just these issues: the legitimacy of enslavement by war, and whether Englishmen or Africans were responsible for it. He also drew attention to the fact that 'The whole transaction was beyond sea.' Neither he nor the affidavits presented to the court mentioned the third and most dangerous issue of all: whether slavery could or did exist in England.

A fourth issue related to the question of ownership. If the brothers were legitimately bought as slaves in Calabar, then they were equally legitimately sold as slaves in Dominica. But what of the subsequent chain of ownership? There is no evidence to show that, after they had run away, they were recaptured and sold by their owner; on the contrary, it seems more likely that they were befriended by someone who promised to return them to Calabar, but who then sold them into slavery in Virginia.[23] Could this be a valid sale? Existing case law suggested that the question of ownership could be crucial. In *Rex* v. *Stapylton*, Mansfield had stressed precisely this issue. Stapylton was tried in the King's Bench in 1771 for kidnapping Thomas Lewis. He justified his actions by stating that Lewis was his slave, but there was no proof of his claim. Mansfield made it clear to the jury that even if it had once been good, the chain of ownership had been broken when Lewis was captured and removed from Stapylton's custody by a Spanish privateer; his subsequent return to Stapylton's service did not necessarily indicate a return to slavery.[24] In an informal discussion of the Robin John case, Mansfield stressed that 'there was a fair purchase by the Virginia planter'. But did this allow him to acquire rights not legitimately available to the vendor? Could any of the usual considerations concerning the transfer of title apply to human beings? Little wonder that 'His Lordship thought the case was not without difficulty.'[25]

Avoiding the issues

Lord Mansfield's judgment in *Somerset* had been a masterpiece of decisive insubstantiality. The case of the Robin John brothers could have threatened this achievement, but, perhaps fortunately for Mansfield's

[23] Clarkson, *Substance of the evidence*, p. 8.
[24] Oldham, *Mansfield manuscripts*, vol. II, pp. 1225–8, 1242–3.
[25] Hutchinson, *Diary and letters*, vol. II, pp. 274–5.

reputation, it did not. The protagonists in *Somerset* had been obdurate: the West India planters, because they were confident of victory; the abolitionists, because they needed clarity and publicity for their cause. This was not so in the Robin John case. The failure of the West India faction to obtain the unambiguous judgment they had anticipated in *Somerset* sounded a warning to all those whose prosperity depended upon the slave trade, and that included *all* the protagonists involved in the Robin John case.

It was only to be expected that those responsible for their imprisonment were slave traders. Perhaps less to be expected is that Thomas Jones, the man who sought their freedom, was also one (and would continue to be so until his death in 1795).[26] More unexpected still is the realization that the two Africans were themselves slave traders. They were members of one of Old Calabar's wealthiest trading houses and closely related to Grandee Ephraim Robin John,[27] who became king of Old Calabar after the massacre of 1767.[28] Mansfield had good reason to refer to them as African 'princes'.

Grandee Ephraim Robin John had an apparently well-deserved reputation for savagery and duplicity; he was said to be 'guilty of so many bad actions, no man can say anything in his favour'.[29] Little Ephraim Robin John and Ancona Robin Robin John worked with him in the family business: it was as slave traders that they had first become acquainted with Thomas Jones. They thus had advantages that were denied to the majority of their fellow-Africans in bondage: both were literate, spoke either English or pidgin English fluently, and were well acquainted with some of the principal figures in the Atlantic slave-trading community. We have no reason to believe that their own experiences led them to question the institution on which the wealth and status of their family depended. On the contrary, they were prepared to offer ten slaves as the price of their redemption.[30]

[26] Richardson, *Bristol, Africa and the eighteenth-century slave trade*, vol. IV, pp. xxxvi–xxxvii. Thomas Jones had probably been involved in the slave trade even longer than Richardson believes, since he refers to negotiations at Old Calabar as early as 1763. P.R.O., KB 1/19, Mich. 1773, affdt. Thomas Jones, 21 October 1773.

[27] Thomas Jones thought them to be sons of Grandee Ephraim Robin John, but then learned that they were his brothers. Anthony Benezet described them as his brother and nephew: Gloucester Record Office, D3549/13/1/B19, Benezet to Sharp, 18 November 1774. The genealogy is somewhat indistinct since the Europeans involved clearly did not understand the nuances of the family and clan relationships of the Efiks.

[28] *Minutes of the evidence: select committee on the slave trade* (London, 1790), p. 537, reproduced in S. Lambert, ed., *House of Commons sessions papers of the eighteenth century*, vol. XV (Wilmington, Del., 1975) [hereafter *Select committee, 1790*].

[29] Quoted in Gomer Williams, *History of the Liverpool privateers and letters of marque with an account of the Liverpool slave trade* (London, 1897; 1966 edn), p. 541.

[30] Clarkson, *Substance of the evidence*, p. 8.

Given, on the one hand, a judge who wished to avoid making a ruling and, on the other, a set of protagonists whose own economic self-interest was best served by assisting such avoidance, it is scarcely surprising that the case was compromised without a hearing. On 6 November 1773 the defendants asked to delay returning the habeas corpus for a further ten days. It is not now possible to track the course of the negotiations that took place, but Thomas Jones must have remained firm in his refusal to pay compensation, for the brothers made their affidavit, with its explicit allegations of illegal enslavement, on 9 November.[31]

Thomas Jones' obduracy is in itself intriguing, implying the existence of reciprocal ties of loyalty between himself and his African colleagues that were more important than possible alliances with those whose friendship, on a purely simplistic racist analysis, one might have expected him to prefer. He did not automatically identify all blacks either as inferior or as potential slaves. Other Europeans exhibited a similar sympathy with Africans and African culture, had warm relationships with black merchants and even joined African secret societies. But for Henry Lippincott and William Jones – who probably had closer ties with America than with Africa – the maintenance of trading relationships with Africans was of little consequence. It is tempting to speculate whether their American focus was responsible for what, on the face of it, seem to be more overt, and perhaps more modern, racist attitudes.

On 15 November a compromise was agreed. The captain responsible for removing the two Africans from Calabar agreed to pay £120 to their alleged owners and the Robin John brothers agreed to return to Calabar 'in a vessel called the *Maria* now about to be fitted out for the said coast of Africa'. Significantly, all pretence of detaining them as debtors was now abandoned and it was openly stated that the £120 was 'for the purchase money or value of the said two Africans'. Equally significant is the fact that the compromise was not a simple private arrangement, but was submitted to the King's Bench 'subject to the Order and Direction of this Honourable Court'.[32] On 19 November the compromise was formally accepted.[33] Clearly neither Lord Mansfield nor his 'Honourable Court' were as convinced as more recent commentators have been that *Somerset* had indeed abolished slavery in England.

---

[31] ibid., p. 11; this gives the year as 1783, which must be a misprint for 1773.
[32] P.R.O., KB 1/19, Mich. 1773, affdt. Thomas Jones, 15 November 1773. The *Maria* sank on the outward voyage, but the brothers survived and returned to Calabar early in 1775. Richardson, *Bristol, Africa and the eighteenth-century slave trade*, vol. IV, pp. 53, 57; evidence of Capt. John Ashley Hall, *Select committee, 1790*, p. 517.
[33] P.R.O., KB 21/40, Saturday next after the morrow of All Souls, 14 George III [6 Nov. 1773]; Friday next after the octave of St Martin, 14 George III [19 Nov. 1773].

Somerset was destined to become a piece of legal mythology almost from the beginning. The West India interest and the abolitionists both contended for publicity, publishing and distributing learned tracts on the state of the law. It became one of the 'principal topics of conversation' of the day, but the subject matter of those conversations was the debate over slavery, it was *not* the narrow question of 'Whether the Captain has returned a sufficient cause for the detainer of Somerset?' upon which Mansfield actually pronounced judgment. Little wonder, therefore, that contemporary newspaper reports ignored the subtleties of Mansfield's wording and so misrepresented the extent to which the wider issues had been addressed.[34]

Mansfield's successors on the bench clearly understood the limitations of *Somerset* and were reluctant to expand upon it. In 1812 the King's Bench was asked to issue a habeas corpus for ten negro crewmen held on Portuguese merchantmen in Truro harbour. The judges were informed that these men were slaves, that they were held against their will, that some or all of them had set foot on English soil, that they wished to remain in England and that they had not entered into any form of contract to provide unpaid labour. The writ was refused, possibly because, as transients, they fell outside the provisions of the 1679 act.[35] As late as 1824, when the judges of King's Bench delivered their verdict in *Forbes v. Cochrane*, the arguments they advanced were not entirely without ambiguity. This was a case, arising from events in the war of 1812, in which Cochrane, a commander in the Royal Navy, refused to return a group of escaped slaves who had taken refuge on his ship to their owner. In upholding his decision the judges expressed clear anti-slavery sympathies and referred to *Somerset* as though it had indeed established that slavery did not exist under English common law. But their judgment stressed other issues: that Cochrane was a public servant constrained by the realities of war; that the standard of proof required to establish a wrongful course of action was higher for him than for ordinary citizens; that since the slaves had refused to return to their master voluntarily, Cochrane would have had to remove them forcibly; that Cochrane had acted honourably by conveying the slaves to a place of safe-keeping pending advice from his superiors and had not delivered an outright refusal to return them.[36]

---

[34] James Walvin, *Black and white: the negro and English society, 1555–1945* (London, 1973), pp. 117–31.

[35] P.R.O., KB 1/37, Easter 52 Geo. III (2), affdts. Thomas Laurance, 25 April and 4 May 1812; Thomas May, 5 April 1812. No reason for the refusal is recorded.

[36] *Forbes v. Cochrane*, 2 Barn. and Cress. 448–73, *English Reports*, vol. CVII, pp. 450–602.

Interpreting *Somerset*: the role of the higher courts

The tone of previous legal debates, coupled with Mansfield's own record
as a judge, leaves one in little doubt of the ease with which he could
have supported Somerset's detention. Slaves were, after all, customar-
ily treated as merchandise, as was explicitly recognized in the charter of
the Royal African Society. Granville Sharp had had good reason to be
pessimistic about *Somerset*; his success should not blind us to the risk
he had taken. *Somerset* simply added another ingredient to an already
murky legal cocktail. It is precisely because its consequences were so unclear that historians have found it so difficult to agree on a precise date
at which slavery could be said to have been abolished in England. Such
difficulties have been compounded by a fundamental misunderstanding
of the nature of the English legal system and of the precedential value to
be assigned to individual examples of the experiences of black slaves in
English courts. All historical research requires a knowledge of and sympathy for the social and administrative context in which actions occurred,
but the interpretation of legal events and the records they create requires
particularly careful attention, since their meanings are rarely transparent
to those untrained in the discipline of the law.

For lawyers and laymen alike, the post-*Somerset* confusion is summed
up by Blackstone's famous gloss on the verdict: 'a slave or negro, the
moment he lands in England, falls under the protection of the laws, and
so far becomes a freeman; though the master's right to his service may
possibly still continue'.[37] The question of the obligation to serve – and to
serve without pay – is central to any discussion of the legal status of slaves
after 1772. For some, this is unremarkable. Cotter, who is convinced that
Somerset genuinely did end slavery (both de facto and de jure), inter-
prets continuing restrictions on the freedom of slaves to negotiate wages
and conditions of service and to remove their labour from one master
to another as being akin to apprenticeship, pointing out that, 'Apprentices, indentured servants and others normally laboured without any
expectation of wages, but rather for room and board, clothing, medical assistance and sometimes for the training or experience.'[38] For most

---

[37] William Blackstone, *Commentaries on the laws of England*, 4th edn, 4 vols. (Oxford, 1770),
vol. I, p. 127. In the third edition (4 vols. (Dublin, 1769), vol. I, p. 127) the word
'probably' appeared instead of 'possibly'. The first edition has no such gloss – 'a slave or
negro, the moment he lands in England falls under the protection of the laws, and with
regard to all natural rights becomes instanti a freeman' – but was nevertheless equivocal:
'Yet, with regard to any right which the master may have acquired, by contract or the
like, to the perpetual service of John or Thomas, this will remain exactly in the same
state as before' (1st edn, 4 vols. (Oxford, 1765), vol. I, pp. 123, 412–13).

[38] Cotter, 'Abolition of slavery', pp. 41–2.

eighteenth-century commentators, however, the provision of training and experience was central to the whole concept of apprenticeship; to this day the primary definition of the word *apprentice* in the *Oxford English dictionary* is 'A learner of a craft; one who is bound by legal agreement to serve an employer in the exercise of some handicraft, art, trade or profession, for a certain number of years, with a view to learn its details and duties, in which the employer is reciprocally bound to instruct him.'

Concept and reality did not, of course, always match and some apprentices ended up as brutalized unpaid victims in situations that they were powerless to control. But as the definition suggests, apprenticeship (unlike slavery) was a contractual relationship, defined by a structured, and theoretically legally enforceable set of rights and duties. The right to an apprentice's service could be transferred, but only with his consent: it could not be bought and sold on the open market. Furthermore, the obligation to serve normally terminated with the master's death, although the apprentice's right to subsistence did not. Most important of all, the apprentice served for a determinate period of time: service was not required for life nor did an individual's obligation descend to another generation.[39] The master's obligations were also clearly defined. Many of the arguments in favour of slavery assumed some reciprocity of obligations: the provision of labour in return for protection and subsistence. But nowhere was this specified. An ill-treated or inadequately trained apprentice could petition the local justices for release. No such remedy was open to a slave. Nor could an owner who had deserted his slaves be required to maintain them. When Charlotte Howe, a slave living on the western fringes of London, applied for poor relief, the two parishes in which she had lived went to law to determine which of them was obliged to support her. Significantly, no one suggested that her owner could or should be compelled to do so. The reciprocity of obligations had no basis in law.[40]

Even before *Somerset*, Sir John Fielding had commented critically on those who brought slaves to England as 'cheap servants having no right

[39] See both T. E. Tomlins, *Law dictionary* (London, 1809), and the various editions of R. Burn, *Justice of the peace*, sub 'apprentice' for fuller details.

[40] Like *Somerset*, Howe's case provides an interesting demonstration of Mansfield's ability to sidestep the real issue. The statement of the case includes the significant information that Howe had been baptized – a process that was widely believed to confer automatic manumission. As the parishes conceived the case, the point at issue between them was whether Howe was capable of entering into a legal hiring, and thus of obtaining a parish of settlement – in other words, whether Howe was or was not a free woman. Mansfield ignored the question of Howe's slavery and her capacity to make a contract by insisting on a strict interpretation of the settlement laws. In ruling that Howe had *not* been hired, he neatly avoided any discussion of whether she *could* be hired. *R. v. Thames Ditton*, 4 Douglas 300–2, *English Reports*, vol. XCIX, pp. 891–2.

to wages'.[41] Doubtless the practice continued. In 1800 a woman was prosecuted for ill-treating a young Jamaican girl 'of colour'. The girl seems to have been a slave rather than a servant, but it is difficult to be sure.[42] As late as 1822, the *Times* reported the arrival in England with his master of a 10-year-old (white) slave.[43] There is no reported case either to confirm the existence of a slave's obligation to serve or to define its limits, but Mansfield took an uncompromising view of the issue: 'Where slaves have been brought here, and commenced actions for their wages, I have always nonsuited the plaintiff.'[44]

But some slaves were also apprentices. Forcing slaves to sign apprenticeship agreements became common after *Somerset*. This not only legitimated the owner's insistence on unpaid labour; it also facilitated the subsequent exportation of the slave concerned. In 1799 there was an application for a habeas corpus for John Hamlet. Hamlet was accused, as an apprentice, of 'unlawfully absenting himself' from his master's service. Hamlet, however, was no ordinary apprentice but a slave who had signed indentures of apprenticeship during the voyage to England. Hamlet left his master, Matthias Dobinson, partly because of ill treatment and partly because of threats to return him to the West Indies for sale as a slave. He told the court that Dobinson 'commands a ship in the Jamaica trade now lying in the River Thames' and that he intended to force Hamlet to serve him on board that ship and thereby return him to slavery in St Christopher. His submission to the court also included an interesting preview of the issues that would arise some thirty years later in the case of the *Slave Grace*:

by the laws of the said island of St Christopher and as this deponent believes of the other West India islands slaves cannot be enfranchised but by deed or wills in the said islands and that if negroes are found at large in the said Islands without being able to produce proof of such Enfranchisement they are by the said laws deemed to be slaves and liable as such to be apprehended and sold and that the said Matthias Dobinson admitted ... that no such deed or instrument of enfranchisement had ever been executed by him.

In other words, even if the court believed Hamlet was free in England, he would revert to slavery if returned to the West Indies. In 1827 the decision in *Slave Grace* turned on precisely this point: the judges held that Grace Allan's stay in England suspended but did not end her slavery.[45] In

[41] J. Fielding, *Penal law* (1768 edn), p. 144.   [42] *The Times*, 26 August 1800.
[43] *The Times*, 5 August 1822.
[44] *R. v. Thames Ditton*, 4 Douglas 300–2, *English Reports*, vol. XCIX, pp. 891–2.
[45] Grace Allan had been brought to England in 1822 and returned to Antigua a year later. Her mistress was then prosecuted for illegally importing a slave, on the assumption that Grace had been freed by residence in England. Like *Somerset*, the case attracted intense

John Hamlet's case, they declined even to consider the matter. The habeas corpus was refused and, *Somerset* notwithstanding, Hamlet was delivered to his master and thereby returned to slavery.[46]

In deciding such cases, the courts deliberately interpreted the law as narrowly as possible. They refused to acknowledge any possibility that apprenticeship could be used to cloak violations of *Somerset*, even when specifically told that this was so. Nor did they enquire into the competence of the parties to make such agreements. It was certainly the case that English youths could bind themselves as apprentices and that as a result they could be forcibly returned to their masters. But those who did so had the advice and support of a parent or other guardian, and stood to gain, in theory at least, clear benefits from the agreement. Slaves who entered into indentures of apprenticeship were unlikely to gain anything at all. They were denied legal advice, and probably did not understand the consequences of their actions, especially if, like John Hamlet, they were illiterate. Even if they did, it is unlikely that they were at liberty to decline the invitation.

Interpreting *Somerset*: the role of the lower courts

The interpretation and enforcement of the law in eighteenth-century England was not a matter for the judges alone. The majority of criminal cases and much routine administrative business was left to the local justices of the peace, meeting in Quarter Sessions, at petty sessions or acting alone. These justices were representatives of the county elite, chosen for their status rather than for their legal knowledge. Some did have formal legal training, but for the most part they administered justice with the aid of manuals and treatises, local knowledge, advice from colleagues and a hefty dollop of what could be termed (depending on one's perspective) either common sense or social prejudice. The decisions they took were not necessarily congruent with the law as conceived by trained jurists.[47]

---

media coverage. Much wider issues would have been opened up if the court had been persuaded to consider whether she had been compelled to return to Antigua against her will. *The Slave Grace*, 2 Haggard, 94–134, *English Reports*, vol. CLXVI, pp. 179–93.

[46] P.R.O., KB 1/30, Easter 39 Geo III, affdt. Richard Walter Forbes and John Hamlet, 26 April 1799.

[47] Discontinuities between the law as practised in local courts and as laid down by the judges in the central court continued for at least a century, and were evident in issues other than slavery. It is instructive, for example, to contrast Carolyn Conley's findings about the way the local courts dealt with offences affecting women, especially battered wives, with Maeve Doggett's study of the way in which the central courts tackled the substantive legal issues during the same period. Maeve E. Doggett, *Marriage, wife-beating and the law in Victorian England* (London, 1992), *passim*; Carolyn A. Conley, *The unwritten law, criminal justice in Victorian Kent* (Oxford, 1991), pp. 68–95.

When, in 1774, John Wilkes, acting as a lay magistrate, used *Somerset* to justify his action in discharging a black slave from his master and recommended that he go to law to recoup fourteen years of back pay, he was interpreting the law as he understood it. But his decision was without precedential value and cannot be used as confirmation that de jure slavery in England was abolished by the 1772 *Somerset* decision. Furthermore, he was almost certainly wrong: it is most unlikely that the judges of the central courts would have reached the same conclusion. Yet his actions did free a slave, and he was not the only magistrate to act in this way. In 1809 six black slave crewmen were jailed for debt by their Portuguese captain, as a means of preventing their escape after he had been told that they 'were free on their arrival in England'. When an abolitionist bailed the slaves, the captain mustered 100 Portuguese sailors to recapture them. A magistrate promptly took him into custody, bound him over for good behaviour 'and [so] restored the poor blacks to the enjoyment of their newly acquired liberty'.[48] Almost all the successful rescues of slaves reported during this period involved the intervention of lay magistrates, interpreting the law as they understood it.[49]

In a legal system in which a substantial degree of legal power was delegated to laymen, it was only to be expected that the confused state of the law, coupled with the misleading publicity accorded to *Somerset* and the growth of popular support for the abolitionist cause, would result in a number of local decisions that would be based on the mythology of *Somerset* rather than on Mansfield's carefully constructed judgment. Furthermore, it is arguable that the activities and decisions of lay magistrates were more influential in shaping experiences and expectations of ordinary people than those of the judges, since for most English people in the eighteenth century a collision with the law was more likely to involve interaction with the lay justices and other amateur representatives of the contemporary criminal justice system than with the higher reaches of the professional legal establishment.

Equally, in the confused and uncertain state of the law after *Somerset*, the sympathetic intervention of lay justices could not be guaranteed. The case of John Hamlet, for example, was originally heard before the Middlesex stipendiary magistrate, George Storey. Storey was legally rather more knowledgeable than most lay magistrates: he had previously practised as a barrister.[50] It may also have been significant that he sat at the Shadwell Police Office, where much of the everyday business was associated with the commercial life of the Port of London, and in an

---

[48] *The Times*, 11 September 1809.   [49] Cotter, 'Abolition of slavery', pp. 48–9.

[50] J. Foster, *Alumni oxonienses* (Oxford, 1888); R. A. Roberts, ed., *Calendar of Inner Temple records* (London, 1936).

area much under the influence of the West India interest. Storey heard arguments on both sides, but professed himself unable to decide whether to hand Hamlet back to his master or not. It was at his suggestion that Hamlet applied for a habeas corpus in order to get the opinion of the judges on the matter.[51] This seems to be a case where, as far as Hamlet's freedom was concerned, a little legal knowledge would have been far less dangerous than Storey's sound grasp of the limits of his legal powers.

Given the paucity of reported incidents, whether in the law reports or in newspaper or pamphlet literature, it is difficult to generalize about the position of slaves after 1772. There can be little doubt that de jure slavery continued to exist. Equally, the misleading publicity given to *Somerset* meant that some black slaves benefited from the resultant confusion and found themselves de facto free. Much of course would depend on the quality of legal advice available to them and on the existence of informal support networks. Although much of the social mapping of British towns and cities has yet to be done, it is clear that most immigrant groups did cluster together: in London, for example, there were several areas that were distinctively Irish.[52] As George has pointed out, however, black slaves did not normally live in supportive communities of this kind: 'their position must have been strangely friendless and anomalous'.[53] Many black slaves in England thought themselves to be free. Many Englishmen agreed with them. But some black slaves, especially those in the country temporarily, may never have known how to take advantage of their supposed freedom. Yet, as the details of *Somerset* faded from immediate judicial memory, the mythology did slowly turn into reality. The judgment in *Forbes* v. *Cochrane* may have been ambiguous but it is nevertheless clear that two of the three presiding judges believed that *Somerset* had indeed abolished slavery in England. When slavery was abolished in 1833, compensation was paid to slave owners; there is no recorded example of such a payment for a slave in England.

Abolition, propaganda and mythology

One of the more intriguing aspects of *Somerset* and its legacy is the way in which publicity about slavery and slave-related issues was carefully manipulated by the abolitionists for their own purposes. In the course of researching this chapter, for example, it has become clear that the case of

[51] P.R.O., KB 1/30, Easter 39 Geo III, affdt. Richard Walter Forbes and John Hamlet, 26 April 1799.
[52] M. Dorothy George, *London life in the eighteenth century* (Harmondsworth, 1966), pp. 120–31.
[53] George, *London life*, p. 139.

the Robin John brothers, although unknown to modern historians, was well known to contemporary abolitionists, and that copies of affidavits, including some not filed in court, were readily available to them. Some were reproduced by Clarkson in his tract, *The substance of the evidence of sundry persons on the slave trade*, in 1789. They were known to at least one witness who testified to the select committee on the slave trade in 1790; they were even available in Old Calabar, as the brothers had taken copies with them on their return to Africa. Yet, despite this widespread knowledge, the information was used in a somewhat partial way, primarily to illustrate the involvement of British slave traders in the massacre of 1767. Wherever the detention of Little Ephraim Robin John and his brother is mentioned, there are suggestions that they were freed as a result of an application for habeas corpus. This is certainly true, but it is not the whole truth, since they were not freed by the due process of law but by means of a compromise that involved recognition of their status as slaves.

If this were an isolated incident, it would be unkind to suggest that the misrepresentation was deliberate. After all, Clarkson did not collect his evidence until some ten years after the event; Granville Sharp does not appear to have known about the case until 1774 and perhaps even then was not fully aware of the legal issues raised. Yet subsequent events certainly make one realize that, not unnaturally, Sharp cared less about the accuracy of his publicity than about the efficacy of that publicity in raising the profile of the abolitionist cause. His castigation of the British government for failing to prosecute in the notorious case of the slave ship *Zong* is a good example of this.

The *Zong* sailed from Africa in 1781 with some 440 slaves on board. Sickness broke out and the master, realizing that the ship's insurance did not cover losses amongst the slaves caused by death from natural causes, had over 100 of them thrown overboard whilst still alive. This action was justified to the underwriters as having been necessary to save the ship because of a lack of water. The case came to public notice when the underwriters refused to pay and were sued by the ship's owners. Initially the owners won their case, but in 1783 the underwriters sought and were granted a second trial when it emerged that the shortage of water was highly exaggerated and that the claim was essentially fraudulent. In allowing a new trial Mansfield stressed that the issue was whether or not it had been a question of necessity, and is said to have remarked that 'the case of slaves was the same as if horses were thrown overboard'.[54]

---

[54] Prince Hoare, *Memoirs of Granville Sharp*, cited in Elizabeth Donnan, *Documents illustrative of the slave trade to America* (Washington, 1930–5), vol. II, p. 555. The report of the case does not attribute these words to Mansfield, but puts similar sentiments into the mouths of counsel opposing the rule for a new trial: 'It has been decided, whether wisely

Even supporters of slavery found it hard to stomach language of this kind, and Sharp seized its propaganda possibilities, campaigning vigorously for the government to launch a murder prosecution against the perpetrators of the crime. Yet he cannot realistically have expected any action. Murder, like any other crime in eighteenth-century England, was not a matter for public but for private prosecution. True, the government did sometimes finance prosecutions for the public good, and murder was precisely the sort of crime in which they were most likely to intervene in this way, but given that the events complained of had taken place two years earlier in colonial waters and that the master of the *Zong* was himself dead, it is difficult to believe that a prosecution would have been successful. If Sharp genuinely did think that there was a case to answer in the English courts and that there were living individuals who could justifiably be brought to trial, there was nothing to stop him from beginning his own prosecution. That he chose to complain about the failure of others to take action rather than to take action himself suggests that he was more interested in using the *Zong* as a means to an end – publicizing the intrinsic evils of slavery – rather than in a genuine attempt to bring the perpetrators to justice.

For Sharp and the abolitionists, the importance of the *Somerset* decision lay not in the decision itself, but in what abolitionist publicity and propaganda could *make* the decision mean. *Somerset* as publicized and interpreted by the abolitionists bore little resemblance to the judgment actually delivered by Mansfield in a corner of Westminster Hall in June 1772. As Wiecek pointed out over twenty years ago: it 'illustrates a legal world where things are not what they seem, a world of deceptive appearances and unforeseen consequences'.[55] It is a case where the myth has become more important than the reality. If one is to ask whether Mansfield really did free the slaves in England, then the answer has to be a clear 'no'. Had he done so, he would never have had to record the formal manumission of his own slave (and illegitimate great-niece), Dido Belle.[56] Some slaves were freed as a result of *Somerset*. Others, like John Hamlet, found that reliance on Mansfield's verdict provided a particularly efficacious return to colonial slavery. But if *Somerset* achieved little else, it certainly helped shape changes in attitudes and expectations (for whites as well as for blacks). Let us return, for example, to the incident of the ten slaves in Truro harbour. The campaign to release them was

---

or unwisely is not now the question, that a portion of our fellow creatures may become the subject of property. This, therefore, was a throwing overboard of goods.' *Gregson* v. *Gilbert*, 3 Douglas 232–4, *English Reports*, vol. XCIX, pp. 629–30.

[55] Wiecek, 'Legitimacy of slavery', p. 87.
[56] Oldham, *Mansfield manuscripts*, vol. II, pp. 1329–30.

led by members of the local white community, who clearly assumed that slavery was not only immoral but also illegal; they had probably already assisted two of the slaves to escape.[57]

We know, as yet, comparatively little about the black population in England in the late eighteenth century: estimates of its size vary from 3,000 to 15,000, some but not all of whom were actually slaves.[58] In practical terms, therefore, *Somerset* had little impact on everyday English life. The paucity of cases relating to slavery is in itself a telling reminder of this. But for those British colonies that were to become the USA, matters were very different. For them, the sheer size of the slave population, coupled with the politicization of the moral and constitutional issues associated with slavery, made it increasingly difficult for the judges to continue avoiding such issues in their courts. Interpretations of *Somerset* were at the heart of those debates on the fate of fugitive slaves and interstate relationships that created continuing accretions of case and statute law, and that were ultimately to contribute to the slide into civil war.[59]

Those developments were neither foreseen nor intended by Lord Mansfield. They resulted not from the judgment itself, but from what the judgment came to mean – and the shaping of those meanings owed as much if not more to the publicity skills of Granville Sharp and his fellow-abolitionists as it did to the judicial skills of Lord Mansfield. Mansfield found the law on slavery in a state of confusion and that is precisely where he left it.

---

[57] P.R.O., KB 1/37, Easter 52 Geo. III (2), affdts. Thomas Laurance, 25 April and 4 May 1812; Thomas May, 5 April 1812.

[58] *Somerset v. Stewart*, 1 Lofft 17, *English Reports*, vol. XCVIII, p. 499; Samuel Estwick, *Consideration of the negro cause commonly so called addressed to the Right Honourable Lord Mansfield* (London, 1772), p. 94; *Candid reflections upon the judgment lately awarded by the court of King's Bench in Westminster Hall on what is commonly called the negro cause by a planter* (London, 1772).

[59] For an introductory overview, see Wiecek, 'Legitimacy of slavery'.

Religion and the law: evidence, proof and 'matter of fact', 1660–1700

Barbara Shapiro

While it has long been recognized that English legal thought had a role to play in political and constitutional thinking, it has less often been noticed that legal thinking played a significant role in English religious discourse. I explore one facet of that influence here as I examine how the legal concept of 'matter of fact' and legal methods of proving 'matters of fact' were applied by Restoration religious thinkers to issues and topics that were far removed from the courts.

The English legal tradition of fact-finding was indebted to the continental Romano-canon legal tradition that had developed a complex evidentiary system during the Middle Ages. In that system witnesses played a key role and criteria were developed to assess the credibility of witnesses and to exclude incompetent, biased or interested testimony. In serious criminal offences where the evidence of two good witnesses or the confession that constituted 'full proof' was lacking, the testimony of less credible witnesses, a single witness or a variety of *indicia* were sufficient for a judge to order judicial torture of the defendant, torture designed to elicit the confession that would constitute full proof. Drawn from the ancient rhetorical tradition, these *indicia* included the age, sex, education, social status and reputation of the accused. Similar criteria were invoked in assessing witness credibility and circumstantial evidence. In some kinds of crimes 'signs', or 'circumstances', treated as presumptions of various strengths might also constitute sufficient proof.

The Romano-canon system distinguished between fact and law. 'Fact' or 'factum' implied actions or events in which human beings participated which might be known, if not directly observed, at the time of adjudication. Such 'facts', established by witnesses, provided the basis for belief and judgment. Some of this legal technology was also to be found in the English common law, most prominently after witnesses became common in jury trials.

Several features of the common law are relevant to this inquiry. The first is the legal usage of 'fact' and the distinction between 'matters of fact' and 'matters of law'. The second is the development of lay jurors as fact evaluators of witness testimony and the criteria for witness evaluation. The third is the value placed on impartial public proceedings and unbiased judgment.

'Matters of fact' and 'matters of law'

The common law, unlike the Romano-canon, separated the determinations of 'matters of fact' from 'matters of law' institutionally, placing the former in the hands of lay jurors and the latter in the hands of professional judges. As a result experience with the concept 'fact' and fact determination became familiar to ordinary individuals eligible to serve on juries and those who attended trials. Widespread public experience and familiarity with the language of fact and methods of fact determination made 'fact' transportable to non-legal contexts and assisted Restoration theologians in employing it in a number of theological and polemical contexts.

The term 'fact' as used in English law had two related meanings. The first referred to a human act or deed of legal significance that had, or would, take place. The second placed 'fact' in the adversarial context of trial. Had or had not the accused person, or a party to a civil dispute, done the act as alleged? The act, the fact, required proof based on evidence. We find references to an accused person being 'taken in the Fact' as well as the 'Heinousness of the Fact' and the still common usage 'before the fact' and 'after the fact' or as William Lambarde's widely read guidebook for justices of the peace would have it, 'precedent', 'present' and 'subsequent' to the fact.[1]

The matter of fact–matter of law distinction developed during the medieval period[2] and in the sixteenth century Sir Thomas More employed the distinction in ways suggesting long-term usage and widespread understanding.[3] From the sixteenth century jurors were 'sworn Judges in matter of fact, evidenced by witnesses and debated before them'.[4] The

[1] William Lambarde, *Eirenarcha* (London, 1614), pp. 218, 219. See also Cicero, *De inventione*, vol. I, 34–43, 48; *Rhetorica ad herennium*, Loeb Classical Library, 2 vols. (Cambridge, Mass., 1954), vol. I, 8.
[2] See Morris S. Arnold, 'Law and fact in the medieval jury trial: out of sight, out of mind', *American Journal of Legal History*, vol. 18 (1974), pp. 268–80; F. F. C. Milson, 'Law and fact in legal development', *University of Toronto Law Review*, vol. 17 (1969), pp. 1–19; James Bradley Thayer, *Preliminary treatise on evidence at the common law* (1898; reprinted New York, 1969), pp. 183–261; Jerome Lee, 'The law–fact distinction: from trial by ordeal to trial by jury', *American Intellectual Property Law Association Quarterly Journal*, vol. 12 (1984), pp. 288–94.
[3] John Guy, ed., *The debellacyon of Salem and Bizance*, in *Complete works of St Thomas More* (New Haven, Conn., 1987), vol. X, pp. xviii ff.
[4] Giles Duncombe, *Tryals per pais*, 4th edn (London, 1702), pp. 1–2.

office of the jury was to find 'the truth of the facts'.[5] Similar statements appeared with some regularity in judicial charges to the jury and in judicial summing up of evidence. The 'fact' or 'matter of fact' was not considered proven until satisfactory evidence had been presented.

Juries and witnesses

The jury went through a considerable evolution as fact decider. Jurors, however, were not initially fact evaluators but rather 'knowers' of the facts, selected locally because they were expected to bring some prior knowledge of the facts and/or the litigants to the trial. Matters of fact in most situations were to be proved either by the testimony of witnesses or 'authentic' documents, sometimes called 'matters of record'.[6] Witness testimony became a regular and accepted part of common law proceedings in the course of the sixteenth century. Thomas More and Christopher St Germain early in that century were already treating the proposition that jurors were not witnesses but judges of fact as if it were common knowledge[7] and justices of the peace were actively involved in the pretrial examination of witnesses.[8] Although jurors retained the right to know personally the facts at issue, they were, for all practical purposes, limited to evaluating the documentary and parole evidence presented to them.

Once witness testimony replaced the jurors' personal knowledge of fact, how the jurors were to discern the truth of the facts at issue from what they heard in court becomes a significant practical question. Early modern English common law courts, however, are rather difficult to analyze in epistemological terms because they are a combination of institutional elements and procedures, some of which, like the jury, had been created in the distant past and some of which, like the witness, were a more recent innovation. Early modern courts incorporated the older device of oaths, grounded in earlier epistemological beliefs, but the relationship between the old oaths and the developing rational criteria for assessing witnesses remained unclear.

A number of assumptions underlay the modes of inquiry of early modern courts. The first was that it was possible to gain adequate if not

---

[5] Edward Leigh, *A philological commentary* (London, 1658), p. 135.

[6] In criminal cases the testimony of witnesses was central, although 'circumstances' might also be relevant.

[7] Sir John Fortescue, *De laudibus legum angliae*, ed. S. B. Chrimes (Cambridge, 1942), chap. 26; J. H. Baker, *The reports of Sir John Spelman* (London, 1978), vol. II, p. 106, citing *Deballacyon of Salem and Bizance* (1533).

[8] See John Langbein, *Prosecuting crime in the Renaissance* (Cambridge, Mass., 1974).

perfect knowledge of events that could not be seen, heard or repeated in court. Neither judges, jurors nor lawyers would actually see a murder. As the author of the first significant treatise on the law of evidence, Geoffrey Gilbert, put it, the law dealt with 'transient things' of no 'constant being'.[9]

First-hand sensory experience of such matters was thought to provide the 'best evidence' for 'matters of fact', but as Sir Matthew Hale noted, it was often unattainable.[10] Courts therefore relied on documents that recorded the actions or rights in question or witnesses who had seen or heard the events in question. If courts were to employ witnesses, it was necessary that their testimony be believable and trustworthy. It was also necessary to develop some way of thinking about what kinds of testimony were likely to be credible and what were not.

All early modern courts were dependent on testimony. Common, civil and canon law developed rules of exclusion and criteria for evaluating testimony. English common law assumed jurors had sufficient intellectual ability and moral probity to assess witness credibility adequately and to reach verdicts of sufficient certitude to satisfy their consciences and the community at large.

Those guilty of certain crimes, for example treason, felony, perjury and forgery, were excluded. Madmen and idiots were excluded for 'want of skill and discernment'.[11] There was controversy about accused co-conspirators and accessaries who were most likely to have first-hand knowledge but were also likely to lie. As Hale indicated, 'It is one thing whether a witness be admissible to be heard, another thing, whether they are to be believed when heard.'[12]

Sir Francis Bacon and Sir Matthew Hale agreed that the law of England left 'the discerning and credit of testimony wholly to the juries' consciences and understanding'.[13] Jurors were both 'judges of the fact, and likewise of the probability or improbability, credibility or incredibility of the witnesses and the testimony'.[14] If it was sometimes asserted that witnesses should be considered 'honeste, good and indifferent, till the contrary be shown',[15] Hale wrote that juries were to judge the 'Quality,

---

[9] Geoffrey Gilbert, *Law of evidence* (London, 1803), p. 3 (1st edn Dublin, 1754).

[10] Sir Matthew Hale, *The primitive origination of mankind* (London, 1677), p. 128.

[11] ibid., p. 144.

[12] Sir Matthew Hale, *Historia placitorium coronae or History of the pleas of the crown*, 2 vols. (London, 1736), vol. I, p. 635.

[13] Francis Bacon, *The works of Francis Bacon*, ed. James Spedding, Robert Leslie Ellis and Douglas Denon Heath (1857–74), vol. I, p. 513. See also Hale, *History of the pleas of the crown*, vol. I, p. 276.

[14] Hale, *History of the pleas of the crown* (1736 edn), vol. II, p. 176. See also vol. I, p. 635; Gilbert, *Law of evidence*, p. 60; Hale, *The history of the common law of England*, ed. Charles M. Gray (Chicago, Ill.), p. 164.

[15] More, *Salem and Bizance*, vol. X, p. 157; Gilbert, *Law of evidence*, p. 147.

Carriage, Age, Condition, Education and Place of Commorance of Witnesses' in giving 'more or less Credit to their Testimony'.[16] Clearly gender, property holding, social status, education and expertise were part of the equation as was the power of the oath taken by witnesses and whether or not the testimony was hearsay.

Justicing manuals contained credibility criteria to assist justices examining witnesses and persons accused of felonies and thus became part of the process through which witnesses and witness credibility became familiar.[17] Building on Romano-canon criteria and classical rhetoric they emphasized ancestry, education, occupation and character.[18]

Summarizing the practice of the early eighteenth century, Gilbert wrote of what might 'render a witness suspected'. A party to a crime or one who swore

for his own safety or indemnity, or be a relation or friend to the party, or the like; or be of a profligate or wicked temper or disposition; and the weight of the probability lies thus; if you think the bias is so strong upon him, as would incline a man of his disposition, figure and rank in the world, to falsify, you are to disbelieve him; but if you think him a man of that credit and veracity, that, notwithstanding the bias upon him, would yet maintain a value for truth, and is under the force and obligation of his oath, he is to be believed.[19]

Although hearsay was clearly viewed as inferior to eye-witness testimony, it does not appear to have been rigorously excluded until the

---

[16] Hale, *History of the common law*, pp. 154, 165.

[17] See Langbein, *Prosecuting crime in the Renaissance*; Barbara Shapiro, *'Beyond reasonable doubt' and 'probable cause': historical perspectives on the Anglo-American law of evidence* (Berkeley, 1991), pp. 148–64.

[18] M. Dalton's *The country justice* (London, 1635), p. 297 included 'two old verses' advising examiners.

    Conditio, sexus, aetas, discretio, fama,

    Et fortuna, fides: in testibus esta requires.

Tancred in the thirteenth century had already noted that when faced with conflicting testimony judges were to 'follow those who are most trustworthy – the freeborn rather than the freedman, the older rather than the younger, the many of honorable estate rather than the inferior, the noble rather than the ignoble, the man rather than the woman. Further, the truth-teller is to be believed rather than the liar, the man of pure life rather than the man who lives in vice, the rich man rather than the poor, anyone rather than he who is a great friend of the person for whom he testifies or an enemy of him against whom he testifies. If the witnesses are all of the same dignity and status, then the judge should stand with the side that has the greatest number of witnesses.' Charles Donahue, Jr., 'Proof by witnesses in the church courts of medieval England; an imperfect reception of the learned law', *On the laws and customs of England*, ed. M. Arnold *et al.* (Cambridge, Mass., 1981), p. 131. For rhetorical origins see Cicero, *De inventione*, II, x, 34–6. See also II, xiii, 43; Thomas Wilson, *Art of rhetorique* (London, 1553).

[19] Gilbert, *Law of evidence*, p. 149.

mid-eighteenth century.[20] Formally excluded or not, second-hand testimony was considered far less valuable than that received 'from those that report their own view'.[21] By the time that Locke wrote it was already a truism 'that any testimony, the further off it is from the original truth, the less force and proof it has'.[22]

On the whole women's testimony was probably undervalued, given the widespread belief that women were the less rational sex. English women appeared as witnesses, but did not serve on juries. A child's testimony was viewed as less credible than that of an adult.[23]

Reputation was a factor in assessing witness credibility, as were 'inclinations' and 'education'.[24] Those with 'habits of falshood and [who] are Comon & Known lyars', and those who lived 'open, vitious scandalous lives', could be heard but their testimony could bind jurors 'no farther' than they believed it in their conscience to be true.[25] In criminal trials defendants often attempted to show that government witnesses were not believable because they were persons of low moral character, of 'ill fame', or lacking in integrity.[26] Thomas Hobbes stated succinctly that testimony involved two beliefs, 'one of the saying of the man; the other of his virtue'.[27]

Moral status and reputation blended into but were not identical to social and economic status in assessments of credibility. The testimony of independent property holders counted for more than that of dependants or the poor, but status considerations might be countered by others. In civil cases those with a pecuniary interest were excluded regardless of status and wealth. Kin might testify but might or might not be considered credible. Juries were also to consider the 'manner' of the witnesses'

---

[20] See John H. Wigmore, 'History of the hearsay rule', *Harvard Law Review*, vol. 17 (1904), pp. 436–58; John Langbein, 'Historical foundations of the law of evidence: a view from the Ryder sources', *Columbia Law Review*, vol. 96 (1996), pp. 1186–90.

[21] Hale, *Primitive origination*, p. 128. See also Sir John Holt, *A report of divers cases* (London, 1708), p. 404. Hearsay might be used to corroborate testimony. See James Oldham, 'Truth-telling in the eighteenth-century English courtroom', *Law and History Review*, vol. 12 (1994), p. 104.

[22] John Locke, *Essay concerning human understanding*, ed. Alexander Frasier, 3 vols. (New York, 1959), chap. 14, §10.

[23] Gilbert, *Law of evidence*, p. 143.

[24] See William Lambarde, *Eirenarcha* (1614), p. 218; Richard Crompton, *L'office et auctoritie de justices de peace* (London, 1606), p. 100r.

[25] M. R. T. Macnair, '"A fragment on proof" by Francis North, Lord Guildford', *The Seventeenth Century*, vol. 8 (1991), p. 143; Hale, *Primitive origination*, p. 128.

[26] Sir Thomas More, on trial for treason, attempted to show that Richard Rich had been notorious as a 'common lyar' and a man of 'no recommendable fame'. Hubertus Schulte Herbruggen, 'The process against Sir Thomas More', *Law Quarterly Review*, vol. 99 (1983), pp. 113–36.

[27] Thomas Hobbes, *Leviathan*, ed. Michael Oakeshott (New York, 1962), p. 57.

testimony, it being 'a probable indication' of whether they speak 'truly or falsely'.[28]

There was a decided preference for multiple witnesses, although the English often emphasized they were not bound by the Romano-canon two-witness rule. Numbers were important but not necessarily decisive.[29] Juries were entitled to 'disbelieve what a Witness swear' and 'may sometimes give Credit to one Witness, tho' opposed by more than one'. One of the 'Excellencies' of the jury trial was that the jury 'either upon Reasonable Circumstances, indicating a Blemish upon their credibility', might pronounce 'a Verdict contrary to such Testimonies, the Truth where of they have just Cause to suspect, and may and do of pronounce their Verdict upon one single Testimony'.[30] Nevertheless the 'concurrent testimonies of many Witnesses ... by their multiplicity and concurrency [made] an evidence more concludent'.[31]

Francis North, Lord Guilford, Chief Justice of Common Pleas, indicated that the 'Probability of [th]e Matter' must be involved in assessing witness credibility[32] and Gilbert noted that the incredibility of the fact 'overthrows' the testimony of a witness and 'set[s] aside' his credit. '[F]or if the fact be contrary to all manner of experience and observation', it was 'too much' to receive upon the oath of a single witness.[33]

Although we know almost nothing about how early modern juries actually reached their verdicts, there is considerable contemporary writing about proper standards for verdicts. From the late fifteenth century onwards, jurors were instructed to give verdicts 'according to your evidence and your conscience'.[34] Sir Thomas More noted that a juror must have a 'sure and certain persuasion & belief in his own conscience', a conscience that has been 'induced reasonably'.[35] Hale wrote, 'it is the

---

[28] Hale, *History of the pleas of the crown*, vol. II, pp. 276, 277. Hale, *History of the common law*, p. 163. See also p. 154. St Germain and Gilbert expressed similar views. More, *Salem and Bizance*, vol. X, p. 157; Gilbert, *Law of evidence*, p. 147.

[29] George Fisher suggests that the number of witnesses testifying on oath was crucial and that credibility considerations counted for little. George Fisher, 'The jury's rise as lie detector', *Yale Law Review*, vol. 107 (1997), pp. 575–714. This finding, however, runs against all the statements concerning credibility assessments we have encountered. No doubt in many trials witnesses on both sides appeared to satisfy credibility criteria. Here numbers might well be decisive. Fisher emphasizes the necessity of believing either prosecution or defence witnesses and so ignores the possibility that only some might be believed. He treats the jury's function as detecting lies rather than coming to a conclusion after consideration of all the evidence.

[30] Hale, *History of the common law*, p. 164.

[31] Hale, *Primitive origination of mankind*, p. 130. See also Gilbert, *Law of evidence*, pp. 104, 147–8, 151.

[32] Macnair, ' "Fragment on proof" ', p. 143.   [33] Gilbert, *Law of evidence*, p. 147.

[34] Baker, *Reports of Spelman*, vol. II, p. 112, citing a case of 1465.

[35] More, *Salem and Bizance*, vol. X, p. 160.

conscience of the jury, that must pronounce the prisoner guilty or not guilty'.[36]

'Satisfied conscience' was the most frequently voiced standard of the common law courts. The process by which the conscience was to become 'satisfied' was a rational and not an emotional one. When jurors entertained reasonable doubts, they were to acquit. Before reaching their verdict the jurors were 'to consider their Evidence . . . [T]hey are to weigh the Credibility of Witnesses, and the Force and Efficacy of their Testimonies'.[37] The verdict in a jury trial 'carries in itself a much greater Weight and Preponderation to discover the Truth of a Fact, than any other Trial whatsoever'.[38] Lord Guilford noted that 'in all cases [tha]t depend on . . . witnesses . . . they who are Judges of [th]e fact are to Consult with themselves, & weigh all Circumstances, and as they in their consciences beleev concerning [th]e testimony so are they to give their verdict'.[39] The 'satisfied conscience' standard was synonymous with the term 'moral certainty' and neither was thought to have the same degree of certainty as demonstration or mathematical proof. Late seventeenth-century judges often used expressions such as 'if you are satisfied or not satisfied with the evidence', or 'if you believe on the evidence'. Judge Vaughan indicated a juror swears 'to what he can infer and conclude from the testimony . . . by the force of his understanding'.[40] Understanding and conscience were concerned with the same mental processes. Over time judges became increasingly likely to mention doubts on the part of the jury. From the mid-eighteenth century the now familiar 'beyond reasonable doubt' terminology of modern Anglo-American law was added to its cognates, 'satisfied conscience' and 'moral certainty'. The meaning of all these phrases was identical and they were often used together.[41]

Despite complaints of biased juries, jurors were assumed to have the qualities of mind necessary to make judgments of matters of fact. They were intelligent enough to consider whether the 'fact' had actually occurred and who had been responsible for it. They were considered capable of evaluating the demeanour of witnesses, comparing testimonies, spotting inconsistencies and contradictions and evaluating the extent to which these factors 'took off' from the credit of witnesses. A property qualification was thought to ensure their independence and impartiality.

---

[36] Hale, *History of the pleas of the crown*, vol. II, p. 314.
[37] Edward Waterhouse, *Fortescue illustratus* (London, 1663), pp. 129, 259.
[38] Hale, *History of the common law*, pp. 165, 167.
[39] Macnair, ' "Fragment on proof" ', p. 143.
[40] *Complete collection of state trials and proceedings*, ed. T. V. Howell (London, 1809–28), vol. VIII, pp. 999, 1005, 1006, 1008, 1110.
[41] See Shapiro, *'Beyond reasonable doubt' and 'probable cause'*, pp. 1–41.

Men of the 'middling sort', jurors, were deemed to have sufficient reason to make sound judgments about matters of fact.

The question of the social status of those responsible for legal fact-finding takes on a special importance to historians of the early modern period, given Steven Shapin's and Simon Schaffer's emphasis on the importance of social status in connection to the construction of knowledge. They suggest that the centrality of prevalent aristocratic and courtier codes established a system of trust and trustworthiness that contributed to the construction of knowledge of scientific 'matters of fact'.[42] While the English certainly exhibited greater inclination to trust the testimony of gentlemen than those of lesser status, those assumptions alone did not determine fact-finding in the courts or, as I shall show shortly, in connection with biblical truths. Societal inclination to trust those of high status was undermined in a variety of ways in the legal setting. Gentlemen engaged in countless lawsuits that pitted the word of one gentleman against that of another. Those with even the slightest financial interest in a civil case were excluded from testifying on the grounds of partiality and interest, gentleman or not. 'Interest' was not a matter of social status. Gentlemen were tried for criminal acts, and upper-class felony defendants were no more permitted to testify on oath than were those of lower class. Although Shapin has suggested that the common people were perceived as 'perceptually unreliable', there is nothing in the legal literature to support such a claim. All normal men were deemed to be perceptually competent, and there was no suggestion that their 'senses' or memories, key elements in matter of fact, were less acute or less accurate than those of higher status. In very high stakes situations, juries, composed of men of middling status, were entrusted with fact-finding.

The norm of impartiality

Efforts to ensure impartiality have always been at the heart of the legal enterprise. The common law attempted to reduce or eliminate partiality and bias in jurors, judges and witnesses, while assuming partiality in the litigating parties and their lawyers. It provided for juror challenges to prevent favouritism, corruption and bias. Jurors were 'Not to be such as are prepossessed or prejudiced before they hear their Evidence'. Only twelve 'indifferent' judges of the fact were to be sworn.[43] Judges are 'to administer the law and justice indifferently without respect of persons'.[44]

---

[42] Steven Shapin and Simon Schaffer, *Leviathan and the air pump* (Princeton, 1985); Steven Shapin, *A social history of truth: civility and science in seventeenth-century England* (Chicago, 1994).

[43] Hale, *History of the common law*, pp. 161, 162–3.

[44] Hale, *History of the pleas of the crown*, vol. I, p. 887.

Hale, enjoining 'an entire absence of affection and passion', insisted that judging required a 'temperate mind totally abandoning all manner of passion, affection, and perturbation'.[45]

The impartiality norm also applied to witnesses. Hale indicated 'that which is reported by persons disinterested' was preferable to 'that which is reported by persons of whose interest it is to have the thing true, or believed to be true'.[46] Witnesses were most credible when 'wholly indifferent and unconcerned'. Indeed their credit was 'to be taken from their perfect indifference to the point in question'.[47] No doubt judges, jurors, and witnesses often violated the norms, but they were constantly reiterated.

In the courts juries, judges, witnesses and counsel participated in a process that was designed to produce 'morally certain' verdicts in 'matters of fact'. By utilizing certain procedures, written documents of specified types, witness testimony produced by certain kinds of persons and under certain conditions and 'circumstances', 'judges of the fact' were thought to be able to produce rational belief in 'matters of fact'. The courts made what society believed to be epistemologically sound findings about events or 'facts' under conditions that were recognized to be imperfect. The security of life and property, deeply held cultural values, depended on these outcomes.

The epistemological assumptions of common law were summarized by Gilbert. First-hand sense data was the best source of knowledge but was of limited usefulness to courts because the law dealt with 'transient things' of no 'constant being'. When we 'cannot see or hear any thing ourselves, and yet are obliged to make a judgment of it', it was necessary to 'see and hear by report from others'. It was reasonable to give 'faith and credibility ... to the honesty and integrity of credible and uninterested witnesses, attesting any fact under the solemnities and obligations of religion, and the dangers and penalties of perjury'. When such conditions had been met the mind 'acquiesces ... for it cannot have any more reason to be doubted than if we ourselves had heard and seen it'.[48]

It was possible to arrive at sound judgments about facts, that is events and deeds, though those events involved actions that could not be observed or replicated by those doing the fact-finding. Sound judgments could be arrived at by examining the testimony of those who had seen or heard the events. In order to do so it was necessary to examine the quality

[45] Maija Jansson, 'Matthew Hale on judges and judging', *Journal of Legal History*, vol. 9 (1989), pp. 204, 206, 207.
[46] Hale, *Primitive origination of mankind*, p. 128.
[47] Gilbert, *Law of evidence*, pp. 122, 155.   [48] ibid., pp. 2, 4.

and quantity of testimony, to be suspicious of hearsay, and to consider any relevant 'circumstances'. Oaths were thought to enhance the probability of testimonial truth, but not to ensure it. Institutional arrangements and procedures, such as the right to challenge jurors or to exclude witnesses with financial interests, would help ensure just and truthful fact determination. During the sixteenth and seventeenth centuries there flourished a legal culture of fact built upon a concept of 'matter of fact'. The legal system was pervaded by the belief that ephemeral 'facts' of human action could be established with a high degree of certitude and that ordinary persons had sufficient ability to arrive at impartial, truthful verdicts. Much of this epistemology and method could be and was transferred to other sites of knowledge.

Testimony, evidence and Restoration religious discourse

Restoration rational theologians and polemicists, particularly those with interests in natural philosophy and of a latitudinarian persuasion, found the legal concept of 'matter of fact' useful in several ways, the most important of which was to provide rational proofs for belief in the central events of the New Testament. 'Fact' also proved useful in supporting several principles of natural religion, and the credibility of Old Testament accounts of the Creation and the Flood, and in proving the existence of 'spirit' in the world. By the end of the seventeenth century a substantial part of the English Protestant edifice was anchored by the concept of 'fact'. If not all English Protestants were as bound to arguments from 'fact' as the rationalizing strand of the Church of England, arguments from fact were not rejected either by most dissenting Protestants or by High Churchmen. English Protestant Christianity would integrate the legal concept of fact and the legal language of establishing facts into its very fabric.

'Matter of fact' and the truth of Christianity

For many generations the truths of the Christian religion and of Scripture were unproblematic. The religious issues and conflicts of the sixteenth and seventeenth centuries, however, brought epistemological issues to the fore. The use of 'fact' or 'matter of fact' to support the fundamental truths of Scripture would be grounded on an approach to knowledge that distinguished various kinds of knowledge, each characterized by different kinds of proof which resulted in varying degrees and kinds of certainty or probability.[49]

---

[49] See Barbara J. Shapiro, *Probability and certainty in seventeenth-century England: a study of the relationships between natural science, religion, history, law and literature* (Princeton,

Although the distinction between mathematical certainty achieved through demonstration and moral certainty that could be gained through direct sense data and credible testimony had medieval and scholastic antecedents, it began to play an important role in religious thought beginning roughly with the publications of Hugo Grotius, the internationally esteemed Dutch jurist whose *The truth of the Christian religion* characterized Christianity as an historical religion resting on 'matter of fact'. It was therefore possible, he argued, to establish the truth of seemingly impossible events, such as those reported in Scripture, if 'testified by ... sufficient Witnesses living in the time when they came to pass'.[50]

William Chillingworth adopted the Grotian line in his 1638 *The religion of Protestants: a safe way to salvation*,[51] designed to refute Roman Catholic insistence on the need for an authoritative judge of Scripture. Chillingworth argued that although civil and criminal cases required an outside authority or judge, Scripture, where plain, did not. Scripture, not itself a judge, provided the rule by which rational individuals could judge or evaluate assertions of religious truth.[52] Although Chillingworth did not spell out the relationship between credible witnesses, 'matter of fact', moral certainty and rational belief, he initiated a mode of argument that would play an important role in the development of English religious thought.

This cluster of ideas was elaborated in Seth Ward's 1654 rational defence of Scripture against radical claims of personal revelation. Ward made good use of the assumptions and arguments that we have traced in the legal community. A committed Anglican, he centred his argument on the nature of evidence and proof for 'matters of fact'. When events reported 'were improbable', as were the central events of the New Testament, it was essential to critically examine the witnesses and the way they related their reports. One considered whether the event in question was knowable, whether the witnesses had the means to obtain the information, whether they were 'eye or ear' witnesses and whether the events were 'publically acted and known'. Ward's criteria for belief in

---

1981); Henry Van Leeuwen, *The problem of certainty in seventeenth-century England, 1630–1690* (The Hague, 1963); Gerard Reedy, *The Bible and reason: Anglicans and Scripture in late seventeenth-century England* (Philadelphia, 1985).

[50] Hugo Grotius, *The truth of the Christian religion*, ed. Simon Patrick (London, 1680), p. 21.

[51] William Chillingworth, *The religion of Protestants: a safe way to salvation*, 2nd edn (London, 1638). See Robert Orr, *Reason and authority: the thought of William Chillingworth* (Oxford, 1967).

[52] Orr, *Reason and authority*, pp. 57, 88, 115. Chillingworth's opponent, Edward Knott, had demanded mathematical certainty or demonstration.

scriptural accounts thus echoed the criteria for the evaluation of legal 'matters of fact'. Invoking the impartiality norm, Ward concluded that 'No impartial person, could reasonably doubt the truthfulness of the matters of fact reported in the History of Holy Scripture'.[53]

It was during the period between 1660 and 1700 that legally derived arguments from 'fact' were most frequently deployed to buttress the truth of Scripture. Now arguments were more likely to be aimed at sceptics who expressed doubt as to the truth of the Scripture and Roman Catholics who emphasized the doctrine of infallibility and the superiority of oral over written tradition. It was largely, though not exclusively, a group of latitudinarian laymen and clerics who deployed the concept of 'matter of fact' most extensively and most effectively in this era. The fate of Protestantism and indeed Christianity itself appeared to hinge on the success of the arguments based on the believability of scriptural 'facts'. By the 1670s, to be convincing to most English audiences these arguments had to be rational, not claims based on authority or divine inspiration.

A well-known and well-established legal tradition for reaching rational belief for 'matters of fact' was readily adopted by rational theologians such as Edward Stillingfleet, John Tillotson, Robert Boyle and Gilbert Burnet. Stillingfleet attempted to provide a 'rational account of the grounds, why we are to believe those several persons . . . imployed to reveal the mind of God to the world'. He did not seek mathematical demonstration, because moral certainty was sufficient, just as it was for 'titles to estates'. It was not reasonable to rely solely on one's own senses and 'question the truth of every matter of fact which he doth not see himself'. Yet steps had to be taken to ensure 'the undoubted certainty of the matter of fact', and to ascertain 'such persons were existent, and did either do or record the things we speak of'. It was necessary to show that 'the certainty of the matter of fact, that the records under the name of Moses were undoubtedly his', as well as to show that he was a person of 'more than ordinary judgment, wisdom and knowledge' with 'sufficient information' of 'the things he undertakes to write of'. Given Moses' impeccable qualifications, as well as his fidelity and integrity, his 'History is undoubtedly true'.[54]

In connection with the testimony of the Apostles and the miracles of the New Testament, Stillingfleet wrote, 'Where the truth of a doctrine

---

[53] Seth Ward, *A philosophical essay toward the eviction . . . of God* [1654], 4th edn (London, 1677), pp. 84–8, 99–101, 102, 107 ff., 117. See also Reedy, *Bible and reason.*

[54] Edward Stillingfleet, *Origines sacrae, or a rational account of the Christian faith* (London, 1662), preface, pp. 120–36. See also Stillingfleet, *A rational account of the grounds of Protestant religion* (London, 1664).

depends upon a matter of fact, the truth of the doctrine is sufficiently manifested, if the matter of fact is evidently proved in the highest way it is capable of.' It seemed obvious that 'The greatest evidence which can be given to a matter of fact, is the attesting of it by those persons who were eye-witnesses of it.' If the report was 'attested by a sufficient number of credible persons who profess themselves the eye-witnesses of it, it is accounted an unreasonable thing to distrust any longer the truth of it'. The Apostles were credible since they had 'no motive to lie and lacked Mean or vulgar motives'. Christ's miracles were visible, no illusion of sense was possible, many saw him raise a man from the dead and many witnessed his resurrection. Although counter-witnesses might 'disparage' testimony, when 'all witnesses fully agree not only in the substance, but in all material circumstances of the story, what ground or reason can there be to suspect a forgery or design in it'? In the case of the key events of Scripture, all witnesses had concurred.[55]

Like the lawyers, Stillingfleet emphasized the nature of the testimony. 'The Apostles had delivered their Testimony with the greatest particularity as to all circumstances. They do not change or alter any of them upon different examination before several persons, they all agree in the greatest constancy to themselves and uniformity with each other.'[56] These qualities were precisely those that the justicing manuals, first published many years earlier, had advised justices of the peace to take into account when examining witnesses and that jurors had long been asked to consider in reaching their verdicts.

In a work designed to shore up Protestant belief in Scripture against Roman Catholic oral tradition, John Tillotson also adopted legal approaches to evidence and assent. Reiterating the position that matters of fact were incapable of demonstration, he argued that belief in past events was reasonable when based on secure grounds rather than 'bare hear-say'.[57] Although the best evidence was immediate sense perception, next was the evidence of witnesses. All witnesses, however, were not equal. Like legal witnesses, they required sufficient mental capacity and impartiality for their testimony to reach the level of moral certainty.[58] For Tillotson, like Ward, scriptural faith was based on the testimony of witnesses and arguments from 'matter of fact'. Using language similar to that of Stillingfleet and Tillotson as early as 1671, John Locke was writing of the appropriate number, credit and condition of witnesses.[59]

---

[55] Stillingfleet, *Origines sacrae*, pp. 260, 285–6, 287–8.   [56] ibid., p. 297.
[57] John Tillotson, *The rule of faith* (London, 1666), pp. 85, 102, 118.
[58] John Tillotson, *The works of the most reverend Dr John Tillotson, late lord Archbishop of Canterbury*, 4th edn (London, 1728), vol. III, p. 411.
[59] John Marshall, *Resistance, religion, and responsibility* (Cambridge, 1994), p. 128.

Arguments from 'matter of fact' were becoming crucial in securing belief in Scripture.

The year 1675 witnessed an outburst of publications employing the concept of 'fact' and 'credible witnesses' to secure rational belief in Scripture. John Wilkins, a leading latitudinarian rational theologian, noted that evidence from testimony 'depends on the credit and authority of the Witnesses' that might be 'qualified as to their ability and fidelity'. When these criteria had been met, 'a man must be fantastical incredulous fool to make any doubt of them'. 'As for matter of fact, concerning Times, Places, Persons, Actions, which depended on story and the relation of others, things are not capable of being proved' by mathematical demonstration. Instead, one must apply the 'best evidence' rule.[60]

Robert Boyle, a leading latitudinarian layman, was similarly committed to showing what kinds of 'Probation' or evidence 'may reasonably be thought sufficient to make the Christian religion fit to be embraced'. Moral certainty, which governed 'the practice of our Courts of Justice here in England', provided the appropriate model. In criminal cases, he argued, though the testimony of more than one witness of itself was not necessarily more credible than that of a single witness, a concurrence of testimonies might amount to a moral certainty.[61] The '[A]rticles of the Christian religion' could be similarly proved by a moral demonstration and could, 'without any blemish to a man's reason, be assented to'. Indeed, although some things of 'unquestionable Truth' might appear incredible if attested by 'slight and ordinary Witnesses', 'we scruple not to believe them, when the Relations are attested with such Circumstances, as make the Testimony as strong as the things attested are strange'. A thing contrary to reason should not be disbelieved 'provided there be competent proof that it is true'.[62]

Some years later Boyle wrote that most knowledge was dependent on the senses, either immediate or 'vicarious', the latter being the primary evidence for matters of fact. By testimony 'we know, that there were such men as Julius Caesar and William the Conqueror, as well as that Joseph knew that Pharaoh had a dream'.[63] Testimony must be provided by witnesses of good moral character who possessed knowledge of the things or events about which they testified.

[60] John Wilkins, *The principles and duties of natural religion* (London, 1675), pp. 9–10.
[61] Robert Boyle, *Some considerations about the reconcileableness of reason and religion* (London, 1675), pp. 93, 95, 96.
[62] ibid., pp. 58, 60.
[63] 'The Christian virtuoso', in *The works of the Honourable Robert Boyle*, ed. T. Birch, 6 vols. (London, 1772), vol. VI, p. 525.

Still another 1675 contribution was Gilbert Burnet's *A rational method for proving the truth of the Christian religion*. Burnet, like Wilkins and Stillingfleet a latitudinarian cleric, insisted that biblical miracles were 'matters of fact ... positively attested by ... many eye-witnesses ... of great probity'. Like Boyle, he explicitly points to the standards of the law courts.

The Apostles ... were men, who upon the strictest tryal of Law must be admitted as competent witnesses; they were well informed of what they heard ... they were plain simple men who could not in reason be suspect of deep designs or contrivances; they in the testimonies they gave do not only vouch private stories that were transacted in corners, but publick matters seen and known by many hundreds; they all agreed in their testimony ... Their testimonies, if false, might have been easily disproved, the chief power being in the hands of enemies, who neither wanted power, cunning nor malice.[64]

Matthew Hale, we should recall, used similar language. Like a lawyer summing up at the end of a trial, Burnet concluded that 'it is as evident as is possible any matter of fact can be, that their testimony was true'.[65]

Religious utilization of the concept of 'fact', however, required some adjustment in the standard for what constituted an ideal witness, because it was forced to rely on the evidence of 'simple plain men'. Although justices of the peace and lawyers sometimes emphasized 'ability and fidelity' and often relied on the testimony of ordinary persons, they were nevertheless inclined to assign somewhat greater credibility to those of higher social status. Those adopting a stance of factual inquiry towards the truth of Scripture were not in a position to stress either the high social status or the experience of their witnesses, and capitalized instead on the Apostles' simplicity and lack of sophistication that rendered them incapable of orchestrating collective misrepresentation of the facts.

Although latitudinarians dominated the discourse on rational proofs of Scripture, they did not monopolize it. Neither Seth Ward nor Richard Allestree were latitudinarians. Allestree noted that the great factual events of Scripture could 'be done but once; he could not be incarnated, and born, and live and preach, and dye, and rise again ... every day, of every age, in every place, to convince everyman by his senses, to all those that did not see the matter of fact'.[66] Belief in such events therefore must be 'made by Witnesses': 'if we can be sure the witnesses that do assert a fact understand it exactly, if the things be palpable ... we can be sure too, that

---

[64] Gilbert Burnet, *A rational method for proving the truth of the Christian religion* (London, 1675), preface, pp. 27–8.

[65] ibid., p. 28.

[66] Richard Allestree, *The divine authority and usefulness of Holy Scripture* (Oxford, 1673), p. 16.

they are sincere, will not affirm that which they do not know, and do not lye, then testimony of it must be most infallible'.[67] There was sporadic publication in this vein for several decades.[68] Another flurry of activity came in the 1690s, when the attacks of deists and sceptics on the need for and reliability of Revelation again elicited a series of fierce defences of the truth of Revelation and of scriptural miracles. Many of the defences were now mounted by non-latitudinarians. John Edwards, a Calvinist minister, harnessed the legalistic proofs associated with matters of fact.[69] Discussion was now taking place in periodicals such as the *Athenian Mercury*.[70] By the end of the seventeenth century proofs of the truth of Scripture based on appropriately verified matter of fact were widely employed, even in non-clerical media and by non-latitudinarian writers.

Natural theology and matter of fact

Proofs for the principles of natural theology, that is the existence of the Deity, his attributes, the immortality of the soul and the existence of future rewards and punishments, also made use of arguments from 'matters of fact', although these were less central than they were to the proofs of scriptural events. 'Facts' could not directly prove the existence of a deity, because 'spirit' could not be observed. 'Facts', however, could be used to infer the existence and attributes of the Creator and to infer the existence of spirit in much the same way as 'signs' and 'circumstances' might be used to infer guilt in certain kinds of unlikely to be witnessed crimes. During the Restoration era, arguments from observed 'matters of fact' were joined to the earlier, more general arguments from design.

The development of a new natural history based on carefully observed 'matters of fact' thus resulted in the union of natural theology and

---

[67] ibid., pp. 16–17.

[68] See Samuel Parker, *A demonstration of the divine authority of the law of nature and of the Christian religion* (London, 1681), and Thomas Tenison, *A discourse concerning a guide in matters of faith* (London, 1681).

[69] John Edwards, *A compleat history or survey . . . of religion*, 2 vols. (London, 1696). Without sense evidence 'all the Passages recorded in the New Testament, concerning Christ's Birth, Life, Miracles, Death, Resurrection, and Ascension are of no Credit: For these are to be proved, as other Matters of Fact are, by the Testimony of Witnesses who heard or saw those things'. The Apostles were neither 'mad or senseless', 'had a share of Understanding as well as others, and their Ears and Eyes were as good as other Mens'. They were 'competent Judges' having the 'Means and Opportunities' of informing themselves about the things they related. The 'Matters of Fact were so frequent, and so often repeated'. The acts were 'done publically'. Edwards emphasized the 'Integrity, Candor, and Simplicity' of scriptural authors. The Apostles were 'Honest, Plain and True-Hearted men', not 'idle and loose persons' (ibid., vol. II, pp. 436–7, 440–1, 443–5, 446, 447).

[70] *Athenian Mercury*, 31 March 1690.

natural history, often called physico-theology. John Ray's popular *The wisdom of God manifested in the works of creation* went furthest in elaborating the argument that natural 'facts', well established by witnesses, demonstrated the existence and wisdom of the Deity. Ray promised readers, 'I have been careful to admit nothing for Matter of Fact or Experiment but what is undoubtedly true, lest I should build upon a Sandy and Ruinous Foundation.' The 'facts' of nature were thus offered as a basis from which to infer the wisdom of the Deity.[71] The argument from design, of course, was a very ancient one, but it had not in the past employed the legally derived concept of fact. The contribution of Restoration theologians and naturalists who adopted legal notions of fact and its proofs was to emphasize that 'matters of fact', now known with greater accuracy and precision, allowed one to observe more accurately the results of God's handiwork and thus to better appreciate his existence, attributes and intelligent design.

Mosaic accounts of Creation, the origin of mankind and the Deluge

Arguments based on 'matter of fact' also played a role in the Restoration campaign against atheists and sceptics who repudiated the biblical accounts of Creation and the Deluge. Such arguments, however, were somewhat difficult to make because of the absence of human witnesses. Nor did the 'facts' from which inferences might be drawn seem as conclusive as they seemed to be in inferring divine design.

The Restoration era nevertheless witnessed a multifaceted campaign to show that the scriptural accounts of the Creation and the Flood were accurate. The jurist Matthew Hale entered the fray to refute the 'Atheistical Spirit that denies or questions the truth of the Fact' delivered in Scripture. In this context, using language strikingly parallel to his own legal writings, he discussed the nature of witness testimony and the need to weigh the veracity of witnesses. In this instance, too, he emphasized the number of witnesses and noted that 'credible and authentic witnesses' were preferable to those that were 'light and inconsiderable'. First-hand

---

[71] John Ray, *The wisdom of God manifested in the works of creation* (London, 1692), preface. See also Wilkins, *Natural religion*; Stillingfleet, *Origines sacrae*, pp. 379, 401–20; Nehemiah Grew, *The phytological history propounded* (London, 1673), pp. 98–101; Nehemiah Grew, *The anatomy of plants* (1682; New York, 1965), p. 8; William Derham, *Astro-theology, or a demonstration of the being and attributes of God* (London, 1715); William Derham, *Physico-theology: or, a demonstration of the being of God from his works of creation* (London, 1724); Lisa Zeitz, 'Natural theology, rhetoric and revolution: John Ray's *Wisdom of God* 1691–1704', *Eighteenth-Century Life*, vol. 18 (1994), pp. 120–33.

testimony was preferable to hearsay and the testimony of disinterested witnesses preferable to that of interested parties.[72]

Hale was unable to build his case exclusively on human testimony, because the history with which he was concerned did not focus on particular acts or deeds associated with proofs from matters of fact. After a long and complex treatment of the nature of proofs available in matters of fact, Hale turned to the 'Origination of Man'. He not only cited several 'Instance[s] of Fact' to show that mankind had a beginning in time, but presented eight 'Evidence[s] of Fact' to show the 'reasonableness of the Divine Hypothesis touching the origination of the world and particularly of Men'. Admitting that each of his eight varieties of 'fact' taken 'singly and apart ... possibly may not be so weighty', yet the 'concurrence and coincidence' of 'many Evidences' carries 'a great weight, even as to the point of Fact; it is not probable that Supposition should be false which hath so many concurrent Testimonies bearing witnesses to it'. He then provided 'probable evidence' that would collectively prove the truth of the Mosaic account of the origin of man 'near six thousand years' earlier.[73]

Although the biblical accounts of Creation and the Deluge were on the whole accepted as believable, some well-observed 'matters of fact' proved difficult to square with Scripture. There followed a variety of efforts, mostly couched in the form of hypotheses, to connect the biblical Deluge and observed matters of fact. The most troublesome of these were fossil forms of sea shells frequently found on mountain tops. Were these the remains of actual sea creatures or simply 'sports' or 'jokes' of nature, perhaps designed by the Deity simply 'to entertain and gratifie man's curiosity'?[74] Thomas Burnet's *Sacred theory of the earth* (1681) initiated an acrimonious discussion which lasted well into the next century and in which legally derived language often played a role. Most participants accepted the veracity of the biblical account of the Deluge and attempted to square their respective theories, explanations or hypotheses both with the 'facts' of the Old Testament and the 'facts' of natural history.[75]

Physico-theology was also linked to a variety of physical observations of and hypotheses about earthquakes and the origins of mountains. Here

---

[72] Hale, *Primitive origination of mankind*, To the reader, p. 129.
[73] ibid., pp. 128–9, 130, 131–2, 139, 151, 162–3, 164, 166, 192, 240, 339.
[74] See Roger Ariew, 'A new science of geology in the seventeenth century?', *Studies in Philosophy and the History of Philosophy*, vol. 24 (1991), pp. 81–94; Roy Porter, 'Creation and credence: the career of theories of the earth in Britain, 1660–1820', in *The natural order: historical studies of scientific culture*, ed. Barry Barnes and Steven Shapin (Beverly Hills, 1979), pp. 97–123.
[75] Thomas Burnet, *The sacred theory of the earth* (London, 1684–90), vol. I, p. 96; John Ray, *Three physico-theological discourses* (3rd edn, London, 1713), p. 5.

again observations of natural facts made by credible witnesses provided the basis for hypotheses designed to achieve consistency with biblical accounts. Because there were no human witnesses who provided testimony to the Flood or the genesis of mountains, there were only signs, effects, circumstances or currently observable 'facts' on which to base inferences. These were roughly analogous to legal arguments based on circumstantial evidence.

If the 'rational' in rational theology of the period was not dependent solely on arguments from 'fact', the appropriation of the language of 'fact', witnessing and circumstantial evidence provided a substantial support for rationalist religious arguments.

Witchcraft, spiritual phenomena and prodigies

But were supernatural events always to be believed when supported by the testimony of seemingly credible witnesses? If the method of proving matters of fact by credible witnesses was appropriate for the law courts and for proofs of Scripture, why should it not be employed to validate contemporary instances of supernatural phenomena? Arguments from matter of fact and credible witnesses had long figured prominently in cases of witchcraft. Witchcraft was a crime and thus like other crimes was a deed or matter of fact to be proved in court to the satisfaction of a jury. Witchcraft and the language of fact became intertwined quite early and remained intertwined long after prosecutions for the crime had abated.[76] Witnesses provided the most desirable form of proof for this crime as well as others, although English courts also allowed indirect or circumstantial evidence because witchcraft was a *crimen exceptum* in which witnesses were unlikely. Frequently recourse was had to inferences from 'signs' or circumstantial evidence. When witnesses were available, the quality and quantity of their testimony was crucial. Early in the seventeenth century John Cotta argued that if the 'witnesses of the manifest magical and supernatural act, be ... sufficient, able to judge, free from exception of malice, partialities, distraction, folly, and if ... there bee justly deemed no deception of sense, mistaking of reason or imagination', the accused should be tried. Richard Bernard similarly advised grand juries to inquire into the wisdom, discretion and credibility of the witnesses.[77]

---

[76] See Shapiro, *Probability and certainty*, pp. 194–226; Shapiro, *'Beyond reasonable doubt' and 'probable cause'*, pp. 51–4, 164–8, 209–12, 320–1; Keith Thomas, *Religion and the decline of magic* (New York, 1971).

[77] John Cotta, *The triall of witchcraft*, (London, 1616), pp. 80–1; Richard Bernard, *Guide to grand jurymen in cases of witchcraft* (London, 1627).

This emphasis on credible witnesses also characterized the views of Restoration clerics like Meric Casaubon, Henry More and Joseph Glanvill, who applied the proof of fact to establish the existence of spiritual phenomena. Their concern was fuelled not by a desire to prosecute witches, but to show the existence of spirit to an age that appeared to them overly attracted to mechanism and materialism. The denial of the existence of spirit would make it difficult to sustain a belief in the soul and in the existence of God. Their defence was grounded on the by now familiar legal concept of matter of fact and focused on the testimony of credible witnesses.

The challenge of atheistical and sceptical thought led Meric Casaubon to consider how the category 'matter of fact' could be used to support religion. He observed that it was often possible to produce 'firm assent' based on observation without knowing the causes of the events observed, and noted that many of 'Nature's Wonders' could not be comprehended or explained. It followed that with 'good attestation ... many strange effects of the power ... of Devils and Spirits' were similarly believable. Faced with reports of 'strange things', it was, however, necessary

to know the temper of the relator, if it can be known; and what interest he had, or might probably be supposed to have had in the relation, to have it believed. Again, whether he profess to have seen it himself, or take it upon the credit of others; and whether a man by his profession, [is] in a capacity probable, to judge the truth of those things, to which he doth bear witness.[78]

While it was sometimes reasonable to suspect the relation of a single person, the testimony of two or three should be sufficient if there was 'no just exceptation against the witnesses'. After all, Casaubon argued, that was all that was required in courts of law. No more should be required to witness the truth of supernatural operations 'by Devils and Spirits'.[79]

Joseph Glanvill was the most prominent figure to employ the proof from 'facts' to defend the possibility of witchcraft and the existence and activity of spirit in the world. In collaboration with Henry More, the leading Cambridge Platonist, who like Glanvill was anxious to prove the existence of spirit as a means of combating atheism and materialism, Glanvill collected witchcraft and apparition narratives to prove that spiritual phenomena existed. Whether or not 'there have been and are unlawful confederacies with evil spirits' was simply a 'Matter of Fact' capable of the 'evidence of authority and sense' and, like other 'facts',

[78] Meric Casaubon, *Of credulity and incredulity in things natural, civil and divine* (London, 1668), pp. 159, 312. See also Meric Casaubon, *A treatise proving spirits, witches, and supernatural operations* (London, 1672).
[79] Casaubon, *Of credulity and incredulity*, p. 164.

could be proved only 'by immediate sense or the Testimony of Others'.[80] History had provided 'attestations of thousands of eye and ear witnesses, and those not only of the easily deceived but of wise and gravely discerning persons of whom no interest could oblige them to agree together in a common Lye'.[81] Although melancholy or imagination could produce false testimony, Glanvill refused to believe that 'All the Circumstances of Fact, which we find in well-attested relations' resulted from deceived imaginations. 'Matters of fact well proved ought not to be denied', simply 'because we cannot conceive how they can be performed.' We must 'judge of the action by the evidence, and not the evidence by our fancies about the action'.[82] He thus attempted to collect experiments and suitably witnessed reports employing the standard criteria for faithful and impartial witnesses.[83] The dissenting clergyman, Richard Baxter, produced a similar collection of 'proofs of invisible powers or spirits'.[84]

John Webster disagreed. The number of persons believing in witchcraft was not satisfactory proof, because few were suitably qualified to search for the truth. Causes were difficult to assign and should not rashly be attributed to the Devil. The proofs provided by witnesses involved hearsay, self-interest, deficient observation and superstition. Proper witnesses must 'be free in the judgements as in *aequilibrio*'. He concluded all known reports were 'too light' to be accepted.[85] John Wagstaffe went even further. Matters of fact necessarily involved the senses. Since spirits were too fine to be perceived by the senses, they simply were not amenable to proof of fact.[86]

Prosecutions and convictions for witchcraft became rarer as grand jurors, jurors and judges became increasingly dubious of the evidence presented to them. The campaign of Casuabon, More, Glanvill and Baxter had largely failed as proofs from matters of fact had lost their effectiveness as support for witchcraft.

Conclusion

An elaborate terminology and technology of matters of fact proven to a moral certainty by credible witnesses had been worked out in English

---

[80] Joseph Glanvill, *Sadducismus triumphatus* (London, 1681), part 2, pp. 4, 10–11.

[81] Joseph Glanvill, *A blow at modern sadducism* (London, 1668), pp. 5–6.

[82] Glanvill, *Sadducismus triumphatus*, vol. II, pp. 11–12.

[83] Glanvill, *A blow at modern sadducism*, pp. 116–17.

[84] Richard Baxter, *The certainty of the world of spirits* (London, 1691), pp. 1, 2, 17. See also *Athenian Mercury*, 31 March 1690.

[85] John Webster, *The displaying of supposed witchcraft* (London, 1677), pp. 55, 57, 60–2, 64.

[86] John Wagstaffe, *The question of witchcraft debated* (London, 1671), pp. 112–13, 123–4, 146.

law in the late sixteenth and earlier seventeenth centuries. Later in the seventeenth century this treatment of fact became central to religious controversies involving Protestant scriptural Christianity and its Roman Catholic, sceptical and atheist opponents, natural religion, the existence of God and of spirit, and Mosaic accounts of the Creation and the Deluge. The common law, which pervaded so many spheres of English life, thus played an important role in the defence of late seventeenth- and early eighteenth-century religious polemic and provided a crucial support for English Protestantism.

10   The press and public apologies in eighteenth-century London

Donna T. Andrew

On 16 November 1769 the following advertisement appeared in London's *Daily Advertiser*:

> Whereas I, Joseph Chandler, of Crofts-Yard, in Princes-Street, Lambeth, did some Time since, without Cause or Provocation, abuse and very ill treat Mrs Ann Cornthwaite, of the Fore-Street, in Lambeth, for which she commenced an Action against me, but being sensible of my Guilt, and on my publickly asking her Pardon in this Paper, she has ordered her Attorney to stop Proceedings; and I do so promise never more to molest, abuse, or disturb her. As witness my Hand, November 15, 1769,
>
> JOSEPH CHANDLER

This apology, and the hundreds more like it that appeared in the London press between the 1740s and 1790s, give us a glimpse into the nature of altercations and one form of conflict resolution in eighteenth-century London. It is not surprising that, given London's urban density, Londoners got into innumerable scrapes with one another. Some of these were serious, and were dealt with by the criminal and civil courts. Many more were resolved by conciliation, involving magistrates, neighbours, friends and family of the involved parties. Such resolution could be a substitute for the more formal avenues of recourse, or could be entered into during the legal processes, as a way of curtailing or bringing them to a close. We know that in the eighteenth century many cases which were brought to the magistrates either did not proceed further or were terminated before the courts delivered a verdict. On the whole, this vast body of wrongdoing and dispute disappears from the historical account when it ceased to leave legal records.[1] And yet if we wish to understand

I would like to thank Richard Gorrie, Suzanne Crawford and Marion Andrew for help in gathering the evidence, John Beattie, Gregory Smith and Nicholas Rogers for sharing their vast expertise in eighteenth-century criminal and legal history with me, and the anonymous external reader at Cambridge University Press for helping me to present my conclusions more clearly.
[1] The existing magistrates' books, scarce as they are, probably contain the most useful accounts of such incidents. See, for example, Ruth Paley, ed., *Justice in eighteenth-century Hackney* (London Record Society, 1991).

both the actions of the courts and 'that large unknown world of acts that might have led [but did not] to charges being laid',[2] we need to find some new ways of recovering these obscure disturbances. The public apology, published as an advertisement in a London newspaper, is one of these few written fragments. The analysis of such advertisements enables us to glimpse, albeit partially, the conflicts and strains of a growing metropolis and one method by which, at least in part, these conflicts were resolved. After a brief introduction to apology advertisements, I will consider four general questions: why were such notices used to aid in settling disputes; what sorts of people used them; for which sorts of contentions were they most frequently used; and how was conciliation achieved. After considering these questions I will advance some thoughts on the relationship between urban disturbance, hierarchical relations and the functions of newspaper apologies. I will neither discuss language patterns, length, typography or context of these advertisements, nor the geography of apologisers and recipients, for this is an introduction to, rather than an exhaustive investigation of, the genre. A few thoughts about the reasons for the virtual disappearance of these advertisements will be offered as concluding remarks.

Although newspaper advertisements were essential for the financial well-being of many eighteenth-century dailies, we still know relatively little about their nature, content and mix in the daily press. Especially under-studied are those notices which communicated information: advertisements which sought marriage partners, which begged for charitable assistance, or which inquired about lost pets or stolen animals. This chapter considers one such form in some detail. It will soon become obvious, however, that this analysis is suggestive rather than conclusive. For these advertisements are tantalizing, but formulaic; they are often only vague and incomplete records of the reconciliation of which they were a part. Having said that, let us see what we can learn from them.

The main source of such advertisements was a remarkable newspaper called the *Daily Advertiser*. Wildly successful, it continued to be London's first and chief advertiser until its demise in 1795.[3] For sixty-five years it (and its later competitors)[4] carried thousands of all sorts of

[2] John M. Beattie, *Crime and the courts in England, 1660–1800* (Princeton, 1986), p. 9.
[3] Of the *Daily Advertiser*, Robert L. Haig writes: 'that paper had become long before 1764 the acknowledged leader in its chosen field: the "advertiser" *par excellence*'. *The Gazetteer, 1735–1797* (Carbondale, Ill., 1960), p. 57. For the little written on the history of the paper, see Lucyle Werkmeister, *The London daily press, 1772–1792* (Lincoln, Neb., 1963), pp. 2–3.
[4] Of the 1,024 apologies considered here, 151 were found in one of London's other papers: *Gazetteer, Morning Herald, Morning Post, Times, World, Oracle, General Advertiser, Public Advertiser, London Chronicle, General Evening Post, St James's Chronicle, Morning Chronicle,*

advertisements yearly, including 1,274 apology notices, which occurred in the six decades between 1745 and 1795.[5] Of these, 250 were duplicate advertisements, printed in successive or close dates to the original. Of these duplicates, most ran for only two issues, though a few appeared as many as six times.[6] All the advertisements cost approximately 2 shillings an entry, although the publisher may have given better rates for repeat entries.[7] At a time when an average working-class male wage was reckoned to be about 2–3 shillings a day,[8] this was a substantial sum. But, as I will show, when compared to some of the possible fines for the offences, as an alternative to other punishment, or as an end to court costs, it may well have seemed that such public apologies were an economical measure.

Why did people come to use the apology advertisement as part of their conflict resolutions? For most apologists, the newspaper advertisement was not an alternative to, but rather a way of ending prosecution. Almost two-thirds of all such advertisements included the statement that some sort of prosecution had been undertaken.[9] In the twenty-eight instances in which the advertisements tell us something of the course of such a prosecution, four of the offenders were taken before a magistrate, one had a warrant taken out against him, seven were in gaol, eight had been indicted, one prosecuted at Quarter Sessions, six sentenced to hard labour

Parker's General Advertiser. Though these were, for the most part, randomly gathered, there is no reason to think that any particular sort of apology or any specific kind of victim was over-represented in this selection. Several (16) of the advertisements which appeared in one of these other papers also appeared in the *Daily Advertiser*. Though I had originally planned to sample advertisements at similar intervals from the *Daily Advertiser*, the appearance and growth of the other newspapers after 1770 led me to supplement my original plan with notices found more broadly.

[5] Although 1,024 advertisements over a 54-year period amounts to fewer than twenty advertisements a year, historians have relied on much smaller samples for longer periods and larger areas. In his two essays based on advertisements, 'The sale of wives' in E. P. Thompson, *Customs in common* (London, 1991), and 'The crime of anonymity' in Douglas Hay *et al.*, eds., *Albion's fatal tree: crime and society in eighteenth-century England* (London, 1975), E. P. Thompson based his conclusions on 218 and 284 such notices.

[6] Of the 250 repeat advertisements, 181 ran for only two issues, 65 for three, 3 for four and 1 for six. Of course, these are just minimal numbers, since it is possible that a complete search would turn up more.

[7] For discussion of this possibility, see C. Y. Ferdinand, *Benjamin Collins and the provincial newspaper trade in the eighteenth century* (Oxford, 1997), p. 184 and James Raven, 'Serial advertisements in eighteenth-century Britain and Ireland', in Robin Myers and Michael Harris, eds., *Serials and their readers, 1620–1914* (Winchester, 1993), pp. 103–22.

[8] These figures are drawn from L. D. Schwarz, 'The standard of living in the long run: London 1800–1860', *Economic History Review*, 2nd series, vol. 38 (1985), appendix 1, p. 37.

[9] Of the 1,024 advertisements 648 state that some form of prosecution had been begun. Beattie notes: 'A number of studies, drawing on a range of intersecting sources at the parish level, have shown how the threat of prosecution could work as an element in the exercise of authority.' Beattie, *Crime and the courts*, p. 8.

in the House of Correction and one found guilty of libel. In most cases we know even less, and might assume that the legal involvement ended with the initial appearance before the magistrate. For the offending parties, the newspaper apology publicly, and in a popular and durable form, admitted the offender's guilt and begged the victim's pardon. It served simultaneously as a record, a punishment and an expiation.

Resolutions involving newspaper apologies tended to share three characteristics, which may help to explain their use. On the whole the conciliation of which they were a part was speedy, relatively inexpensive and flexible.[10] Of those advertisements that include the date of the offence for which they are apologizing, more than one-third of the apologies, and the conclusion of the conflict, came within a week of the original infraction, and more than half within two weeks. More than four-fifths were concluded within two months of the offence.[11] And although an advertisement was not inexpensive, some apologists felt that they had been saved a greater expense in paying for them. For his crime of wheeling a barrow full of gravel, 'along the footpath opposite Mansion house', a paviour's labourer was fined 20s., which was remitted when his apology appeared. Another apology was accepted by its victim, 'in lieu of very great damages and expenses'. In a third case the victims themselves agreed to stop prosecution, 'not wishing the pecuniary damages that would be given in a court of law'.[12] The newspaper apology was also a flexible device, because it could be combined with other forms of restitution or retribution, delayed to maximize expenses or even to assist the offender. Having slandered her neighbour, Mrs Glanvill, Mrs Tufton not only inserted an apology advertisement but noted that she had 'asked pardon [of the victim] on her knees before several witnesses'. In addition to his newspaper apology, Mr Starkey was forced to ask pardon of Mr Barlow, the man about whom he had spread scandalous stories, 'in open court', while Mr Fisher promised the two men he had falsely accused of theft that he would apologize formally before the justice of the peace.[13] Sometimes the advertisement assisted concealment. R. M., one grateful apologist, noted: '[I] do think myself under the highest Obligation to him for his Acceptance of this Acknowledgement as an Atonement for my Crime, without

---

[10] In their interesting recent work, *Rogues, thieves, and the rule of law: the problem of law enforcement in north-east England, 1718–1800* (London, 1998), Gwenda Morgan and Peter Rushton see such advertisements as one way to obtain cheap and local conflict resolution.

[11] There are 496 advertisements which include the date of the original offence: 173 apologies appeared within a week of that date, 272 within two weeks and 410 within seven weeks.

[12] See *Daily Advertiser*, 18 June 1782, 16 November 1786, 31 December 1794.

[13] *Daily Advertiser*, 28 May 1751, 26 Febuary, 1759, 12 September 1755.

exposing my Name, or proceeding against me with Rigour equal to my Fault.' On the other hand, a vengeful opponent could refuse a pardon, as did the passenger whom William Tord had abused. In his apology, Tord wrote that though he had 'begged for pardon ... it was not forthcoming until the Expense amounted to a sum which has almost ruined me, and which I have paid'.[14] In addition to publishing his apology, one young offender was pardoned on condition that he entered the armed services. Other apologists said that their settlements had included recognizances given for future good conduct, and in several cases sums of money from 6s. to £50 penalty to be given to public charities.[15]

These three qualities of reconciliation by newspaper apology – speed, flexibility and inexpensiveness – are the antitheses of what historians of the law have seen in the operations of the courts in this period. W. A. Champion has argued that by the eighteenth century the 'communal embrace' of borough courts 'no longer seemed appropriate for resolving personal interactions'. He emphasizes the demise by 1720 of what he describes as 'the old regulatory regime'. Still, he admits that in the eighteenth century, 'many tradesmen would still have gone to law if it had not been for prevailing costs and delays'. C. W. Brooks agrees, noting that 'fears about the high costs and increasing complexity of litigation go some way towards explaining the low levels of central court business during the eighteenth century'. Brooks' finding, that 'the overall cost of litigation in the central courts doubled between 1680 and 1750', supports this contention. The establishment of courts of request was one solution to this problem; perhaps apology advertisements in newspapers was another. The former seemed to make little difference in total litigation, at least until 1800; the latter may have been one of the few measures available to ordinary folk in the interim.[16]

Some historians have argued that the decline of litigation throughout Britain coincided with, and was perhaps caused by, what they perceive as the weakening of a sense of 'communal obligations'. The apology

[14] *Daily Advertiser*, 9 October 1755, 30 May 1767. Only after 'several repeated Solicitations and Applications' could William Gordon persuade the person he had offended to agree to accept his apology; see *Daily Advertiser*, 31 October 1767.
[15] *Daily Advertiser*, 12 December 1760, 13 September 1773; *Gazetteer*, 9 December 1777, 8 July 1772.
[16] W. A. Champion, 'Recourse to the law and the meaning of the great litigation decline', in Christopher Brooks and Michael Lobban, eds., *Communities and the courts in Britain, 1150–1900* (London, 1997), pp. 195, 197; C. W. Brooks, 'Interpersonal conflict and social tension: civil litigation in England, 1640–1830', in *The first modern society*, ed. A. L. Beier, David Cannadine and James M. Rosenheim (Cambridge, 1989), pp. 377, 382. For more on the decline of litigation and interpersonal disputes, see Craig Muldrew, *The culture of credit and social relations in early modern England* (New York, 1998), and Paul Langford, *Public life and the propertied Englishman* (Oxford, 1991).

Table 1. *Offences apologized for*

	Number	%
Against law officers	93	9
Commotion	41	4
False arrest	19	2
Misc.	80	8
Transport	181	18
Violence or threat	103	10
Words	322	31
Work-related	19	2
Insufficient info.	166	16

advertisements both support and challenge this view. With the proliferation of commercial activity, with the growth of street traffic and street life, with the expansion of London's physical and commercial extent, transport offences often committed by non-resident workers became fruitful occasions for offence and apology. These sorts of apologies perhaps support the notion of a decline in communal coherence. On the other hand, the continued vitality of apologies for scandalous words testify to the on-going importance of both neighbourhood and metropolitan credit-worthiness. For scandalous words remained the most significant activity apologized for. Located between an 'emerging "civil society" of independent associativity' and 'older forms of communal supervision', the apology advertisement contained features of both past and future conflict resolution modes.[17]

Who were these apologists? What characteristics did they exhibit and what spheres of life did they come from? Most apologists included their names, and thus in many cases we know their gender.[18] Women were under-represented in these apologies, as in most criminal prosecutions. This may have been in part a result of their more restricted lives, or as a consequence of the sympathy shown them by the criminal system. Women may also have been seen as less threatening, and their public apologies therefore less necessary for social peace. In addition, their capacity to pay for such advertisement may have been less. There were also group

[17] See, for example, P. Earle, *The making of the English middle class* (London, 1989), p. 335, and P. Clark, *Sociability and urbanity: clubs and societies in the eighteenth century city* (Leicester, 1986), p. 7.

[18] Sometimes the apologists just used initials for themselves, and occasionally gave no indication of whom the offending party was. See, for example, the apology to a woman whom 'several persons' had accused of having informed against another in a customs infraction, *Daily Advertiser*, 1 July 1767.

Table 2a. *Known gender of apologists*

	Number	%
Male	801	78.6
Female	79	7.8
Group-male	106	10.4
Group-male and female	33	3.2
Total	1019	

Source: sample.

Table 2b. *Known gender of recipients*

	Number	%
Male	626	62.2
Female	131	13.0
Group-male	138	13.7
Group-male and female	112	11.1
Total	1007	

Source: sample.

offenders, that is, two or more men or women, or men and women, who appeared collectively as apologists; these also account for slightly more than one-tenth of all advertisers.

Both the majority of apologists and recipients were male. However, the difference in the numbers is interesting. While most apologists were men, a smaller number of those offended were men. Women were much more likely to appear as recipients of an apology than as apologists. Groups of men, or of men and women, were also more likely to appear as objects of offence than offenders, though the difference between these roles for male groups was less extreme.

How did these apologists earn their living? As far as we have self-descriptions,[19] they seemed to have followed an enormous range of occupations. Interestingly, these apologists closely fit John Beattie's description of the prosecutors in the cases he has studied, whom, he notes, were 'drawn overwhelmingly from the middle ranks of society, and included a

[19] Of the total number of apologists, we have self-descriptions for 648, or approximately 63 per cent of the total. Women, when they did not describe their own occupation but their husbands', were counted under that description.

Table 3. *Known occupations of apologists/recipients*

	Apologists		Recipients	
	Number	%	Number	%
Artisans and shopkeepers	206	31.8	149	33.6
Entertainment	12	1.9		
Food and drink	68	10.5	75	16.9
Labourer	23	3.5	5	1.1
Law and officials	35	5.4	133	30.0
Misc.	24	3.7	53	12.0
Servants, porters	41	6.3	12	2.7
Soldiers, sailors and military	11	1.7	13	3.0
Transport	228	35.2	3	0.7
Total	648		443	

Source: appendix a below.

significant number of artisans and labourers'.[20] Apology recipients, the group most analogous to his prosecutors, were more varied in their occupational distribution in the apology advertisements. Though law officials were not immune from prosecution, they appeared more as recipients of apologies than as apologists.

When we attempt to make sense of the events for which these apologists ask pardon, two problems quickly appear. First, in slightly more than one-seventh of all the advertisements, it is impossible to understand what actually happened or why.[21] The most oblique of these apologies merely note that its author is sorry for an unnamed misunderstanding. Many apologies for violent injury, assault or abuse are also very vague. The legal definition of assault was 'a violent kind of injury, offered to a man's person. It may be committed by offering of a blow, or by a fearful speech.'[22] As I shall show, however, in the discussion of scandalous words, the usage of 'assault' in these advertisements seems even more ambiguous and muddled than its legal usage warranted. The second difficulty is the truly assorted quality of about a tenth of the remaining apologies.[23] They

---

[20] Beattie, *Crime and the courts*, p. 9.
[21] Of the 1,024 advertisements found 166 are not considered because they are too vague to allow for any conclusion about the nature of the incident involved.
[22] John Cowell, quoted by Samuel Johnson, *A dictionary of the English language*, 2 vols. (London, 1755), reprinted by AMS Press, Inc., New York, 1967.
[23] Of the remaining 858 advertisements 80 are characterized as miscellaneous.

include disturbing church services, hooliganism, damage to goods in transport, and hindering an auctioneer.[24]

To get a flavour of the range of such assorted apologies, let us consider three such advertisements. The first, inserted by a Mr Allen, apologized for having previously inserted an advertisement announcing a fair to be held at Battersea, and having claimed that his establishment would cater to its visitors. Allen admitted he had no authority to place such a notice, and that it was contrary to the law. In the second, two constables apologized for having entered an inn 'under colour of a warrant from the Commission of the land tax' and for abusing and insulting its patrons. Finally there was the apology of a butcher, Rodrigues, to the inquest of Portsoken ward. Rodrigues explained that he had, in 'open violation of the laws and franchises of this city presumed to keep an open shop without being a freeman'.[25] Though these assorted apologies offer us some very interesting 'snapshots' of everyday life, they do not naturally fall under any general heading. Still, almost six-sevenths of the remaining apologies offer us more general categories and insights into the lives and agitations of a range of ordinary London folk.

The single largest occupational group of men who apologized through the medium of the press worked in a collection of trades which can be called 'transport'. More than a third of the apologists whose occupations we know belong to this group.[26] Included in these trades were those responsible for moving people: hackney and stage coachmen; hackney and private chairmen as well as watermen. Then there were those who carried a variety of goods into, through and out of London: draymen, carters, carmen, drovers, porters and night-soil men. Moving through neighbourhoods, quarrelling between themselves and with others on the road, boisterous and swaggering, such transport workers had a formidable reputation for a sort of devil-may-care rudeness towards their clients and the rest of the world, and relished their prowess and progress on the road. Their offences ranged from driving too fast to hogging the roads to attempting to obtain greater fares than those to which they were entitled. Unsurprisingly, they were also often involved in brawls and altercations with turnpike fee collectors, whom they ran over, 'shamefully

---

[24] The hooliganism involved spraying a water hose at a tallow chandler's wife, see *Daily Advertiser*, 17 January 1761; the items damaged were some sheep, *Daily Advertiser*, 10 June 1775, 26 January 1791.

[25] *Daily Advertiser*, 12 April 1773, 27 March 1779, 15 January 1784.

[26] Though transport workers constituted more than a third of the total number of apologists, less than 23 per cent of offences they apologized for were road offences. This is explained by the varying state of the information given in the apologies. Many apologies from such workers do not state the nature of their offence, or note that it belonged to some other category, such as attacks on law officials.

ill-treated' or assaulted in their anger or while attempting to evade payment.[27] The speed and recklessness of London's traffic was commented on by Matthew Bramble, in Tobias Smollet's *The expedition of Humphrey Clinker*: 'All is tumult and hurry; one would imagine they are impelled by some disorder of the brain, that will not suffer them to be at rest ... The porters and chairmen trot with their burdens ... The hackney-coachmen make their horses smoke, and the pavement shakes under them; and I have actually seen a waggon pass through Piccadilly at the hard gallop.'[28]

The unruliness of transport workers was supposed to be controlled, at least in part, by the commission regulating all licensed coaches, chairs and boats. This group could and did impose heavy fines and suspend or even revoke operators' licences for infractions. In a note to his own apology, a coachman, James Stephens, remarked that 'A Coachman lately prosecuted in the Borough for the like Offence was fined £5. And three Months Imprisonment.'[29] Yet despite any deterrent effect of such punishment, many incidents of gross misbehaviour towards other vehicles, passengers and other pedestrians continued to be reported in newspaper apologies. For many victims a fine, suspension or recompense of expenses was not punishment enough; many wanted the public acknowledgement of fault, the ignominy of public pardon-seeking.

Unsurprisingly, since men of the road were rude to each other as well as to passengers, to pedestrians as well as to folk on horseback, since they obstructed roads and drove on pavements, the largest number of apologies came from this group. Their raucous disrespect is well illustrated in the case of Jonathan Denton, a stage-coach driver. In his apology he begged pardon for having 'willfully, with a mischievous and malicious Intention to overturn, delve[d] against a Gentleman's One Horse Chaise'. Despite the fact that the victim 'was apprehensive of the Danger' and bade him stop, Denton, 'with a Damn you, did drive against and overturn the said Chaise, whereby the Gentleman was thrown out a great Way'. Only his boasting of the feat at a local taphouse allowed the injured gentleman to locate and begin prosecution against the cocky coachman. Another

---

[27] Of the 18 apologies for altercations with tollmen, 16 came from transport workers; a potato merchant and a brickmaker were also in this group. See especially *Daily Advertiser*, 31 January 1776 and 13 February 1771.

[28] For an example of fast driving, see *Daily Advertiser*, 27 April 1771. The driver, picking up two ladies and several children at Chelsea College and delivering them home, confessed that he 'drove part of the way so very fast as to greatly frighten them'. Another coachman drove his vehicle against a woman on horseback, throwing her from the animal and endangering her life, *Gazetteer*, 15 July 1777. For attempts to get more than the set fare, see *Daily Advertiser*, 18 February 1761, 6 February 1751 and especially 18 July 1761. Tobias Smollet, *The expedition of Humphrey Clinker* (1771; Athens, Georgia, 1990), p. 88.

[29] *Daily Advertiser*, 13 December 1786, 20 July 1771.

driver, 'commonly called Daring Dick', also apologized for assaulting both the driver and passengers of a competing coach.[30]

These kinds of offences were also aggravated by bad language, a matter that was acknowledged in the apologies. When begging pardon for damaging a coach with his coal cart, Charles Gibbon also noted that he 'made use of very abusive Language'. Two carmen on a country road, in addition to 'endanger[ing] the lives of all that were then on that road, by driving most furiously' with their team, confessed that when others on the road 'desired [them] to go at a moderate pace' they 'used them with the worse language possible'. In addition to their general pugnaciousness, harsh words were so much expected from these workers that their absence could be noted. In fact, one apologetic coachman remarked that the husband of the woman from whom he had taken more than his proper fare only forgave him because he had not 'given any abusive Language'.[31]

In addition to their incivility and rowdiness on the road, transport men often seemed sadly deficient in deference both towards 'their betters' and to officers of the law. While coachmen or carters, porters or draymen probably also damaged the vehicles and threatened the lives of lowlier folk, they seemed to relish their command of the highways and to be unwilling to cede pride of place even to 'honourable personage[s]', aldermen, judges or ladies.[32] Undoubtedly impulsive and unruly, their apologies were compelled by the threat of loss of occupation and fines. Yet there is no indication that such men were especially or more violent than others.[33] Still, to many contemporaries they must have seemed the epitomes of London's fractiousness, of the bustle and jostle that, even when not criminal, was almost uncontrolled and wore an impertinent and disrespectful face.

If the misdeeds and subsequent apologies of transport men exhibits London in its more transitory aspects, then the apologies for scandalous or abusive words shows us London in its settled, neighbourly mode. It is

[30] *Daily Advertiser*, 6 September 1763, 8 July 1763. When a coach rammed a lady's chaise, her husband, riding his horse nearby, asked the coachman to desist; instead the driver 'grabbed him by the collar and was near pulling him off his horse'. *Daily Advertiser*, 11 June 1788.

[31] *Daily Advertiser*, 29 July 1758; *Gazetteer*, 2 June 1772; *Daily Advertiser*, 18 July 1761. George Peacock, a carman who damaged William Evans' one-horse chaise, was forgiven payment of the damages because he 'gave him no ill Language'; see *Daily Advertiser*, 28 July 1755.

[32] *Daily Advertiser*, 22 March 1755, 9 May 1755, see also *Gazetteer*, 29 October 1773; *Daily Advertiser*, 19 November 1755, 8 May 1761.

[33] See *Daily Advertiser*, 27 March 1762; *The World*, 4 January 1790 for examples of disrespectful behaviour. Transport workers comprised 35.2 per cent of apologists whose occupations were identified (228/648); they comprised only 29 per cent of such identified apologists whose offences included acts of violence (28/93).

clear that in those apologies that include both the address of the victim and the apologist, geographic proximity was the norm. More than half of all advertisements show both parties living in the same parish, often on the same court or street. Still, in cases of apologies for verbal abuse, this propinquity is still more pronounced. More than two-thirds of all apologies that reveal such neighbourliness are for defamatory offences.[34]

How were apologies for scandalous words the same as or different from both the general body of apologies and those involving transport workers? If we consider the social standing of both apologists and recipients, we can see that language offenders and victims were more often of the artisan/shopkeeping strata than the general sample. Of course this may simply be because men of the roads, who comprised more than a third of the total apologists, were almost entirely absent from this sample, though, even as victims, they hardly appeared. It may be that these workers were most likely to offend in their work activities, and to be significantly less visible as gossips or their victims. Apologies for defamatory words also came more often from the miscellaneous category of occupations, and even more of these were found as victims of derogatory language. The most significant difference, however, between the occupational structure of the entire body of apologists, and those of the apologies for words, is the important presence of servants, their masters, employers and their employees. These two categories have, for the purpose of clarity, been collapsed, since it is not always clear from eighteenth-century descriptions when the words were being used as synonyms, and when not. Almost one-fifth of all identified defamatory apologies came from employee/servants; more than 12 per cent of their recipients were masters/employers, while another 6 per cent were other servants/employees. Not only the neighbourhood but the household were important sites for the creation and propagation of such offences.[35]

Unlike apologists in road offences, who were always male, there were some female apologists begging pardon for defamation. In fact, though only about 16 per cent of all apologies for scandalous language were from women, more than half of all women apologists are found in this category. Thus, although women were more prevalent in earlier ecclesiastical defamation cases than they were among newspaper apologists,[36] there is

[34] Of the 343 apologies which contain both the address of the apologist and recipient, 196 reveal residential nearness; of these, 132 are apologies for scandalous language.
[35] See table 4. Of course, though these numbers are very small, they are suggestive.
[36] For defamation in a preceding period, see J. A. Sharpe, *Defamation and sexual slander in early modern England* (York, Borthwick Papers no. 58, 1980), and especially Tim Meldrum, 'A woman's court in London: defamation at the bishop of London's consistory court 1700–1745', *London Journal*, vol. 19, no. 1 (1994), pp. 1–20.

some continuity in such activities. It is important, however, to state from the outset that from this evidence most rumour and gossip were conducted by men against other men. Individual men were responsible for almost three-quarters of such apologies; individual men were the recipients of these more than 60 per cent of the time. Though women defamed other women more frequently than they did men, men defamed other men at an even higher rate.[37] Even in defamation, pre-eminently thought of as a 'female' activity, men predominated, at least in public apologies. Whether this is because men had more financial and business credit to lose than women, that men could better afford such advertisements, or that men found gossip by other men more dangerous than the 'mere tattle' of women, is impossible to know.

Defamation covered a wide variety of offences. However, many of the apologies for defamation were general and non-informatory:[38] we never learn, for example, the nature of the charges that Lazarus Davis made at sundry times against Mr George Hamilton; only that such attacks led Hamilton to begin legal proceedings which Davis' apology ended.[39] What many such apologies did stress, however, was the 'publicness' of the offence, that it had been committed where it could be witnessed by neighbours and customers. Nicholas Delany abused the Hon. Richard Fitzpatrick 'at the door of his house'; others were aspersed 'in publick Company', 'at a public vestry held in the parish church ... before a great number of people', at pubs like 'the Robin Hood and Black Boy in Leather lane' or worse still, the offence was 'repeated ... several times in the presence and hearing of several people'. For, as the widow Sinclair admitted in her apology for traducing the good name and character of a local milliner, the intent of such words was to injure her reputation in her neighbourhood.[40] Local gossip was a potent personal weapon; words could cause great harm. When it was said that Thomas Haynes, a Westminster butcher, had bought and sold a cow that had not been slaughtered but had died of disease, the apologist noted that the rumour had cost Haynes 'several of his customers'. When it was falsely rumoured that Richard

[37] Fifty-five per cent of apologies for defamation (25/45) by women had women as their object; 33 per cent of female defamation (15/45) was directed against men. Seventy per cent of apologies for defamation by men (140/199) had men as recipients, only 17 per cent of male defamation was directed against women (33/199). The missing percentages are apologies to groups of men, or men and women.
[38] Only in 88 apologies for scandalous words do we have a sense of what was said, and what motivated the offence.
[39] See *Daily Advertiser*, 28 January 1780.
[40] *Daily Advertiser*, 12 October 1767, 15 January 1769, see also 27 March 1755, 28 February 1770, 11 December 1771, 3 December 1773; see also *Gazetteer*, 5 March 1785. For the deleterious effect of slander on a neighbourhood, see *Daily Advertiser*, 25 April and 6 October 1760.

Hughes, a waiter at Sadler's Wells, had mixed wine with water, he lost his job as a consequence. The rumour that a master weaver had been unsympathetic to the plight of some of the distressed in his occupation, and opposed a subscription on their behalf, had led, the rumour-monger noted, to 'the most dreadful circumstances against both the property and person' of the victim of such calumny. Thus, in his apology for uttering derogatory words against the Rev. Mr Scott, Richard Fenton, an exciseman, hoped that it would 'be a Warning to others, to be more careful in their Expressions'.[41] Perhaps the public nature of the offence made the publicity of the newspaper advertisement seem like a just and functional punishment.

While malicious gossipers spread all sorts of tales, all such stories were guaranteed to lower the victim's esteem in his or her locale. They were designed, after all, to 'take away the good name' or belie 'the Honour and Credit' of the person slandered. Words themselves were seen as a form of abuse akin to assault. It is likely that it was merely words that were exchanged when James Kilvington 'abused and assaulted' his late wife's surgeon and the surgeon's apprentice, for having neglected her in her last illness, and for demanding payment of outstanding bills. Similarly, when John Shaw, a waterman, refused to carry a passenger to an agreed-upon destination, he apologized for having 'grossly abuse[d] and ill treat[ed] him (as far as words can do)'.[42]

Defamation could occur either in written or in oral form, though there were more apologies for the latter. Apologists for written aspersions had sent letters (for example, one sent to the principal customer of the victim, with the 'vile intent to prejudice him in his business'), handbills (suggesting that a pencil maker and his accomplice had attempted to defraud several merchants by ordering large stocks of their own pencils) or pamphlets (like 'A Cure for Canting' directed against Sir Richard and Rev. Rowland Hill).[43] Far more common were apologies for 'calumnious words', for language which 'falsely slandered' or 'maliciously scandalized' its victim.[44] On the whole, when we have details of such talk, rumours were spread about three subjects: business repute, sexual repute and law-abidingness.

Most aspersions designed to cast doubt on the credit and reputation of an individual could not but have hurt him in his business dealings; some, however, made specific charges about illicit business practices.

---

[41] *Daily Advertiser*, 10 April 1794, 23 February 1780, 7 July 1767. For other servants who lost their places because of malicious gossip, see 8 February 1764 and 15 March 1773.
[42] *Daily Advertiser*, 28 August 1772, 29 February 1772, 6 October 1760, 6 August 1769.
[43] See *Daily Advertiser*, 22 October 1755, 29 October 1772, 23 June 1795.
[44] *Daily Advertiser*, 9 February 1763, 27 March 1761, 14 November 1760.

Table 4. *Numbers of apologies for scandalous words (where the occupation of either apologists/recipients is known)*

	Apologists	Recipients
Artisans and shopkeepers	42	39
Food and drink	13	14
Labourers	3	
Law		4
Misc.	8	17
Transport	7	4
Employees/servants	18	6
Employers		12
Total	91	96

Source: sample.

Both victuallers and butchers were particularly vulnerable to such charges, since their reputation for wholesome food was central to the success of their ventures. Surgeons and doctors were also easily and often criticized; any public doubts about their acumen or skill would have an immediate impact on their income. Other business attacks were more particularized but no less venomous: when John and Elizabeth Warren apologized to John Kitteridge for having 'scandalized and hurt [him] in the Way of his Trade', they took the occasion to repeat the offence, noting that they had claimed that Kitteridge 'kept unlawful Workers, and did not give a lawful Price, and works the worst of Silk'.[45]

There were two further 'false and scandalous' business rumours we must consider: those involving either a breakdown of the relationship between employer/master and his or her servant or employee, and the 'malicious accusation' of actual or imminent bankruptcy. Employee–employer conflict was a frequent source of newspaper apologies for defamation and sometimes exhibited a nastiness characteristic of family disputes. Thus a journeyman employed by a baker, Mr Martin, confessed to having 'go[ne] from house to house and reported that [his] master bought nothing but second flour to make his bread with and other false expressions, whereby Mr Martin has been injured in his business'. Upton, an apprentice watchmaker, used his position within the household to 'insult [his master] by accusing him of an attempt to injure his servant

[45] *Daily Advertiser*, 16 June 1758, 7 January 1773, 27 August 1762. There were several apologies that, under the guise of asking pardon, seemed to repeat the substance of the offence. See, for example, *Daily Advertiser*, 15 February 1755 and 27 August 1762.

girl at the same time demanding £50 to keep the same a secret'. Though we do not know what one Buckram, servant to a hairdresser, Mr Brosier, said 'to the prejudice of his master', we do know he said he was contrite, and begged pardon in a public apology.[46]

Some apologies for defamation came not from within the work-family, but from without, from the envy and malice of competitors. Thus, when one victualler apologized to another whose shop was on the same street, for having accused him of 'making use of short measures in his said business', one might well suspect that the rumour had been raised to gain some of the latter's customers. Mr Hughes, a jeweller, confessed to having started rumours about his competitors, the firm of Shelley and King, 'with a view and intention to prejudice them in their trade and reputation'.[47] Scandal seemed one readily available weapon in business rivalries.

While the tattle of a disgruntled employee or disaffected competitor could do much harm, people may have taken those sorts of conflicts with a pinch of salt, expecting perhaps that such irritations were not uncommon in households or between businesses. In contrast, the charges of bankruptcy, or loss of credit and creditworthiness, was much more grave. When Mary Moad accused Robert Clavering, a carpenter, of owing her money, and 'declaring in the publick street, that he had not more than sufficient to pay [her]', it became necessary for Clavering, if he wished to remain in business, to get an apology as public as the original words had been. It is not surprising that John Field's rumour that William Hammond, a saddler, 'was bankrupt, and not able to pay his creditors' not only led to 'his reputation hav[ing] been so much injured' but also to a prosecution against his defamer.[48] Unchecked, the rumour itself could ruin a tradesman. It was not at all uncommon for advertisements from such slandered individuals to appear in the *Daily Advertiser*, affirming their on-going fiscal health.

The apologies for sexual scandalmongering were just what one might have expected. Men and women engaged in such tattle in almost equal numbers, their aspersions covering the gamut of offences from accusations of prostitution and adultery to varieties of fornication. A third of such apologies were from men who had accused other men of 'unnatural' crimes or acts.[49] But it is clear that financial irregularity had replaced

[46] *Daily Advertiser*, 17 October 1791, 21 January 1780, 10 February 1772.
[47] *Daily Advertiser*, 21 December 1769; *Gazetteer*, 10 October 1775.
[48] *Daily Advertiser*, 3 February 1766, 13 January 1778; see also 7 September 1761 and 17 January 1771.
[49] The apologies for accusations of fornication can be found in *Daily Advertiser*, 1 September 1775, 21 January 1780, for whoredom, 18 May 1763, 27 September 1775

sexual irregularity as the main diet of the rumour-monger; twice as many apologies appeared for business as for sexual defamation. Only two apologists noted that their offence had been the traditional staple of sexual abuse, calling a woman 'a whore'.[50]

It is in the apologies for mistakenly accusing others of crimes that we perhaps get the most detailed sense of the tensions and petty suspicions that could grow within working-class neighbourhoods. The most common charge was theft: sometimes specified, sometimes not. Sometimes the person who thought he had been the victim of the theft apologized for his mistake: for example, a Mr Welsh, after charging a private soldier, John Wilkes, with having stolen £20 from him, ultimately confessed that he had found the money in the lining of his breeches. At other times, third parties spread rumours of reported thefts; the purloining of a tea sample from a tea warehouse, the theft of a calf's head, or of a plank from a felled elm. Unlike the Welsh incident, most apologies revealed the small amount of the alleged thefts. But within a community of people living poorly and working hard, valuing small accumulations of property, these were items of importance. Two other factors need notice, however, in these accusations of wrongful activity. The first, the antipathy to informers was an expression of the solidarity of many within the neighbourhood to the intrusions of outside regulation. For example, when Goddard, a labourer residing at Bell Court, apologized, he explained that he had 'unjustly reported to sundry persons that [the victims] were the informers against a still taken out of Bell Court on the 18 August, which much injured their reputations'. Similarly, when Mr Wiggens tried to blacken the reputation of an enemy, a local publican, he first asserted that the publican had been arrested and taken into custody, and when that proved patently false, he later claimed that the publican was an informer.[51]

The second factor was the relatively small number of apologies which had accused neighbours of more serious charges: rape, murder and highway robbery. While there were a few rumours spread about such significant offences, more had to do with the theft of things like a fishing net, two ale glasses, or a stolen cotton gown. In the world of London's neighbourhoods, the charge of being an informer, or of small theft left unanswered,

and 31 January 1794; for accusations of adultery, 10 November 1772, 19 December 1769. The unnatural acts apologies can be found in 2 October 1766, 11 December 1771, 9 November 1784 and 14 October 1788.
[50] *Daily Advertiser*, 18 May 1763; *Gazetteer*, 27 September 1775.
[51] In 24 of the 32 apologies for accusations of crime, the defamers had claimed that the people they had accused had been involved in the theft or the receipt of stolen goods. For Welsh, see *Daily Advertiser*, 15 December 1763; theft of tea, 29 July 1786; stolen calf's head, 5 May 1772; and the stolen plank, 30 September 1785. For Goddard, 9 September 1784; Wiggen's two charges, 1 November and 2 December 1751.

could be as devastating in terms of day-to-day relations, in terms of trust given and favours extended, as a more serious charge might be in the law courts.[52] Furthermore, one's customers and creditors in other parts of London might also take fright, and such charges could ruin the defamed person.

If much discord arose, as it seems to have, from the pressures of living among gossiping neighbours and envious competitors, these apologies also testify to the role of friends, family, people of local repute, and often the magistrate himself,[53] in resolving these disagreements. The most common intermediaries were usually described as 'friends' by the apologists; such friends could through their intervention either prevent the beginning of a legal action or recommend forgiveness through public apology once it had started. Occasionally, the victim's friends played the role of peacemakers: it was 'the Friends of the injured Party' who mediated a settlement between Joseph Rollinson and the man he drove over in his coach.[54] In yet other cases, it was the offender's own family that brought about a final, informal agreement. Very frequently, members of the community in which the offence occurred, and in which both parties often lived or worked, arranged such a resolution. Without naming either the victim or the offence, in his apology William Peart acknowledges this vital role: 'I likewise return sincere Thanks to those several worthy Persons of the said Parish, who were the means of this favourable Accommodation, by which a Prosecution is prevented that would have been of severe Consequence to me.' James Brereton thanked his friends and neighbours for their intercession; David Holdsworth agreed to pay 'Damages agreed on by the Neighbours'.[55] Sometimes the mediators were respectable gentlemen of the vicinity, the employer or master of the

[52] For the treatment of informers, even those only suspected of being informers, see J. M. Beattie, 'Violence and society in early modern England', in A. Doob and E. Greenspan, *Perspectives in criminal law* (Aurora, Ont., 1985), pp. 40–1. The apology for the accusation of rape can be found in *Daily Advertiser*, 30 September 1767; the two murder charges in 1 July and 25 August 1784; and the highwayman rumour, 31 May 1782. The apology about the theft of the fishing net in 23 November 1780; the ale glasses, 17 July 1786; and the cotton gown, 15 October 1786.

[53] Thus, for example, after having 'raise[d] a great Riot and Disturbance in Bow-Lane', assaulting and abusing the watchmen of the ward, Richard Lance and John Trevors, two journeymen barbers, apologized for their offence, remarking that the magistrate before whom they were brought had recommended 'to the Parties injured to forgive us, on our making Satisfaction and asking Pardon'. *Daily Advertiser*, 8 January 1761.

[54] For the prevention of a suit by the intervention of the offender's friend, see *Daily Advertiser*, 14 September 1771; for reconciliation after the offence see 21 August 1771 and 19 September 1755. For the intercession of the victim's friends in the Rollinson case, see 21 March 1769; for another instance see 7 March 1795.

[55] *Daily Advertiser*, 9 June 1760. For the role of family, see 7 April 1774; for parish and neighbourhood, 28 February 1770 and 7 December 1771.

offender, or even on occasion, the victim himself.[56] Since such conflicts could harm the peaceful fabric of a neighbourhood, it is not surprising that many parts of the community became involved in their resolution. The newspaper apology was a public statement, both to the offended party and to the community, that peace had been in some sense restored.

If the transport offences for which the apologies we have been considering can be thought of, as Nicholas Rogers has suggested, as expressions of 'plebeian self-assertion',[57] and the advertisements apologizing for defamation as evidence for the continuing importance of credit and repute in one's locale, the third major sort of offence apologized for, the attacks on a variety of sorts of law officials, combined these two motives. Most such apologies merely state that the advertiser begs pardon for assaulting, or attempting to interfere with the official in the due execution of his office. Several offenders assaulted a law officer simply because of personal circumstances. When A. S. Wappin had his goods seized to cover his debts, he roughly evicted the officer left to guard them. Though in his apology he regretted the evil example that his violence promoted, his act was essentially an individual one, concerned only with his own welfare.[58] Still, there were many run-ins with law officers that seemed to be less individualistic. In some, local high spirits or drinking practices came into conflict with legal rules. For example two men confessed that on Shrove Tuesday, they were 'unwaringly drawn into association with divers disorderly and idle persons, illegally assembled for throwing at cock and other bad purposes, tending to a breach of the peace ... and when officers appeared to suppress and disperse this assembly, we did in a most daring and outrageous manner assault, oppose, and obstruct them, and endeavour to spirit up the mob to attack and pelt them with stones'.[59] Others seemed more defensive and were perhaps the other side

---

[56] See *Gazetteer*, 12 July 1777. The master of two apologists and the employer of another successfully intervened in their workers' behalf, see *Daily Advertiser*, 14 November 1778 and 28 July 1791. The basket-maker mistress of an erring apprentice argued that, as a widow with small children, his arrest could severely injure her livelihood (6 March 1779). For the intervention of the victim see the Wright case, 13 December 1786.

[57] Nicholas Rogers, 'Confronting the crime wave: the debate over social reform and regulation, 1749–1753', in L. Davison *et al.*, eds., *Stilling the grumbling hive: the response to social and economic problems in England, 1689–1750* (Stroud and New York, 1992), p. 87. Rogers in fact uses barrow women and draymen as his examples of such insubordination (p. 96).

[58] *Daily Advertiser*, 25 January 1772; see also 28 July 1785.

[59] *Gazetteer*, 3 October 1772. For other instances of such local practices, see the apology for attacking a constable who was trying to stop Sunday sales of fruit, *Daily Advertiser*, 3 June 1760, and a similar apology for the attack on 'members of the Society for Preventing the Profanation of the Sabbath', 18 December 1776. See Gregory Thomas Smith, 'The state and the culture of violence in London, 1760–1840' (unpublished Ph.D. thesis, Toronto, 1999), p. 194 for more on violence towards city officials.

of neighbourly conflict. There were a dozen apologies for having taken part in bad conduct towards law officials, either in an attempt to rescue a neighbour or fellow-worker, in an attack on such officials during public punishment, or the refusal to help them apprehend a person charged with a felony.[60] Unusual only for the small number of people involved was the incident that led to the apology of the Squires, husband and wife, and their friend Cork, like Mr Squire, a shoemaker and resident of Oxford Street. When the officers of the Sheriff of Middlesex came to arrest John Squires for debt, the pair attacked them and rescued Squires. Later recaptured and in gaol, the three publicly apologized and hoped that their advertisement would serve as 'a Public Warning to others offending in the like imprudent, outrageous and turbulent Manner'. The apology concluded with an acknowledgement of the justice of the law; 'well knowing now that the Law which punishes us protects us'. An echo of the same refrain can be heard in another apology to a Shadwell justice of the peace, whom a Mr Hay had 'most daringly insulted . . . in the execution of his office'. Hay concluded his advertisement by recommending to all people whatsoever always to shew a due respect to such our superiors, placed in so high an office'.[61]

By the mid-1790s the *Daily Advertiser*, the source of most of these advertisements, discontinued publication. Though such apologies continued to be published in many of the other dailies of the metropolis, their numbers began to decline in the 1770s and 1780s and to dramatically decrease in the 1790s. Perhaps prosecutors or offended parties had become cynical about the power of these declarations to effect change. Perhaps, in the harsh economic climate of the later 1790s, the great majority of offenders, who were poor working people, could no longer afford the expense of the advertisement, whatever the alternative. Perhaps, with the introduction of stipendiary magistrates, some of the cases that would have been informally resolved now went through the courts. Perhaps public and legal opinion had changed, veering from the desire to settle informally to the position that justice must be publicly done and seen to be done rather than privately negotiated or settled. Or perhaps the public apology, like other communicative advertisements, seemed old-fashioned, and suffered a sort of 'genre' decline.[62]

---

[60] For the apology for attacking an official attempting to arrest a fellow-servant, see *Daily Advertiser*, 15 November 1766; for an assault during a public whipping, 24 January 1764; for assaulting officers and refusing assistance in the arrest of a charged felon, *Gazetteer*, 31 October 1772.

[61] The Squires–Cork apology, *Daily Advertiser*, 26 January 1789; Hay, 11 October 1771.

[62] On the change in legal thinking, favouring a more public dealing with offences, see Peter King, 'Punishing assault: the transformation of attitudes in the English courts', *Journal of Interdisciplinary History*, vol. 27, no. 1 (summer 1996), pp. 45–6; Beattie, 'Violence and

Table 5. *Number of*
apology advertisements

	By decade
1740s	11
1750s	78
1760s	345
1770s	272
1780s	230
1790s	88

Source: sample.

If we have seen in the public newspaper apology a part of the process of conflict resolution and of reconciliation, a public effort to stem and regulate the exuberant but often churlish behaviour of London's many transport workers, we must not end without a glance at another aspect of London life that these advertisements reveal. Not only were there no apologies from employers or masters to servants, though there were many, as I have shown, from the latter to the former, but the public apology also functioned as a public caution, as a warning against untoward, insubordinate behaviour.[63] Apologies from transport workers, from labourers involved in illicit wage negotiations, or from those who attacked officials sometimes contained cautions to the public to avoid such transgressions, lest the power of the law should descend on their heads and lives. For while the function of an apology was to restore social relations in the neighbourhoods as well as in the metropolis, it was also to maintain hierarchy, to rehabilitate relations of deference, to restrain unruliness and promote regularity and decorum. Combining mediation with social control, the newspaper apology mirrored the social order of which it was a part.

society', and Smith, 'State and the culture of violence', p. 122. For genre change, see D. T. Andrew, 'To the charitable and humane: appeals for assistance in the eighteenth-century London press', in Hugh Cunningham and Joanna Innes, eds., *Charity, philanthropy and social reform* (London, 1998), pp. 103–4.

[63] In addition to the apologies mentioned in note 57 above, see *Daily Advertiser*, 17 May 1771, 16 September 1791 and 5 December 1788. Almost one-third of all apologies contained some warning or cautionary note. Many were labelled as cautions: 'A caution to watermen' (*Daily Advertiser*, 14 July 1772); 'A caution to porters' (*Gazetteer*, 12 Dec. 1781); 'A caution to gunmakers' (*Daily Advertiser*, 18 Aug. 1786). Of the 295 apology advertisements which contained such warnings, 69 were apologies for wage offences or against legal officials.

APPENDIX A

Artisans and shopkeepers = apothecary, auctioneer, barber, basket-maker, bedscrew maker, birdcage maker, blacking polish maker, black-smith, bookbinder, bookseller, bricklayer, brickmaker, cabinet maker, cane dealer, carpenter, carver, chandler, chinaman, clothworker, coach harness maker, coach joiner, coal dealer, collar maker, cooper, cordwainer, currier, draper, enameller, engine weaver, engraver, farrier, fellmonger, feltmaker, fine drawer, furrier, glass manufacturer, gold and silver button maker, gunsmith, haberdasher, hairdresser, hardwareman, horsedealer, jeweller, lacemaker, lastmaker, lath renderer, mantua maker, marble polisher, medical snuffmaker, oilman, ostler, painter, paper-stainer, pattern maker, pawnbroker, peruke maker, printseller, sadler, sawyer, shipwright, shoemaker, silkdyer, silversmith, skindresser, smith, soapboiler, staymaker, stonemason, tailor, tanner, toyman, turner, un-dertaker, violin maker, warehouseman, watchmaker, weaver, whipmaker, wheelwright, whitesmith, woolcomber

Entertainment = innkeeper, publican, owner of spa, tapster, waiter

Food and drink = brewer, baker, cheesemonger, confectioner, cook, fisher, fruitseller, higgler, miller, poulterer, milkman, potato merchant, sugar baker, turncock, victualler

Labourer = coalheaver, dustman, fireman, groom, labourer, lighterman, mangler, marshman, paviour, postboy, slaughterman

Law and law officers = bailiffs, constables, servants of the court of re-quests, firemen, inspectors, judges, lawyers, letter carriers, local juries, magistrate, marshal's men, officers, overseers/churchwardens, reforma-tion society, sheriff's men, tax collectors, toll collectors, watchmen

Misc. = actor, alderman, ambassador, author, bleeder, broker, church-warden, clergy, clerk, dancing master, farmer, gardener, guide, lottery seller, mayor, medical practitioners, pavement contractor, printer, publisher, student

Transport = carman, carters, chairman, coachmen, draymen, drover, night-soil man, waggoner, waterman

11   Origins of the factory acts: the Health and Morals of Apprentices Act, 1802

Joanna Innes

Most contemporaries agreed that the first factory act – the Health and Morals of Apprentices Act of 1802 – was poorly enforced. In 1819 a House of Lords committee documented this. Though in many counties J.P.s had followed the directions of the act and appointed visitors, appointments had tailed off; such visitors as there were rarely reported. Owners of eligible factories increasingly failed to register with magistrates. Sir Robert Peel was one of the few who continued to do so – but then, he had been the chief promoter of the act.[1]

Recent historians of the factory acts have generally chosen to begin their studies with the act of 1833, the first to provide for salaried inspectors: if the acts ever acquired teeth, it was then.[2] The 1802 act nonetheless deserves our attention. It does so because of its impact by way of *idea*. Subsequent attempts to secure factory legislation took it as a starting point: proponents of regulation argued that Parliament had conceded the principle that factory conditions required its attention; all that remained to be settled was how far regulation should be extended, and how best to give it effect. British factory acts, moreover, provided models for regulation in other parts of the world.[3]

The 1802 act provided a model – but upon what was it modelled? How did the *first* factory act come about? Although some existing accounts engage with this question, more can be done to make its formulation intelligible, by setting it in the context of the concerns and characteristic patterns of action of the later eighteenth century; by attending closely to how it emerged, who was involved, and what parts they played. This chapter addresses these tasks of elucidation, and in so doing presents a case

---

[1] *House of Lords Sessional Papers* (1819), paper 66, pp. 77 ff.

[2] J. T. Ward, *The factory movement, 1830–1855* (London, 1962), and R. Q. Gray, *The factory question and industrial England, 1830–1860* (Cambridge, 1996); cf. such older studies as B. L. Hutchins and A. Harrison, *A history of factory legislation*, 3rd edn (London, 1926), and M. W. Thomas, *The early factory acts* (Leigh-on-Sea, 1947).

[3] P. Bolin-Hort, *Work, family and the state. Child labour and the organization of production in the British cotton industry, 1780–1920* (Lund, 1989), compares British with other legislative histories.

study in the formation of social legislation in a period before government played much part in initiating or forming such measures.[4]

We must first survey the act's provisions.[5]

It applied to cotton and woollen 'and other' mills (in this respect differing from the next significant piece of factory legislation, the 1819 act, which applied to cotton mills only). All such mills employing twenty or more workers, or three or more apprentices, fell within its scope.

As its title – 'health and morals' – suggests, the act had two concerns. Health-related provisions included the requirement that mills be whitewashed and ventilated. Visitors appointed under the act were empowered to call in physicians if infectious disease broke out. Other health-oriented provisions related more particularly to apprentices, who were to have two suits of clothes, one new each year; were not to sleep more than two a bed, or work more than twelve hours a day, or between nine at night and six in the morning.

'Moral' provisions in the act focused entirely upon apprentices. The act provided that male and female apprentices must sleep separately; that they should be instructed in reading, writing and arithmetic (as appropriate to their age and ability) during every working day, during the first four years of their apprenticeship, should attend church on Sundays, receive religious teaching, and, if members of one of the established churches, be prepared for communion.

The enforcement provisions of the act built upon existing models. Eligible mills were to display copies of its text, and register with the clerk of the peace annually. County benches were to appoint at least two visitors, one a justice, the other a clergyman, to report. The visiting principle was adopted over this period in various institutions: justices were already empowered to visit prisons, madhouses and workhouses; voluntary institutions such as infirmaries and Sunday schools also sometimes had 'visitors'.[6]

The act's special (though not exclusive) focus on apprentices suggests that its origins might be sought in a long tradition of legislation empowering J.P.s to regulate apprenticeships. I will suggest that indeed this played a part in setting the scene. But the act was also coloured by a recent flowering of interest in health, morals and education. Concern about health as a public issue had surfaced in the prison reform movement; concern about

---

[4] J. Innes, 'Parliament and the shaping of eighteenth-century English social policy', *Transactions of the Royal Historical Society*, 5th series, vol. XL (1990), pp. 63–92 offers a more broadly conceived survey.

[5] 42 George III c. 73.

[6] 24 George III s. 2, c. 54; 14 George III c. 49; 30 George III c. 49.

education, in the Sunday school movement. In the late eighteenth century these concerns fused to shape a new approach to children's employment.

This chapter will approach its task of elucidation as follows. First, it will set the scene with a sketch of the growth of children's employment in textile factories, in the context of patterns in apprenticeship and children's employment more generally. A second section will trace the growth of concern about the impact of factories upon health; a third, the development of a moral perspective on factories. Health issues especially engaged the attention of medical men; moral issues, that of magistrates, judges and metropolitan philanthropists. Nationally oriented philanthropic societies helped to bring the two together.

A distinctive (though not unique) feature of this legislation (anti-slave-trade legislation also comes to mind) was that it brought public interest concerns to bear on economic activity. The final sections of this chapter explore the workings of that relationship: charting Peel's emergence as the act's chief proponent, the ways in which humanitarian and manufacturing concerns were negotiated in Parliament, and the subsequent rise and fall of manufacturing opposition to the act. In the event, of course, the struggle over this act was to prove only the first instalment of a much longer saga.

Although some children were employed in silk mills in the early eighteenth century, it was only when Richard Arkwright successfully applied millpower to cotton spinning that large numbers were drawn into factory employment. After the overturn of the patent for Arkwright's 'water frame' in 1785, such mills proliferated. By 1787 there were over 200 in England and Scotland, and at least eight in Ireland. Concentrated in Lancashire, Derbyshire, Nottinghamshire and Yorkshire, they could also be found in fourteen other British counties. By 1795 they totalled around 300.[7] Some firms had several mills: Peel's, the biggest, had twenty-three.[8] The successful application of steam power to the alternative technology of mule spinning then opened the way for the rise of large mule-based mills. By 1812, over 600 of these operated in Lancashire, Cheshire and the Halifax region of Yorkshire alone – probably coexisting with several hundred waterframes.[9] New technology was slower to make an impact

[7] R. S. Fitton, *The Arkwrights. Spinners of fortune* (Manchester, 1989). For mill numbers, S. D. Chapman, 'The Arkwright mills – Colquhoun's census of 1786 and archaeological evidence', *Industrial Archaeology Review*, vol. 6 (1981–2), p. 5.

[8] For Peel's enterprise in context, S. D. Chapman, 'Fixed capital formation in the British cotton industry, 1770–1815', *Economic History Review*, 2nd series, vol. 23 (1970), pp. 256 ff.

[9] Chapman, 'Arkwright mills', p. 8, and G. Daniels, 'Samuel Crompton's census of the cotton industry in 1811', *Economic History* (supplement to *Economic Journal*), vol. 2 (1930), pp. 107–10.

in the woollen industry, where spinning was mainly by jenny. At the turn
of the century, although there were some 240 cotton mills in Yorkshire,
there were only about twenty-two worsted-spinning mills. Powered wool
spinning was a still later development.[10]

Arkwright mills often employed high proportions of young workers.[11]
In Robert Owen's New Lanark in 1799, 70 per cent of the workforce
were said to be under 18 years of age, of whom most were under 13.[12]
Mule-based mills employed a higher proportion of adult workers to su-
pervise the mules – but children were still required to piece yarn and
doff 'cops', and indeed, the greater the number of spindles per mule,
the higher the proportion of children required. In 1816, in a number
of mills around Preston some 70 per cent of the workforce were under
18, as against 50 per cent in the Manchester area and 45 per cent for
Scotland.[13]

Evidence as to what proportion of factory children were apprentices is
patchy, and what there is suggests a complex picture. For the purposes of
the 1802 act, 'apprentice' seems to have been understood to imply a child
apprenticed not by his or her parents but by a parish or charity, living
in mill accommodation. It is often suggested that such apprentices were
most sought by rural mills, rural neighbourhoods not supplying enough
young workers. However, town mills also figured among those recruiting
London apprentices. There are indications that larger enterprises were
more likely to employ apprentices, whatever their location.[14] Yet some
allowance has to be made too for the preference of the employer: neither
Arkwright at Cromford nor Strutt at Belper – both large employers in
rural areas – employed apprentices.[15]

In relation to the act, perhaps the point that most needs stressing is
how prevalent 'free' child labour was at its passage – probably being the
norm in most enterprises, if harder to estimate as a proportion of the
child workforce. Wilberforce asserted in 1802 that there were forty mills
near Manchester where there were few or no apprentices; in the whole
of Yorkshire, very few.[16] In 1816 Peel – then supporting the extension of

---

[10] G. Ingle, *Yorkshire cotton. The Yorkshire cotton industry, 1780–1835* (Preston, 1997), p. 18;
D. T. Jenkins, *The West Riding wool textile industry, 1770–1835* (Edington, Wilts., 1975),
p. 75.

[11] Bolin-Hort, *Work, family*, pp. 45–9.   [12] ibid., p. 35.   [13] ibid., p. 40.

[14] ibid., pp. 37–9 suggests that the concentration of apprentices in rural mills became
marked only after 1815. On larger mills, see M. B. Rose, 'Social policy and business:
parish apprenticeship and the early factory system, 1750–1834', *Business History*, vol. 31
(1989), pp. 18–19.

[15] R. S. Fitton and A. P. Wadsworth, *The Strutts and the Arkwrights* (Manchester, 1958),
p. 104.

[16] *Parliamentary Register*, ed. J. Debrett, 45 vols. (London, 1781–96), vol. XVIII (1802),
pp. 184–5. See also James Nield in *Gentleman's Magazine* (June 1804), pp. 494–5;
Parliamentary Papers [hereafter *P.P.*] (1816) III, p. 341.

regulation to 'free' child labour – suggested that their numbers had grown radically since 1802, when, he claimed, apprentice labour had been the norm.[17] Though some employers who had employed apprentices ceased to do so in the early nineteenth century,[18] the indications are that change had been less radical than Peel made out.

Factory children formed a small element in a larger child labour force. Patterns of youthful employment in this period were diverse – differing not only with social status, but with local employment opportunities, the preferences of parents and the policies of local authorities. Ages at starting work varied greatly. Children were not usually put out to work before the age of 6, but might be (if at all) at any time up to their late teens or early twenties.[19]

Youthful work relationships were commonly characterized either in the terminology of 'master and servant' or that of 'master and apprentice'. These latter terms were used in several different contexts.[20] First, in certain boroughs, to designate a period of employment which when completed qualified the apprentice to be free of the town, with the right to do business there. Secondly, in accordance with the Elizabethan statute of artificers, to designate a period of employment involving the learning of a trade, within a framework of regulations laid down by that act. Thirdly, to designate a period of employment organized by parish officers on the authority of Elizabethan poor laws: all householders could be compelled to receive as 'parish apprentices' children aged between 5 and 14 whose parents could not support them.

Apprenticeship provisions, statutory and otherwise, were normative. Practice was always more improvisatory and untidy. Ilana Ben Amos, thus, suggests that throughout the early modern period most apprentices did not complete the term for which they had been indentured.[21] We must be wary of supposing – as contemporaries sometimes did – that eighteenth-century practice represented a degeneration from an older pattern in which most young people were maintained for an extended period under quasi-parental discipline and care.

[17] *P.P.* (1816) III, p. 140.   [18] Horn, 'Traffic in children', p. 182.

[19] H. Cunningham, 'The employment and unemployment of children in England, *c.* 1680–1851', *Past and Present*, no. 126 (1990), pp. 115–50 and J. Humphries and J. Horrell, ' "The exploitation of little children": child labor and family economy in the industrial revolution', *Explorations in Economic History*, vol. 32 (1995), pp. 485–516.

[20] J. Lane, *Apprenticeship in England, 1600–1914* (London, 1996); C. Brooks, 'Apprenticeship, social mobility and the middling sort, 1500–1800', in C. Brooks and J. Barry, eds., *The middling sort of people: culture, society and politics in England, 1550–1800* (London, 1994), pp. 522–83; K. Snell, *Annals of the labouring poor: social change and agrarian England, 1660–1900* (Cambridge, 1985), pp. 228–319; and J. Rule, *The experience of labour in eighteenth-century industry* (London, 1981), pp. 95–123.

[21] I. Ben Amos, *Adolescence and youth in early modern England* (New Haven, 1994), pp. 130–1.

Eighteenth-century developments may nonetheless have meant that even fewer children's experience approximated to this domestic ideal.[22] So-called apprenticeships increasingly lasted for short terms, with apprentices boarded away from their masters, paid wages, and dismissed when no longer needed. In the Macclesfield silk industry, young workers termed apprentices were taken on for a few years at weekly wages. Such arrangements were also common in the cotton industry, though in the context of debates prompted by Peel's initiative such child workers were distinguished from 'apprentices' and termed 'free children'.[23]

Moralists of all social classes lamented these developments.[24] The tendency of better capitalized masters in both workshop and outwork trades to take on unprecedentedly large *numbers* of apprentices also aroused concern – and not only from a moral perspective. Adult workers complained that jobs were reserved for the young, who within a few years were turned adrift in flooded labour markets. Workers' protests against such practices found expression not only in industrial action but also in lawsuits brought under the Statute of Artificers, and applications to Parliament.[25]

Most apprenticeships were probably organized by parents. Charity trustees also played an important part in some parishes. Parish officials, by contrast, routinely apprenticed out only a fraction of children, often a mere 5 per cent of the relevant age group.[26] When occasionally they employed their powers more vigorously, they found plenty of scope for doing that. In the hundred of Ongar, Essex, in 1801, magistrates ordered parish officers to apprentice or put out as servants all children aged 12 and over who were not in work. More than 500 were put out in the first year, between 150 and 200 in each of the following years, probably representing the vast majority of the age cohort.[27]

For most of the eighteenth century, as earlier, children of the better-off were most likely to be sent long distances, to pick up prized skills

[22] See note 20 above and K. Snell, 'The apprenticeship system in British history: the fragmentation of a cultural institution', *History of Education*, vol. 25 (1996), pp. 303–21.

[23] G. Malmgreen, *Silk town: industry and culture in Macclesfield, 1750–1835* (Hull, 1985), pp. 34–40; A. Redford, *Labour migration in England* (London, 1926); [T. Bernard,] *Reports of the society for bettering the condition of the poor*, 6 vols. (London, 1798–1814), vol. IV, appendix, pp. 179–80.

[24] cf. Sir Robert Buxton in Debrett, *Parliamentary Register*, vol. XVII, p. 448; vol. XVIII, p. 64, and the printers' circular cited by Rule, *Experience of labour*, p. 101.

[25] Rule, *Experience of labour*, pp. 110–19.

[26] Local studies of Butler's Marston and Tysoe, Warwickshire, and Old Swinford, Worcestershire, supply both numbers apprenticed and population data, making rough estimation possible. For variations in practice, see S. Hindle, 'Power, poor relief and social relations in Holland Fen, *c.* 1600–1800', *Historical Journal*, vol. 41 (1998), pp. 86–7, and P. Sharpe, 'Poor children as apprentices in Colyton, 1598–1830', *Continuity and Change*, vol. 6 (1991), p. 259.

[27] [Bernard,] *Reports of the society*, vol. V, pp. 110–15.

and make valuable contacts; poor children, by contrast, were retained in their own or neighbouring parishes. The growth of a long-distance traffic in poor apprentices to the industrial Midlands and north was a new departure, shadowing industrial take-off: this got underway in the 1760s and picked up speed from the 1780s.[28]

The scale of this traffic in the early nineteenth century was illuminated by an 1815 parliamentary inquiry into the destinations of the 5,800 children apprenticed by London parishes from 1802 to 1811.[29] The total represented the usual few per cent of the age cohort – most poor London children must have been dealt with in other ways. Most of those apprenticed (65%), moreover, remained within the metropolis. Those sent 'into the country' had, however, commonly gone to textile trades, three-quarters into cotton trades, the majority of these probably to spinning factories.

Parish children sent to spinning factories thus constituted a minority of a few per cent of the capital's youthful population, yet a large proportion of those disposed of through parish apprenticeships, and we know that some London charity apprentices, such as Foundling Hospital apprentices, went the same route. London may have contributed disproportionately to the trade. Yet other places certainly contributed too – from Chelmsford, Essex, and Brighton, Sussex, to Witney, Oxfordshire, and Oswestry, Shropshire.

This traffic in children generated criticism and resistance. Not all need have been rooted in generic reservations about industrial working environments. The Witney residents hauled before Quarter Sessions for trying to obstruct the cart removing local children northwards, the couple who wrote to Wilberforce to lament their son having been barbarously torn from them and sent to a distant factory, may have been chiefly moved by the fact of the children's removal.[30] Member of Parliament, Wilbraham Bootle, arguing the case for a register of apprentices in 1802, stated that among other things it would make it possible for friends to find out where an apprentice had been taken – not always easy as things stood.[31] Overseers or charity officers might develop reservations about one industrial employer, but happily consign children to another in the same trade; there had always been thought to be good and bad masters. However, increasingly concern was associated with specific reservations about factories. To the formation of these we now turn.

---

[28] See Rose, 'Social policy and business' for the origins of the trade.
[29] *P.P.* (1814–15) V, pp. 1569–71.
[30] Lane, *Apprenticeship in England*, p. 279; R. I and S. Wilberforce, *The life of William Wilberforce*, vol. III (London, 1838), p. 45. See also G. Unwin, *Samuel Oldknow and the Arkwrights*, 2nd edn (Manchester, 1968), p. 171.
[31] Debrett, *Parliamentary Register*, vol. XVII, p. 199.

It was as reputed breeding grounds for typhus that factories first attracted concern. Spread by lice, and flourishing most among populations weakened by malnutrition, typhus – one of the more common endemic, intermittently epidemic diseases of the period – was especially visible in residential institutions, hence its sobriquets camp fever, hospital fever and gaol fever. Epidemics often followed years of harsh weather, poor harvests and high prices, occurring in 1709/10, 1728, 1741, 1783, 1790, 1794/5 and 1800/1.[32]

Eighteenth-century doctors could not confidently distinguish typhus from other 'fevers'. But a body of preventive medicine grew up around some of its evident characteristics. Early experiments in prevention focused especially on institutions, both as perceived centres of disease, and because susceptible to hygienic regulation. Prisons attracted reforming effort during the 1770s and 1780s – in part because of the campaigns of John Howard, in part because disease flourished during the crisis of overcrowding that followed the collapse of transportation during the American war.[33] In this context it is not surprising that proliferating factories also attracted concern – especially factories with apprentice houses, where children slept in crowded conditions. Wilder fears also gained some currency. Just as it was sometimes suggested that typhus originated in spoilt grain, so it was rumoured that it was being carried into the country in raw cotton.[34]

It was in 1784 that a possible connection between factories and fever first attracted wide notice. In that year, neighbours became concerned about the prevalence of a 'low putrid fever of a contagious nature' among the poor of the township of Radcliffe, near Bury, Lancashire. Some believed that it had begun among children employed in the Radcliffe mills of Peel and Yates (the future Sir Robert Peel).[35] A local magnate, Lord Grey de Wilton, drew the matter to the attention of Manchester magistrates – that is, magistrates of the Salford division of the Lancashire

[32] C. Creighton, *A history of epidemics in Britain*, 2 vols. (Cambridge, 1894), vol. II, pp. 43–180.

[33] R. Evans, *The fabrication of virtue: English prison architecture, 1750–1840* (Cambridge, 1982), chap. 3.

[34] *Manchester Mercury*, 2 February 1796: letter from John Ferriar.

[35] Peel's Radcliffe works is described in F. Collier, *The family economy of the working classes in the cotton industry, 1783–1833* (Manchester, 1964), chap. 4 and S. Chapman and S. Chassagne, *European textile printers in the eighteenth century* (London, 1981), pp. 57 ff, pp. 96–7. The best modern account of the 1784 incident is 'The putrid fever at Robert Peel's Radcliffe mill', *Notes and Queries*, vol. 203 (1958), pp. 26–35. A contemporary account is Revd. Sir W. Clerke, *Thoughts upon the means of preserving the health of the poor* (London, 1790); cf. D. Campbell, *Observations on the typhus, or low contagious fever* [Lancaster, 1785].

bench, acting under the energetic chairmanship of Thomas Butterworth Bayley, a proponent of various reforming causes. Bayley had already begun to show a probing interest in the state of Manchester's prison: the building of a new prison, called the 'New Bayley' in his honour, was to begin in 1785. The magistrates asked Manchester infirmary physicians to investigate and report.[36]

The physicians reported that conditions in the factory might indeed have contributed to make the children vulnerable. They made suggestions about ventilation and fumigation, also stating that '[i]t may also be advisable to bathe the children occasionally'. They furthermore urged that children under the age of 14 not be made to work for more than ten hours a day, or at night, and that 'the rising generation should not be debarred from all opportunities of instruction' (another lively concern of the moment – the Sunday school movement had hit Manchester in January 1784, when a letter detailing initiatives in Gloucester had appeared in the *Manchester Mercury*; the first Manchester Sunday school would open that autumn).[37]

On receiving this report, the magistrates resolved to cease forthwith approving the binding of parish apprentices to any mill not meeting these conditions. They printed both report and resolution in the *Manchester Mercury*, and sent copies to the magistrates of seven neighbouring counties. In practice they clearly received wider circulation: thus the Manchester Chamber of Commerce sent copies to its Glasgow counterpart.[38] The magistrates' focus on apprentices may reflect their dominance in Peel's child workforce, but it probably also reflects the limits of magisterial power. Magistrates arguably had discretion to consent or not to apprenticeships, in the light of circumstances (though no such power was specifically assigned by statute). It is hard to see on what basis they could have claimed to determine how free children might be employed. However, the care they took to give publicity to the physicians' conclusions suggests that they hoped to make a wider impact.

Peel meanwhile responded defensively, writing to the *Mercury* to assert that while he accepted the need to take precautions, the fever had more

---

[36] T. Percival, 'Biographical memoirs of the late Thomas Butterworth Bayley Esq.', in *Works. Literary, moral, medical*, new edn (1807), vol. II, pp. 287–302. The magistrates' concern about fever in the Manchester house of correction was noted in the *Manchester Mercury*, 3 February 1784.

[37] The report was printed in the *Manchester Mercury*, 19 October 1784. For Sunday schools, see A. P. Wadsworth, 'The first Manchester Sunday schools', *Bulletin of the John Rylands Library*, vol. 33 (1951), pp. 299–326, and for Bayley's support for these, G. Fisher, 'The birth of the prison retold', *Yale Law Journal*, vol. 104 (1995), pp. 1303–8.

[38] Lancashire Record Office [hereafter Lancs.R.O.], Quarter Sessions Order Book 1784–6 (MF 10/24) October 1784; also printed in the *Manchester Mercury*, 26 October 1784. For the communication with Glasgow, see I. Donnachie and G. Hewitt, *Historic New Lanark* (Edinburgh, 1993), p. 42.

probably originated in Preston (the site of a county prison). He was not prepared to stop night working in the mill.[39] Identifying one of the concerns that was to fuel subsequent interest in compulsory legislation, he argued that since he had to compete with other manufacturers, he could not afford to constrain himself by rules not generally observed.

The 1790s saw the return of typhus fever. In the interval, the interests and ambitions of medical men had broadened. Modifying their initial fixation on large residential institutions, they now turned to the shortcomings of urban housing, and to ways of combating the spread of fever through urban neighbourhoods. In Manchester, a meeting of concerned parties in January 1796 gave rise to a 'Board of Health' – chaired in its early days by Bayley – which drew up regulations prescribing whitewashing, and established an initially controversial 'Fever Hospital'.[40]

Factories however continued to figure among objects of concern – not surprisingly, given that they had begun to multiply within Manchester itself.[41] Dr John Ferriar of Manchester began pressing manufacturers to cease night working and to adopt other hygienic practices during the 1790 epidemic. Several proprietors of large mills reportedly attended the meeting that founded the Board of Health. Doctors were nonetheless uneasily aware of the limits of mere moral influence. In a report to the board, Dr Thomas Percival accordingly proposed an application to Parliament to sanction good practice. (As in the 1784 report, which he had helped to write, he coupled the health and educational status of factory children as subjects of concern.)[42]

In 1800/1 high prices returned and typhus with them, and the debates of a few years before were renewed in Manchester and elsewhere.[43] In Nottinghamshire, thirty apprentices in Topliss & Co.'s mill died – prompting the London parish which had sent them to reconsider their

---

[39] *Manchester Mercury*, 26 October and 9 November. Correspondence continued until 30 November.

[40] For responses to typhus in the 1790s see *Proceedings of the Manchester Board of Health* (Manchester, 1805) – I have been able to consult only the manuscript copy held in Manchester Central Library, MF 1834. J. Ferriar, *Medical histories and reflections*, 3 vols. (Warrington and London, 1792–8); J. Pickstone and S. Butler, 'The politics of medicine in Manchester, 1788–92', *Medical History*, vol. 28 (1984), pp. 227–49.

[41] See J. Bohstedt, *Riot and community politics in England and Wales, 1790–1810* (Cambridge, Mass., 1983), p. 71 for suggested numbers of town mills: 1790 – 2; 1795 – 17 plus; 1800 – 'dozens'; 1803 – 65.

[42] Ferriar, *Medical histories*, vol. III, p. 46 for mill-owners at the initial meeting; Percival's proposals were reprinted in *P.P.* (1816) III, pp. 139–40.

[43] For typhus in Manchester, see *Proceedings of the Manchester Board of Health*, fos. 130–45; *Cowdroy's Manchester Gazette*, 14 November, 12 December 1801. This was the first typhus epidemic since the establishment of the SBCP (for which, see below), and appropriate forms of response to it bulk large in their reports: [Bernard,] *Reports of the society*, vol. IV, pp. 95 ff, pp. 131 ff *et passim*.

practices.[44] In 1816, by contrast, Manchester witnesses at least were to claim that, since the turn of the century, the intensity of epidemic fever had diminished. Peel attributed this to the operation of his act. Others were more inclined to give credit to the fever hospital.[45] (In 1816/17 a new epidemic wave would put such confidence to the test.)

The medical men who shaped early thinking about health in factories, as I have shown, intermixed medical with moral concerns. Others also contributed to the development of moral concern about factory children. Three distinguishable though overlapping groups deserve attention: magistrates and judges; philanthropists; and members of moral and social reforming societies.

As I have described elsewhere, the 1780s saw the emergence of a new form of magisterial activism, spearheaded by a scattered group of high-profile magistrates who developed a network of communications with each other, having as its object what might be summarized as moral renewal.[46] Some of their initiatives involved the more vigorous discharge of their own duties: for example, the building of new model, supposedly reformative prisons. Others relied on mobilizing wider energies. Thus, in the early 1780s several county benches issued 'Rules for the good ordering of society', urging lesser officeholders to take their responsibilities seriously, and attempting to stimulate a range of voluntary initiatives, from Sunday schools to friendly societies. Thomas Butterworth Bayley, the Manchester magistrate, moved in these circles.

Magistrates had at law various responsibilities in relation to apprentices, particularly parish apprentices.[47] The binding of parish apprentices required their authorization, as the binding of others did not. The Elizabethan Statute of Artificers gave some powers over apprentices and their masters to magistrates in Quarter Sessions. In 1747 an amending act began the process of transferring protective powers over poorer apprentices to pairs of magistrates out of Sessions.[48] Magistrates sometimes pushed beyond what the law clearly sanctioned. Manchester magistrates' action in the Radcliffe case followed earlier initiatives: in 1772 and again

[44] Horn, 'Traffic in children', p. 182.   [45] *P.P.* (1816) III, pp. 133, 315–16.

[46] J. Innes, 'Politics and morals: the late eighteenth-century reformation of manners movement', in E. Hellmuth, ed., *The transformation of political culture. Late eighteenth-century England and Germany* (Oxford, 1990), pp. 57–118.

[47] Statute law and legal precedent are summarized in such handbooks as F. Const, *Decisions of the Court of King's Bench upon the laws relating to the poor, originally published by E. Bott Esq., now revised*, 3rd edn (London, 1793). See also Lane, *Apprenticeship in England*, pp. 2–6.

[48] 20 George II c. 19.

in 1780 they had ordered overseers of the poor to visit parish apprentices to ensure they were tolerably well treated.[49]

The activist mood of the 1780s encouraged magisterial initiative in relation to apprentices. For those concerned to strengthen the moral fibre of society, apprenticeship clearly deserved attention. It provided a framework within which, ideally, the young could be raised in habits of industry and discipline. Conversely, as the Manchester magistrates thought, abusive apprenticeships might sap the physical and moral potential of 'the rising generation'.

In the 1780s enthusiasm for the potential of the institution seems to have been the dominant note. Thus, Gloucestershire magistrates' resolutions of 1788 suggested that those who neglected 'to execute the laws, which direct the apprenticing of poor children ... are in great degree answerable for the consequences of early depravity'.[50] In the bad harvest years of the 1790s and early 1800s a number of counties directed that children be set to work (as apprentices or otherwise); the Ongar initiative, already mentioned, was a product of these years.[51] In 1802 a Kent magistrate devoted a published charge to the powers of magistrates and overseers in apprenticing children, emphasizing their extent and utility.[52]

Manchester magistrates' emphasis on apprentices' vulnerability, and magistrates' special responsibility for the welfare of parish poor children, was not initially widely echoed.[53] But they were backed by the Court of King's Bench: first implicitly, later explicitly. In 1789, adjudicating a settlement dispute, Lord Chief Justice Kenyon hinged his verdict on the assertion that the apprenticing of poor children was 'one of the most serious subjects which fall to the decision of justices', who in effect took the place of the children's parents. In endorsing such apprenticeships, magistrates therefore acted judicially and not merely ministerially: that is, they were bound to exercise independent judgment about the merits of actions.[54] Kenyon's judicial conduct was persistently shaped by a

[49] Fisher, 'Birth of the prison', p. 1296, citing local newspapers.

[50] Gloucestershire Record Office, Q/SBb 340/61. See also W. Godschall, *A general plan of parochial and provincial police* (London, 1787), pp. 6–9, 20–5.

[51] W. Le Hardy, *Hertfordshire records. Calendar of Sessions books*, vol. VIII, *1752–99* (Hertford, 1935), p. 452; R. Wells, *Wretched faces. Famine in wartime England, 1793–1801* (Gloucester, 1988), pp. 304–5.

[52] G. Lamoine, ed., *Charges to the grand jury, 1689–1803*, Camden Society, 4th series, vol. XCIII (London, 1992), pp. 593–600.

[53] There are no signs of action in Cheshire, Denbighshire or the West Riding of Yorkshire at this time. I have not been able to check other Quarter Sessions' order books. Derbyshire and Warwickshire both adopted such resolutions at some point I have not dated.

[54] *King* v. *Inhabitants of Hamstall Ridware*, 27 June 1789, 3 T.R. 380, *English Reports*, vol. C, pp. 631–3.

powerful moral vision; his judgment was certainly not just a technical one, but expressed real concern.

In 1801 he gained a better chance to publicize this concern when a Middlesex muslin weaver, Jouvaux, was charged with mistreating seventeen apprentices. According to newspaper reports – the case was reported at unusual length in some provincial as well as London papers – Kenyon 'discovered great anxiety in the business and examined most of the witnesses himself'. Reprimanding local authorities for having allowed abuse to remain so long undiscovered, he contrasted their conduct with that of the Manchester magistrates, observing that 'Mr Baillie and [his fellows] have thought it worthwhile to pay great attention to such objects.'[55]

Breaking with the initial pattern of reluctance to follow Manchester's lead, in 1796, in the context of anxiety about typhus, and with some prompting from Bayley, West Riding magistrates bestirred themselves.[56] In September – having noted by way of preamble that their responsibilities in this sphere had been pronounced to be judicial and not merely ministerial – they resolved not to allow 'apprenticing to cotton mills or other works of this kind where children are obliged to work at night, or out of the parish, except in special circumstances'. They also ordered that two petty sessions be held every year in each division, to obtain a general return of the poor, and a report as to 'the state, condition and treatment of parish apprentices'. They ordered this resolution to be printed, and inserted in West Riding papers, where it was reprinted annually for several years.[57] In Middlesex, the Jouvaux case prompted action. Middlesex magistrates' subsequent resolution – observing, among other things, that the health of children was damaged by apprenticeship to tambour weaving and other such sedentary trades – was read out in court at the conclusion of Jouvaux's trial, and circulated to neighbouring counties.[58]

Heightened emphasis on official responsibilities must have played a part in stirring overseers to greater vigilance. Some may have had their consciences pricked; they were also exposed to pressure from children's relatives. There is evidence by the end of the century of parishes following up on their apprentices (indeed, Jouvaux's dealings were first exposed by parish officers from Greenwich). Some who sent children to northern

[55] A whole column of the *Leeds Mercury*, 30 May 1801, was devoted to this case; see also report of judgment on 27 June.

[56] West Yorkshire Archive Service, Wakefield: QS 10/33, September 1796; Bayley's presence is recorded. In a letter to Bayley of 21 January 1797, copied in *Proceedings of the Manchester Board of Health*, fo. 122, Bernard refers to 'your Yorkshire resolution of 8 September last'.

[57] For similar action in Warwickshire and Derbyshire, date unspecified, see *P.P.* (1816) III, pp. 121–4; [Bernard,] *Reports of the society*, vol. V, pp. 179–80.

[58] *Leeds Mercury*, 30 May 1801. S. and B. Webb, *English poor law history*, vol. I, *The old poor law* (London, 1927), pp. 204–5.

factories made trips to check on their charges. Some apparently decided all this was more trouble than it was worth, and opted to apprentice children locally instead – though as late as 1811, when a bill to prohibit the sending of children at a distance was mooted, it was reported that London vestries were poised to oppose the action with all their power.[59]

The growth of judicial concern about the conditions of apprentices must be set alongside broader developments in thinking about children. Charitable awareness of children's special needs had been given new expression at mid-century, when a series of high-profile, child-oriented charities were established in the metropolis, including the Foundling Hospital and the Marine Society. In the 1760s Jonas Hanway, who had been involved with several such projects, campaigned for new arrangements to safeguard the lives of parish poor children.[60] In the 1780s child-oriented projects began to be pursued across the nation, most notably in the Sunday school movement.[61]

An interesting feature of child-oriented philanthropy at this time was that philanthropists increasingly concerned themselves not merely with providing material and moral care, but with how such things might *best* be provided: with what the most nurturing environment for children might be. This question engaged interest across a wide spectrum of opinion, from those influenced by Rousseau to those influenced by the Evangelical revival (no doubt some were influenced by both). Of particular interest to us must be the growing concern that poor children not merely be set to work (as had long been urged) but set to work in an appropriate setting. Some contemporaries who promoted 'schools of industry' – non-residential workshops for children – favoured these not just as cheap alternatives to the workhouse, but as intrinsically better than workhouse, apprenticeship or other employment – at least for the youngest children.[62] The lively interest expressed by many in David Dale's provision for child workers at his New Lanark mills (subsequently taken over by Robert Owen) reflected the same concerns.[63]

---

[59] For parochial inspection, Horn, 'Traffic in children', *passim*, and Rose, 'Social policy and business', p. 21; *P.P.* (1816) III, p. 131, for an unfavourable report from Birmingham overseers on one of Peel's mills in 1800. For vestry opposition: Hansard, *Parliamentary Debates*, vol. XX (London, 1811), p. 519, and Webb, *Old poor law*, p. 205n.

[60] I. Pinchbeck and M. Hewitt, *Children in English society*, 2 vols. (London, 1973) for background; D. Andrew, *Philanthropy and police* (Princeton, 1989), chaps. 2–4, and J. S. Taylor, *Jonas Hanway* (London, 1985).

[61] T. Laqueur, *Religion and respectability* (New Haven, 1976).

[62] The SBCP reports contain much information about schools of industry. See also M.G. Jones, *The charity school movement* (Cambridge, 1938), pp. 154–62. For their advantages, see S. Trimmer, *Oeconomy of charity* (London, 1801), pp. 193–201.

[63] For visitors to Dale: Donnachie and Hewitt, *Historic New Lanark*, pp. 46–8. *Proceedings of the Manchester Board of Health*, fos. 62–71 gives Dale's response of February 1796

In the metropolis, the harm children might suffer by ill-conceived apprenticeships in particular was widely canvassed during the agitation over chimney sweeps' boys, launched in the early 1770s by a concerned sweep, David Porter, with Hanway's assistance.[64] Hanway gave this campaign a public dimension by writing to the newspapers, publishing pamphlets and making representations to local and national authorities. He emphasized the boys' youth; their unprotected state – some were parish apprentices, others had poor parents more concerned to make an income from their sons than for their welfare; the injury and disease to which they were subject (particularly cancer); their failure to acquire skills for adult life, and lack of access to education and religious instruction. After Hanway's death, in 1786, M.P. Robert Burton secured an act which laid down that no boy under the age of 8 be apprenticed to the trade; his parents' consent must be obtained; he must be provided with suitable clothing and living conditions, and the opportunity to attend church on Sundays. Nor did the campaign stop there. In the 1790s it became one of the causes espoused by the Society for Bettering the Condition of the Poor (SBCP). Thomas Bernard, the society's initiator, in 1797 urged further voluntary regulation, recommending that a society for the protection of climbing boys institute a system of inspection for their beds, clothing and domestic accommodation.[65]

These first stirrings of concern about children's work were associated with a focus on common *local* forms of work: thus, factory work in Lancashire and Yorkshire, tambour weaving and chimney sweeping in the metropolis. But newspapers, pamphlets and books dispersed concern more widely. The dispatch of London children to northern factories may have helped to direct metropolitan attention to those factories, but the printed word did so too. Between the mid-1780s and the early 1800s a number of moral, topographical and medical pamphlets and books drew Manchester physicians' and magistrates' worries about factory children to the attention of a wider public.[66] Growing southern awareness is

to a questionnaire from Bayley about his regime, also noted in *Historic New Lanark*, pp. 43–6.

[64] K. H. Strange, *The climbing boys: a study of sweeps' apprentices 1773–1875* (London, 1982).
[65] [Bernard,] *Reports of the society*, vol. I, pp. 146–56; vol. II, pp. 149–57, app. p. 70; *P.P.* (1817) VI, p. 7.
[66] B. Porteus, *Letter to the clergy of the diocese of Chester in relation to Sunday schools* (London, 1786), pp. 21–2; T. Gisborne, *Enquiry into the duties of men in the higher and middle classes of society*, 2 vols. (London, 1795), vol. I, p. 421n.; vol. II, p. 363n., pp. 368–72; J. Aikin, *Description of the country for thirty to forty miles around Manchester* (London, 1795), pp. 219–20, see also p. 456. For relevant medical writings: Campbell, *Observations*; Clerke, *Thoughts*; Ferriar, *Medical histories and reflections*; Percival, *Works*. Bayley evidently drew the writings of Gisborne and Ferriar to David Dale's attention in 1796; Dale responded that he had seen Gisborne's *Enquiry*, but that Ferriar's *Medical histories* were 'not to be got here' (*Proceedings of the Board of Health*, fo. 63).

evidenced by the writings of metropolitan philanthropist Sarah Trimmer. In the first, 1787 edition of her *Oeconomy of Charity*, 'Mrs Trimmer' praised factories for putting productive work in the way even of very young children. By 1801, however, she had developed reservations, and argued that schools of industry provided a better working environment (she cited particularly a pamphlet about precautions against typhus by Manchester physician John Ferriar, reprinted by the SBCP).[67]

In 1802, when Peel was defending his bill in Parliament, he was to claim that a great majority not only of the House but 'of the country' had 'unequivocally declared in its favour'.[68] Whatever the basis for this claim, he evidently expected his audience to find it plausible. While discussions provoked by the bill itself must have helped to create this climate of opinion, concern about the circumstances of working children fostered by initiatives of the previous two decades had prepared the ground.

Important in harnessing for reforming causes the energies both of the magistracy and of the socially concerned at the end of the eighteenth century were two societies: Wilberforce's Society for the Enforcement of His Majesty's Proclamation against Vice and Immorality (or Proclamation Society), founded in 1787, and the aforementioned Bettering Society, or SBCP, founded in 1796 – an offshoot of the by-then flagging Proclamation Society, incorporating many of its more active members and carrying forward some of its concerns.[69] Both societies showed an interest in children's welfare issues in general and the fate of apprentices in particular.

Each represented something of an *omnium gatherum* of the socially concerned elite – and included among its members numerous figures already encountered. Thus, Manchester magistrate Thomas Butterworth Bayley attended a magistrates' convention organized by the Proclamation Society in 1790, and subsequently became a member; he was one of the first provincial members of the Bettering Society. Kenyon was an early member of the Proclamation Society, and, though he resigned upon becoming Lord Chief Justice, remained a supporter. Robert Burton, who introduced the chimney sweeps' bill, was a member. Among those who helped to publicize Manchester doctors' and magistrates' concerns in

[67] Trimmer, *Oeconomy of charity* (London, 1787), pp. 59–80; 2-volume edition (1801): vol. I, pp. 193–201. The pamphlet was Ferriar's *Advice to the poor in manufacturing towns*, also reprinted in his *Medical histories and reflections* of 1792–8.

[68] Debrett, *Parliamentary Register*, vol. XVIII, p. 591.

[69] Innes, 'Politics and morals' for the Proclamation Society; for relations between the two societies: p. 99. On the Bettering Society, J. R. Poynter, *Society and pauperism* (London, 1969), pp. 91–8.

their writings, Bishop Porteus in 1792 became the Proclamation Society's president; Thomas Gisborne was an early member of the SBCP.

The Proclamation Society was the less child-oriented – though it did in 1789 distribute to county benches material relating to Sunday schools, and its 1792 pamphlet on the duties of overseers *inter alia* covered apprenticeship.[70] The society may have helped promote two acts, passed in 1792 and 1793, extending magistrates' summary powers in relation to poor apprentices (certainly members were involved in both cases).[71]

Children loomed larger among the concerns of the Bettering Society – perhaps reflecting the preoccupations of Thomas Bernard, who was treasurer of the Foundling Hospital,[72] perhaps as a result of this society's focus not on immorality but on poverty, and more specifically, on how the poor might be helped to help themselves. While the society's reports trumpeted the merits of a wide range of initiatives, from cow-keeping schemes to fever hospitals, a striking number were concerned with children's education or work.

A letter from Bernard to Bayley reveals that the state of parish and especially manufacturing apprentices featured on the society's initial agenda.[73] On the evidence of its reports, for some years such concern was nonetheless almost exclusively focused on climbing boys. The only report prior to 1802 devoted to factory children was one of 1800, describing a visit by Bernard to David Dale's celebrated mills – in which he observed that in point of humanity it would have been better if cotton mills had never been invented, but that since they had been, their proprietors had to be pressed to achieve standards as high as Dale's.[74] Given the society's concerns, and the Bayley connection in particular, it is nonetheless not surprising that when Peel prepared to lay before Parliament a factory apprentice regulation bill growing out of Manchester discussions, he should have thought it useful first to lay his proposals before the society.

It is not clear precisely what the proposals that Peel laid before the Bettering Society were. The first state of the bill to have survived is that which emerged, already amended, from its first Commons select

[70] West Yorkshire Archive Service, Wakefield, QS 1/131 Sessions roll July 1789, letter from Richard Mawhood to Mr Bennett; 'A country magistrate', *The duty of overseers of the poor* (London, 1792).
[71] 32 George III c. 57 and 33 George III c. 55, building on the 1747 act, already discussed. Each may alternatively have arisen out of the concerns of particular counties. *Report of the committee of the society for carrying into effect his majesty's proclamation against vice and immorality for the year 1799* (London, 1800), p. 25, emphasizes the society's interest in the topic.
[72] Rev. J. Baker, *Life of Sir Thomas Bernard Baronet* (London, 1819) offers the fullest account.
[73] *Proceedings of the Manchester Board of Health*, fo. 122.
[74] [Bernard,] *Reports of the society*, vol. II, pp. 363–74.

committee hearing. It seems certain that it related only to cotton mills (its extension to other mills was effected on the floor of the House). Given what we know of the Manchester discussions, it seems probable that it included provisions relating to ventilation and cleanliness; that it related chiefly to 'apprentices'; that it proposed that these be forbidden to work at night, or more than twelve hours a day; and that some provision be made for their general and religious instruction. The society's contribution probably took the form of helping to give these intentions definite shape. It is also possible that members pressed Peel to widen his bill – above all, to extend it to 'free' children. We know that Wilberforce for one would have preferred it to be so extended. If so, then, as later in Parliament, Peel resisted this pressure.[75]

Peel's own role now claims our attention. How had Bayley, Ferriar and Percival's concerns given rise to a bill brought into Parliament by the very man whose factory had prompted their first expressions of disquiet? How had 'humanitarian' concerns come to find a champion from within the manufacturing interest?

Though the idea of seeking legislation seems to have started with Bayley and the doctors, Peel at some point seized the initiative. When he brought his bill into Parliament, Manchester magistrates told Lancashire county members of Parliament that in their view, his scheme did not go far enough.[76] They would like to have seen restrictions on the hours of all children, and a more rigid ban on night work, coupled with a restriction on the number of apprentices any one employer might maintain. Peel was to argue that such restrictions were objectionable in principle – men of large capitals should not have their operations cramped in this way, and free workers should be allowed the 'privilege possessed by all the people of this country' of determining their hours of work. He also argued – probably correctly – that many manufacturers thought that even his proposal conceded too much; no one was as well placed as he to judge what might obtain their support, or to elicit that support by his own example.

Though Peel had substantial business interests in Manchester, he was not a resident member of its business community.[77] In the mid-1780s,

[75] Peel referred to his consultation of the society in debate: Debrett, *Parliamentary Register*, vol. XVIII, p. 185. See also Wilberforce, *Life*, vol. III, pp. 44–5.

[76] Debrett, *Parliamentary Register* omits this, but see *Senator*, vol. V, cols. 1292, 1556–7, and reports in *Manchester Mercury*, 25 May 1802; also *P.P.* (1816) III, p. 140.

[77] Manuscript sources on Peel are scanty. For the family fortunes S. Chapman, 'The Peels in the early English cotton industry', *Business History*, vol. 11 (1969), pp. 61–89, and for additional details, Chapman and Chassagne, *European textile printers*, part 2. R. Thorne, ed., *History of Parliament. The Commons, 1790–1820*, vol. IV (London, 1986), pp. 740–4 for his parliamentary activities.

moved in part by a desire to escape from the wage demands of Lancashire cotton printers, he had shifted his main base of operations from Bury to Tamworth in Staffordshire. Having bought up a major local estate, in 1790 he entered Parliament as Tamworth's member. In practice, he often presented himself as a spokesman for Manchester interests, but he played no conspicuous part in local affairs – and economically, Manchester was in truth a battleground between diverse interests. In a recent controversy, which had split and indeed destroyed its Chamber of Commerce, for example, representatives of cotton weaving interests had urged a ban on the export of cotton twist – which representatives of spinning interests had fiercely opposed. Peel, who had interests in all stages of cotton manufacturing, in this instance sided with the weavers.[78]

Peel had clearly not been any kind of campaigning reformer in 1784 – though, even at that date he had protested his good intentions as an employer. His early troubles may have motivated him subsequently to keep abreast of evolving notions of good practice. In the mid-1790s his Radcliffe works earned the praise of Chester physician John Aikin, who in other contexts wrote critically of factories as working environments.[79] If Peel had indeed tried to adapt to changing standards, he had not done so alone. Manufacturers would shortly argue that much of what his bill required had become standard practice. As individuals, many must have been touched by changing attitudes. They had practical reasons to wish to avoid disease, and may have hoped that education would promote work discipline. Of course they varied in terms of their ability and willingness to accept the extra costs attention to health and morals entailed, but some had both the means and the inclination to address these tasks.

Some contemporaries accused Peel of pursuing narrowly sectional interests: of promoting measures which, because of the costs they entailed, advantaged large manufacturers over small. Alternatively, they charged him with sacrificing the interests of spinners to those of weavers, inasmuch as his measure could be expected to hold down yarn production and thus limit quantities available to foreign enterprise – in effect achieving indirectly what Peel (among others) had sought to achieve by a ban on the export of twist. Some historians have echoed these charges.[80] Yet they

---

[78] R. Lloyd-Jones and M. J. Lewis, *Manchester and the age of the factory* (London, 1988), p. 64; his brother Lawrence, who was more prominent in Manchester affairs, by contrast took the spinners' side.

[79] Note also Chapman, *European textile printers*, p. 97.

[80] H. P. Marvel, 'Factory regulation: a reinterpretation of early English experience', *Journal of Law and Economics*, vol. 20 (1977), pp. 379–402 develops the first argument with reference to the 1833 act; Gray, *Factory question*, pp. 104–9, 164–84 questions such analyses. J. Foster, 'The making of the first six factory acts', *Society for the Study of Labour History Bulletin*, vol. 18 (1969), pp. 4–5 suggests Peel was promoting weaving over spinning interests; see also Lloyd-Jones and Lewis, *Manchester*, chap. 5.

seem over-elaborate. Moreover, as Peel himself observed, had either been his aim, he might better have pursued it by striving to regulate free child as well as apprentice labour, thus affecting many more, especially smaller enterprises. Yet, at this stage he consistently set his face against that.[81]

It seems improbable that Peel, with major interests in both spinning and weaving, was indifferent to the impact of his measures on the industry. Yet his act, once passed, encountered a storm of opposition from manu-facturers, which it seems that he anticipated to some extent. If his aim was not to advance his own interests over those of fellow-entrepreneurs, how can we explain why he should have backed this controversial measure?

It is important to note that not all later opponents of the bill opposed it initially. Thus, one man who later campaigned for repeal initially urged his M.P. to support Peel, stating that he saw 'no objection to it on the system he wishes to see realized'. What he did urge his M.P. to resist were any amendments presented on a 'mistaken plea of humanity'.[82] This suggests that what was at issue was not some relatively straightforward question of sectional advantage, but, rather, a more delicate matter of judgment: how best to protect the interests of the industry in the face of humanitarian lobbying.

Peel's actions, I suggest, are best understood in more or less the terms in which he represented them: as an attempt to find a middle way be-tween humanitarian hopes and manufacturing fears. He intended his bill to embody existing ideas about good practice, while fending off 'hu-manitarian' calls for tougher, as he saw it, untried and impractical re-strictions. Some people – medical men, magistrates, humanitarians – clearly favoured more radical action.[83] Most threatening to someone like Peel must have been any scheme (such as Manchester magistrates reportedly favoured) limiting the number of apprentices an employer might take on.[84] Potentially devastating in practice, such a proposal might (in the worst scenario) have given heart to, and even attracted support from, militant workers – of whom Peel, like his father before him, had all too much experience.[85] In this context it is not hard to imagine

---

[81] *Manchester Mercury*, 8 June 1802 for Peel's observation that restrictions on apprentice labour would in fact affect large more than small manufacturers, and the claim that he would be 'ashamed to take any advantage of poorer manufacturers'.

[82] Lancs.R.O., DDK/1741/10, fo. 44.

[83] For one such opinion not elsewhere cited, Lancs.R.O., DDK/1741/10, fos. 50–1.

[84] See Peel's comments on the other apprenticeship bill, Debrett, *Parliamentary Register*, vol. XVIII, pp. 63–4. When, in 1811, it was proposed to prohibit metropolitan appren-tices going to any employer with more than nine apprentices, Peel objected. This clause was dropped from the bill as passed in 1816: *P.P.* (1810–11) I, pp. 89 ff; Hansard, *Parliamentary Debates*, vol. XIX, p. 749; vol. XX, p. 517 f; 56 George III c. 139.

[85] For worker militancy associated with the apprenticeship issue, and Peel's experience of it, see Chapman, 'Peels', pp. 77–8. For worker militancy around Manchester at this period, Bohstedt, *Riot and community politics*, chap. 6; R. Glen, *Urban workers in the early*

him calculating that the best way forward lay in seizing the initiative and determining the terms under which factory apprenticeship might continue.

Twenty years later, his son and namesake was to write, apropos the reform of the Scottish judicial system, that he had tried to persuade his fellow-Tories 'that it was the best Policy to take to ourselves the credit of the Reform and that by being the authors of it, we should have the best chance of preserving limits to the Innovation'.[86] I suggest that twenty years before, his father had calculated similarly. But the father, like the son, was to see the necessity of the strategic concessions he had promoted challenged by those he claimed to serve.

It remains to consider the parliamentary history of the bill.[87]

In March 1802 Wilbraham Bootle and Viscount Belgrave (the latter the son of Lord Grey de Wilton), both members of Parliament for the north-west, brought into Parliament a bill requiring magistrates to keep a register detailing to whom and on what terms parish apprentices were apprenticed.[88] That bill was already advanced when, in April, Peel brought his – more radical if more narrowly directed – Health and Morals of Apprentices Bill into the Commons. Peel was candid about his bill's moderating intent, presenting it as an attempt to find a compromise between reformers' and manufacturers' wishes.[89] The difficulties of the project were nonetheless quickly exposed, as it came under pressure from several directions.

Within Parliament, the most persistent and most (though not invariably) successful pressure was directed at extending the bill's provisions. It was argued successfully that it was inappropriate that it should apply to cotton only. Wilberforce helped to secure its extension to woollen and 'other' industries, asserting that 'he was sure that those manufacturers with whom he himself was connected [as county member for Yorkshire] would be pleased with having provisions so useful extended

industrial revolution (London, 1984), pp. 68–81, and in the cotton industry generally, J. L. and B. Hammond, *The skilled labourer* (revised imprint 1927; reprinted London, 1979), chap. 4.

[86] Cited in: Elaine Reynolds, *Before the bobbies: the night watch and police reform in metropolitan London, 1720–1830* (London, 1998), p. 128.

[87] This can be traced through the *Commons* and *Lords Journals*, and *P.P.*, where two draft versions of the bill survive. There is no record of the debate in Hansard, *Parliamentary Debates*, but varying accounts in newspapers served as a basis for differing reports in Debrett's *Parliamentary Register*, *Senator*, *Manchester Mercury* and *Cowdroy's Manchester Gazette*. Wilberforce's diary provides additional insights: see below, note 93.

[88] 43 George III c. 46; two drafts survive in *P.P.* For the debate, see Debrett, *Parliamentary Register*, vol. XVII, pp. 199, 217, 395; vol. XVIII, pp. 63–4.

[89] *Senator*, vol. V, cols. 1292–3.

to themselves'. (Henry Lascelles, his fellow-member, read the situation differently, and spoke against the bill.[90])

When it came to its first reading, the extent to which it fell short of the aspirations of Manchester magistrates immediately became an issue. Precisely how Peel responded was later contested, but according to some accounts, while expressing 'respect for the Manchester justices when they confined themselves to their proper sphere', he questioned their 'right to dictate to the House of Commons'. He argued that his measure went as far as it was practicable to go in terms of the politics of the situation, and as far as it was fair to go by way of experiment.[91] Members of Parliament in general seemed willing to accept some form of compromise. However, many were unpersuaded that only apprentices stood in need of protection; they would have wished to see the bill extended to 'free children'. Wilberforce, who had been prepared not to press this had it not arisen, added his voice to the chorus. Peel refused to shift, arguing that humanity should advance slowly on the basis of experience. 'If the provisions of the bill were more extended, that would be going forward entirely in the dark.'[92]

The rapid pace at which the measure proceeded gave opposing manufacturers little chance to make themselves heard. John Douglas of Holywell later claimed to have written urging Peel to delay until the next session, to give opponents time to marshal evidence, but if so, Peel paid no heed.[93] One of Wilberforce's key Yorkshire friends and supporters, the Evangelical doctor and magistrate William Hey, sent him a glowing report on working conditions in a Yorkshire cotton mill he had just visited, and argued that Peel was actuated by 'improper motives'. Wilberforce refused to credit these insinuations, being more disquieted by what he described as Peel's sad 'shuffling' on the free labour issue.[94] In the final stages of the debate – on the bill's third reading – Henry Lascelles uttered a last protest on behalf of opposing manufacturers. But by then Peel was on a roll, confident enough to assert the predominance of both parliamentary and public opinion in his favour. Passing through the Lords, the bill received the royal assent at the end of June.

[90] Debrett, *Parliamentary Register*, vol. XVII, pp. 447–8. William Wilberforce Bird, Wilberforce's cousin and a leading figure in the Coventry silk industry, affirmed that he would welcome its extension to the silk industry (vol. XVIII, pp. 183–4).

[91] *Senator*, vol. V, cols. 1556–7; *Manchester Mercury*, 25 May 1802, and for Peel on poor reporting of the debate, 22 February 1803.

[92] Debrett, *Parliamentary Register*, vol. XVIII, pp. 183–5, 457–9.

[93] Lancs.R.O., DDK/1741/10, fo. 200.

[94] Bodleian Library, Wilberforce MSS, C35, fos. 51–2. Wilberforce's sons excluded such opprobrious material from extracts in their *Life*. For Hey, see J. Pearson, *Life of William Hey* (London, 1822). For his comments on this occasion, see [Bernard,] *Reports of the society*, vol. IV, appendix pp. 16–19.

Over the months that followed magistrates moved to put the act into effect, advertising in newspapers to draw manufacturers' attention to the need to register, appointing inspectors and undertaking inspections.[95] It seems plain however that the act was not aggressively enforced – and inspections did not become routine: some magistrates later admitted to having forgotten the act, while arguing that notorious abuse would surely have come to light.[96]

A number of developments meanwhile underlined the precariousness of the ground on which the bill stood. First to come into play were the manufacturers, whose voice had theretofore been little heard. William Hey's representations formed the basis of an attempt to get the SBCP to reconsider – and in December 1802 it set up a subcommittee to consider whether the bill had been well judged. This however concluded that the fact that many factories were already well run demonstrated that compliance with the act should *not* prove impossibly burdensome; the subcommittee further expressed the hope that men such as Hey would serve as visitors.[97]

Early in 1803 – when Parliament reassembled after the summer's general election – the act's manufacturing opponents convened in their localities to petition for its repeal. Like Hey, they had a difficult case to argue. They did not wish to repudiate Peel's humanitarian project. On the contrary they started to collect evidence to show how far existing practice conformed to its requirements. The act was nonetheless objectionable, they averred. First, because some of the detail of its provisions was excessively demanding, an objection which may have come into focus only when they saw the full text of the bill, and when magistrates moved to put it into effect. Secondly, and more importantly, it instantiated regulation at the heart of an industry whose strength had been its freedom: 'creating an unquestionable power of inspection over and interference with the manufacture of the country which hitherto has flourished free'. It seems plain that coincidental alarm about efforts to ban the export of yarn had helped to give force to these anxieties. A Manchester-based committee co-ordinated a campaign which elicited petitions from Manchester itself, Scotland, Yorkshire and the south-west all denouncing the act as

[95] The SBCP circularized county benches urging them to alert manufacturers to the need to register. Cheshire magistrates acted in response (Cheshire Record Office, QJB 3/18, Dec. 1803). Quarter Sessions' order books generally note the appointment of inspectors, but other documentation – registration books, reports – more rarely survive. Were it not for a later inquiry by Parliament, we would have little evidence of action beyond the appointment of inspectors. Parliament did not seek evidence of prosecutions. Since these could be brought to any two justices, they too would be hard to trace.

[96] *P.P.* (1816) III, pp. 416, 420.

[97] [Bernard,] *Reports of the society*, vol. IV, appendix pp. 1–22.

injurious and oppressive. After a fiery start, however, the campaign fizzled out. The feebleness of the act's enforcement must have helped to dampen opponents' ire.[98]

If manufacturing opposition quickly rose and fell, the contrary view – that the act was not radical enough – proved slower to take form, but was more tenacious. In 1804 Yorkshire magistrates reiterated their belief that magistrates should discourage if not ban all sending of parish apprentices far from their parish of origin, and Wilberforce at their behest brought in a bill to extend magistrates' supervisory powers over both overseers and masters. This proposal, however, became entangled with an overlapping West Country debate, and no legislation emerged.[99] In 1811 Wilbraham Bootle returned to the fray to push further the policy of cutting off manufacturers' access to apprentices at the point of supply. In 1816 a part of this scheme was embodied in legislation forbidding the sending of parish apprentices more than forty miles from their homes – effectively ending at least the metropolitan traffic in children.[100] Peel spoke out against the measure, arguing that it represented an unwarranted interference with manufacturers' liberty – but in the same year he nonetheless again emerged as something of a trimmer, bringing into Parliament a bill to do what he had previously held the line against doing, regulating the working conditions of 'free' children in cotton factories.[101]

Considered as a case study in the genesis of social legislation before government played much part in such matters, the story of the passage of the first factory act has some characteristic and some more unusual features.

Characteristic, first, were the bill's origins in a particular, locally rooted set of concerns. When we bear in mind the fact that it was most ambitiously implemented in Lancashire, we might almost be tempted to class it as a piece of local legislation, masquerading as a national measure. Yet

---

[98] *Commons Journal*, vol. LVIII, pp. 149, 160, 191, 206. For the campaign, Lancs.R.O., DDK/1741/10, fos. 198–209.

[99] West Yorkshire Archive Service, Wakefield, QS 10/34, 18 April, 2 June 1803, 23 February 1804; Debrett, *Parliamentary Register during the first session of the second Parliament of George III*, 3 vols. (London, 1803–4), vol. III, pp. 32–3; *P.P.* (1803–4) I, p. 297 ff.

[100] *P.P.* (1810–11) I, p. 89 f; Hansard, *Parliamentary Debates*, vol. XIX, p. 749; vol. XX, p. 517 f; S. Romilly, *Memoirs*, 3 vols. (London, 1840), vol. II, pp. 378–81, 398–99. The inquiry into the fate of parish apprentices, cited in note 29 above, arose from these efforts; the final bill was 56 George III c. 139.

[101] The background to the 1819 factory act has not been explored in any detail, but see Donnachie and Hewitt, *Historic New Lanark*, p. 115 f, and works listed in notes 2 and 80 above. Typhus and a renewed campaign against the export of cotton twist revived some of the circumstances that had formed a background to the 1802 act – but by the war's end organized labour was also involved: A. Fowler and T. Wykes, eds., *The barefoot aristocrats. A history of the amalgamated association of operative cotton spinners* (Littleborough, 1987), p. 19.

this would be an overstatement. The localist orientation of legislation at this period can be, and sometimes has been, exaggerated. I have shown that both county magistrates and philanthropists were plugged into wider networks. Parliament, the most powerful resource available to local activists, was moreover a national body. Concerns brought there were canvassed before, subject to modification by, and dependent on the support of representatives of all parts of the nation.

Characteristic, secondly, were many of the categories of people involved in shaping the bill: public-spirited professional men, magistrates, philanthropists, members of national philanthropic societies. I have found no indications of ministerial involvement, though it cannot be ruled out. People active in local government and in voluntary activity were, however, clearly the ones making most of the running.

A more unusual feature of this act was that it brought moral and philanthropic concerns to bear on economic activity. If magistrates and philanthropists had much experience of bringing their concerns to Parliament, many economic interest groups had as much, and often more. Manufacturers had given Pitt's government a hard time in the 1780s. One might have expected them to make a formidable showing against a 'humanitarian' measure, which they thought inimical to their interests. That they did not succeed in blocking the 1802 act may be explained in part in terms of one of their best-placed spokesmen having sponsored it. Peel was able to present himself to the Commons as the voice of the manufacturing interest (although, as I have noted, that claim did not go unchallenged). Their failure perhaps owed something too to Parliament's failure to consult more widely. Yet in the 1810s, when factory regulation came on to the table again, and there was wider consultation, still a further act was passed, against much manufacturing opposition. And if Peel could be seen as then having sold the pass again – showing that some manufacturers thought further regulation practicable – yet in 1816, parish apprenticeship had been further regulated against even Peel's opposition. If, as I have suggested, Peel's actions were motivated in important part by the conviction that the 'humanitarian' lobby was a strong one, deserving respect, then the pattern of events in the next two decades leaves that conviction looking like one an intelligent political operator might reasonably have held.

If Peel's intention was at one and the same time to promote and contain the philanthropic impetus, his initiative might in retrospect be reckoned a success. For Parliament, having endorsed his style of limited paternalism, was in the course of the next few decades decisively to reject attempts – attempts inspired by workmen, but invoking broader, moral and humane considerations – to breathe new life into Elizabethan protective regimes.

Attempts to entrench idealized old-style, domestic apprenticeship were rejected as incompatible with progress. The way was left clear for the factory system to advance.[102]

Yet in other senses Peel's was a pyrrhic victory. His act *had* legitimated new forms of intervention; during the next few decades he and his fellow-industrialists – cotton industrialists most particularly – were to be forced, usually reluctantly, to cede more ground. The whole train of factory acts, moreover, though they did imprint the figure of the humane industrialist upon public consciousness, did not imprint his image as vividly as that of the exploited and abused factory child. The most lasting effect of the acts was probably to plant the figure of the abused factory child at the heart of common understandings of what was entailed in the British experience of industrialization.

---

[102] For the immediately ensuing battle over this issue in the Yorkshire woollen industry, see Hammond and Hammond, *Skilled labourer*, pp. 140–8; E. P. Thompson, *The making of the English working class* (rev. edn, Harmondsworth, 1968), pp. 576–9.

John M. Beattie's publications

BOOKS

The English court in the reign of George I (Cambridge: Cambridge University Press, 1967)

Ed., *Attitudes towards crime and punishment in Upper Canada, 1830–1850: a documentary study* (Toronto: Centre of Criminology, University of Toronto, 1977)

Crime and the courts in England, 1660–1800 (Princeton: Princeton University Press, 1986)

Policing and punishment in London, 1660–1750: urban crime and the limits of terror (Oxford: Oxford University Press, 2001)

ARTICLES

'The court of George I in English politics', *English Historical Review*, vol. 81 (1966)

'Towards a study of crime in eighteenth-century England: a note on indictments', in P. Fritz and D. Williams, eds., *The triumph of culture: eighteenth-century perspectives* (Toronto: A. M. Hackert, 1972)

'The pattern of crime in England, 1660–1800', *Past and Present*, no. 62 (1974), reprinted in Eric Monkkonen, ed., *Crime and justice in American history: the colonies and early republic*, 2 vols. (Westport, Conn.: Meckler, 1991)

'The criminality of women in eighteenth-century England', *Journal of Social History*, vol. 8 (1975), reprinted in D. Kelly Weisberg, ed., *Women and the law: the social historical perspective* (Cambridge, Mass.: Schenkman, 1982)

'Crime and the courts in Surrey', in J. S. Cockburn, ed., *Crime in England, 1550–1800* (London: Methuen, 1977)

'Misdaad door vrouwen en de wet' [Women, crime and the law], *Spiegel Historiael* (Dec. 1977)

'Judicial records and the measurement of crime in eighteenth-century England', in Louis A. Knafla, ed., *Crime and justice in Europe and Canada* (Waterloo, Ont.: Wilfrid Laurier University Press, 1981)

'Administering justice without police: criminal trial procedure in eighteenth-century England', in Rita Donelan, ed., *The maintenance of order in society* (Ottawa: Ministry of Supply and Services, Canada, 1982)

'Violence and society in early modern England', in Anthony N. Doob and Edward L. Greenspan, eds., *Perspectives in criminal law* (Aurora, Ont.: Canada Law Book, 1985)

'London jurors in the 1690s', in J. S. Cockburn and T. A. Green, eds., *Twelve good men and true: the English criminal trial jury, 1200–1800* (Princeton: Princeton University Press, 1988)

'The royal pardon and criminal procedure in early-modern England', *Historical Papers* [Canadian Historical Association] (1988)

'Criminal sanctions in England since 1500', in Martin L. Friedland, ed., *Sanctions and rewards in the legal system: a multidisciplinary perspective* (Toronto: University of Toronto Press, 1989)

'Criminal trial in the reign of William III', in Peter Maccubbin, ed., *The age of William III and Mary II: power, politics and patronage, 1688–1702* (New York: Grolier Club, 1989)

'Crime, policing, and punishment in England, 1550–1850: a bibliographical essay', in Jane Gladstone, Richard Ericson and Clifford Shearing, eds., *Criminology: a reader's guide* (Toronto: Centre of Criminology, University of Toronto, 1991)

'Garrow for the defence', *History Today*, vol. 41 (February 1991)

'Scales of justice: defense counsel and the English criminal trial in the eighteenth and nineteenth centuries', *Law and History Review*, vol. 9 (1991)

'The cabinet and the management of death at Tyburn after the revolution of 1688', in L. Schwoerer, ed., *The revolution of 1688–89: changing perspectives* (Cambridge: Cambridge University Press, 1992)

'London crime and the making of the "bloody code", 1689–1718', in L. Davison *et al.*, eds., *Stilling the grumbling hive: the response to social and economic problems in England, 1689–1750* (Gloucester: Allen Sutton, 1992)

'English penal ideas and the origins of imprisonment', in Wendy Barnes, ed., *Taking responsibility: citizen involvement in the criminal justice system* (Toronto: Centre of Criminology, University of Toronto, 1995)

'Women, crime and inequality in eighteenth-century London', in J. Hagan and R. D. Person, eds., *Crime and inequality* (Stanford: Stanford University Press, 1995)

'Women and crime in Augustan London', in Valerie Frith, ed., *Women and history: voices of early modern England* (Toronto: Coach House Press, 1995)

Index